THE HERB COMPANION
WISHBOOK
AND
RESOURCE
GUIDE

BOBBI A. MCRAE

INTERWEAVE PRESS

Neither the author nor the publisher assumes responsibility for accuracy of the information in this book, which was supplied by individual businesses. Nor does either assume responsibility for disappointing or harmful results incurred in using the products, techniques, and methods described herein.

Cover design by Signorella Graphic Arts
Production by Marc McCoy Owens
Design by Marc McCoy Owens & Ann Sabin Swanson
Cover border print is "Willow Bough" wallpaper by William Morris.
  Reproduced by permission of the Victoria and Albert Museum, London.

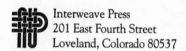 Interweave Press
201 East Fourth Street
Loveland, Colorado 80537

Copyright 1992 by Interweave Press
All rights reserved
Library of Congress Catalog Number 92-2942
ISBN number 0-934026-74-2

Library of Congress Cataloging-in-Publication Data
McRae, Bobbi A., 1956–
    The herb companion wishbook and resource guide / Bobbi A. McRae.
      p.   cm.
    Includes bibliographical references and index.
    ISBN 0-934026-74-2 (paper) : $16.95
    1. Herb gardening--Equipment and supplies--Catalogs. 2. Herb industry--Directories.
    3. Herbs--Bibliography--Catalogs. 4. Herb gardens--Directories. 5. Herbs--Societies,
    etc.--Directories.
    I. Title.
    SB351.H5M353   1992
    635'.7--dc20
                                                    92-2942
                                                      CIP

Foreword

If only *The Herb Companion Wishbook and Resource Guide* had been available when we were developing Hilltop Herb Farm in the piney woods of Texas more than 35 years ago! This was long before herbs became trendy; finding high-quality plants and seeds, essential oils and fixatives for potpourri, even something as simple as rooting compound, were frustrating obstacles.

The world of herbs has seen so much growth and change in recent years that the problem has almost reversed: it has become difficult just to keep up with new products, emerging businesses, and even the correct names of plants! The wealth of information which is now available to herb growers and users is most welcome and appreciated. Bobbi McRae's compendium will make it even easier to satisfy those needs, for both novice and experienced gardeners. Locating publications, even out-of-print books for serious study, is not a task necessarily to be completed on a single rainy afternoon. For those with research on their minds, there are rare, historic herbals to be found in many specialty libraries which are noted. This Guide makes it reasonably simple. Even publishers are listed with addresses!

When you travel with *The Herb Companion Wishbook and Resource Guide* at your side you can keep abreast of the many regularly scheduled public events around the country. Plan your vacations and other travel time to visit the ever-increasing number of public gardens which feature herbs. You can even book a reservation in one of myriad charming bed-and-breakfasts popping up all over the country.

Most valuable to us, *The Herb Companion Wishbook and Resource Guide* is a classic example of that rare American phenomenon called "networking". You will not only find what you need, but make new friends as well, for herb gardeners are the friendliest people in the world. No matter where you grow your herbs, you can check out your herbal needs with others of like interest. You will be exhilarated with the results and the warmth of friendship of those traveling the same path. You will soon call them friends. In the vernacular of user-friendly expressions, networking with herbs is a fine way to begin your day. *The Herb Companion Wishbook and Resource Guide* can be the key to unlocking the door and will be your handbook. We know you will find it as useful and beneficial as we have.

Madalene Hill
Gwen Barclay
Cleveland, Texas

Dedication

For my grandparents

The famous artist, Papaw (Howard Winston) Allen and the
famous artist's wife, Mamaw (Doris) Allen;
Jennie (Mamaw) Neal, who planted the seed of the love of
gardening in my young heart so long ago.
And in memory of B. J. Neal.

Acknowledgements

With love to my husband, Rudy Chukran, a modern Renaissance man, primo loom builder and "budding" herbal chef;
Thanks to Colleen Belk, president of the Austin Herb Society,
for her enthusiasm, friendship, numerous gifts of plants, and
countless hours of volunteer filing; For Sharon, who doesn't
mind a huge phone bill now and then; thanks to Anne Patterson Dee, for always telling me exactly what she really thinks; to
Michael, for general encouragement, ongoing friendship and
legal advice; and to Linda Ligon, for having faith in the idea.

Contents

Introduction 7

1 Plants and Seeds Available by Mail 9

2 A Potpourri of Herbal Supplies and Products 47
   *Herbal craft supplies; herbal bath, beauty, and aromatherapy
   supplies; culinary herbs and spices; herbal gifts and products; mostly
   medicinals; herbal specialty foods*

3 Publications 131
   Magazines, newsletters

4 Bibliography of Books on Herbs 139
   Publishers' directory / 162

5 Mail-order Booksellers of Herb Books 167

6 Educational Opportunities 177
   Classes; workshops; herbal schools; videos

&. Herbs and Etymology 208

7 An Herbal Calendar 209
   Recurring festivals and annual celebrations around the nation

&. A Grower's Guide to Favorite Culinary Herbs 222

8 Public Gardens with Herb Collections 223
   Geographical index

&. Cooking with Favorite Culinary Herbs 254

9 Herb Membership Groups 255
   *Local, national, and international organizations, associations, herb
   societies, and clubs*

10 Additional Resources 271
   *Miscellaneous resources; herbal bed and breakfasts; herb garden
   designers; herbal computer software; writers*

Appendix 280
   A geographical listing of herb businesses

Index 289

Introduction

Dear herb lover,

Do you know what zubrovka is? How about patchouli? Or mugwort? Never mind that, would you know where to find these plants if you knew what they were and wanted them? Well, now you *can* find them with the help of this book. We've collected sources for you for everything from common basils and mints to exotic herbs and spices. We've collected sources for seeds and plants for those who want to plant their own herb gardens, and we've listed hundreds of sources for dried herbs and botanicals for culinary, craft, or medicinal uses. There are lots of books and other publications listed, lots of places to take classes on herbs and herb gardening, and lots of public gardens to visit to inspire your garden designs. Probably everything herbal that you've ever wanted (and some things that you didn't know you wanted until you saw them) is listed here.

When I first started compiling information for this book, I had no idea how many mail order herbal suppliers there really were. Now that it's done (if a book of this type is ever really "done"), I realize how big the world of herbs really is. Going through the several thousand catalogs that came to me over the course of six months was wonderful fun, yet very frustrating! So many varieties of basil to buy and plant, so many books to read, so many classes to attend—so little time! I've found suppliers for everything herbal from seeds for old-fashioned varieties of herbs and everlasting flowers to modern instructional videocassetes. The herb lover's dream lies between the pages of the catalogs offered by the companies listed here. Some of the catalogs are slick affairs with full color pictures; some are hand-drawn masterpieces with plant descriptions carefully lettered. Have fun with them—many include a wealth of herbal information on the plants that's just plain fun to read whether you ever plant the herb or not! Please follow the supplier's requirements for receiving their catalogs (SASE means a self-addressed, stamped envelope with first class postage affixed).

Did We Leave Someone Out?

We have looked through hundreds of publications, used countless mailing lists, and mailed out thousands of letters and questionnaires trying to collect information for this book. In a subject of this size, it's inevitable that someone will get left out. If you know of a mail-order supplier that should be listed in future editions, please let me know. Due to space limitations, we were not able to list retail-only establishments; that was not the purpose of this book. As a mail order guide, we tried to list those companies that sell consistently by mail-order, predominantly to the general public. Some retail-only businesses were included (in Chapter 6) if they offered a substantial number of workshops or classes.

If your favorite supplier is not listed, perhaps it is because they did not answer the questionnaire sent them, or it was returned to us too late to include. Many suppliers had to be left out simply because they did not send the required materials to me.

If you have additions, deletions, address changes, etc., for the next edition, let me know! Just write me a note with the name of the business and their mailing address or phone number, and I'll take it from there.

If you are a mail order supplier and want to be considered for inclusion in future editions of this book, send a SASE for information to:

Bobbi A. McRae-HCWB
Box 49770
Austin, TX 78765-9770

I will contact each of you again when we are ready to begin the updating process.

And for those of you who are included in this edition, please keep me up-to-date on your address changes, new products, etc.

Thanks for your help,

Bobbi A. McRae

P.S. I regret that I do not have the staff or time to answer individual requests to locate sources over the phone or by mail.

1

Plants &
Seeds by Mail

THIS CHAPTER INCLUDES SOURCES for herb seeds and plants—annuals, perennials, everlastings, natives, scented geraniums, antique roses, chili peppers and spices, wild flowers, old-fashioned, rare and not-so-rare varieties. You'll find everything from angelica to zubrovka for culinary, medicinal, decorative, fragrance and craft purposes!

Abundant Life Seed Foundation

Forest Shomer
PO Box 772
Port Townsend, WA 98368

(206) 385-5660
Established 1975
Mail order; wholesale; retail; public garden
Catalog $1.00*

The Abundant Life Seed Foundation is a nonprofit corporation formed to acquire, propagate and preserve the plants and seeds of the native or naturalized flora of the North Pacific Rim area. The Foundation specializes in species that are not commercially available, including many rare or endangered species. All seeds are open-pollinated and fungicide-free. The list focuses on heirloom medicinal and culinary herbs, vegetables, small grains and edible seeds, wildflowers and old-fashioned flowers. Some of the herb seeds listed in this extensive catalog are fennel, amaranth, ambrosia, basils, borage, chia, chickweed, cumin, fenugreek, lamb's-quarters, vervain, asafetida, burdock, catmint, coltsfoot, elecampane, horehound, Joe-Pye weed, lovage, milkweed, speedwell and many more. Roots such as comfrey and osha are offered as well. Seeds are available in packets or in bulk. Accessories include cleaning screens, cloth bags and hand-operated seed threshers.

A long list of books is also available from here; see Chapter 4.

*Memberships are available in the Abundant Life Seed Foundation starting at $8.00 per year. For this you will receive the current seed/book catalog, a periodic newsletter and bulletins. Check the catalog for further information.

Alberta Nurseries & Seeds, Ltd.

Chris Berggren
PO Box 20
Bowden, Alberta
Canada T0M 0K0

(403) 224-3544
Established 1922
Mail order
Catalog $2.00 in U.S., free in Canada

Alberta Nurseries & Seeds, Ltd. offers a number of seeds for everlastings (including an everlasting bouquet collection), Oriental vegetables, flowering shrubs, perennials, and herbs.

American Ginseng Gardens

Billy E. English
100 Mountain Meadow Lane
Flag Pond, TN 37657

Established 1951
Mail order
Catalog $1.00

Want to grow your own ginseng? Here's the place to find both stratified seed and roots for planting, both in small numbers and in larger quantities. Also available are goldenseal roots, goldenseal powder and dried ginseng roots.

Antique Rose Emporium

Mike Shoup
Rt. 5, Box 143
Brenham, TX 77833

(409) 836-4293
Established 1983
Mail order; wholesale; retail
Catalog $5.00

The full-color catalog from the Antique Rose Emporium in Brenham, Texas, is a rose-lover's delight. Specializing in antique or heirloom roses, owner Mike Shoup offers a huge collection of roses that have, for the most part, been propagated from plants found growing near old homes and historic sites in Texas and the South. These include species roses, china roses, noisettes, bourbons, tea roses, polyanthas, rugosas, floribundas, hybrid musk roses and lots more. Also offered are a number of perennials and perennial herbs (santolinas, lamb's ears, rosemary, thyme, bearded iris, scented violets, yarrows, purple coneflowers, etc.) that complement old roses.

Books on old roses and miscellaneous gardening supplies are also available from the Antique Rose Emporium.

The Banana Tree

715 Northampton St.
Easton, PA 18042

(215) 253-9589
Established 1964
Mail order; retail
Catalog $3.00

The Banana Tree specializes in seeds for rare plants, most of which are tropical. Most seeds are shipped as they are freshly harvested. Ever wanted to grow your own cinnamon trees? The Banana Tree has seeds from time to time. They also carry ginger rhizomes and seeds of flax, banana passionfruit, silver dollar eucalyptus, allspice tree and black pepper vine seeds, to name just a few.

Barney's Ginseng Patch

Barney L. Frye
Rt. 2, Box 43
Montgomery City, MO 63361

(314) 564-2575
Established 1965
Mail order; wholesale; retail by appointment
Planting guide/price list $2.00

Barney L. Frye offers ginseng seeds, roots and plants for sale by mail order. His price list and catalog is an informational booklet titled "Grow Ginseng for Profit". Also for sale are books, goldenseal seed and roots, bloodroot roots and mayapple roots.

Blue Springs

Mary Hidalgo
236 Eleanor Ave.
Los Altos, CA 94022

(415) 948-3787
Established 1987
Mail order
Catalog $2.00

In addition to a variety of dried herbs, spices and potpourris, Blue Springs carries herb plants and packaged herb and vegetable seeds, some of which are imported from France. The herb plants include angelica, bergamot, burnet, lemon balm, mugwort, pennyroyal, summer and winter savory, southernwood, verbena and wormwood. Seeds are available for angelica, anise, caraway, cardoon, chervil, coriander, cumin, fennel, sweet marjoram, safflower, sesame, tabasco peppers and more.

Bluejay Gardens Herb Farm
Viola Jay
Rt. 2, Box 196
Haskell, OK 74436

(918) 482-3465
Established 1981
Mail order; wholesale; retail; public garden
Catalog $1.00; refundable with purchase

Viola Jay's Bluejay Gardens is a source for organically grown herb plants such as angelica, artemisias, baby's-breath, basils, borage, calendula, chamomile, comfrey, fennel, scented geraniums, elephant garlic, germander, lovage, blue flax, mints, mullein, parsley, perilla, pennyroyal, pyrethrum, statice, thymes and many more. Flowering plants especially for crafting include celosias, ammobium, Chinese lantern, fuller's teasel, love-in-a-mist, money plant and bittersweet. Living herb wreaths, dried flowers and culinary herbs are also available. (Also see listing in Chapter 6.)

Bluestone Perennials
W. N. Boonstra
7211 Middle Ridge Rd.
Madison, OH 44057

(800) 852-5243
Established 1972
Mail order
Catalog free

Bluestone Perennials offers plants in sets of three or six plants at reasonable prices (single and mature plants are more expensive). Some of the plants listed in the full-color catalog are yarrows (eight types), ajuga, artemisias, lady's-mantle, coreopsis, foxglove, dianthus, echinaceas (four types), baby's-breath, pyrethrum daisies, salvias, rue, santolinas, thymes, ground covers, ornamental grasses and shrubs.

Botanic Ark Nursery
Steve La Valley
Copeland's Road
Warragul, Victoria
Australia 3820

Phone 056-235268
Established 1981
Mail order; retail
Catalog $1.00 U.S.

The Botanic Ark Nursery does not export plants to the U.S., but will exchange some seed (if you have something they don't have and want).

Bountiful Gardens
A Project of Ecology Action
Betsy and Bill Bruneau
19550 Walker Rd.
Willits, CA 95490

Mail order
Catalog free in U.S.; $1.50 to foreign addresses

The Bountiful Gardens catalog includes seeds for herbs, flowers, grains, cover crops and heirloom vegetables. The herb seeds include angelica, anise, lemon balm, basils, borage, caraway, chives, cilantro, cumin, dill, purple coneflower, feverfew, Good-King-Henry, horehound, lovage, oregano, purslane, rosemary, tansy, and wormwood. Also listed in this informative catalog are some everlastings, lots of books, beneficial insects, organic gardening gardening supplies, pyrethrum powder, etc.

Bowman's Hill Wildflower Preserve

Thomas Stevenson, Plant Propagator
Washington Crossing Historic Park
PO Box 103
Washington Crossing, PA 18977-0103

(215) 862-2924
Mail order; retail; public garden
Catalog $.10

Bowman's Hill Wildflower Preserve offers small quantities of seeds from native Pennsylvania plants. The species vary from year to year. A recent catalog lists purple giant hyssop, agrimony, pearly everlasting, wild blue indigo, cohosh bugbane, Joe-Pye weed, horsemint, wild senna, various coneflowers and others.

Brushy Mountain Bee Farm, Inc.

Steve Forrest
Rt. 1, Box 135
Moravian Falls, NC 28654-9906

(919) 921-3640
Established 1984
Mail order
Catalog free

If you are looking for herbs to attract bees, or as a source of nectar for your own bees, this company has the seeds for them! The Bees' Garden seed collection includes anise hyssop, catnip, English lavender, horehound, lemon balm, lemon mint, meadowsweet, oregano, and creeping thyme. Brushy Mountain Bee Farm also carries a large assortment of general beekeeping supplies.

W. Atlee Burpee & Company

300 Park Avenue
Warminster, PA 18974

(215) 674-4900
Mail order; wholesale
Catalog free

Burpee supplies a large number of seeds and plants of vegetables, herbs, perennials, flowers, ornamental plants, etc. The current herb list includes angelica, anise, basil, chamomiles, chives, coriander, upland cress, dill, fennel, horehound, lavender, lovage, mint, oregano, parsley, pennyroyal, safflower, savory, sesame, thyme, watercress and wormwood. Perennial plants include yarrows, artemisias, foxglove and lavender. The catalog also lists general gardening supplies such as seed starting supplies, materials to make space-saving gardens, earthworms, organic controls, T-shirts and books.

D. V. Burrell Seed Growers Co.

Rick Burrell
PO Box 150
Rocky Ford, CO 81067

(719) 254-3318
Established 1899
Mail order; wholesale; retail
Catalog free

Burrell's carries a few herb seeds and a large number of flower seeds, many of which are everlastings.

Cactus Patch Herbs

Rosalyn Haag
RR 2, Box 33
Seymour, IN 47274

(812) 523-8305
Established 1985
Mail order; wholesale; retail
Catalog for SASE

Cactus Patch Herbs carries a number of herbs and unusual flower varieties, all of which are organically grown.

Cedarbrook Herb Farm

Toni and Terry Anderson
986 Sequim Ave. S.
Sequim, WA 98382

(206) 683-7733
Established 1968
Mail order; retail; public garden
Catalog $1.00

Cedarbrook Herb Farm offers a number of herb seeds by mail order. These include angelica, basils, borage, chervil, chives, sweet cicely, dill, leeks, lovage, parsley, savory and thyme. Seeds for tea herbs and everlastings are also listed. (Also see listings in Chapters 2 and 6.)

Chili Pepper Emporium

328 San Felipe NW
Albuquerque, NM 87104

(505) 843-6505
Established 1984
Mail order; retail
Catalog free

The Chili Pepper Emporium stocks seeds for peppers, both hot and sweet. Some of these are Anaheim, poblano, habanero, serrano, pepperoncini and a chili pepper collection.

Circle Herb Farm

Sue Falco
Rt. 1, Box 247
East Jordan, MI 49727

(616) 536-2729
Established 1984
Mail order; wholesale; retail; public garden
Catalog free

Circle Herb Farm specializes in potted herb plants, fresh cut herbs and edible flowers. Circle Herb Farm offers more than 140 different herbs, perennials and scented geraniums. The herbs include anise hyssop, ten types of basils, borage, Russian caraway, chervil, feverfew, sweet fennel, four types of oregano, summer and winter savory, five types of sage, yarrow, southernwood and Corsican mint.

Scented geraniums include Attar of Rose, Chocolate Mint, Apricot, Old Spice, Cinnamon, Musk, Citronella and others.

Clark's Greenhouse & Herbal Country

Wilma Clark
RR 1, Box 15B
San Jose, IL 62682

(309) 247-3679
Established 1985
Mail order; wholesale; retail; public garden
Catalog $1.00 refundable with order

Wilma Clark lists a large variety of herb plants, scented geraniums and unusual everlastings and selected flowers in her mail-order catalog. The herbs include angelica, anise, numerous basils, boneset, salad burnet, costmary, curry, feverfew, flax, epazote, horehound, our-lady's-bedstraw, lavender (including a yellow variety), lemongrass and mullein. The scented geraniums are divided into groups: citrus, rose, fruit and spice, mint and pungent. Some dried bundles and finished herbal crafts are also listed in the current catalog.

Clark's has an extensive public garden and offers a series of classes; see Chapters 6 and 8 for more information.

Clyde Robin Seed Co., Inc.

Nancy Bulloch
3670 Enterprise Ave.
Hayward, CA 94545

(415) 785-0425
Established 1936
Mail order; wholesale
Catalog free

The Clyde Robin Seed Co., Inc. specializes in wildflower seed. The current catalog includes yarrows, wildflower mixtures, purple coneflowers, red flax, baby's-breath and others. Some seeds are available in bulk to wholesale buyers.

Companion Plants

Peter and Susan Borchard
7247 N. Coolville Ridge
Athens, OH 45701

(614) 592-4643
Established 1981
Mail order
Catalog $2.00

Peter and Susan Borchard offer an abundance of herb and everlasting flower plants and seeds in their current catalog. These include yarrows, hyssops, many artemisias, asafetida, pink and white baby's-breath, basils, bay laurel, betony, belladonna, calendula, seven catnips, chives, coffee plant, Vietnamese coriander, culantro, ephedra, foxglove, many scented geraniums, soapwort, sweet grass, fuller's teasel, thymes, weld, woad and yerba buena.

Comstock, Ferre & Co.

Carol Casey
263 Main St.
PO Box 126
Wethersfield, CT 06109-0263

(203) 529-3319
Established 1820
Mail order; retail; public garden
Catalog $1.00

Comstock, Ferre & Co. carries more than 50 herbs in their current catalog. These include angelica, artemisia, borage, burnet, cardoon, corn salad, fenugreek, lavender, pennyroyal, safflower and sweet woodruff. Also listed are many annual, biennial or perennial flowers, many of which are everlastings. The herbs are packaged in attractively illustrated seed packets which are suitable for framing.

The Cook's Garden

Shepherd and Ellen Ogden
PO Box 535
Londonderry, VT 05148

(802) 824-3400
Established 1980
Mail order
Catalog $1.00

The Cook's Garden offers a large number of seeds of edible flowers, herbs, including ten basils, vegetables and salad greens as well as general gardening supplies and books.

Country Bloomers Nursery

Sharon Gordon
RR #2
Udall, KS 67146

Established 1982
Mail order; wholesale
Catalog free

Country Bloomers Nursery specializes in old garden (heritage) roses, English shrub roses and selected miniatures. Sharon Gordon plans to offer herbs in the near future.

Country Lane Herbs & Dried Flowers

Karen Michaud
RR 3
Puslinch, Ontario
Canada N0B 2J0

(416) 659-7327
Established 1988
Mail order to Canada only; retail; public garden
Write for price list.

Country Lane Herbs & Dried Flowers carries a good selection of culinary herb plants, tea herbs, medicinal herbs, everlastings and scented herb plants for sale by mail order within Canada.

Karen Michaud also sponsors workshops and other special events throughout the year. Call or write for a schedule.

Cross Seed Co.

Dale K. Cross
HC 69 Box 2
Bunker Hill, KS 67626

(913) 483-6163
Established 1943
Mail order; wholesale; retail
Catalog $1.00 refundable with purchase

The Cross Seed Co. offers organically grown seeds of beans, grains and sunflowers. This catalog also lists a nice selection of sprouting seeds for alfalfa, yellow clover, red clover, turnip, black mustard, fenugreek, radish and sesame.

Dabney Herbs

Davy Dabney
PO Box 22061
Louisville, KY 40252-0061

(502) 893-5198
Established 1986
Mail order
Catalog $2.00

The 32-page Dabney Herbs Catalog and Reference Guide lists more than 200 varieties of herb plants categorized by genus.

These include alliums (chives, garlic, shallots, leeks, ramps), artemisias (mugwort, Roman wormwood, Silver King, tarragon), lavenders, mints (14 types), oreganos (six types), patchouli, rosemary, scented geraniums, salvias and thymes. Also listed are several English roses and miniature roses. Seeds are offered, and include anise, basils, bells of Ireland, borage, catnip, chives, coneflower, luffa, mullein and St. John's wort. Gift certificates are available. (Also see listing in Chapter 2.)

William Dam Seeds

Rene W. Dam
Box 8400, 279 Hwy. 8
Dundas, Ontario
Canada L9H 6M1

(416) 628-6641
Established 1949
Mail order; retail; public garden
Catalog $2.00

The William Dam Seeds catalog lists a large number of wildflower, vegetable, flower (including everlastings) and herb seeds. Herb seeds include basils, lemon balm, borage, peppermint, sweet marjoram, Russian tarragon, thymes, sorrel, rosemary, pennyroyal, watercress, dandelion, white mustard, cumin, pyrethrum, clary sage, an herb garden mixture and many more.

Davidson-Wilson Greenhouses

Barbara Wilson
Rt. 2, Box 168, Dept. 16
Crawfordsville, IN 47933-9423

(317) 364-0556; FAX (317) 364-0563
Established 1980
Mail order; wholesale; retail
Catalog $2.00

Davidson-Wilson Greenhouses specializes in house plants, and carries a wide variety of scented geraniums: Copthorne (cedar),

Lemon Meringue, Snowy Nutmeg, Apple, Finger Bowl (citronella), Chocolate Mint, Attar of Roses, Ginger and many more. This company also carries growing supplies.

Daystar
Marjorie A. Walsh
Rt. 2, Box 250
Litchfield, ME 04350

(207) 724-3369
Established 1950
Mail order; retail by appointment
Catalog $1.00

Daystar carries a number of small shrubs, uncommon trees and New England perennials. The perennials include yarrows, artemisias, coreopsis, echinaceas and mustards.

DeGiorgi Seed Company
Duane Thompson
6011 N Street
Omaha, NE 68117

(402) 731-3901
Established 1905
Mail order; retail
Catalog $2.00

The DeGiorgi Seed Company catalog offers a large number of traditional open-pollinated and hybrid seeds for annuals, perennials, wildflowers, grasses, vegetables and herbs. The herbs include angelica, anise, basils, bay, borage, caraway, chamomile, garlic chives, coriander, fennel, fenu-greek, hyssop, oregano, black and yellow mustards, nasturtiums, peppermint and thyme.

The catalog includes recipes, planting charts and information and a grid for planning your own garden. DeGiorgi also sells garden art, books and general supplies.

Diana's Designs
Diana Sammataro
PO Box 240
Litchfield, OH 44253

(216) 722-2021
Established 1984
Mail order
Price list for SASE

Diana Sammataro specializes in seeds for bee plants (anise hyssop, horehound, lamb's-ears, etc.) and plants for weavers (bouncing bet, coreopsis, Hopi sunflower, teasel, etc.).

Elixir Farm Botanicals
Lavinia McKinney and Susan Wiseheart
Elixir Farm
Brixey, MO 65618

(417) 261-2393
Established 1986
Mail order; retail by appointment
Catalog $1.00

Elixir Farm Botanicals offers a number of indigenous and Chinese medicinal plant seeds in its highly educational catalog. Some of these are Oriental garlic, great burdock, mugwort, leopard flower, beefsteak plant (perilla), Chinese pink flower, four types of coneflower (echinaceas), purple prairie clover, purple bergamot, wild quinine, compass plant, spiderwort, mullein, and Culver's root. Elixir Farm also carries organic garlic bulbs and bare-root comfrey and purple coneflower plants. A flower press and refills, Florammune echinacea tincture, and several books are also listed in the current catalog.

Euroflax, Inc.

Claire C. Westerink
PO Box 241
Rye, NY 10580-2451

(914) 967-9342
Established 1985
Mail order; wholesale
Catalog $2.00 (includes flax samples)

In addition to its line of flax fibers and yarns, Euroflax also offers top-quality flax seed used by Belgian flax growers.

Farmer Seed & Nursery

Don Prodoehl
818 NW 4th St.
Faribault, MN 55021

(507) 334-1623
Established 1888
Mail order; retail
Catalog free

Farmer Seed & Nursery specializes in hardy varieties of plants, especially those adapted to the northern regions of the U.S. Listed in the current catalog are roses, pyrethrum daisies, perennials, some everlastings, peppers, parsley and general gardening supplies.

Henry Field's Seed & Nursery Co.

Keith Lapour
415 N. Burnett St.
Shenandoah, IA 51602

(605) 665-4491
Established 1892
Mail order
Catalog free

Henry Field's catalog offers a little bit of everything, including a good listing of herb seeds. Among these are an old-world herb garden collection, summer savory, borage, catnip, horseradish roots, sage, chamomile and woolly applemint. Everlasting seeds include strawflower, cockscomb, candytuft and others. Interesting, fun and novel

Herbs do comfort the wearied brain with fragrant smells which yield a certain kind of nourishment.

—William Coles,
1656

seeds are included for giant gourds, mammoth sunflowers and luffa sponges.

Filaree Farm

Ron Engeland
Rt. 1, Box 162
Okanogan, WA 98840

(509) 422-6940
Established 1977
Mail order; wholesale; retail
Catalog free

Filaree Farm has been growing specialty garlics for 15 years. The current list includes more than 50 different strains, many from the former Soviet Republic of Georgia or from eastern Europe.

Flowers & Spice World

Robert J. Hilliard
2276 M-37 S.
Traverse City, MI 49684

(616) 943-8273
Established 1984
Mail order; wholesale; retail
Catalog $1.00

Flowers & Spice World offers over 400 varieties of perennials, all available in either three- or six-packs at reasonable prices. These include some herbs, everlastings and old-fashioned flowers.

The Flowery Branch Seed Company

Dean Pailler
PO Box 1330
Flowery Branch, GA 30542-1330

(404) 536-8380
Established 1978 (formerly Catnip Acres Herb Farm)
Mail order; wholesale
Catalog $2.00 for two-year subscription

The Flowery Branch carries a large assortment of seeds for perennials, herbs and everlastings. The catalog lists plants by Latin name and includes full descriptions as well as information on ease of germination and care.

The seeds in the current catalog include 12 yarrows, five dills, 26 peppers, 18 sages, 15 basils and much more.

Forestfarm

Ray and Peg Prag
990 Tetherow Rd.
Williams, OR 97544-9599

(503) 846-6963
Established 1974
Mail order
Catalog $3.00

Forestfarm carries a huge selection of herbs, perennials and everlastings in its 144-plus-page catalog. These include eucalyptus, sweet woodruff, elecampane, osage orange, sassafras, baby's-breath, bee balm, betony, carob, purple coneflower, dittany, elderberry, ephedra (Mormon tea), mallow, tea tree, sunflower and lots more.

Fox Hill Farm

Marilyn Hampstead
444 W. Michigan Avenue
Box 9
Parma, MI 49269

(517) 531-3179
Established 1975
Mail order; retail
Catalog $1.00

Fox Hill Farm supplies a large number of herb plants by mail order. Included are 20 types of basil, 11 lavenders, lots of mints, 12 varieties of oregano and many others.

Fox Hollow Herbs & Heirlooms

Tom and Carol Porter
PO Box 148
McGrann, PA 16226

(412) 763-8247
Established 1987
Mail order; wholesale
Catalog $1.00; refundable with purchase

Fox Hollow Herbs & Heirlooms, owned by Tom and Carol Porter, carries a large number of herb and flower seeds for cottage and alpine gardens. Small, inexpensive seed-sampler packages as well as larger packages are available. Herbs include angelica, anise, basils, borage, calendula, caraway, cardoon, chervil, chives, coriander, cumin, fennels, lobelias, lovage, mullein, parsleys, Mexican oregano, pyrethrum daisies, rosemary, sage and tansy. Old-fashioned flowers for cottage gardens are included as well. Also available are vegetable seeds and books.

Fragrant Fields

Carol Hanson
128 Front St.
Dongola, IL 62926

(618) 827-3677 or (800) 635-0282
Established 1978
Mail order; wholesale; retail; public garden
Catalog free

Fragrant Fields offers more than 80 varieties of potted herbs, scented geraniums, perennials and everlasting flower plants and is one of the largest herb growers in the Midwest. Plants include basils, garlic, Greek oregano, caraway, English thyme, lemon basil, burnet, borage, 14 mints and many medicinal and decorative herbs. A small number of books and herb seeds are also available.

Fragrant Fields is also a supplier of herbal craft materials; see listing in Chapter 2.

The Fragrant Path

Ed Rasmussen
PO Box 328
Ft. Calhoun, NE 68023-0328

Established 1982
Mail order; retail
Catalog $1.00

The Fragrant Path specializes in seeds for fragrant, rare and old-fashioned plants. The herbs listed in the current catalog include angelica, anise, borage, caraway, chervil, garden cress, fennel, fennel flower, fenugreek, lovage, curled-leaved mallow, nasturtium, poppyseed, rocket, safflower (false saffron), summer savory, sesame and rocambole. Perennial herbs include bee balm, catnip, chicory, giant fennel, lavender, oregano, rosemary, rue, sage, sorrel and thyme. Many interesting climbers, fragrant annuals and perennials, prairie flowers and grasses and a few exotics are listed.

Garden Perennials

Gail Korn
Rt. 1
Wayne, NE 68787-9785

(402) 375-3615
Established 1981
Mail order; retail; public garden
Catalog $1.00; refundable with purchase

Gail Korn offers a large number of perennial plants, including many herbs, everlastings and daylilies. A few of these are baby's-breath, bellflower, chamomile, chives, clove pinks, coneflower, heliotrope, lamb's-ears, loosestrife, pearly everlastings, scabiosa, artemisias and yarrows.

Garden Place

John Schultz
PO Box 388
Mentor, OH 44061-0388

(216) 255-3705
Established 1945
Mail order; wholesale; retail by appointment
Catalog $1.00

Garden Place carries a large number of perennial plants: yarrows, ajuga, artemisias, senna, coreopsis, dianthus, coneflowers, feverfew, baby's-breath, chives, sweet woodruff, lemon verbena, rue, salvias, thymes and lots more. Although the plants are listed by their Latin names, the common names are also given as well as a handy pronunciation guide to the Latin.

Gardens of the Blue Ridge

Betty H. Robbins
PO Box 10
Pineola, NC 28662

(704) 733-2417
Established 1892
Mail order; retail; public garden
Catalog $2.00

Gardens of the Blue Ridge specializes in hardy, native plants. These include blue cohosh, wild ginger, bittersweet, citronella, angelica, witch hazel, alumroot, St. John's wort, bee balm, ginseng, bloodroot and many others.

The Gathered Herb

Shelley Carlson
12114 N. State Rd.
Otisville, MI 48463

(313) 631-6572
Established 1988
Mail order; retail; public garden
Catalog $2.00

In addition to a large number of herbal products (see listing in Chapter 2), Shelley Carlson of The Gathered Herb grows and sells a good selection of herb, perennial, everlasting and scented geranium plants through mail order. These include aloe vera, nine types of artemisias, bee balm, Roman chamomile, black and blue cohosh, purple coneflower, dianthus, eucalyptus, five colors of globe amaranth, heather, lady's-mantle, lemon verbena, lovage, 13 mints, soapwort, statice, strawflower and 11 thymes.

Glade Valley Nursery

Rudy Hamilton
9226 Links Rd.
Walkersville, MD 21793

(301) 845-8145
Established 1971
Mail order; wholesale; retail
Catalog $2.00; refundable with purchase

The Glade Valley Nursery offers an extensive variety of herbs, perennials and everlastings by mail order. These include 17 mints, patchouli, eight sages, 11 thymes and many unusual or hard-to-find plants. The plants are shipped year round, weather permitting.

Good Seed Company

Charlene Rich and Miquel Guizar
Star Rt. Box 73A
Oroville (Chesaw), WA 98844

(509) 485-3605
Mail order
Catalog $1.00

The Good Seed Company is a family business that believes in the preservation of old seed and tree varieties. The current catalog includes bulbs of garlic and elephant garlic and seeds for everlastings, parsley, peppers, cardoon, hyssop, salvias and many more. Some books and general gardening supplies are also offered.

Goodwin Creek Gardens

Jim and Dotti Becker
PO Box 83
Williams, OR 97544

(503) 488-3308
Established 1977
Mail order; retail
Catalog $1.00

Goodwin Creek Gardens is a small family farm located in the foothills of the Siskiyou Mountains of southwestern Oregon. The Beckers specialize in raising herbs, everlasting flowers and fragrant plants. Many native American herbs are propagated in the Goodwin Creek nursery, too. All plants are organically grown and shipped in 2¾-inch pots. Seeds are available as well. Some of the plants offered are agrimony, alkanet, aloe, angelica, artemisias, balloon flower, bay laurel, bee balm, boneset, butterfly weed, calamint, cardoon, celandine, Chinese lanterns, dyer's broom, Egyptian onion, hops, gotu kola, jojoba, lemongrass, 20 lavenders, madder, maypop, pennyroyal, prickly pear, pyrethrum, 12 rosemaries, 18 thymes, yerba buena and hundreds more. More than 60 varieties of herb seeds are also listed in the catalog.

Jim and Dotti Becker are the authors of *A Concise Guide to Growing Everlastings* ($7.95 +.75 postage from the address above). (See Chapter 4 for comments on the book.)

Great Lakes Herb Company

Ron Holch
PO Box 6713
Minneapolis, MN 55406

(612) 722-1201
Established 1988
Mail order; wholesale; retail
Catalog $1.00

In addition to thousands of herbal products (see listing in Chapter 2), Great Lakes Herb Company carries herb seeds from Abundant Life Seed Co. and bulk sprouting seeds. Some of the more unusual seeds are breadseed poppy, epazote, wild Aztec tobacco, alfalfa and red clover.

Greenmantle Nursery

Marissa Fishman
3010 Ettersburg Rd.
Garberville, CA 95440

(707) 986-7504
Established 1983
Mail order; retail and/or garden tours by appointment only
Catalog $3.00; rose list only, legal size SASE

Greenmantle Nursery offers a wide range of old and unusual fruit varieties in addition to 250 types of classic roses. The plants are all organically grown with no chemical fertilizers or pesticides. The roses include species roses, rugosas, gallicas, damasks, tea roses and hybrid musks.

Gurney Seed & Nursery Co.

Anita Gross
110 Capital St.
Yankton, SD 57079

(605) 665-1930
Established 1866
Mail order
Catalog free

Gurney is an all-around seed and plant supplier whose current catalog includes a limited number of herb and seasoning plants (leek, horseradish, French shallot, garlic, elephant garlic, chives, ginger, mint, French tarragon) and herb seeds. The seeds include borage, caraway, catnip, chamomile, lemon balm, rosemary and more. Also offered are a wide variety of annual and perennial flowers, many of which are everlastings.

Hartman's Herb Farm

Lynn and Pete Hartman
Old Dana Rd.
Barre, MA 01005

(508) 355-2015
Established 1975
Mail order; wholesale; retail; public garden
Catalog $2.00

Hartman's Herb Farm is a family business that offers a wide range of herbal products. More than 200 varieties of herb plants are available, including seven artemisias, 13 basils, chervil, echinacea, hops, indigo, ten lavenders, 17 mints, shallots, alpine strawberries, 20 thymes and eight yarrows. A large number of perennials are available (shipped bare root), including hollyhock, alkanet, columbine, baby's-breath, cornflower, flax, bee balm, pyrethrum and more. More than 60 scented geraniums are also listed.

The Hartmans also create and sell herbal gifts as well as a beautiful "Herbal Calendar" each year. (Also see listing in Chapter 2.)

Havasu Hills Herb Farm

Cynthia Stratton, Jan Dunn and Val Myrick
20150-A Rough & Ready Trail
Sonora, CA 95370

(209) 536-1420
Established 1985 (new owners 1990)
Mail order; wholesale; retail
Catalog $1.00

Havasu Hills Herb Farm carries a number of herb plants, scented geraniums and seeds that are available by mail order. These include betony, catnip, clary sage, comfrey, curry plant, dittany of Crete, fennel, germander and lemongrass.

Heirloom Garden Seeds

Arie Raysor
PO Box 138
Guerneville, CA 95446

(800) 745-0761 or (707) 869-0967
Established 1972
Mail order; wholesale
Catalog $2.50

Heirloom Garden Seeds' catalog is a delightful collection of tidbits of legend and lore illustrated with quaint antique woodcuts. Seeds include adonis, agrimony, alfalfa, alkanet, amaranth, angelica, arugula, balloon flower, basil, yellow bedstraw, campion, chickweed, cilantro, dill, elecampane, epazote, gourds, immortelle, lunaria, marigolds, mignonette, milkweed, nasturtium, orach, scarlet and blue pimpernel and many more.

The Herb Barn

Sandy Nelson
Trout Run, PA 17771

(717) 995-9327
Established 1977
Mail order; retail
Brochure for SASE

Sandy Nelson offers a variety of herb plants including angelica, artemisias, bay, bedstraw, bugleweed, horseradish, lavenders,

mints, parsley, dwarf pomegranate, rosemary, sages, many scented geraniums, tansy, thymes, lemon verbena and yarrow.

The Herb Garden

Steve and Ann Beall
PO Box 773
Pilot Mountain, NC 27041-0773

(919) 368-2723
Established 1983
Mail order; retail
Catalog $3.00

The Herb Garden's catalog includes information on growing, fertilizing, harvesting and preserving herbs as well as a list of several hundred herb plants. These include ten artemisias, 16 basils, four fennels, nine lavenders, 18 mints, 17 yarrows and many more. The Bealls also carry a large number of botanicals, oils and dried herbs; see listing in Chapter 2.

Herbamed Medicinal Herb Nursery

Barbara Miller
PO Box 209
Bermagui South
NSW Australia 2547

Phone: 0641 934 896
Established 1986
Price list free (Ask for the seed list.)

Herbamed offers a number of seeds for medicinal herbs, wildflowers, wild vegetables and spices.

The Herbary & Stuff

Mary Lou Hamilton
Rt. 3, Box 83
Jacksonville, TX 75766

(903) 586-2114
Established 1989
Mail order; retail
Catalog $2.00

The Herbary & Stuff sells plants with more than 70 varieties of herbs, 20 varieties of old-fashioned flowers and more than 15 kinds of peppers. The retail shop on the farm sells unusual jams and jellies, wreaths, bulk herbs and spices, etc.

The Herbfarm

Carrie Van Dyck and Ron Zimmerman
32804 Issaquah-Fall City Rd.
Fall City, WA 98024

(206) 784-2222
Established 1978
Mail order; retail; public garden
Catalog $3.50 includes plant list; $2.00 refundable with purchase

The Herbfarm's plant catalog lists more than 600 herbs and related plants: agrimony, aloe vera, alyssum, anchusa, angelica, artemisias, astilbe, baby's-breath, lemon balm, basils, bleeding heart, Canterbury bells, purple coneflower, crocus, many scented geraniums, feverfew, horseradish, germander, knotweed, mints, mullein, onions, rosemary, poppies, saxifrage, self-heal, stock, St. John's wort, statice, thymes, woad, wood betony and hundreds more. A small number of culinary herb and edible flower seeds (mostly annuals) are also listed. (Also see listings in Chapters 2, 6 and 8.)

Herbs-Liscious

Carol Lacko-Beem
1702 S. 6th St.
Marshalltown, IA 50158

(515) 752-4976
Established 1987
Mail order; wholesale; retail; public garden
Catalog $2.00

Herbs-Liscious carries a wide variety of herb plants, dried herbs and herb products. All 250+ varieties of herbs are organically grown. These include 11 basils, chicory, chamomile, centaury, coltsfoot, ginger, ginkgo, heliotrope, foxglove, 16 mints, perilla, pimpernel and many more.

Carol Lacko-Beem also offers a custom growing service; you tell her what you want and she'll grow it for you! (Also see listing in Chapter 2.)

Heritage Rose Gardens

Joyce Demits and Virginia Hopper
16831 Mitchell Creek Drive
Ft. Bragg, CA 95437

Established 1981
Mail order
Catalog $1.00

Heritage Rose Gardens supplies two-year-old, field grown plants on their own roots that are shipped bare root. Included in the current catalog are species roses, gallicas, damasks, perpetual damasks, centifolias, albas, moss roses, ramblers and climbers, bourbon roses, China roses, noisettes, rugosas, polyanthas, hybrids and many others.

Heritage Seed Program

Canadian Organic Growers (See listing in Chapter 9).

Hidden Springs Herbs

Kathleen Lander and Mark Smith
Rt. 14, Box 159C
Cookeville, TN 38501

(615) 268-9354
Established 1976
Mail order
Price list for SASE

Hidden Springs Herbs offers herb plants by mail order, including some annuals and many perennials. Among the latter are 12 mints, 11 thymes and a good number of scented geraniums.

High Altitude Gardens

Bill McDorman
PO Box 4619
Ketchum, ID 83340

(800) 874-7333
Established 1984
Catalog $2.00

High Altitude Gardens is a bioregional seed company dedicated to saving and expanding the genetic resources of the "alta-region" by selling open-pollinated varieties of seeds. As the Gardens are located at 6000 feet, Bill McDorman focuses naturally on the challenge of gardening in harsh climates. The catalog lists vegetables, herbs, wildflowers, native grasses and more—many of which have been recently brought from Siberia. The herb seeds include Italian and regular sweet basil, borage, calendula, chamomile, cilantro, catnip, chives, dill, garlic chives, mole-plant, lemon balm, sawtooth mountain mint, true Greek oregano, Italian parsley, curled parsley, Japanese parsley, sage, thyme and wormwood. Books, soil amendments and other items are also offered.

Hilltop Herb Farm

Beverly Smith
PO Box 325
Romayor, TX 77368

(713) 592-5859
Established 1957
Brochure free

For three decades, the Hilltop Herb Farm has been serving specialty foods using only fresh ingredients and seasonings, many of which are grown right on the farm. Now a list of plants and seeds is available by mail order, as are a number of gourmet foods and gift baskets (see listing in Chapter 2). Plants include scented geraniums, thymes, mints, rosemaries, sages and many others. Seeds are available for basils, cilantro, chives, dill, fennel, parsley, salad burnet, tansy and sage.

Historical Roses

Ernest J. Vash
1657 W. Jackson Street
Painesville, OH 44077

(216) 357-7270
Brochure for SASE

E.J. Vash specializes in heritage roses, including old-fashioned shrub roses, climbers, hybrid perpetuals, floribundas and hybrid tea roses. All roses are two years old and field grown.

Holbrook Farm and Nursery

Allen Bush
PO Box 368
Fletcher, NC 28732-0368

(704) 891-7790
Established 1980
Mail order; retail; public garden
Catalog $2.00; refundable with purchase

The informative Holbrook Farm and Nursery catalog includes hundreds of perennials, grasses, wildflowers, ferns and woody plants. A few of these are bee balm, cone-

At spring (for the summer) sow garden ye shall,
at harvest (for winter) sow not at all;
Oft digging, removing and weeding (ye see) makes herb the more wholesome, and greater to be.

—from *Tusser's Calendar*, 1573

flowers, yarrows, bugleweed, lady's-mantle, hollyhock, artemisias, coreopsis, lily-of-the-valley, foxglove, milkwort, meadowsweet and baby's-breath.

The Hollow, Orchids & Herbs
Joane Molenock
71 German Crossroad
Ithaca, NY 14850

(607) 277-3380
Established 1975
Mail order; retail at greenhouse
Herb list for SASE

Joane Molenock carries a variety of herbs, including 14 basils, six lavenders, seven rosemaries, 14 thymes and many others.

Honolulu Community Action Program, Inc.
Mr. Lono M. Lauahi, Herb Project
Coordinator
99-102 Kalaloa St.
Aiea, HI 96701-3801

(808) 487-7404
Established 1984
Wholesale only
Call or write for information.

The Honolulu Community Action Program, Inc., is a non-profit human service agency employing senior citizens and handicapped workers. The workers grow the herbs, and the agency processes and ships them to wholesale accounts. Sweet basil is their biggest seller, but other herbs are available also: rosemary, opal and cinnamon basil and others. The growing season in Hawaii runs from October 1 through June, but the group has items for sale all year. A catalog is not available at this time; call or write for more information.

Hortico, Inc.
Harry A. de Vries
723 Robson Rd.
Waterdown, Ontario
Canada L0R 2H1

(416) 689-6984; FAX (416) 689-6566
Established 1970
Mail order; wholesale; retail
Catalog $2.00

Hortico carries a large number of herbs, wildflowers, bog plants, and grasses, not to mention more than 450 varieties of roses (hybrid teas, floribundas, miniatures, shrub and tree roses) and more than 500 varieties of perennials.

Horticultural Enterprises
PO Box 810082
Dallas, TX 75381-0082

Established 1973
Mail order; retail
Catalog free

Horticultural Enterprises carries seed for chili peppers, including anchos, Anaheims, pasillas, jalapeños, serranos, cayenne, pepperoncini and others. A few other Mexican herbs, seasonings and vegetables are listed, including tomatillos, chia, cilantro and tatume squash. (Shipments to U.S. only.)

Hsu's Ginseng Enterprises
PO Box 509HC
Wausau, WI 54402-0509

(800) 826-1577
Established 1981
Mail order; retail
Catalog free

Hsu's Ginseng Enterprises lists ginseng seeds, rootlets and other ginseng products in its current catalog.

Hubble Hill Herbs

Roselynn Hubble
PO Box 2083
Loveland, CO 80539-2083

(303) 669-0756
Established 1988
Mail order
Catalog $2.00; refundable with order

Hubble Hill Herbs offers seeds for a limited number of herbs, ornamental gourds and ornamental grasses. Some of the herbs listed in the small but very informative catalog are anise, seven basils, borage, caraway, catnip, coriander, hyssop, lamb's-ears and marjoram.

Roselynn Hubble's fact-filled booklet titled *Herbal Spotlight* includes lots of fascinating "herbal secrets" such as "Culinary Herbal Recipes", "Old Timey Uses" for herbs, "Garden Tips", "Companion Planting Instructions" and more. The booklet currently sells for $10.00 postpaid.

J. L. Hudson, Seedsman

PO Box 1058
Redwood City, CA 94064

Established 1911
Mail order; retail
Catalog $1.00

J. L. Hudson stresses open-pollinated seeds and the preservation of our genetic resources, in addition to supporting the free and unrestricted worldwide exchange of seeds and knowledge. Many of the rare or unusual seeds offered here are listed by Latin names; you may need to search to find the many herbs scattered throughout the catalog. It is worth the time, however. Hudson's "Zapotec collection" includes seeds for chilis, epazote, wild marigolds, and many other interesting varieties.

J. L. Hudson will sometimes exchange seed from the wild or from unusual plants in your garden for credit on orders. Ask for the "Seed Exchange" pamphlet for further information.

Ed Hume Seeds

Mail Order Clerk
PO Box 1450
Kent, WA 98035

FAX (206) 859-0694
Established 1977
Mail order; wholesale to retailers
Catalog free

Ed Hume Seeds carries a variety of seeds for vegetables, herbs, flowers (including everlastings), as well as garlic bulbs. The herbs include anise, borage, caraway, catnip, dill, fennel, sweet marjoram, sage, peppermint, arugula (roquette) and thyme. Ed Hume has a weekly syndicated gardening show, "Gardening in America".

Hundley Ridge Farm

Tom and Loretta Hundley
Box 253 Squiresville Rd.
Perry Park, KY 40363

(502) 484-5922
Established 1985
Mail order; wholesale; retail; public garden
Catalog free

The Hundleys offer a number of herbs, everlastings, perennials and scented geraniums in their current catalog. All plants come in 3½-inch pots. Wooden herb baskets, herb markers and market baskets are also for sale.

Iden Croft Herbs

Rosemary Titterington
Frittenden Rd.
Staplehurst, Kent
England TN12 0DH

Phone: 0580 891 432 or FAX 0580 892416
Established 1970
Mail order; retail; wholesale; public garden
Catalog £3.00 overseas

Iden Croft Herbs has one of the most beautiful catalogs that I've seen in a long time. It's a "Year Book" that lists plants with growing requirements, cultivation hints, recipes and loads of other helpful information. Separate lists of herb seeds and plants include companion plants, common herbs, wild (native) flowers and old-fashioned cottage garden flowers. (Also see listing in Chapter 8).

Rosemary Titterington has also written a book titled *Growing Herbs—A Guide to Management* (see description in Chapter 4). The book is available from the address above; write for current price.

Enter then, the Rose-garden when the first sunshine sparkles in the dew, and enjoy with thankful happiness one of the loveliest scenes of earth. What a diversity and yet what a harmony of colour! . . . What a diversity, and yet what a harmony of outline!

—Dean Hole, 1895, in
A Book About Roses.
Reprinted in the
Antique Rose Emporium
catalog

In Harmony with Nature

Donna Hollopeter
RD #1, Box 109 North St.
Rockton, PA 15856-0040

(814) 583-7887
Established 1986
Mail order; retail
Catalog $3.00; refundable with purchase

Donna Hollopeter carries more than 300 varieties of perennials and 300 varieties of herbs as well as some native plants (shipped in spring only). In addition, she offers herbal products, natural foods products, books and small sizes of organic gardening fertilizers and other organic gardening products.

It's About Thyme

Diane Barnes
PO Box 878 (729 FM 1626)
Manchaca, TX 78652

(512) 280-1192
Established 1979
Mail order; wholesale; retail
Catalog $1.00; refundable with order

Diane Barnes offers a large number of herb and everlasting plants by mail order, most grown and shipped in 4-inch pots. These include yarrows, aloe vera, ambrosia, arugula, a number of artemisias, lots of basils, borage, cardamom, chervil, cilantro, cumin, epazote, purple coneflower, several eucalyptuses, scented geraniums, germanders, heliotrope, henna, hoja santa, indigo, bay laurel, lavenders, lovage, 11 mints, Greek and Italian oregano, rue, rosemaries, speedwell, tansy, lots of thymes and wormwood. Everlastings include celosias, sea holly, globe amaranth, strawflowers, statice and others.

The company also offers custom garden design and installation.

Johnny's Selected Seeds

Barbara Kennedy and Rob Johnston
Foss Hill Rd.
Albion, ME 04910

(207) 437-4301; FAX (207) 437-2165
Established 1973
Mail order; retail
Catalog free

Johnny's Selected Seeds is an all-around garden seed supplier with a good listing of herb seeds: basils, bee balm, borage, calendula, chervil, dill, lavender, garlic chives, lemon balm, mint, pennyroyal, rosemary, perilla, creeping thyme, wormwood and others. The catalog also lists a number of wildflowers, edible flowers and everlastings together with seed starting supplies, floral materials and other garden tools and equipment.

John's Gourmet Gardens

A. John Gaige
9010 Burnett Dr.
Boise, ID 83709

(208) 362-4439
Established 1984
Wholesale only
*Write on company letterhead for more
information.*

John's Gourmet Gardens provides a number of herb plants in flats, scented geraniums and vegetables to wholesale accounts only.

J. W. Jung Seed Company

J. C. Jung
335 S. High Street
Randolph, WI 53957

(414) 326-3121
Established 1907
Mail order; retail
Catalog free

The J. W. Jung Seed Company is a general garden supply company that carries a number of everlastings, perennials and herbs (both plants and seeds) in its current catalog.

Kingfisher, Inc.

Liz Bair
PO Box 75
Wexford, PA 15090-0075

(412) 935-2233
Established 1989
Mail order; wholesale
Catalog $2.00

Kingfisher, Inc. (formerly Halcyon Gardens) offers a number of herb seeds, seed collections, and specialty items. The seeds include alpine strawberry, opal basil, lemon catnip, Russian comfrey, echinacea, edelweiss, heliotrope, horehound, lovage, mignonette, opium poppy and many others. Collections include culinary, indoor kitchen, herb tea and Shakespeare garden.

An herb nursery kit contains a seed collection, pots, seed starting trays, growing medium and herb booklet. Kitchensill herbs include a ceramic growing container with a color graphic on front depicting the plant, seed, a plastic pot with drainage and a cork stopper for later use in storing the herbs in the growing container. The indoor cat garden is similar but includes catnip or grass oats, and the jars are decorated with cat motifs.

A Kiss of the Sun Nursery

Pamela Johnson
5273 S. Coast Hwy.
South Beach, OR 97366

(503) 867-6578
Established 1981
Mail order; retail; public garden
Catalog $1.00

A Kiss of the Sun Nursery offers a large variety of herbs and perennials, including some unusual ones. Angelica, anise, ballota, bayberry, betony, cardamom, cardoon, cat thyme, chervil, sweet cicely, citronella, comfrey, costmary, saffron crocus, cumin, horehound, many lavenders, garden mace, more than 20 mints, myrtle, patchouli, rampion (the "Rapunzel" plant), nine rosemaries, samphire, many artemisias, dianthus, echinacea, scented geraniums and violets are some of their offerings. Books are also listed.

Krystal Wharf Farms

Burt Israel
RD 2, Box 2112
Mansfield, PA 16933

(717) 549-8194
Established 1985
Price list free; write for more information.

Krystal Wharf Farms offers organically grown vegetables, dried goods, herbs and garden seeds.

D. Landreth Seed Co.

Shirley Gastrell
180–188 West Ostend St.
Baltimore, MD 21230

(301) 727-3922
Established 1784
Catalog $2.00

D. Landreth Seed Co. is America's oldest seed house, and boasts some familiar names on its past customer list: George Washington (who was extended 30 days' credit on his seed purchase), Thomas Jefferson and Joseph Bonaparte, among others. Today the company offers a wide variety of seeds for vegetables, flowers, everlastings, fruits and herbs.

Le Jardin du Gourmet

Paul Taylor
PO Box 275
St. Johnsbury Center, VT 05863-0275

(802) 748-1446
Established 1954
Mail order; retail
Catalog $.50

Le Jardin du Gourmet has earned a reputation for its variety of gourmet foods from around the world, sample packets of seeds and live plants. This source offers an assortment of shallots, garlics and onions, as well as herb plants that include angelica, garlic chives, sweet cicely, hyssop, English and French lavenders, pennyroyal, pineapple sage, tansy, sweet woodruff and leeks. A good number of everlastings is also listed.

Seeds of herbs and vegetables are available in both sample packets for $.25 for trial or small gardens, and larger packets. Herb seeds include angelica, anise, *Anthemis tinctoria*, globe artichoke, basil, cardoon, chicory, coriander, fennel, woad, mints, poke root, sesame, fuller's teasel, wormwood, Roman and German chamomile and feverfew. (Also see listing in Chapter 2).

Orol Ledden & Sons

Donald Ledden
Box 7, Centre Ave.
Sewell, NJ 08080-0007

(609) 468-1000
Established 1904
Mail order; wholesale; retail
Catalog free

Orol Ledden & Sons carries a wide variety of annual and perennial flower, vegetable and herb seeds in their current catalog. The herbs include anise, basil, borage, caraway, catnip, chervil, chives, coriander, dill, fennel, lavender, oregano, peppermint, roquette, rosemary, summer savory, spearmint, sweet marjoram and a kitchen herb assortment. A good number of peppers, chicory, and dandelion and many everlasting flower seeds are available as well.

Lewis Mountain Herbs & Everlastings

Judy Lewis
2345 St., Rt. 247
Manchester, OH 45144

(513) 549-2484
Established 1985 (formerly Hopewell Gardens)
Mail order; wholesale; retail; public garden
Catalog free

Judy Lewis lists a large number of herbs, everlastings and scented geraniums in her current catalog. The herbs include a number of thymes, mints and sages; everlastings include yarrows, ammobium, artemisias, baby's-breath, lunarias, salvias and tansy. More than 60 varieties of scented geraniums include rose, spice, mint, fruit, pine and pungent scented plants. Some dried materials are offered; see listing in Chapter 2.

Liberty Seed Co.
Tracy Andrews
PO Box 806
New Philadelphia, OH 44663

(216) 364-1611
Established 1981
Mail order; wholesale; retail; public garden
Catalog free

The Liberty Seed Co. home garden catalog lists vegetables, perennials, annuals, bulbs, herbs and accessories. The herb seeds include anise, borage, catnip, chives, cress, marjoram, mints, dill, summer savory and others. Discounts are given on larger quantities of seeds.

Lily of the Valley Herb Farm
Paul and Melinda Carmichael
3969 Fox Avenue
Minerva, OH 44657

(216) 862-3920
Established 1981
Mail order; wholesale; retail
Catalog $2.00

The Carmichaels' Lily of the Valley Herb Farm catalog is a reference guide to more than 570 species of herbs, scented geraniums, everlastings, perennials and ornamentals as well as "quality herbal products". Among the plants are 18 artemisias, 16 basils, ten lavenders, eight mints, six rosemaries and 15 sages. Orrisroot, patchouli, skirret, gotu kola, ginseng and chicory are some of this source's more unusual offerings.

Special assortments of culinary herbs, fragrant herbs, everlastings and scented geraniums are available. (Also see listing in Chapter 2.)

Logee's Greenhouses
Joy Logee Martin
141 North Street
Danielson, CT 06239

(203) 774-8038
Established 1892
Mail order; retail
Catalog $3.00

The Logee's Greenhouses' 128-page full-color catalog is practically an encyclopedia of rare and unusual plants including begonias, cacti and succulents, ferns and mosses, orchids and others. Twelve descriptive pages of nearly 200 common and unusual herbs include 14 passifloras, seven artemisias and 15 salvias. More than 50 varieties of scented geraniums include a Logee cultivar, "Logeei", that smells like Old Spice aftershave. Logee's also carries a number of books. Visitors are welcome at the greenhouses, and plants are shipped year-round, weather permitting.

Louisiana Nursery
Ken Durio
Rt. 7, Box 43
Opelousas, LA 70570-9110

(318) 948-3696
Established 1940
Mail order; retail by appointment; public garden
Catalog $5.00; refundable with purchase

Although the Louisiana Nursery specializes in magnolias and "other garden aristocrats", the 148-page catalog also lists hundreds of perennials and ground covers that include herbs. Just a few of these are yarrows, carpet bugleweed, artemisia 'Silver Mound', coreopsis, evergreen bittersweet, several mints, bee balm, salvias, spiderwort and vetiver.

Mary's Herb Garden & Gift Shop

Betty Ann Viviano
23825 Priest Rd.
Philomath, OR 97370

(503) 929-6275
Established 1989
Catalog free

Mary's Herb Garden & Gift Shop (formerly Salero Herbs) offers a selection of herb seeds, including borage, curled chervil, cilantro, oregano and others. (Also see listing in Chapter 2.)

McClure & Zimmerman

Vicki Huffman
PO Box 368
Friesland, WI 53935-0368

(414) 326-4220
Established 1982
Mail order
Catalog free

McClure & Zimmerman specializes in flower bulbs and has a good selection of alliums—leeks, garlics, onions, chives and shallots. An Allium Collection is also listed in the catalog.

McCrory's Sunny Hill Herbs

Dolores McCrory
35152 LaPlace Ct.
Eustis, FL 32726

(904) 357-9876
Established 1977
Mail order; wholesale; retail by appointment
Catalog $.50; refundable with purchase

McCrory's Sunny Hill Herbs carries herb plants in 4-inch pots. These include aloe, basils, bergamot, betony, comfrey, fennel, henna, lavender, marjorams, mints, rosemaries, sages, soapwort, statice, tansy, turmeric, yarrows and scented geraniums.

Meadowbrook Herb Garden

Judy Gagel
PO Box 578
Fairfield, CT 06430-0578

(203) 254-7323 (mail order)
(401) 539-7603 (wholesale or retail location)
Established 1967
Mail order; wholesale; retail; public garden
Catalog $1.00

Meadowbrook Herb Garden has an extensive plant and seed list. Herbs and everlastings include agrimony, aloe vera, ambrosia, angelica, many artemisias, baby's-breath, basils, bee balm, calendula, celeriac, chervil, Chinese lantern, coreopsis, eucalyptus, foxglove, gas plant, many scented geraniums, germander, heliotrope, speedwell and thymes as well as several herb seed collections. (Also see listings in Chapters 2 and 6.)

Merry Gardens

Mary Ellen Ross
PO Box 595, Mechanic St.
Camden, ME 04843-0595

(207) 236-2121
Established 1946
Mail order; retail
Catalog $1.00

Merry Gardens offers a large list of herb plants and scented geraniums, most of which are available in 2½-inch pots.

Midwest Seed Growers

Mark Pflumm
10559 Lackman Rd.
Lenexa, KS 66219-1290

(913) 894-0500
Established 1946
Mail order; wholesale; retail
Catalog free

Midwest Seed Growers sells many kinds of seed for flowers and vegetables along with some herbs such as sweet basil, coriander, chives, dill and sage. Flower seeds available from this source include balsam, celosias, dianthus (annual), marigold, pansy and others. This company is unusual in that it sells seed in larger quantities—from fractions of an ounce to one pound of some varieties.

Molbak's Seattle Garden Center

Kathryn Taylor
1600 Pike Place
Seattle, WA 98101

(206) 448-0431
Mail order; retail
Write for more information.

Molbak's Seattle Garden Center is located in the historic Pike Place Market in Seattle. The Garden Center is just starting in mail order, but has been serving the Seattle area for years with herb plants and gardening supplies. The seed selection, which is available by mail order, includes more than 125 varieties. Among these are 18 varieties of basil, damassia (a natural slug and snail killer), culinary herbs and hard-to-find medicinal herbs such as gotu kola, ambrosia and Chinese rhubarb. The Garden Center also offers an extensive list of herbal and gardening books.

Moon Mountain Wildflowers

Donna Vaiano
PO Box 34
Morro Bay, CA 93443-0034

(805) 772-2473
Established 1981
Mail order; wholesale; retail
Catalog $2.00

Moon Mountain Wildflowers offers seed for cornflower, coreopsis, yarrow, chicory, foxglove, purple coneflower, several salvias, crimson clover and more.

Native Seeds/SEARCH

Kevin Dahl
2509 N. Campbell #325
Tucson, AZ 85719

(602) 327-9123 (office phone; no orders)
Established 1983
Mail order; display garden at the Tucson Botanical Gardens
Catalog $1.00

Native Seeds/SEARCH (Southwestern Endangered Aridland Resource Clearing House) is a nonprofit membership seed conservation organization that works to preserve the traditional crops and their wild relatives of the U.S. Southwest and northwestern Mexico. The group sponsors a seed bank of these crops that are adapted to these desert regions. The catalog indicates whether crops have been grown successfully in low desert or high desert plantings, or are suitable for both. Some seeds are sold in bulk. Seeds currently available include amaranth, chilis, chiltepines, cotton, gourds, indigo, onions and sunflowers. Herb seeds include chia roja, cilantro, desert chia, epazote, guarijio conivari, mayo/yaqui basil, Mrs. Burns' Famous lemon basil, Mt. Pima oregano, Tarahumara/Mt. Pima anis (also called Mexican mint marigold) and Tarahumara chia.

Although you don't have to be a member to buy seeds from Native Seeds/SEARCH, members receive a quarterly newsletter, *The Seedhead News,* and can get a 10% discount on purchases and free admission to the annual Chili Fiesta. The organization also has a 30-minute slide/tape program that is available with a $25.00 deposit to groups to borrow as an introduction to seed saving, genetic diversity and the mission of Native Seeds/SEARCH.

Why We Grow What We Do

We grow herbs because too many things in life are difficult and complicated. Herbs are not, and add graciousness and simplicity to our sometimes hectic lives with a minimum of effort on our part. They are ornamental landscape plants, useful culinary plants, and are easily grown given a little soil, sunlight and water. We could hardly ask for more.

—from The Story House Herb Farm catalog

New Hope Herb Farm

Carolee Bean
Rt. 1, Box 660
Spencer, IN 47460

(812) 829-6086
Established 1985
Catalog $1.00

New Hope Herb Farm supplies a number of herb, everlastings and perennial plants by mail order: alkanet, ambrosia, angelica, aloe, arugula, baby's-breath, bachelor-button, balm of Gilead, many basils, bells of Ireland, bergenia, butterfly weed, cardoon, catchfly, coltsfoot, coreopsis, dill, foxglove, mammoth fennel, germander, scented geraniums, lavender, sages, vanilla grass, and many other unusual or rare varieties.

From time to time, the Farm also offers a number of dried everlastings for sale. (Also see listing in Chapter 6.)

Niche Gardens

Kim and Bruce Hawks
1111 Dawson Rd.
Chapel Hill, NC 27516-8576

(919) 967-0078
Established 1986
Mail order; retail by appointment
Catalog $3.00 (includes periodic newsletter)

Kim and Bruce Hawks of Niche Gardens specialize in nursery-propagated southeastern native plants. They also offer other North American natives, some perennials, ornamental grasses and underutilized trees and shrubs. Available plants from this source include bee balm, black-eyed Susan, butterfly weed, coneflowers, coreopsis, fennel, foxglove, goldenrod, Joe-Pye weed, milkweed, compact oregano, prickly pear, Queen-Anne's-lace, salvia and others. The Hawkses also offer landscape design services. Call or write for details.

Nichols Garden Nursery

Rose Marie McGee
1190 North Pacific Hwy.
Albany, OR 97321-4598

(503) 928-9280
Established 1950
Mail order; wholesale; retail; public garden
Catalog free

Nichols Garden Nursery offers a large selection of herbs, flowers and vegetables in their current catalog. Ten basils, fleabane, goatsbeard, Jerusalem oak, black lovage, meadowsweet, two perillas, and a lemon-flavored agastache are among the 112 herbs offered as seed. Among the 88 kinds of herb plants are six lavenders, nine mints, 12 thymes, Labrador violet, and lemon verbena. Herb teas, potpourri kits, homebrew and winemaking supplies, garden tools and sourdough starter are some of the other offerings in this fascinating catalog.

NORTHPLAN/Mountain Seed

Loring M. Jones
PO Box 9107
Moscow, ID 83843-1607

(208) 882-8040
Established 1978
Catalog $1.00

This company offers several herb seeds in its general catalog: anise, sweet basil, burnet, caraway, coriander, dill, fennel, lavender, peppermint, sage, spearmint and several others.

An additional catalog of native wildflowers, shrubs, trees, grasses and legumes is available for an additional $1.00. Ask for the native species seed list.

Owen Farms

Lillian and Edric Owen
2951 Curve-Nankipoo Rd.
Rt. 3, Box 158-A
Ripley, TN 38063-9420

*(901) 635-1588 (between sunset and 10:00
p.m. CST)*
Established 1986
Mail order; wholesale; retail
Catalog $2.00

Owen Farms supplies trees, shrubs and perennials in its mail-order catalog. Perennials include yarrows, sneezewort, anise hyssop, carpet bugleweed, wormwood, milkweed, coreopsis, sweet woodruff, Greek oregano, mints, salvias, thymes and others.

George W. Park Seed Co.

Joyce Reagin, Public Relations
Cokesbury Rd.
Greenwood, SC 29647-0001

(800) 845-3369
Established 1868
Catalog free

The Park Seed Co. is one of the country's oldest all-purpose garden suppliers. They carry everything from flowers, herbs, vegetables and fruits to small composters and other garden equipment. The herb seeds included are both perennials and annuals, as well as several herb seed collections. A number of perennial herb plants are offered, including ginseng and horseradish roots.

The Park Seed Company also offers a book, Gertrude Foster and Rosemary Louden's *Park's Success with Herbs* (see Chapter 4 for comments).

Peace Seeds

Alan M. Kapuler, Ph.D.
2385 SE Thompson St.
Corvallis, OR 97333

(503) 752-0421
Established 1975
Mail order; retail
Catalog $3.50

Peace Seeds, "A Planetary Gene Pool Resource and Service", offers a number of organically grown, wild-collected, heirloom, traditional or rare seeds for flowers, herbs, vegetables, trees, etc. Just a few of these are amaranth, ambrosia, angelica, arnica, bloodroot, borage, burdock, carob, clover, coneflowers, dandelion, ephedra, flax, frangipani, ginseng, jojoba, luffa, milkweeds, mullein, orach, purslane, tobacco and yerba santa. All plants are listed by family, but a handy common name index will clear up any confusion. It is interesting and educational to see plants listed this way. For instance, did you know that ginseng is related to carrots?

The Pepper Gal

Jenny Jacks
PO Box 12534
Lake Park, FL 33403-0534

Established 1970
Mail order
Price list for SASE

The Pepper Gal is a good source for pepper seeds of all kinds—ornamentals such as Deep Purple, Firecracker, Orange Blossom, Peter peppers (regular and extra large), Red Missiles, Royal Black, Thais and many more. Hot varieties include Anaheim, ancho, cayenne, chile de arbol, jalapeño, habanero, Ring of Fire, serrano, tabasco; sweet varieties include California wonder, cubanelle, giant yellow banana, paprika, pepperoncini, pimiento, red cherry peppers and lots more!

Pinetree Garden Seeds

Dick Meiners
Route 100
New Gloucester, ME 04260

(207) 926-3400
Established 1979
Mail order; retail
Catalog free

Pinetree Garden Seeds caters to the home gardener with less space and less need for large seed packets. The catalog lists more than 700 varieties of seeds as well as tools and plants. The herb seed list includes about 50 varieties; the everlasting seed list includes just as many. Also in this quaint, informative catalog are bulbs, garlic, many vegetables, sprouting seeds, flower presses, kitchen gadgets and numerous books.

Plants of the Southwest

Ingrid Olson
Agua Fria, Rt. 6, Box 11A
Santa Fe, NM 87501

(505) 983-1548
Established 1979
Mail order; wholesale; retail
Catalog $1.50

Ingrid Olson's Plants of the Southwest supplies native seeds and plants for ancient American vegetables, modern vegetables, herbs, cover crops and grasses, trees, shrubs and wildflowers. A few of the plants listed in this encyclopedic catalog are amaranth (golden grain and purple), chili peppers, Hopi dye sunflowers, basils, borage, catnip, chia, chives, comfrey, cota (Navajo tea), epazote, nasturtiums, oregano, osha, curled peppergrass, rosemary, poppy (breadseed), sage and mother-of-thyme. Also listed are beneficial insects, fertilizers and biological pest controls, wildflowers (senna, jimsonweed, coreopsis, yarrow, bee balm) and much more.

Ingrid Olson also offers a landscaping service for people in her area.

Prairie Moon Nursery

Alan Wade
Rt. 3, Box 163
Winona, MN 55987

(507) 452-1362
Established 1982
Mail order; retail by appointment
Catalog $1.00

The Prairie Moon Nursery carries both plants and seeds of native species indigenous to North America prior to European settlement: yellow and purple giant hyssops, wild garlic, wild leek, false indigo, columbine, swamp milkweed, many asters, wild senna, New Jersey tea, bittersweet, sand or prairie coreopsis, coneflowers, Joe-Pye weed, false boneset, spotted bee balm, violets, goldenrods and hundreds more. Also offered are grasses and sedges as well as many seed mixes. All plants are grown organically at the nursery, not dug from the wild.

Prairie Seed Source

Robert Ahrenhoerster
PO Box 83
North Lake, WI 53064-0083

Established 1972
Mail order; retail
Catalog $1.00

Prairie Seed Source specializes in prairie restoration and offers seed that is representative of southeastern Wisconsin prairie plants. These include wildflowers, grasses and shrubs. Some of the wildflowers offered are tall cinquefoil, blue-eyed grass, lupines, meadow rue, spiderwort, pale purple coneflower, wild bergamot, boneset and many others.

Chamomile was once known as "The Plants' Physician" by colonial housewives since sickly plants would recover if chamomile was planted nearby.

Putney Nursery, Inc.

C. H. and Ruth Gorius
Rt. 5
Putney, VT 05346

(802) 387-5577
Established 1923
Mail order; retail; public garden
Catalog $1.00; refundable with purchase

The Putney Nursery's "Old Tyme Seed Catalog" features wildflowers, herbs, perennials and alpine plants. Seeds listed include a wildflower meadow seed mix for different regions, yarrows, butterfly weed, purple coneflower, baby's-breath, Queen-Anne's-lace, lunaria, bee balm, lamb's-ears, creeping thyme, violets, dill, chives, wormwood, coriander, hyssop, lavender, lovage, mints, anise and others.

Rasland Farm

Dick and Sylvia Tippett
NC 82 at US 13
Godwin, NC 28344-9712

(919) 567-2705
Established 1981
Mail order; wholesale; public garden; retail
Catalog $2.50

Rasland Farm offers a wide variety of culinary, fragrant, medicinal and ornamental herb plants and many scented geraniums. These include aloe vera, anise hyssop, Australian rosemary, basils, bay laurel, bergamot, cedronella, chamomile, chervil, comfrey, purple coneflower, costmary, curry plant, lemongrass, horehound, hyssop, lady's-mantle, lavenders, mints, patchouli, rosemaries, rue, sages, skullcap, sorrel, sweet flag, thymes, lemon verbena, sweet woodruff and yarrows. All plants are well-rooted and shipped in 3-inch pots by UPS in April, May and early June. (Also see listing in Chapter 2.)

Rawlinson Garden Seed

Bill Rawlinson
269 College Rd.
Truro, Nova Scotia
Canada B2N 2P6

(902) 893-3051
Established 1979
Mail order; retail (from February through June)
Catalog $1.00 to U.S.; free in Canada; $1.50 overseas

Rawlinson Garden Seed carries a number of seeds for vegetables, herbs and flowers. Herb seeds include anise, lemon balm, basil, borage, chamomile, catnip, chervil, chives, garlic chives, coriander, fenugreek, sweet marjoram, rosemary and others. A planting instruction booklet is sent free with all seed orders.

Redwood City Seed Company

Craig and Sue Dremann
PO Box 361
Redwood City, CA 94064

(415) 325-7333
Established 1971
Mail order; wholesale; retail
Catalog $1.00; catalog supplement $2.00 for one year (lists seasonal items, rare or unusual seeds that are available only in smaller quantities).

The Redwood City Seed Company specializes in "useful plants"—those that have more than purely an ornamental use (food, dye, medicinal, etc.)— and is the world's oldest alternative seed company. The Dremanns do not sell hybrids; they concentrate on the older varieties, obtaining seeds from many countries and cultures. Just a few of the seeds listed in this fascinating catalog are amaranths, edible burdock, chicory, Florence fennel, garlic chives, garlic sets, nasturtiums, parsley, many hot and sweet peppers, shallots, ajwain (a Near Eastern and African herb), basils, cumin, epazote, black mustard, mugwort, perilla, comfrey, flax, pyrethrum, safflower, sesame, shepherd's-purse, jojoba, luffa and many more.

A number of books and informational pamphlets (many of which are by Mr. Dremann) are available, as well as garden consultations within the San Francisco Bay area. Call for details.

Rabbit Shadow Farm

Mary and Charlie Gibbs
2880 E. Hwy. 402
Loveland, CO 80537

(303) 667-5531
Established 1980
Mail order; retail; wholesale
Catalog $1.00

Herbal topiaries in shapes both standard and fanciful are a specialty of Rabbit Shadow Farm. Their list also includes a broad selection of culinary herbs and antique roses.

Richters

Inge Poot
Box 26
Goodwood, Ontario
Canada L0C 1A0

(416) 640-6677; FAX (416) 640-6641
Established 1971
Mail order; wholesale; retail
Catalog $2.50

Richters has one of the largest selections of herb seeds, plants and dried herbs around. Its extensive list includes aconite, adonis, agrimony, alfalfa, allheal, angelica, arnica, Vietnamese balm, many basils, bloodroot, belladonna, dyer's broom, calamus (sweet flag), cardamom, castor bean, chicory, clivers, blue cohosh, cotton, devil's-claw, ephedra, garlics, many scented geraniums, ginseng, jojoba, madder, mandrake, mints, orris, psyllium, Queen-Anne's-lace, sarsaparilla, sunflowers, tansy and hundreds more! Also listed in the 74-page catalog are books, posters, oils, garden supplies, potpourri

kits, beneficial insects, wildflowers, herb seed collections and everlastings.

An unusual offering is a "Gift Collection of Live Herbs"—an herb garden of 12 live herbs to be shipped anywhere in Canada or the continental U.S. between April to September.

Rose Acres

Muriel and William Humenick
6641 Crystal Blvd.
Diamond Springs, CA 95619-9636

(916) 626-1722
Established 1980
Mail order; retail by appointment
Catalog for SASE

Rose Acres carries several hundred varieties and classes of roses, including climbers, floribundas, miniatures, old garden roses, tea roses and many others.

Rose Hill Herbs and Perennials

Joan R. Rothemich
Rt. 4, Box 377
Amherst, VA 24521

(804) 277-8030
Established 1976
Mail order
Catalog $2.00; refundable with order

Rose Hill Herbs and Perennials carries a number of herb plants, including 17 artemisias, basils, yellow bedstraw, catmint, chamomile, chives, costmary, fennels, feverfew, many scented geraniums, germander, horehound, lavenders, lemon verbena, lovage, ten mints, oreganos, parsley, 13 rosemaries, salvias, santolinas, sorrel, tansy, 13 thymes, sweet woodruff and yarrows. Several special collections are also offered—a Bounty of Basils, A Salad Lover's Collection, a Vinegar Maker's Delight and a Scented Geranium Special.

The Rosemary House

Susanna Reppert, Manager
120 South Market Street
Mechanicsburg, PA 17055

(717) 697-5111
Established 1968
Mail order; wholesale; retail; public garden
Catalog $2.00

Susanna Reppert and her mother, Bertha Reppert, offer a huge assortment of herbal products in their catalog. They sell herb plants and seeds of everything from aconite to zubrovka, with scented geraniums and saffron bulbs in between. (Also see listing in Chapter 2.)

Roses of Yesterday and Today, Inc.

Mrs. Patricia Wiley
803 Browns Valley Rd.
Watsonville, CA 95076-0398

(408) 724-3537 or 724-2755
Established 1952
Mail order; retail; public garden
Catalog $3.00

The 84-page illustrated catalog from Roses of Yesterday and Today lists more than 200 varieties of roses—old, rare, unusual and selected modern roses. These include gallicas, damasks, moss roses, hybrid rugosas, climbers, floribundas, shrub roses, China roses, tea roses, noisettes and many others. Each plant is fully described with size, color, fragrance and ideal climate for that particular rose. Roses are shipped dormant, bare root, between mid-January and late May.

St.-John's Herb Garden, Inc.

Sydney Vallentyne
7711 Hillmeade Rd.
Bowie, MD 20720

(301) 262-5302 or 262-5303
Established 1977
Mail order; wholesale; public garden open May through September
Catalog $5.00

St.-John's carries a number of seeds for vegetables, Victorian flower gardens (annuals and perennials), herbs (from alfalfa to yarrow), spice seeds and bulbs as well as thousands of dried botanicals and other herbal items. (Also see listing in Chapter 2.)

Sandy Mush Herb Nursery

Fairman and Kate Jayne
Rt. 2 Surrett Cove Rd.
Leicester, NC 28748

(704) 683-2014
Established 1976
Mail order; retail
Catalog $4.00

The Jaynes' encyclopedic, hand-calligraphed catalog contains a large number of herb seeds and plants, including many uncommon varieties. The plant list includes elephant garlic, rocambole, aloe, angelica, baby's-breath (white and pink), bayberry, eight bee balms, burnet, cardamom, six catnips, lawn chamomile, costmary, dianthus, flax, purple coneflower, a large number of scented geraniums, ramie, Good-King-Henry, heathers, old-fashioned hollyhock, 16 lavenders, madder, 26 mints, oregano maru (Bible hyssop) and hundreds more. Seeds are available for a number of culinary herbs, gourmet vegetables, everlastings and seeds for dyes, natural fibers and repellents. A good listing of books is also included in the Sandy Mush catalog.

Seeds Blüm

Jan Blüm
Idaho City Stage
Boise, ID 83706

(208) 342-0858
Established 1982
Mail order; retail
Catalog $3.00

Jan Blüm (pronounced "bloom") specializes in heirloom seeds of flowers, vegetables and grains, and carries a good selection of herbs, too, including eight basils, chives, mints, sage, winter and summer savory, anise hyssop, burnet, caraway, chervil, coriander, cumin, hyssop, Greek and Mexican oregano, safflower, tansy, thyme, perilla, nettles and epazote. The catalog is full of interesting information on all the seeds, and lists many books.

Seeds Blüm sponsors several seed-saving programs for gardeners. Write for further information.

Select Seeds—Antique Flowers

Marilyn Barlow
180 Stickney Hill Rd.
Union, CT 06076

(203) 684-5655
Established 1987
Mail order; wholesale; retail by appointment
Catalog $2.00

Select Seeds is a small, home-based business that grew out of Marilyn Barlow's desire to create a period flower garden to complement her 1835 home. Now she specializes in seeds for heirloom plants and offers close to 100 old-fashioned flower varieties, selected for their fragrance and use as cut flowers. These include red yarrow, monkshood, single hollyhock, lady's-mantle, columbine, thrift, swallowwort

(butterfly weed), double feverfew, black cohosh, sweet William, foxgloves, coneflower, baby's-breath, forget-me-not, soapwort, sweet violet, heliotrope, flowering tobacco, mignonette and many more. Also listed are notecards by Julia Bell and several books.

Shady Hill Gardens

Charles F. Heidgen
821 Walnut Street
Batavia, IL 60510

Established 1974
Mail order; wholesale; retail
Catalog $2.00; refundable with purchase

Shady Hill Gardens specializes in geraniums and carries more than 1100 different varieties in its descriptive catalog! More than 65 of these are scented geraniums that include such scents as almond, apple cider, apricot, attar of roses, bitter lemon, chocolate mint, citronella, ginger, lime, nutmeg, peppermint, strawberry and many more. Special prices are given on collections of ten or 20 plants of Shady Hill's choice. Some seed is also available for apple, coconut, mint and mixed scented geraniums.

A book, *Everything You Ever Wanted to Know About Scented geraniums*, is available from Shady Hill Gardens for $3.95 + $1.00 handling.

Shepherd's Garden Seeds

Renee Shepherd
6116 Highway 9
Felton, CA 95018

(408) 335-6910
Established 1984
Mail order; retail; wholesale
Catalog $1.00

Renee Shepherd offers a wide range of carefully tested gourmet vegetable and culinary herb seeds in her extensive catalog, many of them open-pollinated varieties and heirloom cultivars. The charming catalog is a trove of information on different types of herbs, vegetables and flowers, and even includes recipes for using the plants. The seed packets themselves are printed with complete growing and harvesting instructions.

Flower seeds offered by Shepherd's include everlastings (there's a new peach-colored statice), heirloom and old-fashioned cutting flowers, flowers with edible blossoms, and varieties for growing in containers. The herb seeds offered include ten basils, epazote, bronze fennel, French sorrel and three parsleys, one of which is an Italian heirloom seed. Specialty seed collections include a Southwest Seed Collection, the Herbal Tea Collection, the Nasturtium Collection and others. All seeds are also available in individual packets.

Larger quantities of seeds are available for growers, and Shepherd's will accept special orders for seeds that they do not normally stock.

Renee Shepherd has also compiled two wonderful cookbooks, *Recipes from a Kitchen Garden*, Volumes I and II (see Chapter 4 for annotations).

Southern Exposure Seed Exchange

Jeff McCormack
PO Box 158
North Garden, VA 22959

Established 1982
Mail order; wholesale (seed racks only)
Price list for SASE; catalog $3.00

Southern Exposure Seed Exchange specializes in open-pollinated, heirloom and traditional varieties of vegetables, sunflowers, flowers and herbs. Many varieties are available by catalog for the first time. The company also offers a selection of heirloom fruit trees, rare perennial multiplier onions, topset onions and shallots. Herbs include eight basils, echinacea,

fenugreek, hops, a huge selection of peppers and much more. General gardening supplies and books are also listed in this extensive catalog.

Stokes Seeds, Inc.

Mark A. Kaminski
PO Box 548
Buffalo, NY 14240

(416) 688-4300; FAX (416) 684-8411
Established 1881
Mail order; wholesale; retail; public garden
Catalog free

Stokes Seeds is an all-around garden supplier that furnishes an extensive number of seeds of vegetables, perennial and annual flowers, and herbs. Herb seeds include anise, borage, Spicy Globe basil, lemon basil, catnip, chives, French dandelion, lavender, nine parsleys, rosemary, sage and others. The seeds are available by the packet, or in larger quantities up to 25 pounds.

Story House Herb Farm

Cathleen Lalicker and Judy Taylor-Clark
Rt. 7, Box 246
Murray, KY 42071

(502) 753-4158
Established 1990
Mail order; retail by appointment
Catalog $2.00

Story House Herb Farm is a mail-order nursery that specializes in "quality organically grown herb plants and superior customer service". The catalog is divided into two sections, perennials and annuals, and the plants are arranged by common name. Perennials include salad burnet, catmint, catnip, lemon catnip, chives, costmary, a number of scented geraniums, lady's-mantle, lavenders, mints, oregano, rosemaries, sages, southernwood, tansy, thymes, valerian and others. Among the annuals are basils, borage, cardoon, cilantro, dill, parsley, and summer savory. Five herb collections are offered: the Tea Time Collection, the Poultry Seasoning Collection, the Italian Renaissance Collection, the Hope Chest Collection and the Salad Dressing Collection.

Sunnybrook Farms Nursery

Timothy Ruh
9448 Mayfield Rd.
Chesterland, OH 44026

(216) 729-7232
Established 1928
Catalog $1.00; refundable with purchase

Sunnybrook Farms Nursery provides plants of herbs, perennials and scented geraniums. Among them are aloes, angelica, balm of Gilead, basils, salad burnet, chervil, curry plant, heliotrope, lady's-mantle, orris, pimpernel, salsify, soapwort, valerian, weld, woad and others. Herb collections are also listed: Culinary Collection, Fragrance Collection, Everlasting Collection, Dye Plant Collection, Rosemary Collection and more. Some dried herbs, books, bee skeps and essential oils are also listed.

Sunrise Enterprises

Lucia Fu
PO Box 330058
West Hartford, CT 06133-0058

(203) 666-8071 or FAX (203) 665-8156 (preferred)
Established 1975
Mail order; wholesale; retail
Catalog $2.00

Sunrise Enterprises offers seed of a large number of Oriental vegetables and some herbs. These include Chinese leeks (garlic chives), Chinese leek flower, Chinese parsley, mustards, Japanese parsley, sweet basil, perillas, peppermint, watercress, and fennel. Lemongrass plants are available, as are several jasmines. The catalog is printed in English and Chinese.

T & T Seeds, Ltd.

Kevin Twomey
Box 1710
Winnipeg, Manitoba
Canada R3C 3P6

(204) 943-8483
Established 1946
Mail order; retail
Catalog $1.00

T & T Seeds is an all-purpose seed and plant supplier that carries a variety of garden tools and supplies as well as herbs, perennials and everlastings. The company also carries Watkins products and a line of herbal teas and health products.

Taylor's Herb Garden, Inc.

Michele Andre
1535 Lone Oak Rd.
Vista, CA 92084-7723

(619) 727-3485
Established 1947
Mail order; retail
Catalog $3.00

Taylor's Herb Garden lists more than 130 varieties of herb plants and more than 200 varieties of herb seeds in its informative catalog. The catalog includes full descriptions of each plant with information on its uses. Included are five garlics, 11 thymes, six types of scented geraniums and eight mints. The catalog also contains recipes and growing tips.

Taylor's Herb Garden of Arizona, Inc.

Jean Langley
PO Box 362
Congress, AZ 85332

(602) 427-3201
Wholesale only
Price list free (inquire on letterhead)

Taylor's Herb Garden of Arizona provides organically grown fresh cut herbs for restaurants, caterers, etc. on a wholesale-only basis. The herbs are packed in 1- or 2-pound bags. Orders in by 9:00 a.m. are delivered the next day, insuring freshness of the herbs.

Territorial Seed Company

Tom Johns
PO Box 157
Cottage Grove, OR 97451

(503) 942-9547
Established 1979
Mail order; wholesale; retail by appointment
Catalog free

The Territorial Seed Company specializes in seeds that grow west of the Cascades. The herbs listed in the current catalog include dill, fennel, oregano, thyme, sweet marjoram, chervil, summer savory, borage, chives, caraway, French sorrel, lemon basil and others. Seeds for flowers, vegetables and grains are listed, as well as general gardening supplies.

Thomas Jefferson Center for Historic Plants

John T. Fitzpatrick
Monticello, PO Box 316
Charlottesville, VA 22902

(804) 979-5283
Established 1987
Mail order; retail; public garden
Catalog free

The Thomas Jefferson Center for Historic Plants offers seeds harvested from the gardens at Monticello, some of which were actually grown by Jefferson when he lived there. These include native columbine, red orach, larkspur, hyacinth bean, globe amaranth, strawflower, heliotrope and a

"Jefferson sampler". Other seeds, which have been packaged by the Center for Historic Plants at Tufton Farm, include hollyhocks, butterfly weed, bachelor-buttons, foxglove, purple coneflower, alpine strawberry, English lavender, honesty, nasturtium and many others. A number of books and other gardening items are also available.

Thyme Garden Seed Company

Rolfe and Janet Hagen
20546 Alsea Hwy.
Alsea, OR 97324

(503) 487-8671
Established 1990
Mail order; retail; public garden
Catalog $1.50; refundable with order

The Thyme Garden Seed Company catalog includes seeds for more than 100 herbs and everlastings. A few of these are ambrosia, angelica, anise, basils, boneset, borage, calendula, catnip, cardoon, chamomile, coriander, dill, fennel, cumin, epazote, feverfew, Good-King-Henry, flax, jimsonweed, Joe-Pye weed, lavender, lamb's-ears, lemon balm, mullein, rue, safflower, sage, self-heal, sweet cicely, valerian and sweet woodruff. Everlastings include baby's-breath, globe thistle, goldenrod, heliotrope, statice, strawflower and others. (Also see listing in Chapter 8.)

Tinmouth Channel Farm

Carolyn Fuhrer and Kathy Duhnoski
Box 428B, Town Hwy. 19
Tinmouth, VT 05773

(802) 446-2812
Established 1985
Mail order; retail
Catalog $2.00

The Tinmouth Channel Farm is, at this time, the only 100% certified organic herb farm in Vermont. They supply seeds and/or plants for anise hyssop, basils, caraway, chives, cilantro, cumin, dittany of Crete, lady's-mantle, lavender, lemon verbena, mints, pennyroyal, sage, santolina, tansy, sweet woodruff, 13 thymes, Welsh onions (red and white) and wormwood. Plants are shipped until the end of October; seeds are shipped year round.

Otis S. Twilley Seed Company, Inc.

Philip A. Lewandowski
PO Box 65
Trevose, PA 19053

(215) 639-8800
Established in 1920
Mail order; wholesale; retail
Catalog free

The Otis S. Twilley Seed Company caters to the fresh market, roadside and larger-quantity growers. It carries a number of herbs, most of which are available by the packet, ounce or pound. These include arugula, basils, borage, chives, cilantro, dill, fennel, lavender, sweet marjoram, rosemary, sage, summer savory and others. The catalog also lists some everlastings and many peppers, both hot and sweet.

Van Bourgondien Bros.

Debbie Van Bourgondien
PO Box A
Babylon, NY 11702-0598

(516) 669-3500; FAX (516) 669-1228
Mail order
Catalog free

Van Bourgondien Bros. is best known for a wonderful selection of Holland and domestically-grown flower bulbs. However, the company's catalog also lists many perennials, such as baby's-breath, balloon flower, larkspur, liatris, lily of the valley (in white and pink), coneflowers, lavender, three pulmonarias, lamium, three monkshoods, sea hollies and yarrow.

Vileniki—An Herb Farm

Gerry Janus
RD #1, Box 345
Olyphant, PA 18447

(717) 254-9895
Established 1979
Mail order; retail
Catalog $1.50; refundable with order

In the lore of eastern Europe, vileniki´are woodspirits who possess great knowledge of the healing properties of every plant under their protection. The Vileniki Herb Farm's current catalog lists plants for aconite, agrimony, chives, garlic chives, angelica, archangel, artemisias, 16 basils, bloodroot, calendula, German and Roman chamomile, comfrey, costmary, curry plant, elecampane, Good-King-Henry, henbane, lavender, lemongrass, lungwort, many mints, orris, pimpernel, rue, St. John's wort, skullcap, sweet cicely, French tarragon, three thistles, 15 thymes, valerian, vervain, weld, woad and yarrow. (Also see listings in Chapters 5 and 6.)

Washington National Cathedral Gardens

Wisconsin and Massachusetts Ave.
Washington, DC 20016-5098

(202) 537-6263
Established in 1940
Brochure $1.00
(ask for the mail-order herb list)

The Washington National Cathedral Gardens Greenhouse (see listing in Chapter 8) offers a good number of herb plants by mail order: anise, artemisias, basils, borage, burnet, calendula, chervil, coriander, curry plant, feverfew, French lavender, mints, parsley, rosemary (three types), sage, santolina and others.

Wayside Gardens

Joyce Reagin, Public Relations
1 Garden Lane
Hodges, SC 19695-0001

(800) 845-1124
Established 1916
Mail order
Catalog free

Wayside Gardens' beautiful, full-color catalogs include a little bit of everything—roses, other flowers, shrubs, bulbs, vegetables, trees and herbs. Some of the herb plants listed in the current catalog are rosemary, chives, sweet bay, thyme, oregano, French tarragon, tricolor sage, four lavenders and coneflowers.

Well-Sweep Herb Farm

Cyrus and Louise Hyde
317 Mt. Bethel Rd.
Port Murray, NJ 07865

(908) 852-5390
Established 1976
Mail order; retail; public garden
Catalog $2.00

Well Sweep Herb Farm's 64-page catalog carries a huge assortment of herbs and herb products. Thirty-eight pages of the informative catalog are given over to herb plants, perennials and scented geraniums. These include many unique and hard-to-find herbs such as mandrake, zatar and asafetida, as well as 23 basils, 29 mints, 12 catnips and 18 oreganos! Plants are shipped from April through October. More than 65 varieties of herb seeds are also available. (Also see listing in Chapter 2.)

White Flower Farm

Steven Frowine
Rt. 63
Litchfield, CT 06759-0050

(800) 678-5164
Established 1950
Mail order; retail; public garden
Catalog free

The full-color White Flower Farm catalog is a feast for the eyes! It features a full selection of flowers, bulbs, shrubs and perennials. Some perennial herbs listed in the catalog are yarrows, monkshood, lady's-mantle, artemisias, mints, foxglove and more.

Wildseed, Inc.

John R. Thomas
PO Box 308
Eagle Lake, TX 77434

(409) 234-7353
Established 1981
Mail order; wholesale; public garden
Catalog free

Wildseed, Inc. offers seeds for wildflowers and native grasses. On the list are baby's-breath, butterfly weed, candytuft, chicory, coneflowers, cosmos, crimson clover, desert marigold, coreopsis, foxglove, yarrow, lemon mint, sweet William, tickseed, toadflax and others.

Woodland Herbs

Leslie Pylant
7306 North Vandiver
San Antonio, TX 78209

(512) 821-5651
Established 1988
Wholesale only
Price list free

Woodland Herbs provides more than 60 varieties of "Texas Grown" herbs on a wholesale basis. The herbs are in 3-inch containers and are sold in flats of 36 or half-flats of one variety. Labels are provided.

Girls, do not scrub and cook and scour until you have no time left to plant a tree, a vine, or flower.

—Jane G. Swissholm in *Letters to Country Girls*, 1853

Wrenwood of Berkeley Springs

John and Flora M. Hackimer
Rt. 4, Box 361
Berkeley Springs, WV 25411-9413

(304) 258-3071
Established 1981
Mail order; wholesale; retail; public garden
Catalog $2.00

The Wrenwood of Berkeley Springs catalog offers 52 pages of herb plants, perennials and everlastings, the largest collection of herbs in West Virginia and the tri-state area. The Hackimers have everything from ambrosia to yarrow as well as 31 varieties of scented geraniums. The informative catalog gives tidbits about each plant, hints on usage and cultivation tips. The shipping season is from April through November, or as weather permits.

Wyrttun Ward

Gilbert A. Bliss
18 Beach St.
Middleboro, MA 02346

(508) 866-4087
Mail order; retail (call first)
Established 1983
Catalog $1.00

Wyrttun Ward offers a number of herb and wildflower plants. These include absinthe, agrimony, borage, bedstraw, bergamot, basil, caraway, chamomile, chives, cinquefoil, foxglove, germander, goat's rue, horehound, Jacob's-ladder, lady's-mantle, lovage, mint, motherwort, nettle, Welsh onion, rosemary, rue, salad burnet, senna, speedwell and others. Herbs are sold in lots of six or multiples thereof, but there is no minimum number of any one species required per order.

2

A Potpourri of Herbal Supplies and Products

THIS CHAPTER INCLUDES EVERYTHING you could ask for in the way of materials for herbal and floral crafts; culinary herbs and spices; herbal bath, beauty and aromatherapy products; gifts; medicinal herbs and herb blends; specialty foods; and tools and general gardening supplies of special interest to herb enthusiasts. There is some overlap between suppliers when it comes to dried herbs and spices; check them all to find what you're looking for!

Herbal Craft and Floral Supplies

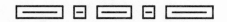

Allen's Basketworks

Allen Keeney
8624 SE 13th
Portland, OR 97202

(503) 238-6384
Established 1986
Mail order; wholesale; retail
SASE with 2 oz. postage for catalog

If you use baskets in your herb work, you'll want to take a look at the catalog from Allen's Basketworks. Mr. Keeney carries everything from materials for making your own baskets (including sea grass, raffia, pine needles and cornhusks), basket kits, tools and lots of books. A number of classes and workshops on basketmaking are also offered.

Ashcombe Farm and Greenhouses

Kathryn Weaver
906 Grantham Rd.
Mechanicsburg, PA 17055

(717) 766-7611
Established 1961
Mail order; wholesale; retail
Catalog free

Kathryn Weaver's Ashcombe Farm and Greenhouses offers dried everlastings such as ambrosia, statice, oats, celosia, curly dock, eucalyptus, globe amaranth, globe thistle, larkspur, nigella, roses, santolina, artemisia and others. Also available are dried flower bouquets, baskets and wreaths.

Aviva Design

15100 Monterey Hwy.
Morgan Hill, CA 95037

(408) 778-1354
Established 1985
Mail order; wholesale; retail
Free price list

Aviva Design grows and dries large numbers of everlastings and herbs. Among these are ammobium, artemisia, caspia, feverfew, globe amaranth, larkspur, roses, nigella, safflower, salvia, statice and strawflowers. The minimum order is $75.00.

Barker Enterprises

Mabel Barker
15106 10th Ave., SW
Seattle, WA 98166

(206) 244-1870
Established 1955
Catalog $2.00, refundable with purchase

If you've always wanted to make your own herbal scented candles, Barker Enterprises sells the candlemaking supplies that you'll need—molds (metal and plastic), waxes, wicking, candle scents, accessories, candle holders, containers (votive glass, square jars), floral decals and more.

Bay Laurel Farm

Glory H. Condon
West Garzas Rd.
Carmel Valley, CA 93924

(408) 659-2913
Established 1979
Mail order; wholesale; retail
Catalog $1.00

Glory Condon of Bay Laurel Farm offers fresh bay laurel wreaths, pepperberry wreaths, fragrant herbal wreaths and Victorian tussie-mussies by mail order. The bay laurel wreaths are made on a floral foam to retain water and keep them fresh longer. Also available is an instructional videocassette, "Making Fresh Bay Laurel Wreaths" as well as fresh bay laurel branchlets, fresh pepperberries and California peppergrass. Write for further information.

Becker Greenhouse & Herb Farm

Jan Becker
1118 Killian Rd.
Akron, OH 44312-4730

(216) 644-3408
Established 1986
Wholesale; public garden
Write for information.

Becker Greenhouse features herb plants (year round), wreaths, books and dried everlastings on a wholesale basis.

The Berry Tree

Cathy and Kurt
24 E. Burd St.
Shippensburg, PA 17257

(717) 532-2566
Established 1976
Mail order; wholesale; retail
Catalog $1.00

The Berry Tree offers a wide variety of herbal products in the current catalog, including potpourris, potpourri accessories (bags, jars, baskets), simmering potpourris, simmer cups, pomanders, Christmas ornaments, sachets, scented magnets, dried flowers, scented wreaths, natural pet products, herbal bath sachets, luffa sponges, fragrance oils, potpourri refresher oils and essential oils. Culinary herbs and spices, herbal teas and tea blends, traditional medicinal herbs and herbs for smoking are also listed, as are potpourri ingredients, craft supplies, books, tapes, natural household products and more.

Dorothy Biddle Service

Lynne Dodson
Dept. HC
Greeley, PA 18425-9799

(717) 226-3239
Established 1936
Mail order; wholesale; retail
Catalog $.25

Dorothy Biddle Service stocks supplies and equipment for working with flowers and plants in the home: flower holders of all types, tools, books, silica gel and glycerin for preserving, and all basic floral supplies (wires, picks, pins, wreath rings, tapes, cutting tools, etc.). Also listed in the catalog are mosses, decorator fans, Floralife cut flower preservative, candle holders, flower presses, wreath hangers and Aqua-Blum underwater stem cutters.

Blossoms & Bevels

Kerrie Badertscher
6326 Corinth Rd.
Longmont, CO 80503

(303) 772-5818
Established 1983
Mail order; wholesale; retail
Price list free

Like the look of pressed flowers, but don't have the time to do your own? Kerrie Badertscher has done the work for you and offers a number of pressed herbs and flowers at very reasonable prices, ready to be used in your craft projects. These include achillea, alfalfa, alyssum, baby's-breath, bindweed, columbine, dill, dusty miller, Johnny-jump-ups, lobelia, marigolds, pansies and many more.

Boone Drug Co.

Kevin Hudson and Gerda Main
113 E. King St.
Boone, NC 28607

(704) 264-3766
Established 1983
Mail order; wholesale
Price list free

The Boone Drug Company sells only two craft items: vials for essential oils and Canadian hemlock cones. The vials are available in three sizes by the gross, and the cones are available by the pound (with 1200–1400 cones per pound). These are very small cones for use in potpourris, wreaths, etc.

Brushy Mountain Bee Farm, Inc.

Steve Forrest
Rt. 1, Box 135
Moravian Falls, NC 28654-9906

(919) 921-3640
Established 1984
Catalog free

In addition to a number of seeds for herbs that attract bees (see listing in Chapter 1), this company also carries an eclectic collection of supplies for making meads, wines, candles, herbal honeys, etc. Many containers are listed here—honey bears, clear plastic jars, glass honey jars, hexagonal shaped jars, labels and tamper-proof seals, lids and a complete line of beekeeping supplies (in case you want to grow your own!).

Bunch's Herbs & Gifts

Kathie M. Bunch
51 E. Water St.
Chillicothe, OH 45601

(614) 773-3909
Established 1984
Mail order; wholesale; retail
Catalog $2.00; refundable with purchase

Kathie M. Bunch offers dried herb and flower arrangements from plants grown on her family farm. These arrangements are available in various themes (Victorian, Christmas, Country, etc.) and include swags, wreaths, heart wreaths, bouquets, hats and others. Kathie also offers a Custom Color Design service; just send her a swatch of fabric or a wallpaper sample and she will coordinate the colors for you. The Bunches also offer various classes and workshops at the farm during the spring.

Cadillac Mountain Farm

Kathleen Seaver
4481 Porter Gulch Rd.
Aptos, CA 95003

(408) 476-9595
Established 1985
Mail order; wholesale; retail
Catalog $1.00; refundable with order

Kathleen Seaver offers a large number of dried flowers, herbs and exotics, including yarrows, ageratums, artemisias, dusty miller, lavender, larkspur, oreganos, ornamental grasses and gourds, poppy pods, roses, salvias, statice and teasels. Custom orders for bouquets, arrangements, wreaths, etc. are welcome.

Cambridge Chemists, Inc.

Joseph Policar
21 E. 65th St.
New York, NY 10021

(212) 734-5678
Established 1941
Mail order; retail
Catalog $1.50

Cambridge Chemists specializes in potpourris and potpourri ingredients. These include allspice berries, cedar chips, cinnamon bark, cornflowers, frankincense, juniper berries, lavender, lemon peel, nutmeg, orris, pinecones, rosebuds and tonka beans. Decorative pinecones and other tree cones are offered along with fragrance oil concentrates and a number of already blended potpourris (some imported).

Country Flower Bin

Sandy Bridenbaugh
344 Furlong Rd.
Laura, OH 45337

(513) 947-1546
Established 1983
Mail order; wholesale; retail
SASE for information

Sandy Bridenbaugh of the Country Flower Bin offers a number of herbal items— wreaths, bouquets, swags, baskets and a large number of dried materials—but specializes in Silver King artemisia.

Country Garden Dried Flowers and Herbs

LeAna Sacrison
1895 Steelbridge Rd.
Kalispell, MT 59901

(406) 756-6892
Established 1989
Mail order; retail
Price list free

LeAna Sacrison offers a variety of dried herbs and everlastings including strawflowers (with or without stems), statice, nigella pods, blue salvia, poppy pods, ornamental grasses, yarrows, lavenders, small roses and pearly everlastings. Also available are dried oregano, basil, sage and summer savory, rose petals, bouquets and wreaths.

One old-fashioned fixative for perfume is labdanum, a substance secreted by the leaves of certain roses which grow high in the hills in Mediterranean countries. Supposedly as sheep graze among the bushes, the labdanum rubs off on their fleece. The shepherds then comb the labdanum off of the sheep and sell it to local perfume makers. Labdanum is supposedly the only substance of plant origin that resembles the smell of ambergris.

—from *The Frugal Housewife* by Mrs. Child, 1833

The Country Shepherd

Dell Ratcliffe
Rt. 1, Box 107
Comer, GA 30629

(404) 783-5923
Established 1986
Mail order; retail; public garden
Catalog $1.00

The Country Shepherd supplies a number of herbal products—fresh cut herbs and flowers in season, dried herb and flower products, wreaths and dried flower bundles in the fall.

Cramers' Posie Patch

Ralph L. Cramer
740 High Ridge Rd.
Columbia, PA 17512

(717) 684-0777
Established 1985
Mail order; wholesale
Catalog free

Cramers' Posie Patch offers a number of dried flowers and herbs, including sweet Annie, chives, crested celosia, globe amaranth, rosebuds, sage, strawflowers and more.

Creative Craft House

897 San Jose Circle
HC 62 Box 7810
Bullhead City, AZ 86430

(602) 754-3300
Established 1973
Mail order; retail
Catalog $2.00

Creative Craft House offers a variety of general craft supplies, including floral materials, chipwood boxes, miniature straw and wood chip baskets and more.

The Florist Brokerage, Inc.

Richard and Rose DeLong
107 N. Maple
Lamoni, IA 50140

(515) 784-7885
Established 1988
Mail order; wholesale
Catalog free

Richard and Rose DeLong of The Florist Brokerage offer a select variety of freeze-dried preserved botanicals such as flowers, fruits and vegetables and foliage. These are coated with polymer after drying which makes them waterproof and crushproof. Materials available include roses, miniature carnations, lilacs, rose hips, statice, eucalyptus, anise hyssop, salvia, flax, marjoram, oregano, pennyroyal, sage, tansy, yarrow and others. Floral freeze-drying machines are also available if you really want to "do it yourself".

Fragrant Fields

Carol Hanson
128 Front St.
Dongola, IL 62926

(618) 827-3677 or (800) 635-0282
Established 1978
Mail order; wholesale; retail; public garden
Catalog free

In addition to a large number of herb plants, Carol Hanson of Fragrant Fields also carries dried flowers and herb bunches, essential oils, fragrance oils, wreaths, herbal moth sachets, beeswax, orrisroot, dried herbs and teas, cinnamon sticks, whole vanilla beans, posters, smudge sticks, natural pet care products and a cute terra-cotta cat catnip planter. (Also see listing in Chapter 1.)

Gingham 'n Spice, Ltd.

Nancy M. Booth
Box 88
Gardenville, PA 18926-1304

(215) 348-3595
Established 1979
Mail order; wholesale
Catalog $2.00

Nancy M. Booth supplies a number of potpourris and glass jars for them, coordinating potpourri fragrance oils, essential and fragrance oils, stovetop spicescents, Fresh 'n Vac mixtures, culinary spice blends, salt and sugar-free herb blends, Christmas ornaments, herbal hot pads and more.

Good Earth Farm

Eric and Ann Brandt-Meyer
55 Pleasant Hill Rd.
Freeport, ME 04032-6441

(207) 865-9544
Established 1984
Wholesale only
Price list free; write on letterhead for more information.

Good Earth Farm is a family farm on the coast of Maine that specializes in dried everlastings and herbs. These include fillers such as ambrosia, silver artemisia, caspia, eucalyptus, statice and sweet annie. Flowers include celosia, feverfew, globe amaranth, liatris, nigella, salvia, strawflowers and heather. Dried herbs include anise hyssop, dill, sweet marjoram, sage and summer savory. The Brandt-Meyers also carry bayberry branches, rose hips and some pressed flowers. The minimum order is $40.00; discounts are given for quantity orders.

Good Scents

Donna Metcalfe
23 South Sixth St.
Redlands, CA 92373

(714) 335-6160
Established 1985
Mail order; wholesale; retail (call for hours)
Catalog $1.00

Good Scents carries fragrance oils, perfume ring kits, herbal bath blends, bath crystals, soaps, lots of teas (in bags or bulk dried), bulk dried herbs for potpourris, dried culinary and medicinal herbs and more. Many other items are available at the retail store.

Donna Metcalf has also written and published an informative 24-page booklet, *A Beginner's Guide to Potpourri* ($5.00 postpaid).

Greenfield Herb Garden

Arlene Shannon
1135 Woodbine
Oak Park, IL 60302

(219) 768-7110
Established 1980
Mail order; wholesale; retail; public garden
Catalog $1.50

Arlene Shannon of Greenfield Herb Garden carries dried herbs and spices, everlastings, fragrance oils, essential oils, hard-to-find tussie-mussie holders, finished herbal craft items, potpourris, pomander kits, glycerin, silica gel, culinary herbs and spices, whole herb bunches, and more than 300 herb books. Ms. Shannon also offers a number of workshops and classes on herbs.

The Herbal BodyWorks

Jeanne Rose
219 Carl St.
San Francisco, CA 94117

(415) 564-6785 (leave message) or
FAX (415)564-6799
Established 1978
Mail order; wholesale; retail
Catalog $2.50, includes gift

Jeanne Rose's Herbal BodyWorks provides ingredients and supplies for making your own body care products at home. These include reusable bags, unscented salts, almond meal, beeswax, clay (white, green or yellow), cocoa butter, epsom salts, glycerin, unpetroleum jelly and essential oils.

Herbal Gardens

Pat Hurt
4645 South Drive West
Fort Worth, TX 76132

(817) 292-7670
Established 1988
Mail order; wholesale
Catalog for SASE

Herbal Gardens is a source for concentrated fragrance oils for potpourris, per-

fumes, scented soaps, candles, etc. More than 40 scents are available, from Allspice to Ylang Ylang. A new Holiday Oil is also listed. The oils are available in 1-ounce, 4-ounce and 8-ounce sizes.

Herbitage Farm

Barbara Radcliffe Rogers
686 Old Homestead Hwy.
Richmond, NH 03470

(603) 239-6231
Established 1976
Mail order; wholesale
Catalog $1.00

Barbara Radcliffe Rogers of Herbitage Farm offers a collection of handcrafted gifts and kits "in the folk art tradition". These include a cornhusk doll kit, a hand spinning kit, a lavender lady kit, a lavender bag kit, a spice wreath kit, a moth bag kit and catnip mouse kit. Also available are fragrance oils for potpourri, myrrh beads in strings, dried flowers, pods and grasses and pinecones. A short list of books is also available, including Barbara Rogers' own *Fresh Herbs*, and *The Little Herbal Library* series and other titles.

High Desert Growers Wholesale

Korby Lawrence
PO Box 249
Newberry Springs, CA 92365

(619) 257-4126
Established 1987 (formerly Sunshine Farms)
Mail order; wholesale
Catalog free

High Desert Growers specializes in preserved and dried florals, including gypsophilas, statices, dried roses and other seasonal blooms. Flowers are available in either natural or dip-dyed colors.

Give your stored, dried herbs and spices the "sniff test" every spring. If herbs don't smell pure, pungent, and full of heady aromas, then replace them and use the old ones in your vacuum cleaner as a room freshener.

—contributed by Paula Johnson, Herb Country Gifts & Collectibles, Belmont Center, Massachusetts

Hillhouse Naturals Farm

Peggy Batts
Rt. #1, Box 28A
Wickliffe, KY 42087

(502) 335-3585
Established 1986
Mail order; wholesale
Catalog $2.00; refundable with purchase

Peggy Batts of Hillhouse Naturals Farm supplies dried flowers and everlastings, garlic bulbs, dried cinnamon apple slices, preserved oak-leaf or princess pine wreaths, chili pepper strings and wreaths, garlands, bulk spices and botanicals, as well as some craft and floral supplies.

International Manufacturing Co.

Martha Arnold
216 Main St.
Whitesburg, GA 30185

(404) 834-2094
Established 1972
Mail order; wholesale
Catalog $5.00; refundable with order

International Manufacturing Co. imports hundreds of dried flowers, floral craft supplies and wreathmaking materials. These include grapevine wreaths and hearts, twig baskets, dried flower bouquets, wreath bases (moss, pinecone, pine-straw, statice, eucalyptus, dogwood, oak-leaf, etc.), decorated swags and a large selection of general craft supplies. This company also does custom manufacturing of dried items.

Lavender Lane

Donna Madora Mitchell
6715 Donerail Dr.
Sacramento, CA 95842

(916) 334-4400
Established 1987
Mail order; wholesale; retail by appointment
Catalog $2.00

Lavender Lane carries many different containers and other herbal craft supplies. These include glass bottles and jars with corks and/or lids, plastic containers with snap-on lids, glass vials with lids, fancy perfume bottles, tester vials, funnels, oil droppers, flip-top squeeze bottles, perfume sampler vials, tamper-proof seals for wines, vinegars and oils, empty tea baglets for filling with your own herbal blends, muslin drawstring bags and more. Also listed are fragrance oils, designer-type perfume oils and potpourri magic fixative.

Donna Mitchell has also written and published a delightful booklet filled with recipes for making your own teas, vinegars, remedies, floral waters, massage oils, etc.: *Crafting with Fragrance Makes Scents*. It is available for $8.50 postpaid.

Lewis Mountain Herbs & Everlastings

Judy Lewis
2345 St., Rt. 247
Manchester, OH 45144

(513) 549-2484
Established 1985 (formerly Hopewell Gardens)
Mail order; wholesale; retail; public garden
Catalog free

In addition to a large number of herb plants (see listing in Chapter 1), Judy Lewis also carries dried everlastings such as ammobium, baby's-breath, blue salvia, caspia, celosia, statice, goldenrod, globe amaranth, tansy and yarrows. Artemisia wreath bases, potpourris and books are also available.

Dody Lyness Co.

Dody Lyness
7336 Berry Hill (D-4)
Palos Verdes, CA 90274-4404

(310) 377-7040
Established 1979
Mail order; some wholesale; retail
Price list of potpourris for SASE; catalog of dried floral accessories $1.50 (refundable with order)

Dody Lyness offers a selection of supplies for making your own potpourris, including fragrance oils, fixatives (benzoin gum powder, oak moss, orrisroot), dried blossoms, herbs and spices, silica-dried mini and standard roses, and her specialty, silica-dried pansies.

Dody Lyness also offers an entire catalog of dried floral home accessories, which includes a Victorian Dove wall hanging, "The Queen" 19-inch wreath, smaller heart wreaths, tussie-mussies, potpourris, ceramic wallpots, Victorian oval wreaths, hanging grapevine baskets, wedding herbs for strewing and showering and flower and lace fans.

Berry Hill Press, also owned by Dody Lyness, publishes the *Potpourri Party-Line Newsletter* (see listing in Chapter 3) and the booklet *Potpourri. . .Easy as One, Two, Three!* The 64-page book (see Chapter 4) is currently available for $6.00 per copy; dealer rates are available.

Magnolia Herbs

Patricia Cameron
7513 Roster Dr.
Baton Rouge, LA 70817-5524

(504) 753-2980
Established 1988
Mail order; wholesale; retail
Catalog $1.00

Patricia Cameron of Magnolia Herbs offers herb plants, seeds, fresh and dried herbs, dried flowers, potpourris, oils, herbal wreaths, dried floral arrangements, pressed herb samplers, topiaries and gift baskets.

Magnolia's

Linda Lee Purvis
318 Main St., N.
Markham, Ontario
Canada L3P 1Z1

(416) 294-6919
Established in 1985
Mail order; retail; some wholesale (botanicals and oils) with proof of business
Catalog $2.00

Magnolia's supplies a good selection of dried botanicals and flowers, potpourri fixatives and oils, dried foliage and mosses and wreaths. Ms. Purvis also carries pods, fungus and other "neat weird stuff" such as lotus pods, cattails and assegai poles. Floral supplies include pins, foams, picks, silica gel and raffia. Pure essential oils, blended potpourri, simmer pots and books are also available.

Maine Balsam Fir Products

Wendy and Jack Newmeyer
16 Morse Hill Rd.
PO Box 9
West Paris, ME 04289-0009

(800)-5-BALSAM (national);
(800) 675-2094 (in Maine)
Established 1983
Mail order; wholesale; retail at selected craft
shows
Catalog $1.00

The Newmeyers make and sell balsam-filled handcrafted screen-printed pillows with wildlife designs. They also offer pure balsam fir tips and balsam-wood potpourri. The Newmeyers are the nation's leading source for balsam fir products.

McFadden's Vines & Wreaths

Betty, Joe and Tammy McFadden
RR 3, Box 2360
Butler, TN 37640

(615) 768-2472
Established 1986
Mail order; wholesale; retail
Catalog $1.00

The McFaddens supply wreaths, vines and cones for herbal crafts. Wreaths are available in honeysuckle, birch or grapevine. Also available are cones of Carolina hemlock, white pine and Princess pine, "curly Q's", door arches, round wreaths, grapevine hearts, brier wreaths, wall baskets and more.

Meadow Everlastings

Sharon Challand
Rt. 1, #149 Shabbona Rd.
Malta, IL 60150

(815) 825-2536
Established 1986
Mail order; wholesale; retail; public garden
Catalog $2.00; refundable with order

Meadow Everlastings is a good source for dried flowers and everlastings, wreath bases and a variety of floral supplies. The air-dried everlastings listed include baby's-breath, hyssop, German statice, strawflowers, nigella pods, ambrosia, bergamot flowers, rosebuds, oregano, sage, bells-of-Ireland, and horehound. Floral supplies include grapevine wreaths, straw wreath bases, tussie-mussie holders, straw hats, floral picks, cinnamon sticks, and Spanish moss. Finished arrangements are also available, and include swags, bouquets, wreaths, topiaries, and pomanders. Potpourri ingredients and blends are also listed.

Mountain Valley Farms

Judy Higgins
348 Bowman Rd.
Hamilton, MT 59840

(406) 363-2543
Established 1976
Mail order; wholesale; retail
Price list free

Judy Higgins of Mountain Valley Farms says that they "only sell what we grow and we only grow German statice". Mountain Valley Farms sells the dried German statice in bulk or by the package. Quantity discounts are available; write for details.

Nature's Finest

Jen Mescher
PO Box 10311, Dept. HCWB
Burke, VA 22009-0311

(703) 978-3925
Established 1984
Mail order; wholesale; retail
Catalog $2.50

Nature's Finest carries an incredible number of herbal crafting supplies (not for culinary use) and miscellaneous items. Jen Mescher's encyclopedic catalog gives precise descriptions of all products. These include dry ingredients (alder cones, angelica root, cedar shavings, cellulose, chili peppers, globe amaranth, orrisroot and others), oils (essential and fragrance oils, simmer oils, perfumes), potpourris and herbal blends, Christmas items, simmer potpourris and pots, bath items, bottles, cloth bags, scent rings, eyedroppers, sachet stones, pewter top jars, ornaments, pomander jars and baskets.

Jen Mescher has also written several detailed information sheets on essential oils, herbal baths and potpourris. These are also listed in the Nature's Finest catalog.

New England Cheesemaking Supply Company, Inc.

Ricki and Robert Carroll
85 Main St.
Ashfield, MA 01330

(413) 628-3808
Established 1978
Mail order
Catalog $1.00

Ever thought about making your own herbal cheeses? You can do it with materials from Ricki and Bob Carroll's catalog. Bob Carroll, the author of *Cheesemaking Made Easy* (see Chapter 4), has gathered together all the ingredients that you need to make your own cheese, yogurt and kefir. The catalog includes cheesemaking kits, presses, cultures, molds and other supplies.

Northstar Freeze Dry

PO Box 409
Nisswa, MN 56468

(800) 551-3223
Established 1977
Brochure free

Northstar Freeze Dry manufactures freeze drying machines for flowers, herbs, vegetables, etc. These machines are available in several sizes and prices— none is cheap— but if you absolutely need one, take a look at Northstar's brochure.

Out of the Woods, Inc.

Denise Stutz
11947 U.S. 12
White Pigeon, MI 49099

Established 1989
Mail order; wholesale
Write for more information.

Denise Stutz offers a variety of dried materials, including rose-hip wreaths, bittersweet wreaths, bunches of sweet Annie, cinnamon fern, Silver King artemisia, etc. Also available are large grapevine and twig arches, blueberry, red twig and pin oak branch swags, etc. All products are handmade from materials that grow around the business's 1885 schoolhouse workshop.

Ozark Basketry Supply

Pamela Janus
PO Box 9HCRG
Kingston, AR 72742

(501) 665-2281
Established 1985
Mail order
Catalog $1.00

Pamela Janus of the Ozark Basketry Supply carries a wide assortment of supplies for basketmaking: kits, reed, books, bases, molds, cane webbing, handles, rims and hoops, bark, rattan and cane.

Petite Fleur Essence

Judy Griffin
8524 Whispering Creek Trail
Fort Worth, TX 76134

(817) 293-5410
Established 1984
Mail order; wholesale; retail
Catalog $2.00

Judy Griffin of Petite Fleur Essence offers 84 different flower essence extracts, sets containing 64 or all 84 of these concentrates, handmade skin care products and a number of specialty books.

Pettengill Farm

Jan Richenburg
121 Ferry Rd.
Salisbury, MA 01952

(508) 462-3675
Established 1982
Mail order; wholesale (limited); retail
Write for price list.

During the Christmas season, Pettengill Farm offers balsam fir wreaths, preserved pine wreaths and several ornaments by mail order. An unusual vanilla bean bottle is available all year.

PolyBags Plus, Inc.

Ernestine Schmelzl
3602 Harbor Blvd.
Port Charlotte, FL 33952

Established 1980
Mail order; wholesale
Free brochure

PolyBags Plus is a good source for small quantities of cotton muslin drawstring bags in six different sizes, cellophane bags and poly zipclose bags—in various thicknesses and sizes.

Potpourri and Sachet Supplies

Peter and Anna Hunt
PO Box 53
Northcote, Victoria
Australia 3070

Phone: 03 4822677
Established 1980
Mail order; wholesale; retail
Catalog free

Peter and Anna Hunt offer supplies for making potpourri and sachets. These include dried botanicals, plastic and cellophane bags, celluloid boxes and unfilled sachets. Also listed are potpourris, fragrant sachets, pomanders, potpourri cottages, an unusual rose petal confetti, Elizabethan wash balls, fragrant pots and more.

Potpourri by Martha

Martha Cline
4207 Mulberry Lane
Fairmont, WV 26554

(304) 366-8313
Established 1988
Mail order
Catalog free

Martha Cline offers a good list of materials for making your own potpourris and perfumes. These include cellophane bags in various sizes, glass vials with stoppers, droppers and glass pipettes, muslin bags, filters, fixative oils, fancy perfume bottles and other items.

According to legend, the red or purple flower in the middle of the Queen Anne's lace flower cluster represents a drop of blood shed from Queen Anne when she pricked her finger while making lace.

Preservations

Frank Holder
78 Freedom Rd.
Pleasant Valley, NY 12569

(914) 635-8471
Established 1981
Mail order; wholesale; retail
Catalog $1.00

Preservations is a source for dried botanicals and herbs in bunches—ageratum, ammobium, basil, calendulas, corns, dill, eucalyptus, globe amaranth, hydrangea, hyssop, mosses, poppy pods, rosebuds, strawflowers, tansy, yarrow and more.

Preserve the Memories

Jeannette Czerwinski
1070 Marion Ave.
Marion, CT 06444

(203) 260-0477
Established 1989
Mail order; wholesale
Price list for SASE.

Preserve the Memories offers freeze-dried flowers and vegetables. The flowers include roses, baby's-breath, bells-of-Ireland, calla lilies, carnations, liatris, stephanotis and others.

Radcliffe Farms

Cyndy Radcliffe and Maggi Roth
250 Airport Rd.
Bedminster, NJ 07921

(908) 526-0505
Established 1984
Mail order; wholesale (dried flowers and herbs); retail
Price list/workshop schedule for SASE

Radcliffe Farms offers kits for herbal wreaths, wall arches and sprays, herbal arrangements, topiaries and baskets. Cyndy Radcliffe also teaches workshops on how to make these objects.

River's Bend Farm

Becky Wuthrick
24696 Hartley Rd.
Alliance, OH 44601

(216) 821-4095
Established 1985
Mail order; wholesale
Catalog free

River's Bend Farm provides dried everlastings, herbs and bouquets in addition to dried arrangements and wreath bases. Also listed are flower heads and Indian corn.

St.-John's Herb Garden, Inc.

Sydney Vallentyne
7711 Hillmeade Rd.
Bowie, MD 20720

(301) 262-5302 or 262-5303
Established 1977
Mail order; wholesale; public garden open May through September
Catalog $5.00

St.-John's Herb Garden carries an incredible number of herbs, spices, potpourris and other herbal products in the 136-page catalog. Among these are incenses (bulk, powdered or stick), ten pages of essential oils, special oils used to make incense and soaps, fragrance samplers, four pages of dried flowers, herbal craft supplies (ribbons, raffia, wood chips, silica gel, floral supplies), wreaths (grapevine, eucalyptus, statice, straw, sweet Annie, others), potpourris (including stove-top scents and warmers). Other items include pomanders, dream pillows, Christmas items and lots of containers, gift packaging and storage bags.

St. John's also carries bath and beauty aids, herbal soaps, cosmetics, hennas, bath salts and pet care products. Culinary items include herb vinegars, honeys, food extracts and edible flavor oils, eight pages of dried spices, 14 pages of dried herbs (everything from absinthe powder to zubrovka), herbal extracts, empty capsules and capsule fillers, ginseng products, herbal and black teas and tea accessories. Many books are also offered, and herb and spice seeds are also available (see listing in Chapter 1).

Shields Organic Herb & Flower Farm

Mr. Leigh Shields
Rt. 218, RD 1, Box 120
Spraggs, PA 15362

(412) 435-7246
Established 1981
Mail order; wholesale; retail
Catalog $1.00

Shields offers a nice selection of dried everlastings in bunches for sale by mail order. These include yarrow, starflower, sweet Annie, basil, salvias, catnip, eucalyptus, foxtail grass, baby's-breath, lavender, strawflowers, tansy, and others. Live herb plants are available at the retail location only.

Claudia Simeone

105 Harker Ave.
Liftwood
Wilmington, DE 19803

(302) 764-8101
Established 1966
Mail order; wholesale
Newsletter/price list free for SASE

Claudia Simeone (formerly Roberta Moffitt Designs) provides a number of dried everlastings (artemisia, baby's-breath, celosia, eucalyptus, larkspur, love-in-a-mist, plumosa, statice, sweet Annie, thistle and more) and single dried flowers. Other supplies include Petalast drying agent, foam bricks, waterproof green tape, floral pins and clays. A book, *Roberta Moffitt's Step-by-Step Book of Preserving Flowers*, is available from the above address for $6.95.

Simply De-Vine

Meri Gerber
654 Kendall Rd.
Cave Junction, OR 97523

(503) 592-3752
Established 1982
Mail order; wholesale; minimum order $25.00;
winery with tasting room
Catalog $1.00; refundable with purchase

Simply De-Vine manufactures handwoven grapevine products from canes grown at Foris Vineyards in southern Oregon. Shapes available include hearts, ovals, baskets, swags, open wreaths, matted and pocket wreaths, bows and several others.

Solargraphics

Audrey Wittig, Sales Manager
PO Box 7091
Berkeley, CA 94707

(800) 327-9869
Established 1979
Mail order; wholesale
Catalog free

Solargraphics supplies sun-sensitive papers for making art and nature prints. The papers are available in large or small print-making kits as well as note card kits.

According to the Romans, a man who accepted a sprig of basil from a woman would love her forever.

Spider Web Gardens

William L. Stockman
Rt. 109A
Center Tuftonboro, NH 03816

(603) 569-5056
Established 1938
Brochure for SASE

During the Christmas season, Spider Web Gardens offers Christmas wreaths made from freshly cut balsam fir, "pee wee" wreaths, partridgeberry wreaths and living ornaments by mail order.

Stonegate Gardens

Zin Marie Matheny
13128 Old Sno-Monroe Rd.
Snohomish, WA 98290

(206) 568-7046
Established 1985
Mail order; wholesale; retail by appointment
Price list free

Stonegate Gardens offers dried peonies by the dozen in shades of pink at reasonable prices.

Timber Rock Farms

Ms. Marty Ryan
RD #2, Box 290E
Emporium, PA 15834

(814) 486-7685
Established 1981
Mail order; wholesale; retail; public garden
Catalog $1.00

Timber Rock Farms carries a wide selection of natural dried flowers, herbs and spices, essential oils and fixatives along with their own blends of culinary herbs, vinegars, potpourris and sachets. Also available are wreaths, wood products (drying racks, flower presses and spice racks) and potpourri supplies. Timber Farms features "all natural" herbal weddings, and can custom-design bouquets and floral arrangements for their customers.

Val's Naturals

Valerie Hatcher
PO Box 832
Kathleen, FL 33849-0832

(813) 858-8991
Established 1987
Mail order; wholesale
Catalog free

Val's Naturals offers dried naturals for potpourris and herbal crafts including birch cones, Everglades ball grass, garlic braids, miniature roses, tea roses, oyster plant pods, pepperberries, pinecones and Spanish moss.

Vine Arts

Janet Schuster
PO Box 83014
Portland, OR 97203

(503) 289-7505
Established 1975
Mail order; retail
Catalog $2.50; refundable with purchase

Vine Arts carries supplies for topiaries as well as finished topiaries. Frames made from galvanized steel wire and treated with rustproof paint are available, and include a rabbit, elephant, pig, fox, Egyptian cat, penguin, ducks and baskets in various sizes. Topiary frames are available unplanted, filled with moss or already planted with "needlepoint" ivy. Custom topiaries are also available.

Warmbier Farms

Mary Ellen Warmbier
7328 Buck
Freeland, MI 48623

(517) 695-5044 or 695-9583
Established 1974
Mail order; wholesale; retail
Catalog $1.00

Warmbier Farms provides a number of dried florals: German statice, strawflowers, baby's-breath, ammobiums, globe thistles, artemisias, penny cress, oats, flax, ambrosia, celosia, carnations, Chinese lanterns and more. Minimum order is $15.00.

Samuel Wells & Co.

Paula Wright
7190 Pondlick Rd.
Seaman, OH 45679

(513) 927-5283
Established 1826
Mail order; wholesale; retail; public garden
Write for more information.

Samuel Wells & Co. offers dried everlastings (statice, strawflowers, globe flowers, etc.) as well as foraged herbs and roots. Some of these include ginseng, blackberry root, bloodroot, burdock root, goldenseal root, lobelia herb, sassafras leaves, slippery elm bark, wild gingerroot, wild sarsaparilla root and others.

Herbal Bath, Beauty & Aromatherapy Products

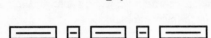

Auroma
John Fergeus
68 Burwood Rd.
Hawthorn, Victoria
Australia 3121

*613 796 4833 (Australia) or 613 796 4966
(International); FAX 613 796 4966
Established 1982
Mail order; wholesale; retail
Price list free*

Auroma offers the following materials by mail order: professional aromatherapy essential oils, standard essential oils, "healing oils", extracts, balsams and resinoids, gums, resins and waxes, vegetable oils, tinctures, essences and floral waters, dried botanicals, pottery and books.

Avena Botanicals
Deb Soule
PO Box 365
West Rockport, ME 04865

*(207) 594-0694
Established 1985
Mail order; wholesale; retail
Catalog $2.00 (free with order of $10.00 or more)*

Avena's products are all made from certified organic and wild-collected herbs. They include simple herb extracts, herbal tea blends, compound extract formulas, dried herbs, extracts especially for women, oils and salves (made with organic cold-pressed olive oil), flower essences for people and animals and herbs for animals. Non-animal tested body care products include skin tonic, face creams and benton-ite clay. A listing of herb books and pamphlets is also available.

Deb Soule also offers a number of workshops and is available for consultations or referrals by appointment.

Baudelaire, Inc.
Joe Marks
Forest Rd.
Marlow, NH 03456

*(800) 327-2324
Established 1987
Mail order; wholesale
Catalog free*

Baudelaire offers an extensive line of fine imported cosmetics and body care products. The company's goal is to offer unique products from small regional producers who use ingredients and formulas indigenous to their region. The company prefers to sell all-natural products, none of which is ever tested on animals. These include Swiss bee products (soaps, creams, lotions and shampoos), English herbal vegetable oil soaps, German herbal bath oils, Jacob Hooy products from Holland, McClinton's Barilla soaps from Ireland, Taylor Turkish Bath soaps from Canada, Gregory skin oils and soaps from England and more.

The Bayou Blending Co.
Pam Bradley
210 Leonpacher Rd.
Lafayette, LA 70508

*(318) 234-0433
Established 1987
Mail order; wholesale; retail by appointment
Catalog $2.00 (includes oil sample); refundable
with purchase*

The Bayou Blending Co. offers a good selection of herbal products: Hera's Bath Herbs, scented bath salts, herbal inhalants, facial steams, facial oils, scented body oils, aromatherapy oils, foot soaks, potpourris and linen sachet sprinkles.

Belle Star, Inc.

23151 Alcălde, #C4
Laguna Hills, CA 92653

(714) 768-7006
Established 1972
Mail order; wholesale; retail
Catalog free

Belle Star supplies duplications of designer perfumes, low-smoke incenses, lotions, soaps, light-bulb rings, oils, exclusive handblown glass perfume bottle necklaces and more.

Culpeper Ltd.

Ian Thomas
Hadstock Rd., Linton
Cambridge, England CB1 6NJ

(44) 223 891196; FAX (44) 223 893104
Established 1927
Mail order; wholesale; retail
Catalog $1.00 to the U.S.

Culpeper Ltd. was founded in 1927 by Mrs. C. F. Leyel, and is still the only company in Great Britain to grow its own herbs for use in cosmetics, foods and potpourri blends. Their wonderful catalog includes natural herbal blends, herbal tonics and remedies, lotions, hair preparations, talcum powders, soaps, soap leaves, bath salts and preparations, essential plant oils, cosmetic nut oils (apricot kernel, sweet almond, carrot seed, avocado, etc.), aromatherapy massage oils, pomanders and potpourris, sleep pillows, sachets, apothecary jars, culinary herb and spice blends, whole and ground spices and herbs, fresh herb jellies, English herb vinegars, books and much more! The Culpeper Herb Plant Collection is also listed in the catalog.

Culpeper Ltd. is always interested to hear from anyone who has old herb books for sale, particularly those published before 1800. Any editions of Nicholas Culpeper (1616–1654) or material relating to Mrs. C. E. Leyel and/or the Culpeper shops are of particular interest. Write or call for more information.

Devonshire Apothecary

Nancy "J. J." Levy
PO Box 160215
Austin, TX 78716-0215

(512) 442-0019
Mail order
Catalog $1.00

Devonshire Apothecary provides a large number of herbal items by mail order. These include a number of dried botanicals and spices, spice blends, culinary teas, herbal tea blends, tinctures, body products (bath herbs, herbal tooth powder, massage oils, super salve, green clay), specialty items (massage oil, smoking blends, etc.), simmering potpourris and sachets, beautiful scented floral jewelry, essential oils, incense and gum resins.

Dry Creek Herb Farm

Shatoiya Jones and Kim Rutter
13935 Dry Creek Rd.
Auburn, CA 95603

(916) 878-2441
Established 1988
Mail order; wholesale; retail; public garden
Brochure free

Shatoiya Jones of Dry Creek Herb Farm uses wild-collected and organically grown herbs to make her line of herbal skin care products. Chemical preservatives, alcohol, mineral oil or animal products do not appear in her formulas. These items include cleansing grains, an herbal splash, dry skin cream, body lotions, massage oils, bath herbs, herbal balm, "eye kare" moisturizer, Shatoiya's "Trauma-Aid" and an introductory kit with samples of several products. Also available are bulk, organically grown and wild-collected herbs.

A Few Ideas for Introducing Aromatherapy Oils in Your Environment

• Place a few drops on a light bulb.
• Place a few drops in a cup or bowl of boiling water.
• Sprinkle a few drops on a tissue and place on the dashboard of your car.
• Carry around a small vial and pull out and sniff occasionally.
• Place a few drops on a hankie in your pocket.
• Place it in the bath tub, hot tub, or sauna.
• Mix with your favorite shampoo.
• Put a few drops in a pot of simmering water on your stove.

—courtesy of Victoria Edwards, Leydet Oils & Aromatherapy Products, Fair Oaks, California

Earth Herbs

Tom or Betty Tropper
PO Box 23306
Ventura, CA 93002

(805) 659-5158
Established 1975
Mail order
Catalog $2.00

Earth Herbs carries a large number of herbal products from around the world: bulk herbs, spices, coffees and coffee substitutes, teas, extracts (including Chinese herbs); skin care and beauty products, cosmetics, bitters, oils, soaps; incense, potpourris, books, cassettes, videos (see Chapter 6), massage tools, pet products and more.

The Fragrant Garden

Michael Bailes
Portsmouth Rd.
Erina, NSW Australia 2250

Phone 0011-61-43-677322
Established 1976
Catalog $2.00

The Fragrant Garden specializes in "fragrance for home and garden". The catalog includes foaming herbal bath oils, shampoos, hair conditioners, dried herbs, essential oils, floral waters and colognes, perfume light rings, candles, jars, natural flavorings and edible essences and oils, perfume concentrates, potpourris and much more.

Frog Park Herbs

John and Bonnie Dobmeier
151 Frog Park Rd.
Waterville, NY 13480

(315) 841-8636
Established 1977
Mail order; wholesale; retail
Catalog free

The Dobmeiers offer herbal teas, gourmet herb blends (including several no-salt blends), dried herbs and spices, various gift baskets and samplers, herbs for pets, herbal moth repellents and gourmet spices. Other merchandise includes simmering potpourris, fragrance oils, scent rings, bath herbs, essential oils and some hard-to-find potpourri supplies: calamus, frankincense, myrrh, orrisroot, patchouli, sandalwood chips, etc.

The Gathered Herb

Shelley Carlson
12114 N. State Rd.
Otisville, MI 48463

(313) 631-6572
Established 1988
Mail order; retail; public garden
Catalog $2.00

The Gathered Herb is a small, family-owned business that offers a wide variety of products from bulk herbs and botanicals to books, herbal teas, essential oils, fragrance oils, herbal teas, traditional medicinals, herbal seasonings and potpourris. The Gathered Herb also offers a number of herb plants. (See listing in Chapter 1.)

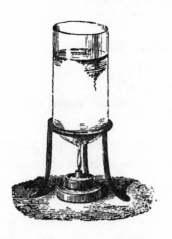

Great Lakes Herb Company
Ron Holch
PO Box 6713
Minneapolis, MN 55406

(612) 722-1201
Established 1988
Mail order; wholesale; retail
Catalog $1.00

The Great Lakes Herb Company catalog contains more than 3000 products including dried herbs, bath products, seeds, pet products, organics, cosmetics, books and other items. The company does not knowingly sell any irradiated items or products from companies that use animals for testing. Great Lake Herb Company's products include certified organic bulk herbs, Chinese herbs and Ayurvedic herbs, prepackaged teas and coffees (black, herbal and medicinal). Other items offered are potpourris, essential oils, aromatherapy products, ginseng products and herbal preparations (extracts, tinctures, syrups and single herbs in capsules, lotions, etc.). Also available are homeopathic remedies, bulk teas, incense and burners, and hundreds of bath, pet and miscellaneous items. The latter include bee pollens, beeswax and royal jelly, capsule filler machines, charcoal disks, spice jars with labels, grinding mills and refiller blades, mortar and pestles, scoops, sprouters and tea accessories.

The Herb Barn
Nancy Johns
1955 Greenley Ave.
Benton Harbor, MI 49022

(616) 927-2044
Established 1989
Mail order; wholesale; retail; public garden
Catalog $1.00; refundable with purchase

Nancy Johns of The Herb Barn carries an assortment of herbal products. Among these are packaged culinary herbs, spices and seasonings, essential oils, fragrances, herbal vinegars and spice blends. Nancy also carries a number of beauty and personal care products, all of which are "cruelty free" and have not been tested on animals. These include Bellmira liquid baths and shampoos, Bee & Flower bar soaps, herbal shampoo bars and Aroma-Vera massage oils. She also offers books, garden markers, candles, potpourri "tarts", spiced tea, Traditional Medicinals teas, dried herb and everlasting bouquets, wedding wreaths, tussie-mussies, gift baskets and customized gift baskets.

The Herb Garden
Steve and Ann Beall
PO Box 773
Pilot Mountain, NC 27041-0773

(919) 368-2723
Established 1983
Mail order; retail
Catalog $3.00

Steve and Ann Beall's Herb Garden offers a large selection of potpourris, herbal bath and beauty products (soaps, shampoo bars, bath salts, body rubs), cosmetic ingredients and natural pet care items. Also available are essential and fragrance oils, tea blends, spices, gourmet seasonings and herb blends. Hundreds of dried botanicals are listed, as are a number of herb books. The Herb Garden also supplies herb plants and seeds (see listing in Chapter 1).

Herb 'n' Renewal

Linda M. Linchester
RR 1
Laura, IL 61451

(309) 639-4145
Established 1991
Mail order; retail
Catalog $2.00

Linda M. Linchester of Herb 'n' Renewal believes in featuring beautiful, environmentally responsible products in her catalog. All items are biodegradable or packaged in recycled or recyclable wrappings. Several hundred dried botanicals are available in bulk (some also offered in smaller quantities). You'll also find soaps, cosmetics (Paul Penders), shampoos and body care items, including Woodspirits handmade herbal soaps. Other items listed are dried botanicals, floral supplies and delightful stationery items by Teesha Moore designed exclusively for Herb 'n' Renewal (letterhead, recipe labels, notepads, recipe cards, etc.).

The company also carries the entire line of Alexandra Avery and Kettle Care body care products, many books and gifts (spice necklaces, porcelain and handmade scented herb bead necklaces with matching earrings), fixative oils and essential oils, hard-to-find ingredients (food-grade oils, glycerin, etc.) and non-toxic incense from Auroshikha (guaranteed non-toxic).

Herbally Yours

Kerry Owens
PO Box 26
Changewater, NJ 07831

(908) 735-4469 or 689-6140
Established 1971
Mail order; wholesale; retail by appointment
Catalog $.50

Kerry Owens carries a wide assortment of herbal products. Herbal bath and beauty products include hair rinses, soaps, massage oils, natural oils and cosmetic ingredients, bath bags, Tiarra skin products, etc. Also offered are dried flowers, potpourris, stove-top simmers, essential oils, culinary blends and seasonings, herbal dips, teas, incense, Nature's Sunshine products, many bulk herbs, herbal pet care products and a good list of books.

The Herbfarm

Carrie Van Dyck and Ron Zimmerman
32804 Issaquah-Fall City Rd.
Fall City, WA 98024

(206) 784-2222
Established 1978
Mail order; retail; public garden
Catalog $3.50 includes plant list; $2.00
refundable with purchase.

The Herbfarm Armchair Sampler catalog is full of unusual herbal and natural products. These include Beeswax Lip Balm, sleep pillows and dream bunnies, nettle shampoo, handmade herbal soaps, Japanese mineral bath brushes, calendula cream, herbal deodorant, a fresh bay wreath, herbal blends, gourmet vinegars, an herb rack, dried bunches of herbs and flowers, Walla Walla shallots, culinary herb wreaths, a tea sampler, books, pet products, videos, bee skeps, sheepskin gloves, T-shirts and sweatshirts, herbal watercolors, cedar sacks, posy pins and tiny potpourri baskets. (Also see listings in Chapters. 1, 6 and 8.)

Herbs and Heirlooms

Jacqueline Wagener
2880 Hassler Rd.
Camino, CA 95709

(916) 622-0141
Established 1987
Mail order; retail
Catalog $1.00

Jacqueline Wagener uses pure essential oils and natural products with no preservatives in her line of herbal cosmetics: peppermint lip balm, vapor balm, herbal creams and salves (pregnancy cream, cleansing cream and antiwrinkle rub), fragrant body powders (Victorian rose and lavender, orange blossom and baby powder), bath herbs, herbal steam cleaning blends for the face and body and bath oils. A number of homemade soaps are also available: mountain sage deodorant bar, frankincense and myrrh for sensitive skin, Swedish sauna and Zanzibar cinnamon soaps.

Herbs Unlimited

M. Vilneff
1111 Davis Dr., Suite G5-320
Newmarket, Ontario
Canada L3Y 7V1

Established 1969
Mail order
Catalog $2.00

Herbs Unlimited supplies a large number of botanicals in various forms, more than 200 herbal extracts and tinctures, and more than 65 essential and perfuming oils and flavor extracts. Also available are bulk potpourris, Chinese tiger balm, ginseng products, empty capsules, herbal teas and more.

Herbs-Liscious

Carol Lacko-Beem
1702 S. 6th St.
Marshalltown, IA 50158

(515) 752-4976
Established 1987
Mail order; wholesale; retail; public garden
Catalog $2.00

In addition to more than 250 varieties of herb plants (see listing in Chapter 1), Herbs-Liscious also has chemical-free, nonirradiated dried herbs and spices, herbal blends (many of which are salt-free), sachets, "airoma" bags, dream pillows, dryer bags, hot pads, herbal bath and facial steams. Other products include personal care items, potpourris, essential oils and fragrances, mortars and pestles, garden markers, herb books and posters, herb craft materials and more.

Hyssop Hill

Beverly Fennell
PO Box 1082
Franklin, TN 37064-1082

(615) 790-6454
Established 1985
Mail order; retail; wholesale
Price list for SASE

Beverly Fennell offers a variety of herbal items, such as "better than salt" seasonings, "Dried Hell" Mexican seasoning, herbal teas, various sizes of wreaths, herbal mustard and vinegars, bath soaks, potpourris, dried flower pictures, sleep pillows, dried flower bouquets, rosemary shampoo, tussie-mussies and more.

Jason Natural Products

Delia Seaman
8468 Warner Dr.
Culver City, CA 90232-2484

(213) 838-7543
Established 1959
Mail order; wholesale; retail
Catalog free

Jason Natural Products offers a line of products that are packaged in recyclable containers and are "cruelty free". These include hair care items, skin care creams and oils, shaving products, hand and body lotions, soaps and bath care products, aromatherapy bath and massage oils, "Aussie Gold" tea tree oil products from Australia, sports products and PABA-free "Sunbrellas" natural sunscreens and tanning lotions.

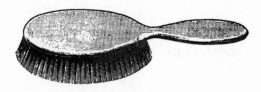

Kauai Flower Perfumes

Kathy S. Palama
PO Box 929B
Kalaheo, HI 96741

(808) 332-7051
Established 1987
Mail order; wholesale; retail
Catalog $1.00

Kauai Flower Perfumes is a small, home-based business owned and operated by Kathy Palama with the help of her family. All products are handmade and handled in very small quantities so that they remain fresh. Kathy's current brochure lists Hawaiian Potpourri, Island Fragrances perfumes (orchid, pikake or plumeria), sachets, a Potpourri basket, Hawaiian Sea Salts Bath, a Hawaiian Herbal Beauty Bath and Facial Sauna Herbs.

Lady of the Lake

Shelley Sovola
PO Box 341575
Los Angeles, CA 90034

(213) 837-2954
Established 1988
Mail order; wholesale; retail
Catalog $1.00

Lady of the Lake carries a large list of cruelty-free herbal products for aromatherapy, bath and beauty care: aromatherapy oil blends, baby skin care products, bath teas and shower gels, body powders, containers, deodorants, facial skin care products, floral waters, hair care products, incense and burners, lip balms, lotions, massage oils, medicinal herbal products, men's skin care products, ointments and balms, perfumes, skin scrubs and masks, soaps, teas, toothpaste, gift baskets and much more.

Leydet Oils and Aromatherapy Products

Victoria Edwards
PO Box 2354
Fair Oaks, CA 95628-2354

(916) 965-7546
Established 1984
Mail order
Catalog $2.50

Leydet supplies a large number of aromatherapy products, including pure essential oils (from angelica to ylang ylang), aroma diffusers, diffuser blends, massage and bath oils, perfumes and anointing oil blends, facial oils, clay masks, aromatic hydrosols (flower waters), traditional and medicinal formulas, books and more.

Liberty Natural Products, Inc.

Jerry Smith
PO Box 66068
Portland, OR 97266

(800) 289-8427
Established in 1982
Mail order; wholesale
Catalog free

Liberty Natural Products manufactures and distributes essential oils, aromatherapy products and health and beauty aids. These include breath fresheners, massage oils, lip balms, bath oils, insect deterrents, tanning oils, aromatherapy diffusers and diffuser kits, eucalyptus products, flavor oils, bulk essential oils and natural cosmetic ingredients and more.

Maple Hill Farm

Karen and Tom Voigts
1224 33rd St., Rt. 4
Allegan, MI 49010

(616) 673-6346
Established 1987
Mail order; wholesale; retail by appointment
Catalog free

Karen and Tom Voigts of Maple Hill Farm make and sell Aunt Karen's handmade complexion soap made from pure, fresh goat's milk, other natural ingredients and pure herbal oil extracts. These soaps, available in various scents including Lavender, Rosemary, Almond, Winter Holiday, Woodsy Bug Away and others, are sold by the set in handmade wooden crates, individually, or in sampler packages.

Also available are a shaving soap set, an herbal bath bag, an old-fashioned bath mitt set and Aunt Karen's Simmering Potpourris.

Meadowbrook Herb Garden

Judy Gagel
PO Box 578
Fairfield, CT 06430-0578

(203) 254-7323 (mail-order)
(401) 539-7603 (wholesale or retail store)
Established 1967
Mail order; wholesale; retail; public garden
Catalog $1.00

The Meadowbrook Herb Garden catalog lists a wide variety of herbal products, including culinary seasonings, herbal recipe blends, books, herb and fruit vinegars, Vermont mustards, drawstring muslin bags, teas and coffees and pottery. Also offered are fresh herbal cosmetics, shampoos and hair tonics, skin care preparations, handcrafted rubber stamps, natural soaps, herbal bath oils, natural essential oils, Olbas herbal remedies from Switzerland, holistic health items, herbal pet care products, herbal insect repellents and lots of books. (Also see listing in Chapters 1 and 6.)

New Age Creations (Ritual Works!)

Jeanne Rose
219 Carl St.
San Francisco, CA 94117

(415) 564-6785 (leave message);
FAX (415) 564-6799
Established 1978
Mail order; wholesale; retail
Catalog $2.50; includes gift

New Age Creations (Ritual Works!) is a very specialized company that sells a complete line of body-care products for personal and ritual use. These include cleansing soaps, ritual rubbing oils, colored and aroma-scented potpourris and ritual herbal bath mixtures.

To produce sleep, wash the head in a decoction of dill seeds and smell it frequently.

—from *The Ladies' Indispensible Companion,* 1854

Next to Nature

Rae Ann Gomez
361 Forest Ave., Suite 106
Laguna Beach, CA 92651

(714) 497-1355
Established 1990
Mail order; retail
Catalog free

Next to Nature offers natural hair and skin care products which use no animal-derived or animal-tested ingredients. These include facial cleansers, toners, creams and treatments, shampoos and hair treatments, bath and shower products, body lotions and sun lotions. Also available are a number of products for men, massage oils, lotions and aromatherapy oils. Sea sponges, luffas, brushes, cotton pads, bath "tea bags" and bulk herbs are also available.

He who bears chives
on his breath
Is safe from being
kissed to death.

—Martial, Roman poet,
c. A.D. 100

Norfolk Lavender Ltd.

Barbara Starr Mott
PO Box 602
Dawsonville, GA 30534-0602

(800) 352-8777
Established 1932
Mail order
Catalog $3.00; refundable with order

Norfolk Lavender is a family firm founded in 1932 and is now England's only full-scale lavender farm. The company offers a beautiful line of lavender products made in England and imported to the United States: bath products, colognes, soaps, skin care products, quilted Victorian designs, sachets, scented pillows, sacks of pure English lavender, flower oils, potpourris, tea towels, travel-sized products and more.

A booklet, *Norfolk Lavender, England's Lavender Farm*, is available, as is Lois Vickers' *The Scented Lavender Book*.

Original Swiss Aromatics

Julie Hovar
PO Box 606
San Rafael, CA 94915

(415) 459-3998
Established 1985
Mail order; wholesale
Catalog $1.50

Original Swiss Aromatics offers a number of aromatherapy products: essential oils, cleansing masks, treatment blends, hydrosols (floral waters), an aromatherapy poster and inhalers.

Penn Herb Co., Ltd.

Robert J. Klug
603 N. 2nd St.
Philadelphia, PA 19123-3098

(215) 925-3336
Established 1924
Mail order; wholesale; retail
Catalog $1.00; refundable with purchase

The Penn Herb Company carries a large number of herbal items—everything from acne products to wart remedies! The catalog lists Olbas herbal products, herbal teas, homeopathic creams and preparations, ginseng items, dried herbs (whole, cut or powder) and herb capsules, special herbal formulas, bath products, hair preparations, tonics and conditioners, skin creams, vitamins and supplements, oils, empty capsules, potpourris, some seeds, herbal extracts, essential oils, incense, gums and waxes and a large number of books, charts and magazines.

Progressive Self-Care Systems

Michele Donohue
Rt. 1, Box 56B
Helper, UT 84526

(801) 472-5650
Established 1989
Mail order
Brochure free

Michele Donohue of Progressive Self-Care Systems carries Crane & Cross self-care products from England. These include hair products (jojoba and avocado shampoo, chamomile shampoo, rosemary and sage conditioners), skin products (cleansers, masques, lotions, oils), eye products, bath products (bath oils, deodorants, mouthwashes, vegetable soaps, talcum powder) and more.

Quintessence Aromatherapy, Inc.

Ann Berwick
PO Box 4996
Boulder, CO 80306-4996

(303) 258-3791
Established 1990
Mail order; wholesale; retail
Catalog free

Ann Berwick of Quintessence Aromatherapy offers a line of high-quality perfumes made without chemical colorants, stabilizers or animal testing. Also available are many essential oils and blends.

The Secret Garden

Renee Troyer Campbell
1100 Chicago Ave.
Goshen, IN 46526

(219) 533-6151
Established 1989
Mail order; wholesale; retail
Write for more information.

The Secret Garden carries everlastings, herbal arrangements and wreaths, potpourris, teas, bath salts, their own blends of culinary seasonings and books. Renee Campbell also offers a gift basket service and sponsors classes on various herbal subjects.

Sandy Smith's Magical Herbs

Sandy Smith
PO Box 2346
Sebastopol, CA 95473

(707) 829-3853
Established 1988
Mail order; wholesale
Catalog free

Sandy Smith offers "ritual herbs, magical oil blends, talismans and amulets" in her mail-order catalog.

The Soap Opera

Chuck Bauer
319 State St.
Madison, WI 53703

(608) 251-4051
Established 1972
Mail order; wholesale; retail
Catalog free

The Soap Opera carries an extensive collection of body care products made of natural ingredients, all of which are biodegradable and free of animal testing. These include essential perfume oils, designer-inspired fragrances, rare essential oils (Chinese sandalwood, Italian bergamot, true English lavender, myrrh and frankincense), a perfume base for mixing your own perfumes or colognes, environmental oils for potpourris, perfume rings, scented glycerin soaps and massage oils (including Jeanne Rose's bath and body oils).

Also offered are bath and shower gels, moisturizers, lotions, hair and complexion care products and creams, an extensive variety of pure herbal baths, oils and vegetarian soaps, perfume bottles and atomizers, potpourris, incense and scented candles in addition to the entire line of products by Crabtree & Evelyn and Scarborough and Company.

Customized gift baskets and boxes are also available.

Sunfeather Handcrafted Herbal Soap Co.

Sandy Maine
HCR 84, Box 60A
Potsdam, NY 13676

(315) 265-3648
Established 1979
Mail order; wholesale
Catalog $1.00; refundable with purchase

Sandy Maine carries a variety of lovely herbal bath and beauty products. These include floral soaps, men's soaps, shampoo bars, herbal body powders, herbal and mineral ocean bath salts and more. A portion of profits from Sunfeather's "Help the Earth" soap and shampoo bars are donated to seven different environmental and peace organizations. Gift baskets are available, as are "Soft Scrubber" washing mitts. Sunfeather even has a soapmaking kit, complete with everything you need to make 7½ pounds of your own herbal soap!

Sandy Maine will also custom-manufacture and label soaps for wholesalers and retailers.

Sweet Woodruff Farm

Evelyn or Mel Shahan
Rt. 27
Boothbay, ME 04537

(207) 633-6977
Established 1989
Mail order; wholesale; retail
Write or call for information.

Sweet Woodruff Farm is a source for various herbal items: plants, dried bunches, wreaths, potpourris, swags, etc.

Victoria's Herb Shoppe

Victoria Wheeling
Rt. 4, Box 286
Titusville, PA 16354

(814) 827-7823
Established 1990
Mail order; retail; public garden
Catalog $1.00

Victoria Wheeling offers an eclectic mixture of herbal items in her eight-page catalog: dried spices, pet products, dried botanicals, potpourris and simmering potpourris, herbal bath products, wreaths, bulk teas and several books.

Weleda, Inc.

Christine Murphy
175 N. Route 9W
Congers, NY 10920

(914) 268-8572
Established 1940
Mail order; wholesale; retail
Catalog free

Weleda offers body care products that contain no synthetic preservatives, artificial colors or additives and are not tested on animals. These include an Iris cleansing lotion, moisturizing cream, night cream, face oil, and soap, herbal and plant gel toothpastes, rosemary shampoo and conditioner, chamomile shampoo and conditioner, rosemary hair oil, natural sage deodorant, natural soaps and bath oils. Natural baby care products are also available.

Wild Weeds

Canela Valentine
PO Box 88
Redway, CA 95560-0088

Established 1987
Mail order; wholesale
Catalog free

Wild Weeds' catalog of "herbal delights" includes a wonderfully eclectic mixture of teas, culinary blends, herbal oils, rubs and extracts, baby and women's care products, herbal cosmetics, hair and body care products, potpourris, essential and perfume oils, clays, labels, pet care items and books. A large number of containers for your own mixtures are available: jars and bottles, muslin bags, amber glass dropper bottles, plastic bottles, tins, packaging bags and powder shakers. Gifts include herbal gift baskets, T-shirts, candles and more.

Windrose Aromatics, Inc.

Kate Damian
12629 N. Tatum Blvd., Suite 511
Phoenix, AZ 85032

(602) 482-1814
Established 1986
Mail order; wholesale
Brochure free

Windrose Aromatics specializes in pure essential oils, aromatic body care products and aromatherapy accessories. The current brochure lists more than 60 pure essential oils (no synthetics), essential oil diffusers, oil blends, aromatic body oils and lotions, floral waters, unscented carrier oils and accessories. Also available are several Windrose Samplers containing body lotion, body oil, floral water, bath gel, sea salts and essential oils, as well as a good selection of books on aromatherapy.

Kate Damian teaches workshops on aromatherapy in various locations; write or call for further details.

Woodspirits Soap

Barbara Bobo
1920 Apple Rd.
St. Paris, OH 43072

(513) 663-4327
Established 1979
Mail order; wholesale; retail by appointment
Catalog $1.00

Barbara Bobo, a medicinal herbalist with experience in aromatherapy, makes beautiful handmade soaps from original recipes. These include a Mountain Sage Deodorant Bar, a Frankincense and Myrrh Medicated Bar, a Swedish Sauna Soap, Shepherd's Soap, Kachina's Dream (includes Aztec blue corn!), Wildwood Flower soap, Lemon Geranium soap, exotic Zanzibar soap and others. All soaps are made from 100% food-grade olive oil or a combination of olive oil and coconut oil. Woodspirits can also make custom soaps from your fragrance oils; inquire for details.

Culinary Herbs & Spices

Barbree Beans

Penny Barbree
Red Head Cty. Rd.
PO Box 414
San Ardo, CA 93450

(408) 627-2676
Established 1987
Mail order; wholesale; retail
Price list for SASE

Barbree Beans supplies pesticide-free dried herbs in small packages or bunches, including basil, coriander, oregano, dill, sage, anise, purple basil and others. The minimum order is $100.00.

Blue Springs

Mary Hidalgo
236 Eleanor Ave.
Los Altos, CA 94022

(415) 948-3787
Established 1987
Mail order
Catalog $2.00

Blue Springs carries a nice selection of gourmet spice blends, culinary herbs and spices (including mustard seed, whole nutmeg and Spanish saffron), potpourri blends, soup mixes, gift baskets, herb plants and seeds, vinegars and sauces. (Also see listing in Chapter 1.)

Boston Spice and Tea Company

Greaner and JoAnn Neal
PO Box 38
Boston, VA 22713

(703) 547-3907
Established 1985
Mail order; wholesale; retail; public garden
Catalog free

The Boston Spice and Tea Company offers a number of interesting herbal products, such as potpourris and kettle spices, O'Bannon's Mill Butter Blends, a spice box assortment, wassail and mulling spices, herbal teas (including an interesting Peppermint Rose), aprons and lots of herbal vinegars.

Camelot Herb Gardens

Laurie Southwick
245 Red Schoolhouse Rd.
Coventry, RI 02816

(401) 397-4588
Established 1984
Mail order; wholesale; retail
Catalog $2.00

Laurie Southwick of Camelot Herb Gardens supplies a good list of dried herbs, spices and botanicals as well as essential and fragrance oils, potpourris, a pomander kit, herbal teas, Rhode Island honey, gourmet herbal culinary blends, beeswax candles and sachets. Bath and beauty items include Kappus soaps from Germany, bath salts, bee balm hand and body lotion. Chinese herbs and herbal formulas, gift baskets and a number of books are listed; Camelot Herb Gardens also distributes Sunrider Whole Herb Formulas.

Camelot is also a source of herb and scented geranium plants.

Canyon Country Herbs

Kate Salzler
PO Box 1523
Cottonwood, AZ 86326

Established 1983
Mail order
Catalog $1.00; refundable with order

Canyon Country Herbs (formerly Herb Hollow) carries an eclectic mixture of herbal items: pet products; original seasonings; herbal mustards; teas; aromatics such as potpourris, sachets, moth repellents, hot mats, etc.; health and beauty items (lip balm, bath blends); stationery and note cards; medicinals; plant needs and miscellaneous items.

Caprilands Herb Farm

Darlene Lee
534 Silver St.
Coventry, CT 06238

(203) 742-7244
Established 1953
Mail order; public garden; retail
Catalog free

Caprilands Herb Farm offers a number of items by mail order including potpourris, essential oils, pomander balls, potpourri and pomander kits, herbal seasonings and blends, hot mustards and herbal jellies, herbal vinegars, herb and spice dip mixes, note cards, wreaths, Christmas decorations, herbal teas, dolls, garden ornaments and books (including all those by founder Adelma Grenier Simmons). (Also see listing in Chapter 6.)

Garlic is as good as having ten mothers.

—Teluga Indian proverb

Clement Herb Farm

Diane Clement
Rt. 6, Box 390
Rogers, AR 72756

(501) 925-1603
Established 1979
Mail order; wholesale; retail; public garden
Catalog $1.00

Diane Clement offers a number of hand-blended herbal products. Culinary blends contain no sugar or preservatives, and many of them contain no salt. Also listed are dried culinary herbs and spices, herbal teas, bulk herb teas, herbal moth bags, wine garlic vinegar, and an assortment of gifts.

Diane Clement is a trained home economist and worked as a hospital dietitian for ten years. When she realized that the public was interested in learning more about growing and using herbs in cooking, she wrote *The Clement Herb Farm Cookbook*, which is available for $3.95 + $2.00 postage/handling.

Pepper is blacke
And hath a good smacke
And every man
doth it bye.

—John Heywood,
Proverbs

The Country Merchants

Linda C. Bales
Rt. 2, Box 199A
Cheney, KS 67025-9659

(316) 542-3293
Established 1986
Mail order; retail by appointment
Catalog $3.00

Linda Bales offers a large number of dried herbs and spices in 1-ounce or 1-pound quantities. A number of organic herbs and spices are listed as well as herbal blends, baking goods (arrowroot, carob powder, lecithin granules, saffron), accessories (capsule filler, garlic keeper, nutmeg grater, wooden spoons), bottles and jars and books. Craft botanicals are listed with a handy reference chart on how to use them. Also available are essential oils and fragrances, several varieties of herb seeds, herbal bath blends and perfume rings.

Country Thyme

Betty Jo Quinn
PO Box 13
Francestown, NH 03043

(603) 547-2725
Established 1985
Mail order; wholesale
Catalog free

Country Thyme is a source of salt-free culinary gift packs, catnip toys, note cards, potpourris, bath bags and more.

Ebert's Herbs & Wheat

Carol Ebert
14415 Louisville Rd.
St. George, KS 66535

(913) 456-2841
Established 1980
Mail order; wholesale; retail by appointment
Catalog $1.00; refundable with order

Ebert's Herbs & Wheat carries dried herbs and spices, herbal tea blends, herbal salt-free seasonings, potpourris and stove-top potpourris, herbal wreaths, potpourri ingredients and "herbal treasures" such as herbal hot pads, sachets, cedar bags, dream pillows, clothes fresheners, pomander kits and more.

Wheat Country Health Delights, a book that contains lots of wheat recipes, is available for $4.95 + $1.60 postage/handling.

Edgewood Herbs

Katharine Bush
RD #1, Box 53
Kane, PA 16735

(814) 837-7704
Established 1985
Mail order; retail; public garden
Brochure free

Edgewood Herbs' mail-order brochure lists herbal culinary blends, nutmeg graters, garlic keepers and presses, ginger graters, mortar and pestle sets, herbal teas and tea accessories, potpourris, pomander balls, hops pillows, bath sachets, essential oils, fixatives, bulk herbs and spices, custom gift baskets and arrangements, wreaths, everlasting bundles and more.

England's Herb Farm

Yvonne England
RD #1, Box 706
Honey Brook, PA 19344

(215) 273-2863
Established 1978
Mail order; retail; public garden
Catalog $2.00

England's Herb Farm (formerly Giunta's) offers herbal products such as vinegars, mustards, oils, sachets, love charms, moth repellents and more.

Yvonne England gives garden tours for groups by appointment for a fee; she also gives lectures and workshops and offers herbal consultation and design services.

Fox Fern Herb Farm

Margaret M. Smith
588 Bremen Rd.
Waldoboro, ME 04572

(207) 832-4721
Established 1985
Mail order; retail; public garden
Price list for SASE

Fox Fern Herb Farm offers culinary herb blends (bouquet garni, dip mixes, fines herbes, salsa mix and saltless salt), teas, potpourris, herbal scented items, moth chasers and more.

Frontier Cooperative Herbs

Patly Konzen
Box 299
Norway, IA 52318

(319) 227-7999
Established 1976
Mail order; wholesale
Catalog free

Frontier Cooperative Herbs is an herb and spice cooperative that provides bulk organic herbs and spices, Chinese herbs, spice blends, specialty foods, packaged herbs, spices and seasonings, packaged flavorings and seasonings, ginseng, herb and spice accessories, potpourris and oils, teas and coffees, health and beauty aids and more. Frontier's 104-page catalog includes everything you will ever need in the way of herbs and spices! Since Frontier is a cooperative, there are membership requirements and minimum orders required to get quantity discounts. Write for more information. The "Frontier Direct" catalog offers herbs and spices directly to the consumer in smaller quantities with no minimum order required.

An informative guide to more than 265 herbs that Frontier carries, *The Herb & Spice Handbook*, is available. Write for current price and ordering information.

Gaia Botanicals

PO Box 8485
Philadelphia, PA 19101

(215) 222-5499
Established 1989
Mail order; wholesale; retail
Catalog $2.50

Gaia Botanicals offers more than 800 varieties of dried bulk herbs and spices for culinary, healing, spiritual or crafts uses. Also available are herb teas and accessories, herbal cosmetics, ginsengs, herbal jewelry, wreaths, essential and fragrance oils, beeswax candles, floral waters, posters, potpourris and pomanders and other gifts. Many herb books are included on such subjects as allergies, aphrodisiacs, aromatherapy, Chinese herbs, cookbooks, gardening, and medicinal uses.

Beer is a good family drink. A handful of hops, to a pailful of water, and a half-pint of molasses, makes good hop beer. Spruce mixed with hops is pleasanter than hops alone.

—from *The Frugal Housewife* by Mrs. Child, 1833

Golden Meadows Herb Farm & Emporium

Jacque Owens
431 S. Saint Augustine
Dallas, TX 75217

(214) 398-3479
Established 1984
Mail order; retail
Catalog $2.00; refundable with purchase

Jacque Owens's catalog is crammed full of herbal products and other wonderful stuff—bulk herbs, sprouting seeds, herbal teas, tea balls, muslin bags in three sizes for packaging your own teas, bulk teas, amber bottles for storing herbs, mortar and pestles, charcoal disks, beauty and bath items, essential oils, potpourris, Dr. Goodpet's products for animals, Swedish bitters and Nature's Herbs products. There's more—liquid herbal extracts, herbal supplements and blends along with Golden Meadows' own nutritional supplements.

Good Scents of Louisiana

Arlene Kestner
11655 Highland Rd.
Baton Rouge, LA 70810

(504) 766-3898
Established 1979
Mail order; wholesale; public garden
Catalog $1.00

Arlene Kestner's Good Scents of Louisiana specializes in traditional Cajun and Creole herb recipe mixes and herb crafts produced in Louisiana. All culinary herb blends are salt-free and contain no flavor enhancers. The catalog lists a number of potpourris, herbal wreaths and decorative accessories. Free shipping is available on all retail mail orders.

Herb Patch Ltd.

Diane Copley
PO Box 1111
Middletown Springs, VT 05757-1111

(802) 235-2466 or (800) 282-HERB
Established 1979
Mail order; wholesale; retail
Brochure free

Herb Patch offers such specialty herbal products as herbal culinary blends (lemon pepper, salt-free herb "salt", Italian Secret, Herb Rice, etc.), herbal teas, "Country Cow Cocoas", herbal vinegars and honeys, scented hot pads and potpourri refills and gift boxes.

The Herb Shop

Barbara Zink
20 E. Main St.
Lititz, PA 17543

(717) 626-9206
Established 1978
Mail order; retail
Catalog free

The Herb Shop offers dried herbs, spices, teas and coffees, pastas, specialty foods, potpourris and sachets, bath products, essential oils, pet products, books and special "Herb Shop Blends". Gift baskets are also available.

Herbal Effect

Richard Hilton
616 Lighthouse
Monterey, CA 93940

(408) 375-6313
Established 1970
Mail order; wholesale; retail
Catalog $2.00

Herbal Effect is a good source for both rare and common culinary spices, exotic teas, medicinal herbs, Oriental herbs and more. Also listed in the extensive catalog are black teas, culinary spice blends, Chinese herbs and botanicals, ginseng products, flower essences, extracts, essential oils and fragrances, potpourris and sachets, herbal pet products, Shepherd's Garden Seeds, books and accessories (tea bags, incense charcoal, mortar and pestle, muslin bags, storage jars, etc.).

Lily of the Valley Herb Farm

Paul and Melinda Carmichael
3969 Fox Ave.
Minerva, OH 44657

(216) 862-3920
Established 1981
Mail order; wholesale; retail
Catalog $2.00 (includes updates)

In addition to hundreds of herbs, scented geraniums, everlastings and perennials, Lily of the Valley Herb Farm also carries bulk potpourri ingredients, fragrance oils, finished potpourris and Christmas products. Also listed are bulk medicinal, tea and culinary herbs, herb and spice blends, traditional medicinal and therapeutic herbal products, pet care products, wreaths and arrangements, T-shirts and books. (Also see listing in Chapter 1.)

Maple River Herb Gardens

Debra A. Raiche
Box 92
Mapleton, MN 56065

(507) 524-3408
Established 1988
Mail order; wholesale
Price list free

Maple River Herb Gardens carries a number of herbal culinary blends (soup blend, fines herbes, bouquet garni, No Salt Herbal Seasoning, Salad Dressing, etc.), dried culinary herbs and bulk herbal teas.

Mari-Mann Herb Co., Inc.

Michael L. King
RR #4, Box 7
N. End of St. Louis Bridge Rd.
Decatur, IL 62521-9404

(217) 429-1555
Established 1977
Mail order; wholesale; retail; public garden
Catalog $1.00

Mari-Mann Herb Co. sells a wide variety of herbal fragrance and culinary items, including fragrance crystals, fragrance oils, designer-inspired oils, gourmet jellies, herb vinegars, dip and salad mixes, bread mixes, culinary seasoning blends, spices and no salt seasonings. Also listed are hard-to-find oils and flavorings for making hard candies, herb teas, traditional medicinal teas, pet care products, homeopathic remedies, ointments, Nature's Way products and beauty fragrances (bath herbs, colognes, the Norfolk Lavender Collection), and lots of craft supplies, everlastings and herb blossoms and wreathmaking supplies. (Also see listing in Chapter 6.)

May Apple

Eugene and Margery Kirsch
211 N. Center St.
Hartford, MI 49057-1138

(616) 621-6024
Established 1982
Mail order; retail
Catalog $1.00

May Apple is a good source of dried botanicals, teas, and culinary herbs and spices. Also available are empty gelatin capsules and ingredients for potpourris: dried flowers, fixatives, spices, essential oils and perfume oils.

Proper Storage of Herbs and Spices

Always store spices, herbs, and seasonings away from heat and sunlight. After opening containers, store them in either glass or specially designed plastic spice jars, never in poly plastic bags (including Ziploc) as they will lose their strength, freshness, and flavor rapidly.

Mt. Sopris Scents and Seasonings

Lydia McIntyre
1625 Rd. 111
Carbondale, CO 81623

(303) 963-1929
Established 1986
Mail order; wholesale
Catalog free

Mt. Sopris Scents and Seasonings carries a line of herbal seasonings, dip mixes and salad dressing mixes. Also available are potpourris, simmering potpourris, sachets, refresher oils, sneaker stuffers, apple ornaments and more.

Lydia McIntyre also offers the "Scent of the Month". Each month a different scented potpourri or herbal product will be sent to the person of your choice.

Nature's Herb

Emma
1010 46th St.
Emeryville, CA 94608

(415) 601-0700
Established 1915
Mail order; retail
Catalog $.50

Nature's Herb carries dried botanicals, Chinese herbs, black and green teas, books, baking needs, culinary spice blends, designer simmerscents and refresher oils, dried vegetables, essential oils, extracts, gelatin capsules, herbal tea blends, mortars and pestles, organic botanicals, potpourri blends and oils, books, sprouting seeds, tinctures and much more.

New Forest Gardens

Wayne Bisso
PO Box 1673
West Babylon, NY 11704

(516) 226-7967
Established 1987
Mail order; wholesale; retail
Catalog free

New Forest Gardens (formerly Raven Cove Enterprises) carries culinary spice blends, teas and tea accessories. Special herbal preparations include "Raven Cove PMS Comfort" formula, Swedish bitters, Swedish bitters kit and an herbal diet kit. Essential and fragrance oils are also listed, including a pure almond oil for cooking or massage. A number of books are also available from New Forest Gardens.

Other services offered are herbal health and Bach Flower Remedy counseling.

No Common Scents

Mary Purdin
Kings Yard
Yellow Springs, OH 45387

(513) 767-4261
Established 1979
Price list free

Mary Purdin offers a good list of dried culinary herbs and spices, bulk herbs, spices and botanicals, specialty foods, natural flavorings, herbal extracts, black and green teas, herbal teas, potpourris, potpourri oils, perfumes and exclusive-blend oils, candles, incense and other oils (castor, jojoba, sweet almond, etc.).

Northwestern Coffee Mills

Harry Demorest
217 N. Broadway
Milwaukee, WI 53202

(414) 276-1031
Established 1875
Mail order; retail
Catalog free (donations accepted)

Northwestern Coffee Mills imports, roasts, blends and grinds 45,000 pounds of high-quality coffee, teas and spices each year. This busy company offers whole bean or ground blends of more than 50 types of coffees (including decaffeinated), all types and sizes of filters, herb teas, grain beverages, gifts and sampler packs, many black, green and oolong teas, dried culinary herbs and spices, peppers, seasoned blends, salt-free herb and spice blends, vanilla extract and beans, natural food flavors and extracts and more—a great place to shop for that coffee or tea lover on your gift list!

Old Hill Herbs

Barbara D. Hawkes
29 Norman St.
Marblehead, MA 01945

(617) 631-4323
Established 1979
Mail order; wholesale; retail by appointment
Product and price list $.50

Old Hill Herbs offers culinary herb products including dips and spreads, salt replacements (featuring an "Instead of Salt Sampler"), spice mixtures (mulled cider and apple butter spice), herb blends, teas, vinegars and jellies. All herbal blends are offered in bulk for those who would like to package them under their own label or use or sell them from the jar.

Nonfood items include sleep pillows, potpourri sachets, repellents and many miscellaneous items. Gift baskets are also listed.

Smoke Camp Crafts

Dot Montgillion
Rt. 1, Box 263-SS
Weston, WV 26452

(304) 269-6416
Established 1978
Mail order; wholesale; retail
Price list for SASE

Dot Montgillion of Smoke Camp Crafts offers a number of traditional herbs and unusual jellies and herbal items, including Sassafras Jelly, Dandelion Blossom Jelly, Rose Petal Jelly and others. Herbal tea blends, organically grown culinary herbs and blends, simmering potpourris, soaps and books are also listed. A 52-page booklet, *Modern Uses of Traditional Herbs*, is available for $4.75 + $1.00 for postage.

The Spice Cabinet

Annita Bannerman
RR #1
Colgan, Ontario
Canada L0G 1G0

(416) 936-2621
Established 1981
Price list free

The Spice Cabinet offers dried herbs, spices and other supplies for potpourris as well as culinary herbs and spices. Also available are low-sodium blends, glycerin and natural soaps, herbal teas, commercial barbecue mixes and herbal bath baglets.

Spice It Up

Robin and Kevin Martin
135 Amory St.
Cambridge, MA 02139

(617) 354-8496 or 800-BUY SPICE (for orders)
Established 1991
Mail order; retail
Catalog free

This new business is a source for custom-milled seasonings—herbs, spices and specialty blends: allspice, anise seed, basil, bay leaf, caraway seed, cardamom seed, cayenne pepper, chervil, chives, cinnamon, cilantro, cloves, cumin seed, dill, fennel seed, garlic, ginger, lemon zest, mace, mint, mustard, nutmeg, onion powder, orange zest, lots of different peppercorns, saffron, sage, sesame seed, shallots, vanilla beans and more. The Martins hope to educate their customer on how to use these seasonings in ways that they may not have thought of before, and so the Spice It Up catalog is a complete reference guide to the uses of these seasonings. Shatterproof spice bottles and a good selection of pepper mills are also available from Spice It Up.

Spices 'N Things

Mary E. Baker
6485 West 1000 South-HCW
South Whitley, IN 46787-9747

(219) 723-4571
Established 1986
Mail order; retail; wholesale to business owners;
special orders available
Catalog $1.00; refundable with order

Mary Baker of Spices 'N Things offers a wide variety of spices, herbs, seasonings, baking supplies and herbal craft materials. These include spices (from allspice to vanilla bean), teas, spice jars, 100% cotton bags, dried flowers, extracts, essential oils, dropper caps, fragrance oils, scent rings, cedar wood shapes, more than 30 different potpourri blends and supplies for making your own potpourris. Several books are also available; a leaflet on "Basic Potpourri Blending" is $1.00.

Strawberry Meadow Herb Farm

Carol Huntington
RFD #3, Box 3689
Pittsfield, NH 03263

(603) 435-6132
Established 1981
Mail order; wholesale; retail
Catalog $1.00; refundable with order

Carol Huntington offers a number of tempting herbal products including culinary mixes, herbal butter mixes, salad dressing mixes, dip mixes, herbal teas and mulled mixes for cider or wine. Also listed are potpourris, simmering potpourris, vacuum scents and more.

Sugar 'n Spice

Alberta Levengood
2819-I Willow Street Pike
Willow Street, PA 17584

(717) 464-0747
Established 1984
Mail order; wholesale; retail; party plan
Catalog $1.75; refundable with $25.00 purchase

The Sugar 'n Spice catalog lists a large number of herbal products, including many hard-to-find items for the gourmet cook; herbs and spices for medicinal purposes; culinary herbs and spices; herbal gift baskets; South of the Border mixes and blends; soup, bases and gravy mixes; salad dressings, mixes and toppings; gourmet vinegars; specialty gourmet mustards; teas; essential oils; health and beauty items and more.

Alberta Levengood also offers an unusual herbal party plan; inquire for details.

Sweet Woodroffe Herb Farm

Pam Woodroffe
11222 SW 238th St.
Vashon, WA 98070

(206) 463-5871
Established 1987
Mail order; wholesale
Price list for SASE

Pam Woodroffe offers a number of "Herbal Folklore Beverages" including two herbal teas, a summer punch mix (Lavender Lemonade), a winter fireside drink (Cranberry Mulling spices) and others. One of the teas, Prosperi-Tea, won first place for herbal teas in a national contest. Also available are "Herbal Folklore Beverage" gift packs.

Twin Ridge Farm

Nancy J. Nieder
RFD #1, Box 1409 Pumpkin Hill Rd.
Warner, NH 03278-9338

(603) 456-2354
Established 1982
Mail order; retail
Brochure free

Twin Ridge Farm offers products that are based on authentic colonial New England recipes, carefully researched and reproduced in the Farm's 18th-century keeping room. Some concessions have been made to 20th-century tastes, however; all but four of the 15 herb blends are completely salt-free. Also available are handmade herbal and floral soaps, soap gift boxes, culinary mixes and herb teas.

The Ultimate Herb & Spice Shoppe

Karen Miller
111 Azalea, Box 395
Duenweg, MO 64841-0395

(417) 782-0457
Established 1986
Mail order; retail
Catalog $2.00

Karen Miller's Ultimate Herb & Spice Shoppe is a good source for bulk herbs, spices, teas, coffees and dried botanicals in powdered, whole or cut and sifted form. Also listed in the extensive catalog are clays (bentonite clay powder, French clays), crushed chili powders, seasoning blends, tree cones for potpourri, dried everlasting flowers, baking needs, certified organic grains, dried vegetables, sprouting seeds, ginseng products, herb and spice accessories, gums and resins (arabic powder, benzoin powder, frankincense, guar powder, tragacanth powder, etc.) and sachet blends. The company also carries essential, fragrance and cosmetic oils, capsulized herbs from other companies, health and beauty aids, salves, weight products, herbal soaps and many books.

United Society of Shakers—Herb Department

Br. Arnold Hadd
RR #1, Box 640
Poland Spring, ME 04274

(207) 926-4597
Established 1799
Mail order; wholesale; retail
Price list for SASE; booklist $2.50

The Shaker Museum at Sabbathday Lake offers a number of herbal products by mail order, including Shaker herbal teas, culinary herbs, rose water, fir balsam pillows, vinegars, potpourris and other interesting items. An extensive book catalog is also available.

Wonderland Tea and Spice Herb Shop

Linda Quintana
1305 Railroad Ave.
Bellingham, WA 98225

(206) 733-0517
Established 1976
Mail order; wholesale; retail
Catalog $1.00

Linda Quintana of Wonderland Tea and Spice carries dried botanicals in bulk, tea and spice accessories (strainers, tea bags, gelatin capsules, etc.), culinary herbs and spices, nutmeg graters, aprons, culinary blends, tea blends, black and green teas, herb pillows, massage and body oils, salves, concentrated herbal drops, arnica oil, bentonite clay, herbal bath and beauty products, essential and perfume oils, potpourris, books and containers. (Also see listing in Chapter 6.)

Herbal Gifts & Products

Amaranth Stoneware, Ltd.

Marilyn King
PO Box 243
Sydenham, Ontario
Canada K0H 2T0

(613) 541-0799 or (800) 465-5444
Established 1986
Mail order; wholesale; custom work
Catalog free

Marilyn King of Amaranth Stoneware offers a delightful stoneware "Garden Collection" including garden plaques, unusual garden hangers for markers, letter and number tiles, garden saints, pot markers, pantry labels, garden stake sets, blank markers, garden title markers such as "butterfly garden", "perennial garden", etc., as well as custom markers. Amaranth Stoneware also has a hand-painted stoneware "Herbs of Christmas" ornament collection and a "Symbols of Christmas" collection.

Andalina, Ltd.

Janet Scigliane Garcia
Tory Hill
Warner, NH 03278-0057

(603) 456-3289
Established 1981
Mail order; wholesale; retail by appointment
Brochure $1.50 plus SASE

Andalina offers herbal soaps, salves and moth chasers in addition to culinary blends, sleep herbs and shoe deodorizers. Products are also available in gift baskets.

Back of the Beyond

Bill and Shash Georgi
7233 Lower E. Hill Rd.
Colden, NY 14033

(716) 652-0427
Established 1983
Brochures for $.75

Shash Georgi offers a hand-crafted flower press, notepapers, a "peace pillow", potpourri, herbal hot pads, herbal teas, fabric lavender rolls and more in her brochure.

There are also classes throughout the year at Back of the Beyond (see Chapter 6) and Bed and Breakfast accommodations (see Chapter 10).

Bird of Paradise Designs

Margo Davis
Box 16
Colebrook, CT 06021

(203) 738-9620
Established 1984
Mail order; wholesale
Brochure free

Margo Davis, artist, offers attractive contemporary-design posters from her Bird of Paradise Designs studio. Among her subjects are traditional healing herbs, Chinese herbs, herbal teas, wild edibles, everlastings, chilis, the English herb garden, culinary herbs and more.

• Store essential and fragrance oils away from direct light and heat, and keep the lids tightly closed when not using them.

• Store potpourri in its unopened bag or in a tightly closed glass jar away from sunlight and heat to maintain its full fragrance until you are ready to use it.

—contributed by Mary Baker, Spices 'N Things, South Whitley, Indiana

Bittersweet Farm

Mary Lou
6294 Seville Rd.
Seville, OH 44273

(216) 887-5293
Established 1983
Mail order; wholesale; retail; public garden
Catalog $2.00

Bittersweet Farm supplies handmade herbal products and flower arrangements. The full-color catalog includes wreaths, wall baskets, an herbal wedding bouquet, bee skeps, swags, hats and a eucalyptus tree.

Calvert Homestead

Barbara Burnett
4555 Sixes Rd.
Prince Frederick, MD 20678

(301) 535-5393
Established 1980
Mail order; wholesale; retail
Call for details

Barbara Burnett's Calvert Homestead offers handcrafted brooms, freshly made potpourris and stove top scents, dried flowers and floral accessories for your own arrangements or the Homestead's own floral or herbal wreaths and arrangements.

Botanical Impressions

Mari Thomas
RR 2, Box 1400
Lubec, ME 04652

(207) 733-2856
Established 1985
Mail order; wholesale with tax number; retail
Write for information.

Mari Thomas of Botanical Impressions designs note cards (blank inside) with plant designs. Each card is handmade by embossing sprigs of plants onto paper, leaving a subtle and delicate impression. The cards are colored by the "juices" of the plant. The name of each plant is written next to the design in italic calligraphy. Each card is unique; there are about ten different designs.

Candlesby Herbs

J. Stafford Allen
Cross Keys Cottage
Candlesby, Spilsby
Lincolnshire, England PE23 5SF

Phone: (0454 85) 211
Established 1981
Mail order; wholesale; retail; public garden
Catalog for self-addressed envelope; do not stamp

John and Jane Stafford Allen of Candlesby Herbs offer culinary products such as herbal blends for meats, a barbecue mix, a mulled wine mix and herbal tisanes (teas). Aromatics available include potpourris, refresher oils, sachets, sleep pillows, bath bags and oils and lavender. The Allens also carry pottery potpourri pots and cottages, pestle and mortar sets, perfume burners, herbal writing papers, posters, herb choppers and tea towels. "Garden Nurse" items include insect and fungus repellents, herbal compost activators and herbal fertilizers.

Procure quantity of petals of any fragrant flower; card thin layers of unprocessed cotton, which dip into finest Florence or Lucca oil; sprinkle a little fine salt on flowers, and lay them on a layer of cotton until an earthen vessel or a wide mouthed glass bottle is full. Tie top closed with a bladder, and lay the vessel in a south aspect to heat of sun, and in fifteen days, when uncovered, a fragrant oil can be squeezed away from the whole mass.

—*Family Receipt Book,*
1819

Cedarbrook Herb Farm

Terry and Toni Anderson
986 Sequim Ave. S.
Sequim, WA 98382

(206) 683-7733
Established 1968
Mail order; retail; public garden
Catalog $1.00

Terry and Toni Anderson of Cedarbrook Herb Farm offer finished herbal products such as Victorian wreaths, Spanish moss or sweetbriar wreaths, kitchen herb wreaths, garlic braids, nosegays, nine scents of potpourri, lavender wands, hot pads, dried culinary herbs, and many holiday and Christmas items.

Clear Light Cedar Co.

Joshua Peine
S. R. 165
Placitas, NM 87043

(505) 867-2381
Established 1970
Mail order; wholesale; retail
Catalog $1.00

The Clear Light Cedar Co. carries sachets, fragrances, skin and hair care items, incense and potpourris, all with a decidedly "cedar" aroma.

The Complete Body Shop

Susan C. Chavis
PO Box 1324
Hamlet, NC 28345-1324

(919) 582-0792
Established 1990
Mail order; wholesale; retail
Catalog $2.00; refundable with purchase

Susan Chavis offers a line of body and skin care products in addition to her original "Herbal Tees" silk screened T-shirt and clothing designs in both 100% cotton and cotton/poly blends. Other products include massage oils, bath oils, beautiful handmade Woodspirits Herb Shop soaps in more than 20 different scents, Jeanne Rose's Super Duper Seaweed Scrub, potpourri diffusers, essential oil air fresheners, books, note cards, a sample herbal soap assortment and gift baskets.

The Country Gardener

Sandi Fallon
5297 Messing Rd.
Valley Springs, CA 95252

(209) 772-1775
Established 1991
Mail order; wholesale
Catalog $1.00; includes free sample

Sandi Fallon offers herbal gift cards, notepads, Christmas gift tags, note cards with envelopes, etc. All are decorated with lovely herbal drawings.

The Country Herb

Teesha S. Moore
18603 SE May Valley Rd.
Issaquah, WA 98027

(206) 255-1543
Established 1990
Mail order; wholesale (mostly)
Catalog free

Teesha Moore offers a unique collection of paper products with charming herbal designs, including herbal vinegar labels, note pads, bookmarks, stationery, note cards, hand-painted prints, bookplates, gift tags, postcards and recipe cards. All are printed on high-quality paper, most of which is recycled.

Country Manor

Phyllis Swindler
PO Box 520, Dept. HCB
Sperryville, VA 22740

(703) 987-8761
Established 1971
Mail order
Catalog $2.00

Country Manor carries an assortment of gifts for the country home and kitchen. These include coiled straw bee skeps, gardening baskets, Mary Hughes's herb garden prints, garlic baskets, wreaths and more.

Country Roots Shop & Gardens

Gloria Harris
203 Keller Drive
Stroudsburg, PA 18360

(717) 992-5557
Established 1984
Limited mail order; retail; public garden;
lectures and classes; bed & breakfast

Gloria Harris offers the poem "A Servant in the Sun" calligraphed with pressed flowers. Write or call for price and ordering information. (Also see listings in Chapters 8 and 10.)

Countryside Fragrances, Inc.

Cynthia D. Chapman
Pacific First Centre
1420 Fifth Ave., 22nd Floor
Seattle, WA 98101-2378

(206) 386-5886
Established 1979
Mail order; wholesale
Catalog free

Countryside Fragrances supplies the Botanical Garden, Pastel, and Southern Countryside collections, potpourris, lace wardrobe sachets, concentrated fragrance oils, in addition to simmering potpourri packets and botanical potpourri packets. Aromaglow Fragrance Systems (light bulb disks) and refill oils are also available.

Dabney Herbs

Davy Dabney
PO Box 22061
Louisville, KY 40252-0061

(502) 893-5198
Established 1986
Mail order
Catalog $2.00

In addition to more than 200 varieties of herbs, everlastings and perennials (see listing in Chapter 1), Dabney Herbs lists more than 60 books, as well as gift wraps, health and beauty products, bath baskets, pure oils, botanicals, accessories (capsule filler, starch papers, mortars and pestles), teas and accessories, potpourri, bee skeps and oils for potpourris, perfumes, soaps, etc. Gift certificates are also available.

Dragon's Lair

Kristi Marcus
PO Box 274
Olean, NY 14760

(716) 373-3497
Mail order
Catalog $2.00

Kristi Marcus of Dragon's Lair carries an eclectic mixture of products: bulk herbs, crystals and stones, potpourris and supplies, "presents and potions".

Dried Floral Creations

Denise Solsrud
N5583 Rangeline Rd.
Tony, WI 54563

(715) 322-5221
Established 1988
Mail order; 10% discount to retail shops; retail
Catalog for SASE

Denise Solsrud offers interesting gift items: small posy rings or candle rings, rosebud pomanders, 5-inch wreaths covered with miniature roses, blue salvia and other flowers, pressed floral parchment stationery, and pressed herb, flower or leaf "sun-catchers". Special orders are accepted.

The Essential Oil Company

Robert Seidel
PO Box 206
Lake Oswego, OR 97034

(503) 697-5992 or (800) 729-5912
Established 1977
Wholesale (minimum order $50.00)
Catalog free

The Essential Oil Company offers pure essential oils, aromatherapy materials and massage oils. The essential oils include chamomile, citronella, eucalyptus, garlic, nutmeg, patchouli and others. Among the synthetic perfume oils are apricot, bayberry, frangipani, jasmine, lotus and violet. Miscellaneous products include charcoal tablets, porcelain scent rings, various glassware, imported teas and books. (Also see Chapter 6.)

The Farmhouse

10000 NW 70th
Grimes, IA 50111

(515) 986-3628
Mail order; retail
Catalog $1.00

The Farmhouse catalog lists a small, eclectic mixture including a clay herb garden plaque, a wreath, a bee skep, embroidered pillows, an herbal topiary, a glue gun holder (handy!), a tussie-mussie and several birdhouses.

The Flower Press

Linda Rhudy
PO Box 6388
Destin, FL 32541

(904) 837-5011
Established 1989
Mail order
Catalog $2.00

The Flower Press offers beautiful Victorian-design stationery by Bronwen Ross. Available are calling cards, note cards and Victorian wedding stationery decorated in a variety of floral designs that include pansies, roses, lilies-of-the-valley, wisteria and others.

Food for Thought Posters

Kay Reed
1442A Walnut St.
Berkeley, CA 94709

(415) 653-8841
Established 1984
Mail order; wholesale; retail
Price list free

Food for Thought offers a number of posters suitable for framing. Especially interesting are the Vegetable Quartet Posters (tomatoes, onions, peppers and eggplants) and the Cook's Garden of Herbs poster.

The Fragrance Shop

Gail Hayden
RFD 3, Box 476, College Hill Rd.
Hopkinton, NH 03229

(603) 746-4431
Established 1977
Mail order; wholesale; retail; public garden
Catalog free (specify wholesale or retail)

The Fragrance Shop catalog lists stove-top scents and samplers, potpourris, fragrant oils and wreaths (Colonial Herb Wreath, Cottage Garden Wreath, Williamsburg Wreath, Kitchen Wreath, Eucalyptus Wreath, etc). Also offered are a spice ball kit, catnip mice, a pomander kit, Auto-Pourri car air freshener, moth repellent, light-bulb rings, straw bee skeps and a glass potpourri jar with pewter top.

Fredericksburg Herb Farm

Varney's Chemist Laden (retail shop)
Bill or Sylvia Varney
PO Drawer 927
Fredericksburg, TX 78624-0927

(512) 997-8615
Mail order; retail
Catalog $1.50

Fredericksburg Herb Farm and its associated retail shop, Varney's Chemist Laden, offer a number of herbal delights, including herb teas, herbs for the grill, herb seasonings, garden markers, herbal vinegars, Parfum Bluebonnet, herbal note cards, potpourris for every room, tussie-mussies, herbal wreaths, a Texas Hill Country Herb Chart, a clay bee skep, some herb seeds, books, Caswell-Massey products, gift baskets and more.

J. J. Fuessel Custom Tile

Rt. 1
Eldorado, TX 76936

(915) 853-2403
Call for price quote or further information

J. J. Fuessel's 850 tiles with Texas wildflower designs grace the walls of the San Angelo Nature Center and have been featured in *Country Living* magazine. The proprietress says that she can "put anything on a tile", and will do herbal designs, plants, flowers, etc., on a custom basis. Sinks can also be made to match. All tiles are made completely from scratch (not preglazed).

Gatehouse Herbs

Carol Gates
98 Van Buren St.
Dolgeville, NY 13329

(315) 429-8366
Established 1980
Mail order; wholesale (some); retail; public garden
Catalog $2.00

Carol Gates of Gatehouse Herbs offers wreaths, bridal bouquets, tussie-mussies, rosebud pomanders, nosegays, candle rings, potpourri ingredients (fragrant oils, botanicals), potpourris, drawer sachets, spice strings, moth chaser strings, herbal bath preparations, dried culinary herbs and spices, gift baskets, herb blends, herb teas and more. Ms. Gates specializes in fresh and dried herbal and flower weddings.

Gooseberry Patch Company

Jo Ann Martin
PO Box 190
Delaware, OH 43015

(614) 369-1554
Established 1984
Mail order; retail
Catalog $3.00 for a 2-year subscription

The Gooseberry Patch Company carries a large number of "the proper country accessories" for your home. These include a heart-shaped grapevine wreath covered with canella berries, decorative wreath hangers, gift baskets, herbal hot pads, a wire herb rack, a spice Christmas garland, herbal cup cozies, pomander kits, potpourris and fragrant pinecones. Altogether a delightful catalog!

Graven Images

Ron Johnson
4211 Seneca
Chattanooga, TN 37409

(615) 821-7473
Established 1983
Mail order; wholesale; retail by appointment
Catalog $1.00

Graven Images carries a wonderful collection of rubber stamps that include suns, moons, weather images, flowers, gardening images (flowerpots, bee skeps), herbs (38 different ones from allspice to vanilla), wreaths, peppers, trees, etc. Also included in the catalog are animals, an English cottage set, quilt patterns, birds, cats, the Twelve Days of Christmas and more. If you love rubber stamps as I do, you'll want to get this catalog!

Gail Grisi Stenciling, Inc.

Donna Walker
PO Box 1263
Haddonfield, NJ 08033

(609) 354-1757
Established 1978
Mail order; wholesale; retail
Catalog $2.00

Gail Grisi Stenciling offers a large number of precut stencils and stencil kits, including many floral designs.

Hartman's Herb Farm

Lynn and Pete Hartman
Old Dana Rd.
Barre, MA 01005

(508) 355-2015
Established 1975
Mail order; wholesale; retail; public garden
Catalog $2.00

Hartman's Herb Farm is a family business that offers a wide range of herbal products as well as a large number of herb plants. Craft supplies include dried herbs and flowers by the bunch, fragrance and essential oils and herbs for making your own potpourris. Dried culinary herbs and spices are listed along with herb teas, Hartman's Herb Dip mix and dried salad herb blends. Herbal Christmas items include an everlasting Christmas tree, decorations and ornaments. The "Hartman's Country Look" line, handmade by family members, include grapevine wreaths, wedding or birth wreaths, folk dolls, tussie-mussies, door hats, sachet baskets, a long list of herbal and everlasting wedding flowers and accessories, wall baskets, swags, garlic braids, gift boxes, T-shirts and herbal note cards.

The Hartmans also create a beautiful "Herbal Calendar" each year.

It is easy to have a supply of horse-radish all winter. Have a quantity grated, while the root is in perfection, put it in bottles, fill it with strong vinegar, and keep it corked tight.

—from *The Frugal Housewife* by Mrs. Child, 1833

Heart's Ease Herb Shop & Gardens

Sharon Lovejoy
4101 Burton Drive
Cambria, CA 93428

(805) 927-5224
Established 1981
Mail order; public garden; retail
Catalog $1.00

Heart's Ease Herb Shop & Gardens is owned by Sharon Lovejoy, author of *Sunflower Houses: Garden Discoveries for Children of All Ages* (Interweave Press, 1991). Sharon's delightful catalog includes flower presses, a bronze sundial, a solid copper arbor for your garden, videos, heart-shaped trellises, herbal pillows, handmade soaps, rose necklaces and miniature wreaths, potpourri and perfume oils. Also listed are potpourri blends, clay herb markers, note cards, birdhouses and feeders, herbal bath grains, bee skep candles, catnip mice and much more.

Heartscents

Barbara Irwin
PO Box 1674
Hilo, HI 96721-1674

(808) 959-3468
Established 1979
Mail order; wholesale; retail by appointment
Catalog $1.00

Barbara Irwin carries herbal hot pads, rose potpourri, "mind clearer" herbal sachets, Heartscent bath salts, catnip mice and the "Pampering Princess" gift basket. Barbara also offers an intriguing "Sweetheart Dinner-Bath Fantasy" package. Call or write for details.

Hedgehog Hill Farm

Mark and Terry Silber
RFD 2, Box 2010
Buckfield, ME 04220-9549

(207) 388-2341
Established 1972
Mail order; retail; public garden
Catalog $1.00

Hedgehog Hill Farm is a small diversified organic farm located in the western mountains of Oxford County, Maine. The 160 acres at Hedgehog Hill Farm are mostly wooded, with eight acres of cleared fields where the Silbers harvest a variety of herbs and flowers, perennials, everlastings and vegetables. The Hedgehog Hill catalog includes information on workshops given at the farm in addition to several mail-order items: herbal wreaths (these can be custom-designed to your specifications), country hats, everlasting arrangements and bouquets, decorated baskets, the "Cook's Collection" gift box, herbal tea and honey gift box, herbal vinegar gift box and the Hedgehog Hill Sampler gift box. Several books are also available.

Terry Silber is the author of *A Small Farm in Maine*, the story of Hedgehog Hill and the Silbers' move to the country. The Silbers are coauthors of *The Complete Book of Everlastings—Growing, Drying and Designing with Dried Flowers*. Both books are listed in the Hedgehog Hill catalog.

The Herb Bar

Connie Moore
200 W. Mary
Austin, TX 78704

(512) 444-6251
Established 1985
Mail order; wholesale; retail
Catalog free

The extensive listing of herbal products in The Herb Bar's mail-order catalog includes essential oils, dried herbs, moth repellent potpourris, herbal flea powders, pyrethrum insect powder, lots of books, tinctures and tincture blends, tea blends and accessories, dried herbs, herb and spice jars and racks, essential and fragrance oils, wreaths, drying racks, mortar and pestle sets and much more. Connie Moore offers classes throughout the year at her shop.

Also available is Connie Moore and Janette Grainger's new book, *Natural Insect Repellents for Pets, People and Plants* (see description in Chapter 4). Write or call for price and ordering information.

Herb Gathering, Inc.

Paula Winchester
5742 Kenwood Ave.
Kansas City, MO 64110-2732

(816) 523-2653
Established 1979
Mail order; wholesale; retail
Brochure free; specify retail or wholesale (send tax number)

Paula Winchester of Herb Gathering, Inc. offers unique "Forget-Me-Not" gift baskets through mail order. Each gift basket contains an assortment of herbal items packed along with fresh cut herbs! Custom assortments are also available.

The Herb House

Becky Fowler
340 Grove St., Dept. HCWB
Bluffton, OH 45817

(419) 358-7189
Established 1986
Mail order; wholesale (bee skeps only); retail
Brochure for SASE

The Herb House offers a large assortment of stoneware herb markers (from angelica to yarrow), title garden markers, garden signs and vinegar labels. Also listed are straw or vine bee skeps/hives, a bee skep cross-stitch, and a vine birdhouse.

The Herb Merchant

Timothy L. Newcomer
70 W. Pomfret St.
Carlisle, PA 17013

(717) 249-0970
Established 1987
Mail order; wholesale; retail; public garden
Brochure for SASE

The Herb Merchant carries an eclectic assortment of essential oils, rubber stamps, Caswell-Massey soaps, gourmet coffees, several hundred books on herbs, gourmet foods, potpourris, incense, greeting cards, pet products and custom gift baskets and boxes.

Herb N' Ewe

Barbara Wade and Susan Mills
11755 National Rd., SE
Thornville, OH 43076

(614) 323-2264
Established 1988
Mail order; retail; public garden
Price list for large SASE

Herb N' Ewe, an "herbal farm for gardeners n' shepherds", lists wreaths, tussie-mussies, gift baskets, ladder drying racks, sheep ornaments and other assorted items in the mail-order brochure. Lectures and workshops are also offered; see listing in Chapter 6.

Herb Products Co.

PO Box 898
N. Hollywood, CA 91603-0898

(213) 877-3104 or (818) 984-3141
Established 1972
Mail order; wholesale; retail
Catalog free

Herb Products Co. offers dried botanicals, extracts and tinctures, high-quality oils and fragrances, empty capsules and books.

Hickory Hill Herbs

Paula Jones Hill
307 W. Ave. E.
Lampasas, TX 76550

(512) 556-8801
Call or write for more information.

Paula Jones Hill of Hickory Hill Herbs offers herbal oils, dried herbs and spices, plants, wreaths, potpourris and more by mail order. (Also see listings in Chapters 6 and 10.)

Hilary's Comfort Beads

Hilary Pfeifer
1134 Van Buren
Eugene, OR 97402-4734

(503) 683-7111
Established 1989
Mail order; wholesale
Brochure $1.50; refundable with purchase
(specify retail mail order or wholesale)

People have long used beads to take their minds off worries by either feeling them or counting them. Even today in Greece, many men carry "worry beads" in their pockets, and Roman Catholics carry rosary beads as an aid in prayer. Hilary Pfeifer has taken this idea one step further by making strands of beautifully colored, smooth-as-river-stones porcelain beads with a word on the end bead which serves as a point of focus for the owner. Hilary's Comfort Beads began as a gift for a friend who was recovering from cancer surgery. Next came a line of beads especially for gardeners. Hilary's Garden Beads are to be held in "hopes of prolific growth, compromising weather and abundant harvest". The last bead in these strands say "carrots", "flowers", "growth", "harvest", "herbs", etc. Custom beads are available with almost any word printed on them. (I have a beautiful "harvest" strand. I can't say whether it's improved my garden this year or not, but it sure is fun to "feel" and to tease the cat with!)

Hill Crest House, Ltd.

Joanne Anthony
17 Coopers Lake Rd.
Bearsville, NY 12409

(914) 679-2340
Established 1990
Mail order; retail
Brochure free

Joanne Anthony has combined her love of stitchery with her love of gardening by collecting the best designs devoted to herbs. All items are in kit form, and include samplers, sachet bags, an afghan, and individual herbs in stitchery. Joanne also offers a stitching frame and scissors.

Homespun Gatherings

Susan Rose Cummings
PO Box 3758
Syracuse, NY 13220

(315) 458-4569
Established 1987
Mail order; wholesale; retail
Catalog $1.00

Susan Rose Cummings offers herbal wreaths, arrangements and baskets in various styles and sizes. Customers are encouraged to send wallpaper or fabric swatches with their orders, since everything is handmade to individual specifications.

Mary Hughes Designs

Mary Hughes
28 R. W. Ross St.
Wilkes-Barre, PA 18701

(717) 826-0729
Established 1985
Mail order; wholesale
Catalog $5.00; refundable with purchase

Mary Hughes offers beautiful hand-watercolored pen-and-ink drawings of botanical, herbal and garden designs. The drawings are matted and framed in your choice of several color combinations, and are fully illustrated in the artist's full-color catalog/folder.

Illuminations

Ann R. Erickson
699 Miller Circle
Indian Springs, AL 35124

(205) 980-8311
Established 1988
Mail order; wholesale
Catalog $1.00; refundable with purchase

Illuminations is a one-woman calligraphy business that offers a number of gifts for herb lovers. Ann Erickson's charming herbal designs are printed on T-shirts, labels and bookplates, gift enclosure cards, memo pads and other stationery, tote bags and garden and kitchen aprons.

The artist will also do custom calligraphy of garden quotes, poems, business cards, logos, certificates, etc. Call or write for additional information.

Indiana Botanic Gardens

Tim Cleland
PO Box 5
Hammond, IN 46325

(219) 947-4040
Established 1910
Mail order; wholesale; retail
Catalog free

Indiana Botanic Gardens carries a wide variety of botanical health and beauty products including ointments, salves, Nature's Way products, bath products, essential oils, potpourri supplies, herb bags, Hyland's Homeopathic remedies, hundreds of loose herbal teas, and a huge list of dried botanicals including everything from acacia gum to yerba santa leaf. The catalog also lists a number of herb seeds, liquid herb extracts and much more!

Sinnament, Ginger,
nutmeg and cloves
And that gives me my
jolly red nose.

—author unknown

Island Aromatics

Marylou Miller
SR 13504
Keaau, HI 96749

(808) 966-8478
Established 1986
Mail order
Price list $1.00; refundable with purchase

Island Aromatics is a source for Tropical Fragrance Essence perfume oils. The oils are blended and bottled in Hawaii, and contain no alcohol in their production. Varieties available are gardenia, pikake, lotus, plumeria, night queen, sandalwood, orange blossom, tiare, orchid, tuberose, passion flower and white ginger. Oils are available in 1-dram or 1/2-ounce bottles. Tester sets are also available with your choice of either six or 12 scents.

Johanna's

JoAnne Fajack
2575 Dogwood Drive
Youngstown, OH 44511-1311

(216) 793-9523
Established 1986
Mail order; wholesale; retail
Catalog $3.00; refundable with order

JoAnne Fajack offers gift baskets, wreaths in various sizes and designs, and herbal arrangements, as well as popular folk art dolls called Cellar Babies that carry herbs and garden tools or baskets filled with herbs. Custom herbal arrangements and wreaths are also available.

Keepsake Hearts & Flowers

Ruth McCully
PO Box 49
South Bend, WA 98586

(206) 942-5956
Established 1981
Mail order; wholesale; retail
Catalog $2.00; refundable with purchase

Keepsake Hearts & Flowers is a source for dried and preserved flowers, wreaths, baskets, botanicals, dried herbs and spices, seasonings, jellies, vinegars and much more. Ms. McCully also handcrafts floral jewelry—one-of-a-kind keepsake pins, earrings, hair combs and barrettes made from preserved natural flowers and miniature roses.

la dama maya herb and flower farm

Maureen Messick
Rt. 5, Box 82
Luray, VA 22835

(703) 743-4665
Established 1977
Mail order; wholesale; retail; public garden
Newsletter/brochure free

Maureen Messick of la dama maya herb and flower farm offers dried herb and flower wreaths, a Victorian basket, a decorated hat, a decorated heart wreath and potpourri by mail order. Ms. Messick will match colors to your home decor if you include a swatch of fabric or color samples. She offers a number of workshops at the farm. See Chapter 6 for further information.

Legacy Herbs

Sue Lukens
HC 70, Box 442
Mountain View, AR 72560

(501) 269-4051
Established 1986
Mail order; wholesale; retail; display garden
Catalog $.50

Sue Lukens and her husband, Dave Mc-Kellep, grow, craft and market herbs and herbal products, stoneware pottery and woodenware. Their catalog is a delightfully eclectic mixture of herbal jellies, herb teas, culinary blends, herbal cosmetics, potpourris and refresher oils, scented craft items, remedies and preparations, bath items, etc. A large number of annual, biennial and perennial herb plants and everlastings as well as several miniature roses are also available by mail order.

The catalog also includes a selection of original stoneware mortars and pestles, bowls, garlic jars, honey pots and garden markers. Handcrafted woodenware include mortars and pestles, cedar garden markers, spice racks, spoons, scoops and toys.

Although not listed in the catalog at this time, Legacy Herbs also carries a wide variety of bulk herbs for medicinal or craft uses, as well as essential oils and fragrances by the 1/2-ounce bottle. Write for additional information.

Litl' Mack's Herb Shoppe

Lisa Macklin
9308 E. 68th St.
Raytown, MO 64133

(816) 353-0493
Established in 1987
Catalog free

Litl' Mack's began in 1987 as a hobby. In the few years since then, it has blossomed into a small but growing herbal craft business specializing in herbal gift items such as herbal trivets, potpourris, sachets, herbal mug rugs, scented padded hangers and a variety of gift baskets containing these items. Also listed are teas, spices and blends.

The Little Farm Press

Jane Conneen
820 Andrews Rd.
Bath, PA 18014

(215) 759-5326
Established 1970
Mail order; retail by appointment
Catalog $2.50

Jane Conneen is an herb gardener who has the skill to capture her plants on paper. Nationally recognized as an outstanding botanical artist, she specializes in miniature hand-colored etchings of wildflowers, herbs, berries and many other charming subjects. The etchings range from 3/4" × 1/2" up to 1½" × 6¾" (I told you they were small!). The artist has had one person and group exhibitions, and has participated in many art festivals. She has won numerous awards for her work and is represented in public and private collections.

Offshoots of the tiny miniature etchings are small books (about 2" × 2½") printed entirely by etching press, hand-colored and hand-bound.

Lynn's

22375 SW Francis
Hillsboro, OR 97123-6573

(503) 642-5469
Established 1989
Price list for SASE

Lynn's is a supplier of bulk dried herbs, Chinese herbs, seasoning blends, sprouting seeds, essential oils, precious oils (German chamomile, jasmine, neroli, etc.), fragrance oils and potpourris.

The soapwort plant is also called "Bouncing Bet" because of the shape of the flower which looks like the backside of a laundress as she bobs up and down scrubbing clothes with her skirts and petticoats pinned up.

Maryland's Herb Basket

Maryland Massey
PO Box 131
Millington, MD 21651-0131

(301) 928-3301
Established 1983
Mail order; wholesale; retail; public garden
Catalog $1.00; refundable with purchase of
$10.00 or more

"I think . . . we're finally realizing that God's gifts are the best ones," says Maryland Massey. "We don't have to manufacture something plastic to have something worthwhile." The Maryland's Herb Basket catalog proves this statement, with its eclectic mixture of culinary herbs, spices and teas, Maryland's Own Herb Basket Blends and Maryland Potpourri, inspired by the business's home state. Also listed are other potpourris, sachets, incense, essential oils, simmering scents, candles, books, herbal bath products and fragrant body oils. A collection of garden supplies includes markers, statues, planters, baskets, bee skeps and more.

Mary's Herb Garden & Gift Shop

Betty Ann Viviano
23825 Priest Rd.
Philomath, OR 97370

(503) 929-6275
Established 1989
Catalog free

Betty Ann Viviano carries culinary herbs and spices, culinary herb blends, herbal vinegars (including a champagne vinegar) and herb teas. Also available are herbal candles, materials for making your own potpourris, wreaths, sachets, spice trivets, candle wreaths, T-shirts, aprons and tote bags. Bath blends, potpourris and gift baskets are also offered. (Also see listing in Chapter 1.)

Mendocino Arts & Gifts

Mary and Glenn Stinson
PO Box 1063
Mendocino, CA 95460-1063

(707) 937-3524
Established 1988
Catalog $2.00

Mendocino Arts & Gifts' gift and decorative items include a fall/winter cone wreath, Obester herbal oils and vinegars, Emandal Farms herbal jams and jellies, herb windowsill gardens, Mendocino Mustards, cedar potpourris, lotions and sachets, Fuller's Herbal Vinegars, McFadden Farms Basilwood, garlic braids, herbal blends, hot pepper jellies and more.

Mr. McGregor's Garden

Joyce Holway
347 White's Path
S. Yarmouth, MA 02664-1214

Established 1990
Mail order; wholesale
Catalog $1.00

Joyce Holway of Mr. McGregor's Garden offers a number of potpourris, simmering blends, moth repellents and hot pad fillers in her catalog. Gifts and handmade items include pomanders, bath bags and mitts, auto refreshers, scented hot pads, tea cozies, bayberry iron waxers, pottery and wooden items.

Mountain Rose Herbs

Julie Bailey
PO Box 2000
Redway, CA 95560

(707) 923-3941
Established 1989
Mail order; wholesale; retail
Catalog free

Mountain Rose Herbs offers herbal "healing" teas (Immunity, Peace Tea, Throat Soother, Women's Balancing Blend), beverage teas, tea brewing utensils, cosmetics (facial steams, tooth powder, bath salts), baby products (baby's balm, body powder and oil, bath herbs), herbs for children, compound rubs and herbal oils. Also available are unscented oils, amber bottles, tins, cardboard powder containers, glass perfume bottles and more.

Nathan's Forge

Nick Vincent
3476 Uniontown Rd.
Uniontown, MD 21157-3558

(301) 848-7903
Established 1983
Mail order; wholesale; retail
Catalog $2.00

Nick Vincent, blacksmith, makes "all sorts of Ironwork in the best and neatest manner, and on reasonable terms". The Nathan's Forge catalog includes hooks for hanging dried herbs and pots, arched plant hangers in assorted sizes, an herb dryer to hang candles or herbs for drying and more. According to the proprietor, "Orders for Ironwork of any kind thankfully received and promptly attended to."

Nature's Acres

Jane Hawley
840 FM 550
Forney, TX 75126

(214) 771-4320
Established 1985
Mail order; wholesale
Brochure free

Jane Hawley's herbal products are all handmade from natural ingredients with organically produced herbal plant materials. These include soaps (peppermint/aloe, rosemary/oatmeal, lavender/Vitamin E, almond/sage scrub), hand creams, lip balm, body oils, herbal flea collars and Nature's Acres salve. A number of herb plants are available at the farm; call for appointment.

The Need'l Love Company, Inc.

Renee Nanneman
PO Box 672
Liberty, MO 64068

(816) 781-4833
Established 1984
Mail order; wholesale
Catalog $1.00

The Need'l Love Company specializes in cross-stitch designs. One, "The Herb Garden", is available as a graph only or kit. The design shows a bee skep surrounded by different herbs, and makes an attractive finished piece of "herbal needlework".

Nu-Life Cards

Joyce Phenicie
N66 W30751 Red Fox Run
Hartland, WI 53029

(414) 367-7463
Established 1975
Price list free

Joyce Phenicie of Nu-Life Cards offers note card packs featuring herbs, plants and fruits of the Bible as well as other special occasion cards.

Olive's Hearth & Haven

Olive Curtis
5481 Doren Rd.
Acme, WA 98220

(206) 595-2485
Established 1991

Olive Curtis sells a set of four herbal note cards depicting thyme, garlic, sage and leeks. The cards are enhanced with color photographs, gardening tips and recipes and come with matching envelopes. The set is currently $5.50 postpaid. (Also see listing in Chapter 8.)

Our Family's Herbs & Such

Lana Sims
702 Llano
Pasadena, TX 77504

(713) 943-1937
Established 1990
Brochure for SASE

Lana Sims offers herbal gifts such as a Silver King artemisia wreath, herbal closet fresheners, potpourri cards, a drying rack with herbs, antique rose potpourri, herbal teas and cooking herbs with recipes.

Park Seed Co.

Joyce Reagin, Public Relations
Cokesbury Rd.
Greenwood, SC 29647-0001

(800) 845-3369
Established 1868
Catalog free

In addition to herb seeds and plants (see listing in Chapter 1), Park also offers an "Herb Dial". Just dial the food being prepared and you are shown suggestions of herbs to use with the specific dish you're preparing.

Patricia's

Patty Levine
41 Alexander St.
Eureka Springs, AR 72632

(501) 253-6589
Established 1983
Mail order; wholesale; retail by appointment

Patty Levine designs original dried floral and herbal arrangements, and specializes in the design of wreaths. These are available in five basic styles: Victorian, Country Kitchen, Southwestern, Wild Floral and Ozark Wildwood.

Also available are basket arrangements, topiaries, swags, herbal braids and bundles, tussie-mussies and other items.

Pine Creek Herbs

Kathleen Gips
152 S. Main St.
Chagrin Falls, OH 44022

(216) 247-5014
Established 1979
Mail order
Catalog $1.00

Kathleen Gips of Pine Creek Herbs specializes in tussie-mussies and the language of flowers. Her delightful catalog features preserved tussie-mussies, posy holders, bud pins, tussie-mussie kits, Victorian rose-scented heart necklaces, herbal bath bags, potpourris, many fragrance oils and original fragrance blends. Also available are potpourri ingredients: botanicals, spices, potpourri kits, etc. Ms. Gips is the author of *The Language of Flowers: A Book of Victorian Floral Sentiments* (see Chapter 4 for annotation).

Pressed for Time

Tauna Anderson
238 South 100 East 68-7C
Ephraim, UT 84627

(801) 283-4788
Established 1990
Mail order; wholesale; retail
Catalog $2.00

Tauna Anderson of Pressed for Time offers a collection of lovely handmade floral pictures from pressed flowers. These include designs such as the alphabet, butterflies, hearts, stars, personalized wedding invitations, a wreath and a bouquet. Prices are reasonable, and all designs are available framed or unframed.

Rasland Farm

Dick and Sylvia Tippett
NC 82 at U.S. 13
Godwin, NC 28344-9712

(919) 567-2705
Established 1981
Mail order; wholesale; public garden; retail
Catalog $2.50

In addition to herb and scented geranium plants (see listing in Chapter 1), Rasland Farm offers herb drying racks, braided garlic ropes, mortars and pestles, bee skeps, herbal wreaths (hearts, rosemary, kitchen, Silver King/sweet Annie), garlic wreaths, decorate-your-own solid wreath bases, wedding and bridal gifts (tussie-mussies, bouquets, etc.). Also listed are a number of potpourris, essential oils and potpourri supplies such as cinnamon chips, star anise, whole cloves, sandalwood chips and fixatives. Culinary herb blends, fresh herb teas and blends, bouquet garni, muslin bags, pottery jars, pet items and bath and beauty products are included.

Dried bunches of hanging herbs and bouquets as well as dried flowers (baby's-breath, ammobium, globe amaranth, statice, strawflowers, yarrow, etc.) are also listed.

Sylvia Tippett's booklet, *A Comprehensive Guide for Making Potpourri*, is available for $2.50.

Rathdowney, Ltd.

Louise Downey-Butler
PO Box 357
3 River St.
Bethel, VT 05032

(802) 234-9928
Established 1982
Mail order; wholesale; retail; public garden
Catalog free

Rathdowney, Ltd. is an herb shop and apothecary that carries a full range of herbal products and books that are hard to find elsewhere.

Remember there is a difference between one bay leaf and two bay leaves; and the difference between one clove of garlic and two cloves of garlic is enough to disorganize a happy home.

—*New Orleans City Guide*, Federal Writers' Project, 1938

Raven's Nest

Terry Craft
4539 Iroquois Trail
Duluth, GA 30136-4284

(404) 242-3901
Established 1987
Mail order; wholesale; retail
Catalog $1.00

Terry Craft's Raven's Nest carries a large number of dried herbs, barks and roots, herbal accessories (gel caps, capsule fillers, tea accessories), spices and cooking blends, Chinese herbs, herbal extracts, black and green flavored teas, essential oils, bottles, designer oils, potpourris and simmering potpourris (no wood chip fillers) and simmering pots. Also listed are gifts for the home such as vacuum scent packages, bee skeps, unique "simmerice", pomanders, hot mats, lace sachets, gift baskets, Victorian dream pillows, bath salts, herbal bath blends, luffa sponges and more.

Marilyan Roberts Collection

Marilyan Brown
PO Box 3471
Beverly Hills, CA 90212-0471

(213) 820-1872
Established 1980
Mail order; wholesale
Brochure free

The Marilyan Roberts Collection carries a line of herbal note cards, floral notelets, herb prints, charming adhesive labels, bookplates, and spice ceramic trivets. Orders less than $105.00 will incur a $6.00 handling charge.

Rocky Retreat Herb Farm

Norma Phelps
Rt. 1, Box 109A
Shenandoah Junction, WV 25442

(304) 876-6653
Established 1990
Mail order; wholesale
Write for information.

Norma Phelps offers hand-blended potpourris made from herbs and flowers grown on her farm, with no added dyed wood chips. Scents include Peach, Thyme, Woodsy Rose, Victorian Rose, Mountain Rain, French Vanilla, Orange Spice and Wildberry Spice. Also available are miniature handmade stoneware vases for scenting rooms or cars, fragrance lamp rings, fragrance oils, bunches of dried baby's-breath, lamb's ears and fairy roses. Ms. Phelps will also custom-blend any potpourri to customers' specifications.

The Rosemary House

Bertha and Susanna Reppert
S. Market St.
Mechanicsburg, PA 17055

(717) 697-5111
Established 1968
Mail order; wholesale; retail; public garden
Catalog $2.00

The Rosemary House is a family business that believes in providing as many herbal products as possible! In addition to many seeds and plants (see listing in Chapter 1), the Reppert family also carries just about every herbal product: salt-free herb blends, bouquet garni cook bags, seasonings, gourmet cookware, herbal napkin rings and placemats, kitchen gadgets, mortars and pestles, aprons, imported herbal tiles, many herbal teas and recipes, herbal sugars and herbal wedding supplies. Also listed are "rosemary" gifts, mail-a-herb greeting cards, stationery, potpourris and potpourri supplies, fragrance and essential oils, bee skeps, herbal pet products and much, much

Than the mayor's kid and loaf more dainty far
Are our poor herbs, self earned, and vinegar.

—Sadi, from Gulistan, c. 1258

more! And books—they have books! Bertha Reppert (the mother) has written and published more than 14 books and booklets herself, and they and many others are listed here.

The retail shop is, according to Susanna Reppert (a daughter), "filled to the gills with herb products and goodies". A tea room next door to the shop, Sweet Remembrances, is operated by Nancy Reppert (another daughter). Sweet Remembrances is open for private groups only (minimum ten) for teas or herbal events. Call for more details. The Rosemary House also sponsors many workshops and classes. See listing in Chapter 6.

Sanders Unlimited
Mary Jo Ruilova
2030 McGregor Blvd.
Ft. Myers, FL 33901

(813) 334-8852
Established 1990
Mail order
Catalog free

Sanders Unlimited offers a full-color brochure full of garden gifts. These include pressed glass bottles; terracotta labels for vinegars; topiary frames; herb, mushroom and greens keeper bags; lavender sachets; assorted pots; herb markers; garden aprons and kneeling pads; bird feeders, gardening books, potting bench, canvas carry-all and more.

Stone Well Herbs
Jan Powers
2320 W. Moss
Peoria, IL 61604

(309) 674-1781
Established 1980
Mail order; retail
Brochure $1.00

Jan Powers of Stone Well Herbs offers an eclectic assortment including herbal stencils, a bee skep cookie cutter, a sterling silver posy pin, a ceramic bee skep pendant, a ceramic wall pot, potpourri jar and crock, theme garden markers handcrafted from clay, a stone bunny statue and several books.

Ms. Powers has written and published two booklets: *Decorating with Herb Stencils*, 27 pages of herb facts, ideas and herb stencils to cut out ($5.00), and *A Victorian Herbal*, a 17-page collection of teas, traditions and Victorian heirloom gardening information ($3.00).

The Studio of Claudia Walker
Claudia Walker
8306 Rainrock Rd., NE
Newark, OH 43055

(614) 745-2419
Established 1976
Mail order; wholesale; retail
Catalog $2.50

Claudia Walker has designed a complete line of gifts for herb enthusiasts. These include herbal prints, aprons, identification tags, note cards, stationery, bookmarks, labels, gift tags, memo pads and herb botanicals.

Herbal designs, paintings, etc., are also available by commission.

The Sunny Window

Nancy Engel
Box 199H
Southboro, MA 01772

(508) 485-8132
Established 1983
Mail order; wholesale
Catalog $2.00

The Sunny Window carries a selection of finished herbal crafts including eucalyptus swags, various wreaths and wall baskets. Also offered are cinnamon sticks, a nutmeg grater set, a spicy stove-top simmer mix, handmade potpourris, herbal hot pads, catnip bags, herbal bath bags, cedar sachets, Christmas items, decorated hats and fans, pomanders, moth repellant mix, herbal car refreshers, etc. (The minimum opening order is $75.00.)

Swinging Bridge Pottery

Bob van Kluyve
HCR 2 Box 395
Madison, VA 22727-9366

(800) 992-4244 (locally (703) 923-4244)
Established 1973
Mail order; wholesale
Brochure free

Swinging Bridge Pottery offers porcelain and stoneware pottery items, including herb and spice jars, herb jar racks, larger herb, garlic or honey pots, herbal lotion and soap bottles, potpourri pots, mortars and pestles, pot and garden markers, scent rings, trivet tiles, lapel pins/refrigerator magnets, planters, unusual ring planters and clocks. Items are decorated with various herbal designs; custom designs are also available.

Tanglewood Gardens

Norma or Dennis Coney
Box 1215, RD #1
Pennellville County Rt. 10
Pennellville, NY 13132

(315) 668-3675
Established 1983
Mail order (dried florals only); wholesale; retail

Tanglewood Gardens offers 62 different dried floral designs including wreaths, topiaries, straw hats, kissing balls, garlands, Christmas trees and baskets, all following a variety of themes such as "Victorian Fancies", "Rustic Country Accents" and "Colonial Decoratives", to list a few. All materials used in the pieces are organically grown. The Coneys also offer landscape consultations by appointment.

Teasel Weed

Darr Littlefield-Fortin
RR 3, Box 1046
Wells, ME 04090

(207) 646-5172
Established 1979
Mail order; wholesale; retail
Catalog $1.00; refundable with purchase

Teasel Weed carries a mixture of herbal items, including a garlic basket, rosebud necklace, a wedding herb potpourri, moth deterrents, large glass jars, muslin bags, essential oil perfumes, various herbal amulets and whimsical "Teasel Trolls".

Oh, better, no doubt,
   is a dinner of herbs,
When season'd by love,
   which no rancour
   disturbs,
Than turbot, bisque,
   ortolans, eaten in
   strife!

—Owen Meredith in
   Lucile, 1860

There's Always the Garden
Linda Cole
32 W. Anapamu St., #267
Santa Barbara, CA 93101

(805) 687-6478
Established 1985
Mail order; primarily wholesale
Catalog free

Linda Cole markets a whole line of products with the "there's always the garden" motif. These include sweatshirts, T-shirts, tote bags, a sports watch, wall plaques, note cards, sunvisors and aprons.

Thistle Hill
Norma B. Gervaise
59 Evans St.
Mayville, NY 14757

(716) 753-7692 (noon until 4:00 p.m.,
Eastern time)
Established 1983
Mail order; wholesale; retail; public garden
Catalog for SASE

Norma B. Gervaise of Thistle Hill carries handcrafted herbal gifts including potpourris and simmering potpourris, herbal moth chasers, lavender heart sachets, sachet bags, potpourri bears, herb and spice hot mats, handcrafted sachet dolls and several Christmas items—an herbal advent wreath and an herbal Christmas wreath.

Also available is a custom design service for retail lines of sachets, potpourris, herbal wreaths or bouquets. Inquire on letterhead.

Tide-Mark Press
Susan Poole
PO Box 280311
East Hartford, CT 0612 -0311

(203) 289-0363
Established 1979
Mail order; wholesale; retail
Catalog free

Tide-Mark Press publishes a large line of full-color calendars on a variety of subjects. The Herbal Calendar includes delightful watercolor illustrations along with herbal recipes and gardening information. The 1992 Herbal Calendar is $9.95 + $3.50 shipping.

Emelie Tolley's Herb Basket
Emelie Tolley
Box 1332
Southampton, NY 11969

(516) 283-5882
Mail order; wholesale
Catalog $1.00

Emelie Tolley, author of several beautiful books on herbs, now offers potpourris (Christmas Rose, Bitter Lemon, Seashore, Red Red Rose, Santa Fe) bath herbs, dried arrangements, scented candles, calendars and books by mail.

Ms. Tolley's books, *Cooking with Herbs* and *Herbs*, and a new book, *Gifts From the Herb Garden*, as well as her herb calendar, are also available (see descriptions in Chapter 4).

United Communications

644 Merrick Rd.
Lynbrook, NY 11563-9815

(516) 593-2206
Mail order
Brochure free

United Communications offers a good number of posters with gardening and herbal themes: the Wall Flowers collection from the New York Botanical Garden Print Series, a Culinary posters series (Culinary Herbs, Mexican Cooking Spices, Wild Edibles, Herbal Teas, Chilis, The English Herb Garden, Sunflower and Chinese Herbs) and the Nature's Secret series that contains wall charts of healing herbs, aromatic herbs and more. Custom framing is also available.

Use a salad spinner to remove excess water from fresh herbs after washing.

—from the brochure of the Memphis Herb Society

Well-Sweep Herb Farm

Cyrus and Louise Hyde
317 Mt. Bethel Rd.
Port Murray, NJ 07865

(908) 852-5390
Established 1976
Mail order; retail; public garden
Catalog $2.00

In addition to a huge number of plants and seeds (see listing in Chapter 1), Well-Sweep Herb Farm also supplies books, dried flowers, essential and fragrance oils, dried arrangements, potpourris, floral supplies, flower presses, herbal bath and beauty products and potpourri supplies.

Western Comfrey, Inc.

Philip L. Peters
PO Box 45
Canby, OR 97013

(503) 266-3788
Established 1969
Mail order; wholesale; retail
Catalog free

Western Comfrey has played a leading role in the commercialization of the comfrey plant and in the development and researching of comfrey as a medicine and food source. Through mail order, Western Comfrey offers several specialty items, including comfrey gels and ointments, teas, liquid root extracts, rootstock, a skin creme, a nail conditioner and strengthener and more.

Probably the largest collection of comfrey recipes anywhere is to be found in *A Comfrey Cookbook* by Phil Peters, also available from Western Comfrey, Inc.

Whole World Recycled Stationery

Janette Lawhorn
400 E. Russell Rd.
Tecumseh, MI 49286

(800) 359-2379
Established 1990
Mail order; wholesale
Catalog $1.00

Whole World Recycled Stationery carries note cards, scratch pads, pocket pads and personal stationery, Christmas cards and other items, all on recycled "postconsumer waste" papers. A number of herbal designs are available: baskets and wreaths, individual herbs, an herb garden and others.

Betsy Williams/The Proper Season

Betsy Williams
68 Park St.
Andover, MA 01810

(508) 470-0911
Established 1970
Mail order; wholesale; retail
Catalog $1.00

Betsy Williams offers lovely herbal items in her full-color mail-order catalog. Moss topiaries, friendship wreaths and herbs, a friendship basket, Faerie Ring wreath, a Cottage Garden Wreath and a Wedding Wreath. Also included are rose necklaces, rose hearts, a wedding basket, wedding herbs (favors, gift box, strewing bag), wall pots, Christmas wreaths and Christmas herbs. Books are also included.

Ms. Williams has also written two small booklets, *Planning a Fresh Herbal Wedding* and *The Herbs of Christmas*, which are available for $3.00 each.

Will's Garden of Knowledge

Lori Willoughby
804 N. Sanborn
Mitchell, SD 57301

Established 1983
Write for more information.

Lori Willoughby offers an interesting array of herbal items by mail order. These include hand-poured ceramic tea sets decorated with herbal leaf prints available with Japanese-style cups, regular teacups or mugs. Also available are labeled spice jars, handprinted T-shirts with herbal motifs, simmering potpourri containers, an everlasting floral heart wreath, a circular everlasting wreath and "Beyond the Season" flower and foliage preservative. Ms. Willoughby also has an informative packet/booklet titled "Basil Through the Ages" for $7.50 + $1.00 postage/handling.

Wind & Weather

Mary Rogers
PO Box 1012
Mendocino, CA 95460-1012

(707) 964-1284
Established 1975
Mail order; retail
Catalog free

Wind & Weather specializes in weather instruments, weathervanes and sundials. Herbalists will especially be interested in this company's assortment of sundials. They include a cast iron or polished brass Williamsburg sundial with pedestal, and Father Time, Helios, Hummingbird and Flowers, Frog on Lily Pad (my favorite) and Fisherboy and Birdbath dials. Also available are several wall dials, compass roses (direction indicators) and pedestals.

Wisteria Press

231 Lawrenceville Rd.
Lawrenceville, NJ 08648

Established 1991
Mail order
Catalog $2.00 (refundable with first purchase)

Wisteria Press carries a line of paper products including beautiful visiting cards, gift enclosures, note cards, sachet envelopes, place cards and more. All designs are adapted from watercolor drawings or chromolithography dating from the 18th and 19th centuries. Available in the future will be animal and English garden designs from Beatrix Potter's Country World.

J. Gaunt Woodman Co.

Janet Woodman
58003 Rd. T
Saguache, CO 81149

(719) 256-4230
Established 1989
Mail order; wholesale

Janet Woodman offers a unique product—an herbal bath greeting card. The full-color greeting card contains an herbal bath tea bag with room to write your own message. The herbal bath tea bags are also available in packages.

Mostly Medicinals

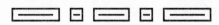

American Indian Herb Co.

Lena Palmer
1735 32nd St.
San Diego, CA 92102

(619) 239-0472
Established 1976
Mail order; wholesale; retail by appointment only
Brochure free

The American Indian Herb Co. offers traditional as well as contemporary herbal teas, herbal extracts and some body care products.

Amrita Herbal Products

Katherine Chantal
Rt. 2, Box 737
Floyd, VA 24091

(703) 745-3474
Established 1982
Mail order; wholesale; retail
Catalog free

Amrita ("immortal" in Sanskrit) Herbal Products carries tinctures, salves and oils made from fresh plant materials. The salves and oils are based on olive oil and the tinctures are alcohol-based. The tinctures include bergamot, boneset, calendula, comfrey root, dandelion root, *Echinacea angustifolia* root, elder flowers, lobelia, bloodroot, chickweed, evening primrose, myrrh, osha root, and others. Salves are made from goldenseal and comfrey. Oils include calendula flower, mullein flower, St.-John's-wort and yellow dock. Jewelweed plantain lotion is also available.

Ellon Bach USA

644 Merrick Rd.
Lynbrook, NY 11563-9815

(516) 593-2206
Established 1979
Mail order; wholesale; retail
Brochure free

Ellon Bach USA carries the entire line of Bach Flower Remedy concentrates, concentrate sets, Rescue Remedy formulas, empty dropper bottles, labels, books, charts and diet kit.

Blessed Herbs

Michael Volchok
Rt. 5, Box 1042
Ava, MO 65608

(417) 683-5721
Established 1985
Mail order; wholesale; retail
Catalog free

Blessed Herbs offers a large number of wild-collected and certified organically grown herbal extracts including black cohosh root, blessed thistle herb, blue cohosh root, boneset herb, burdock root, calendula flowers, cramp bark, ephedra herb, German chamomile, ginkgo leaf, ginseng root, lobelia herb, poke root, slippery elm bark, wild gingerroot, witch hazel bark and yerba santa leaf, to name a few. Also available from Blessed Herbs are several herbal formulas, herbal oils, prepackaged herbs, bulk herbs and books about herbs.

Brooks Enterprises

Marilyn R. Brooks
3436 Red Sails
El Paso, TX 79936-1714

(915) 594-9320
Established 1989
Brochure free

Marilyn R. Brooks distributes the Nature's Remedy line of herbal teas, blends and all-natural herbal soaps and cleansers.

Country Road Herb Farm & Gift Barn

Joeann Hudspath
1497 Pymatuning Lake Rd.
Andover, OH 44003

(216) 577-1932
Established 1986
Mail order; wholesale; retail; public garden
Catalog $2.00

Joeann Hudspath of Country Road Herb Farm carries an extensive listing of live and dried herbs, culinary and medicinal herbs (including Chinese herbs), dried flowers, potpourris, oils, herbal and traditional medicinal teas, flavors and extracts, other baking needs and books. A full selection of homeopathic remedies, salves, tonics, lotions and other products is available. A handy "Craft Botanicals Reference Chart" is included in the catalog.

Down to Earth, Inc.

Garyanna Whitaker
PO Box 1087
Violet, LA 70092-1087

(504) 277-7977
Mail order; retail
Established 1991
Catalog $5.00; refundable with order

Down to Earth distributes more than 4,000 natural health products from more than 375 different manufacturers by mail order. The catalog covers aromatherapy oils, bath and body care items, cosmetics, natural formulas/oils/gels/creams, vitamin and mineral supplements, women's, men's and children's health needs, natural remedy and relief formulas, natural homeopathic herbs, teas and coffees and general mer-

In early New England days, an Indian, called Joe Pye, attracted considerable attention because he effected marvelous cures with herbal medicines. It was said his teas were made mainly of *Eupatorium purpureum*. Although Indian Joe is long forgotten, *Eupatorium purpureum* is known to this day as Joe-Pye weed.

—from *The Herbalist Almanac 50 Year Anthology*, Meyerbooks, Glenwood, Illinois

chandise. Brand names carried by this company include Aura Cacia, Mill Creek, Nature's Gate, Rachel Perry, Kiss My Face, Weleda, Inc., Tom's of Maine, Beauty without Cruelty, Twinlab, Rainbow Light, Nature's Way and more. If you are looking for natural health products, this catalog probably has it!

Down to Earth also offers research services on just about any health-related subject through their National Information Source division. Details are in the Down to Earth catalog.

Earthrise Company

Barbara Duran
PO Box 1196-HC
San Rafael, CA 94915

(415) 485-0521
Established 1979
Mail order
Brochure free

Earthrise manufactures and distributes aquaherbal health supplement products including spirulina, chlorella (a green microalga), barley and wheat grass, as well as herbal blends including these items.

Earthrise also offers the book *Earthfood: Spirulina* by Robert Henrikson.

The Farmers' Museum

Debra Reid, Operations Manager
PO Box 800, Lake Rd.
Cooperstown, NY 13326

(607) 547-2593
Established 1943
Mail order; public garden
Write for price list.

The Farmers' Museum offers a number of historically packaged herbal remedies and pharmaceutical concoctions such as Dr. LaDuke's Infallible Health Pills (sassafras drops), Dr. O'Dell's Euphonial Lubricators (horehound drops) and others. A number of potpourris are also listed.

Golden Earth Herbs

Karl L. Smith
Box 2
Torreon, NM 87061

(505) 384-2916
Established 1986
Mail order; wholesale; retail
Catalog free

Golden Earth Herbs supplies a number of wild-collected, dried herbs, including calendula, cota, elderberry, eucalyptus, hops, ocotillo, sage, uva-ursi, yucca, and others. Sage smudge-sticks are also available from this source.

Green Terrestrial

Pam Montgomery, Herbalist
1651 Rt. 9W
Milton, NY 12547

(914) 795-5238
Established 1986
Mail order
Catalog free

Green Terrestrial is a source for wild-collected or organically grown herbal extracts, oils and salves. The extracts include black cohosh, blue cohosh, chickweed, comfrey, *echinacea angustifolia*, garlic, and osha root. Some of the extracts are available in a vinegar base for those sensitive to alcohol. The oils and salves are based on olive oil.

Harvest Health, Inc.

William Kapla
1944 Eastern Ave., SE
Grand Rapids, MI 49507-2799

(616) 245-5457
Established 1952
Mail order; retail
Catalog free

Harvest Health carries a variety of bulk herbs, spices, teas for crafting and culinary use, as will as a capsule machine, empty capsules, potpourris, refresher oils, essential and perfume oils, liquid herbal extracts, Nature's Way brand herbal combinations, Solgar Company herb capsules and liquid homeopathic medicine combinations by Bioforce.

Haussmann's Pharmacy, Inc.
Irene Paul
534–536 W. Girard Ave.
Philadelphia, PA 19123

(215) 627-2143
Established 1890
Mail order; retail "365 days a year"
Catalog free

Haussmann's Pharmacy carries one of the largest selections of hard-to-fill prescription drugs, medicinals, herbs and imported items in the country. Among these are dried herbs and spices, herbal tea blends, ginseng root and Chinese herb specialties, Boericke & Tafel homeopathic pharmaceuticals and Home Medicine Chest, Alpha remedies and homeopathic specialties, not to mention bath oils, pure herb extracts, gum arabic, stearic acid and coconut oil.

Skin preparations, bath botanics, essential oils and potpourris are also listed in this fascinating catalog. Many supplies for making your own potpourris are included: herbs, oils, chemicals and fixatives (tonka beans, orrisroot, saltpeter, etc.). A full line of imported cosmetics is also available.

Haussmann's will ship to almost any country in the world either directly or through their foreign agents.

Health Concerns
Patty Puckett
2236 Mariner Square Drive #3
Alameda, CA 94501

(415) 523-2029
Established 1985
Mail order; wholesale
Brochure free

Health Concerns offers Chinese Traditional Formulas, herbal supplements and books on Chinese herbal medicine.

Herb-Pharm
PO Box 116
Williams, OR 97544

(503) 846-7178
Established
Mail order
Catalog

Herb-Pharm is a small family-owned business that offers a good selection of herbal products, including concentrated herbal drops, alcohol-free extracts, Chinese herbs, German Mother Tinctures, tea tree oils, ginseng products, herbal compounds, Bioforce Botanical products from Switzerland, bulk herbs, culinary "sprinkles" and herb tea blends, bentonite clay, herbal laboratory equipment, books and pamphlets and more.

Herbal-Ease (OHR & Assoc.)

Viola Ohr
PO Box 330485
Fort Worth, TX 76163

(817) 292-4978
Established 1988
Mail order; wholesale; retail
Catalog free

Herbal-Ease supplies herbal health care products including hand and body lotions, healing balms, massage oils, liniments and facial teas. Other items include moth repellent herbal mixtures and essential oils.

Ms. Ohr will also custom-blend herbal products for health professionals and assist in herbal product development.

Herbalist & Alchemist Inc.

Betzy Bancroft
PO Box 458
Bloomsbury, NJ 08804-0458

(908) 479-6679
Established 1982
Mail order; wholesale; retail
Catalog $1.00

The Herbalist & Alchemist catalog includes an extensive listing of herbal extracts, Chinese herb extracts, glycerites, herbal vinegars, compound herb extracts, herbal oils and ointments, Bach Flower Remedies and ceremonial herbs (sweet grass, bitter root). A large number of Chinese herbs, Earth Spirit tea blends and books are also listed.

The Herbalist, Inc.

Tierney P. Salter
6500 20th NE
Seattle, WA 98115

(206) 523-2600
Established 1984
Mail order; wholesale; retail
Catalog free

Tierney P. Salter of The Herbalist carries a number of herbal self-care products: system tonics, respiratory and flu tonics, cleansing tonics and teas, female tonics, infant and children's tonics, analgesic and muscle relaxing tonics and others. Ms. Salter also offers an interesting Herbalist's Travel-Aid Kit. The minimum order is $25.00. (Also see listing in Chapter 5.)

Herbs of Grace

Herbal Pharmacy of the School of Natural Medicine
Casel Melendy
PO Box 7369
Boulder, CO 80306-7369

(303) 443-4882
Established 1978 (in U.K.)
Mail order; wholesale; retail by appointment
Brochure $.50

Herbs of Grace offers herbal formulas created by Dr. Farida Sharan to herbal practitioners at a discount. A booklet by Dr. Farida Sharan, *Herbs of Grace—A patient/practitioner guide*, is also available for $18.00 ppd. Write on letterhead for further information. (Also see listing in Chapter 6.)

Island Herbs

Ryan Drum
Waldron Island, WA 98297-9999

Established 1977
Mail order; wholesale; retail by appointment only
Price list for SASE

Ryan Drum lives in the San Juan Islands where he has been raising his children, homesteading and harvesting medicinal herbs for the past 10 years. Ryan's mail-order list includes fresh or dried medicinal herbs and sea vegetables by the pound: alder, broom, calendula, comfrey, coralroot, dandelion, grindelia, wild lettuce, nettles, Oregon grape roots, rose hips, shave grass, yarrow flower tops, bladder wrack, kelp, nori, sea lettuce and others. The fresh herbs are shipped as soon after harvest as possible.

LongHerb Health Products, Inc.

Sam Campbell and Sean Wu
607 W. Broadway, 1st Floor, Suite 108
Fairfield, IA 52556

(515) 472-2274
Established 1989
Mail order; wholesale; retail
Catalog free

LongHerb Health Products offers a variety of traditional Chinese herbal health foods, beverages and teas in addition to "Dr. Wu's Chinese Herbal Formulas Assistant" computer software.

Magic Garden Herb Co.

PO Box 332
Fairfax, CA 94930

(415) 488-4331
Established 1970
Mail order
Catalog $.25

The Magic Garden Herb Co. offers tea blends, ginseng products (roots, powder, teas), herbal cigarettes and tobacco, dried herbs by the ounce or the pound, Nature's Way products, herbal facials, books and a small number of herb seeds.

Nature's Apothecary

Debra Nuzzi, MH
997 Dixon Rd.
Boulder, CO 80302

(303) 440-7422
Established 1985
Mail order; wholesale
Catalog $3.00; refundable with purchase

Nature's Apothecary offers a line of fresh fluid herbal extracts, dried extracts, formulas and combinations, oils, salves, herbal syrups, aromatherapy inhalers, a handy Home Herbal Medicine Kit, herbal powders and granules, natural therapy kits and more. (Also see listing for Morningstar Publications in Chapter 6 under Videos.)

Pacific Botanicals

Mark Wheeler
4350 Fish Hatchery Rd.
Grants Pass, OR 97527

(503) 479-7777
Established 1979
Mail order; wholesale
Price list for two first-class stamps

Pacific Botanicals offers a large number of certified organically grown and wild-collected herbs and herb roots. Some are available fresh, while the bulk of them are dried.

Pan's Forest

Loren Cruden
PO Box 218
Orient, WA 99160

Established 1980
Catalog $1.00

Pan's Forest offers an eclectic mixture of herb products: bulk echinacea tincture (organic), sweet grass braids, herbal smoking blend, prairie sage and herbal prayer mixture. Ms. Cruden is the author of *Love is Green: An Herbal for Parents*, which is available for $4.00 retail.

The name "dill" comes from an ancient Norse word, *dilla*, meaning "to lull".

Peter Rabbit Herbal

Peter Michaux
General Delivery
Hornby Island, BC
Canada V0R 1Z0

(604) 335-2385
Established 1989
Mail order; wholesale; retail
Write for price list and information.

Peter Michaux of Peter Rabbit Herbal primarily wildcrafts and cultivates medicinal herbs and makes tinctures and oils.

Present Moment Books and Herbs

Robert Gallagher
3546 Grand Ave. S.
Minneapolis, MN 55408

(612) 824-3157
Established 1980
Mail order; retail
Call or write for further information.

Present Moment Books and Herbs is a whole-line "health and healing service shop" and the largest retailer of homeopathic remedies in the country, offering more than 600 herbs in bulk (western, Chinese and Ayurvedic). They also carry a complete line of tinctures, capsules, essential oils, flower essences and aromatherapy products, as well as thousands of books on herbalism, homeopathy, acupuncture, Chinese medicine and health and healing.

Present Moment offers herbal and homeopathic consultations by trained and qualified herbalists and has a naturopathic doctor on duty every day except weekends.

Simplers Botanical Co.

James and Mindy Green
PO Box 39
Forestville, CA 95436-9706

(707) 887-2012
Established 1980
Mail order; wholesale; retail
Catalog $1.00

A simple is a common health-enhancing plant; a simpler is one who knows how to use these plants. James Green (the herbalist), and Mindy Green (the aromatherapist) offer a catalog of handcrafted herbal and aromatherapy products. Simplers Botanical Co. has been called "The Original Herbal EcoBusiness", and the Greens try to live up to this by using organically grown or wild-collected herbs, using no animal ingredients and trying to use only biodegradable materials. They offer liquid herbal concentrates, compounds, glycerites (glycerin-based extracts) and herbal oil infusions. Aromatherapy products include food-quality pure plant essential oils; therapeutic essential oils; and skin care products such as facial oils, complexion cream, face and body mists, floral waters, bath and body oils and herbal facial kits. Several aromatherapy health specialty oils are listed as are books on herbal medicine and aromatherapy.

James and Mindy Green are instructors at the California School of Herbal Studies, and James Green is the author of *The Male Herbal—Health Care for Men & Boys* (see Chapter 4 for annotation) and *The Herbal Medicine-Maker's Handbook*. Both books are available from Simplers Botanical Co.

If a man want an Appetite to his Victuals the Smell of the Earth new turned up by digging with a Spade will procure it, and if he be inclined to a Consumption it will recover him.

—William Coles

Trout Lake Farm

Linda Condon
149 Little Mountain Rd.
Trout Lake, WA 98650

(509) 395-2025
Established 1973
Wholesale only
Price list free with inquiry on letterhead

Trout Lake Farm is North America's largest producer of certified organic herbs. The herbs and botanicals include alfalfa leaf; anise hyssop; blessed thistle herb; whole calendula flowers; comfrey leaf, root and root powder; dandelion root; nettle leaf; red clover blossom and leaf and more. Also available is an extensive listing of culinary herbs, dehydrated vegetables and other foods. The minimum order is 10 pounds.

Vital Energy

Max Koval
PO Box 846
Brighton, MI 48116

(313) 227-6119
Established 1978
Mail order; wholesale; retail
Brochure for SASE

Vital Energy offers a large list of herbal extracts, most of which have been wild-collected or organically grown. These include aconite root, black cohosh, blood-root, buchu, chaparral, corn silk, echinacea, garlic, various ginsengs, goldenseal, hop flower and much more. Also available are Max Koval's herbal formulas, vitamins, acidophilus tablets, bee pollen, psyllium seeds, oils and seasonings. Mr. Koval is available for iridology, nutrition, or herbology holistic counseling; he is the author of *The Herb Primer*, a 306-page book that details 56 herbs, 15 herbal formulas and other information. The book is available for $40.00 + $3.00 shipping.

Windy Pines Natural Herb Farm

Norman and Una M. French
R. 1, Box 245
Dix, IL 62830

(618) 266-7351
Established 1985
Mail order; wholesale
Catalog free

Windy Pines Natural Herb Farm specializes in the native medicinal plants (roots and herbs) of southern Illinois. All products are free of pesticides and herbicides, and are foraged from the wild.

Wise Woman Herbals

Sharol Tilgner, ND
PO Box 328
Gladstone, OR 97027

(503) 239-6573
Established 1988
Mail order; wholesale; retail
Information for SASE

Wise Woman Herbals carries an extensive line of herbal tinctures, essential oils, non-alcoholic glycerin- and vinegar-based extracts, encapsulations, salves, elixirs and custom preparations. Most of the herbs have been either wild-collected or organically grown. Also available are bentonite clay and pure vegetable glycerin.

WishGarden Herbs

Catherine Hunziker
Box 1304
Boulder, CO 80306-1614

(303) 665-9508
Established 1978
Mail order; wholesale; retail by appointment
Brochure free

WishGarden Herbs supplies general and family health extracts, childbirth and women's health formulas, teas, sitz baths, salves and balms, oils and liniments and a large list of herbal extracts and tinctures. A pamphlet, *Botanical Preparations for Childbearing and Women's Health*, by Ms. Hunziker is available free with your inquiry.

Herbal Specialty Food Products

Alyce's Herbs & Gourmet Herb Vinegars

Alice Petlock Pauser
1901 W. Beltline Hwy. (retail and public garden)
PO Box 9563 (mail order)
Madison, WI 53715

(608) 274-4911
Established 1987
Mail order; retail; wholesale; public garden
Catalog $1.00

Alyce's Herbs manufactures culinary herbal vinegars and flavored infused oils made from organic ingredients. The vinegars are available in 12 flavors, two of which are a red wine raspberry and basil blend and a dill, garlic and nasturtium flower blend. The oils, available in either a safflower or olive oil base, are flavored with herbs, ginger and peppers. Gift packs are available.

Ms. Pauser also custom-designs indoor and outdoor herb gardens.

Aunt Betty's Herbalicious Seasonings

Towns End Herb Farm, Ltd.
Betty Ann Townsend
PO Box 273
Burleson, TX 76028

(817) 295-5513
Established 1987
Mail order; wholesale; retail
Catalog free

Aunt Betty's carries culinary herb and spice blends, made without salt, sugar, or artificial colors or flavorings. Among these are the Chili Con Queso Mix, Hotter'n Hell Salsa Mix, Old Grouch Fixings,

Cajun Stirrings, Texas Party Mix, Happy Thymes Tea, and Pot Likker Mix. Also offered are several herbal gift packs and several herbal skin care products. A cookbook, *Aunt Betty's Herb Cooking*, is also available (write for current price).

Busha's Brae Herb Farm

Dixie Stephen
Rt. 1, Box 232M
Setterbo Rd.
Suttons Bay, MI 49682

(616) 271-6284
Established 1985
Mail order; wholesale; retail; public garden
Brochure free

Busha's Brae Herb Farm is a working farm that grows many of the herbs used in their popular seasonings and herbal vinegars. These include Brae Blend Herb Salt, Herb Mustard Mix, Fines Herbes, Brae Blend Seasoning, Opal Basil, Chive, Garlic/Dill, and Tarragon vinegars. Honey balm hand cream, wild-flower honey and bee skeps are also available. (Also see listings in Chapters 6 and 8.)

Chef's Pantry

Murray Burk
PO Box 3
Post Mills, VT 05058

(802) 333-4141
Established 1988
Mail order
Catalog $1.00; refundable with order

Chef's Pantry features fine specialty foods and ingredients for chefs: fruits and preserves; chocolate and baking supplies; vanilla essence, extract and beans; crystallized flowers; oils; vinegars; mustards; condiments and spices (capers, curry powder, saffron, peppercorns) and more.

Chicama Vineyards

Catherine Mathiesen
Stoney Hill Rd., Box 430
West Tisbury, MA 02575

(508) 693-0309
Established 1971
Mail order; wholesale; retail
Brochure for SASE

Chicama Vineyards is a working winery on Martha's Vineyard, Massachusetts. Catherine Mathiesen offers several herbal, natural and fruit wine vinegars made from the Chicama wines. Also available are salad dressings, flavored oils, mustards, jams, jellies and chutneys, ice cream sauces and gift packages.

Elderflower Farm

John and Kelly Stelzer
501 Callahan Rd.
Roseburg, OR 97470

(503) 672-9803
Established 1982
Mail order; wholesale; retail by appointment
Catalog $1.00; refundable with purchase

John and Kelly Stelzer of Elderflower Farm specialize in organic, naturally preserved, salt-free herbal culinary blends. Among the nine blends available are Fish Blends, Salad Bouquet, Herbes Fines, and Bouquet Garni Aromatique. The blends are sold individually or in sets. The Stelzers are the authors of three books, *Cooking with Culinary Herbs*, *Growing Culinary Herbs* and *Raised Bed Vegetable Gardening*, which are priced at $8.95 each + $2.50 shipping and handling. A Complete Gourmet Set of all nine blends and the *Cooking with Culinary Herbs* book is also available.

We dined on a fine leg of corned pork stufft with green herbs from our garden.

—Martha Ballard, Augusta, Maine, April 7, 1786

Hilltop Herb Farm

Beverly Smith
PO Box 325
Romayor, TX 77368

(713) 592-5859
Established 1957
Brochure free

The Hilltop Herb Farm offers a select list of herbal products by mail order: jams, jellies, conserves, chutneys and relishes, a May wine blend, an herbal salt substitute and personalized gift baskets.

K & S Horseradish

(Keune Produce and Veal Farm)
Steven J. Keune
N6518 Cty. Rd. C
Seymour, WI 54165-8422

(414) 833-2938
Established 1965
Brochure for SASE

Hankering for some hot horseradish? Here's the place to find it! K & S Horseradish is grown on the Keune Produce Farm and is processed fresh as you need it. It's available by direct mail, freshly ground, and is also available to wholesale and food service businesses. The Keunes also offer gift boxes containing their horseradish, veal cuts, Wisconsin cheeses and fruit preserves.

Le Jardin du Gourmet

Paul Taylor
PO Box 275
St. Johnsbury Ctr., VT 05863-0275

(802) 748-1446
Established 1954
Mail order; retail
Catalog $.50

In addition to a large number of seeds and plants, this company carries specialty foods such as shallots, garlics and onions, saffron, crystallized ginger, mustards, herbal teas from Germany, Twinings teas from England and many books on herbs. (Also see listing in Chapter 1.)

Lowelands Farm

Rick and Karen Lowe
Rt. 1, Box 98
Middleburg, VA 22117

(703) 687-6923
Established 1984
Mail order; wholesale; retail
Price list for SASE

The Lowelands Farm is owned and operated by the Lowe family—Karen and Rick (parents) and Jessica and Matthew (children). The Lowes raise Christmas trees, herbs and dried flowers, but their specialty is a line of fine foods using their hand-tended, organically grown herbs. Lowelands Farm products have been judged and accepted into the Virginia Department of Agriculture's "Virginia's Finest" program. They include herbal wine vinegars, herbal cooking sherry, herbal honeys, Savory Worcestershire Sauce and several gift baskets and samplers. Other items include Jessica's Nativity Herbs, garlic baskets and three sizes of imported bee skeps.

Merlin of the Rogue Valley

Wayne Bradd, Manager
PO Box 1340
Merlin, OR 97532

(503) 474-5090
Established 1985
Mail order; wholesale; retail
Brochure free

Merlin of the Rogue Valley offers a number of gourmet food products that do not contain salt, preservatives, MSG or fillers: concentrated garlic powders, garlic jelly, Sweet 'n Sassy Mustard sauce, herb breading mix, tipsy garlic, Garlic Greens, flavored gourmet vinegars and more.

Mozzarella Company

Paula Lambert
2944 Elm St.
Dallas, TX 75226

(214) 741-4072
Established 1972
Mail order
Catalog free

When Paula Lambert returned home after living in Italy, the thing that she missed the most was fresh mozzarella cheese, so she persuaded two friends to become her partner, and the Mozzarella Company was born. Today, it produces a long list of fresh and aged specialty cheeses in a tiny factory near downtown Dallas. The cheeses, all made by hand from fresh cow's, goat's or sheep's milk with no additives or preservatives, have won numerous awards from the American Cheese Society and the American Dairy Goat Association. They include herbed caciottas seasoned with basil, Mexican mint, marigold, sage, dill, rosemary, thyme, Mexican oregano and garlic, or black pepper and garlic, and chili caciottas flavored with various chili peppers and more. Ummm, time for lunch! Cheese baskets are also available, with overnight shipping for those containing fresh cheeses.

Pendery's

Patrick Haggerty
304 East Belknap St.
Fort Worth, TX 76102

(800) 533-1870
Established 1870
Mail order; wholesale; retail
Catalog $2.00; refundable with purchase

Pendery's has been a Fort Worth institution ever since 1870 when DeWitt Clinton Pendery arrived in then untamed Fort Worth. He joined an established family business and soon thereafter began selling his own blends of regional Texas seasonings. The company is still owned by the family, and strives to follow DeWitt's lead by offering probably the largest collection of culinary herbs and spices in Texas. They include allspice, aniseed, star anise, annatto, arrowroot, basil, bay leaves, cinnamon sticks, cloves, epazote, fenugreek, ginger, horseradish powder, juniper berries, mace, mustard seeds and mustard flour, nutmeg, many types of pepper, Spanish saffron, pure vanilla extract with bean and more. Blends and seasonings include biriyani and garam masala, curry powder and many chili pepper blends. Ground hot red peppers, paprikas, ristras and dried chile pods are also available.

Also listed in Pendery's catalog are herbal teas and honey, herbal bath and candy, teas and tinctures, dried vegetables, many botanicals, sachets and potpourris, not to mention quantities of specialty gifts and gift baskets.

Used too many herbs in a recipe?

We've all had the unpleasant experience of preparing a new recipe and getting a little carried away with the herbs, only to find that the finished product is practically inedible.

Have no fear! There are ways to save a dish which has been the victim of overseasoning with herbs. Try one of the following methods:

1. For soups or stews, add a few peeled, uncooked potatoes to the liquid. Potatoes tend to soak up salt and seasonings. After the potatoes are cooked through, serve separately or discard.

2. Wipe off or strain off as much of the seasonings as possible. Add more "bland" liquid such as water, broth, or stock.

3. If possible, try serving the dish cold to hide the overseasoning. Cold dishes tend to taste less harsh.

—from the *Country Thyme Gazette*, El Segundo, California

Penny's Garden

Penny and Don Melton
PO Box 305, Blacks Creek Rd.
Mountain City, GA 30562-0305

(404) 746-6918
Established 1987
Mail order; wholesale; retail; public garden
Catalog free

In addition to potpourris and sachets, Penny and Don Melton offer a good number of gourmet herbal foods. The herb jellies look delicious—apple-rosemary, grape-thyme, opal basil, peach butter with summer savory and tipsy cinnamon basil chutney. Also available are a variety of herb mustards, herb vinegars and combination gift boxes.

Perseus Gourmet Products

Penny Morgan and Kay Hansen
1426 E. 3rd
Kennewick, WA 99336

(509) 582-2434
Mail order; wholesale; retail
Brochure for SASE

Perseus Gourmet Products offers specialty vinegars infused with herbs, herbal olive oils, dried and fresh herbs. The ingredients in the vinegars and oils are organically grown; they are free of sugar and salt, additives or preservatives.

Rafal Spice Company

Donald Rafal
2521 Russell St.
Detroit, MI 48207

(313) 259-6373
Established 1962
Mail order; wholesale; retail
Catalog free

The Rafal Spice Company's 54-page catalog includes an extensive list of spices, herbs, teas, coffees and specialty foods. The spices and herbs include alfalfa leaves, aniseeds, annatto seeds, arrowroot, asafetida powder, birch bark, caraway seeds, cardamon seeds, cassia buds, chicory root (ground and roasted), coriander seeds, corn silk, garlic bulbs, gotu kola, garam masala, hops, hyssop, dehydrated leeks, lovage root, mulling spices, mustard seeds (hot, black or yellow), onion powder, various peppers, pickling spices, saffron (American or Spanish) and much, much more. Also listed are many sauces, mustards and oils, as well as hard-to-find pure extracts and flavors, food colorings, many books, kitchen aids—and still there's more! Potpourris, pomanders, sachets; perfume, fragrance, refresher and fixative oils; essential oils; simmering potpourris; spice jars, storage containers; coffee and tea accessories; herb and spice labels and reusable tea bags are also listed.

G. B. Ratto & Co. International Grocers

Elena Voiron
821 Washington St.
Oakland, CA 94607

(415) 444-7759
Established 1897
Mail order; retail
Catalog free

G. B. Ratto specializes in international foods, and they carry a huge selection! These include flavored extracts and syrups, crystallized flowers from France (violet and rose petals, mint leaves), horehound drops, Ricola natural herb cough drops, flower waters, imported mustards and sauces, and herbs and spices from ancho chili to zatar. The company also carries specialty oils and vinegars (including balsamic vinegar and mustard oil), fresh gingerroot and some gourmet seed packets.

Select Origins, Inc.

Kristi L. Siplon
Box N
Southampton, NY 11968

(516) 924-5447 or (800) 822-2092
Established 1981
Mail order; wholesale
Catalog free

Select Origins offers specialty foods "from where they grow best". Their collection includes garlic bulbs from Gilroy, California; balsamic vinegars from Italy; peppercorns from India; spices, herbs and culinary blends from various locations; seasoning kits and preserves. All herbs are from the most recent growing season and spices are ground just before shipment.

The Snuggery Culinary Herb and Spice Blends

Judy Barnes and Murry Kelso
PO Box 4071
Costa Mesa, CA 92628

(714) 545-1871
Established 1989
Mail order; retail
Price list free for SASE

The Snuggery's culinary herb and spice blends contain no salt, sugar, preservatives or MSG. Their list includes a Boursin-style cheese seasoning, an herb and sesame coating mix, a creamy tarragon béarnaise sauce seasoning and a salsa seasoning. Herbal samplers, dip mixes, vegetarian spaghetti sauce blends and pizza blends are also available. Popcorn lovers will want to try the Sunggery's herbal popcorn seasonings.

Sultan's Delight, Inc.

Charles Farkouh
25 Croton Ave.
Staten Island, NY 10301

(718) 720-1557
Established 1980
Catalog for SASE

Sultan's Delight offers a good mixture of international foodstuffs by mail order including Mideast specialties, imported olive oils, spices, nuts and seeds. Specialty flavorings include zartar with sumac, whole or ground sumac, Egyptian mint leaves, and mastic gum. Also listed are flower waters, Bakhour frankincense, candied and dried fruits, hennas, Turkish coffees and cookbooks. And just in case you need a new belly-dancing costume (and the music to go with it), you can find that here, too!

Paprikas Weiss Importer

Edward Weiss
1546 Second Ave.
New York, NY 10028

(212) 288-6117
Established 1891
Mail order; wholesale; retail
Catalog $3.00

Paprikas Weiss carries a huge selection of imported foods, spices and cookware. Among the thousands of items are imported paprika—"the spice that built our business", imported herbs and spices (including Spanish saffron), peppercorns, meats, cheeses, chocolates, syrups, vinegar, cooking oils, mustards, vanilla beans and many coffees and teas. Baking specialties include pectin, poppy seed, rose water, flavorings and essences for baking and liquor. Useful kitchen tools include a poppy seed grinder and spice mill, a pasta maker, a food grater, a chestnut ricer, coffee grinders, brass mortars and pestles and many more!

Many items not listed in the mail order catalog are available in their retail store. Mr. Weiss can also order hard-to-find items.

If you are substituting dried herbs for fresh in a recipe, use approximately one-third the amount called for.

Windy River Farm/Cottage Garden Herbs

Judy Weiner
PO Box 312
Merlin, OR 97532

(503) 476-8979
Established 1980
Mail order; wholesale; retail; public garden
Catalog $1.00

Windy River Farm is an Oregon Tilth Certified Organic 25-acre farm owned and operated by Peter and Judy Liebes. Their catalog lists dried herb and vegetable blends ("Sprinkles"), teas, gift boxes, individual herbs, herb vinegars and honeys, as well as skin care products and unsulfured, dried fruits and vegetables.

Some Like it Hot . . .

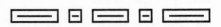

Chili Pepper Emporium

328 San Felipe NW
Albuquerque, NM 87104

(505) 843-6505
Established 1984
Mail order; retail
Catalog free

The Chili Pepper Emporium carries a large inventory of very hot items—red chili pepper jam, diced green chilis, crushed jalapeño, many salsas, dried cilantro, Mexican oregano, chipotle peppers, lots of dried chilis, gourmet mustards and chili powders, chili wreaths and ristras and chili "care packages". Some seeds are also available; see listing in Chapter 1.

Old Southwest Trading Company

Nancy Gerlach
PO Box 7545
Albuquerque, NM 87194

(505) 836-0168
Established 1987
Catalog free

The Old Southwest Trading Company publishes the ultimate catalog for "chili heads". Ms. Gerlach supplies a number of exotic dried chilis including anchos, cascabels, chili pasados, chiltecpins, chipotles, arbols, habaneros, pasillas, piquins and the above varieties in sampler packs. New Mexican red chilis (often called Anaheim chilis) are available prepackaged or strung in ristras. Fresh New Mexico green chilis are available for shipment in August and September. Traditional and nontraditional southwestern foods are also available: red chili sauce mix, blue corn meal, dried masa, garlic oil, hot sauces, canned chilis and tomatillos and numerous gift packs and baskets. Herbs and spices play an important part in southwestern cuisine, and this company has them all: azafran (Mexican safflower), juniper berries, manzanilla (chamomile), epazote, cuminos (cumin seed) and more. A number of Southwestern specialty items (magnets, pot holders, stove-top grills, chili roasters, T-shirts, chili cookie cutters, cookbooks) are also listed in the current catalog.

Nancy Gerlach is the co-author with Dave DeWitt of *The Whole Chile Pepper Book*, *Fiery Cuisines*, and *Just North of the Border*, all available from the Old Southwest Trading Company.

Pecos Valley Spice Co.

Jane Butel
500 E. 77th St.
New York, NY 10162

(212) 628-5374
Established 1978
Mail order; wholesale
Catalog free

The Pecos Valley Spice Co. offers ground and crushed chilis (mild and hot), Mexican herbs and spices (cumin, Mexican oregano, cilantro, etc.) and a number of "Chile Madness" kits. Salsas and southwestern cookbooks are also available. Ms. Butel teaches a Southwestern Cooking School at various locations. Write or call for information.

Santa Cruz Chili and Spice Co.

Armida G. Castro
PO Box 177
Tumacacori, AZ 85640-0177

(602) 398-2591
Established 1943
Mail order; wholesale; retail
Catalog free

The Santa Cruz Chili and Spice Co. offers red chili paste, picante sauces, green salsa, chili powders, barbecue sauces and more.

Texas Gunpowder, Inc.

Janice Pinnell
PO Box 852573
Mesquite, TX 75185-2573

(214) 279-5766
Established 1989
Mail order; wholesale; retail
Price list free

Janice Pinnell offers Texas Gunpowder Ground Jalapeño Powder that contains no salt or preservatives and Mesquite's Own Seasoned Salt. Gift baskets are also available.

General Tools & Gardening Supplies

Ärpe Herb Chopper
Chris and Greg Gang
PO Box 41109
Memphis, TN 38104

(901) 725-7472
Established 1990
Mail order
Brochure free

The Ärpe Herb Chopper is made from high-grade cast iron, and features a boat-shaped base and a cast iron cutting wheel with a handcrafted oak handle. The chopper is used to chop dried herbs by rocking the wheel back and forth.

Bloomsaver Ltd.
Diane Ryason
2049 Paseo Dorado
La Jolla, CA 92037

(619) 456-5086
Established 1987
Mail order; wholesale
Brochure free

Bloomsaver Ltd. offers several tools and accessories for the flower and herb gardener. The Bloomsaver is a handy tool that enables a gardener to gather lots of flowers and herbs at leisure, while protecting them from wilting, crushing and bruising. The easy-to-carry container includes three sections that allows you to sort flowers by size, color or type. The brochure also lists water conditioners and nutrients for cut flowers and a holster that clips onto the Bloomsaver to hold cutting shears. Bloomsaver Ltd. also carries topiary frames in several sizes as well as mock birdcages.

The Crate Shoppe
A. J. De Paola
PO Box 154
Kipton, OH 44049

(216) 985-2008
Established 1984
Mail order; wholesale
Catalog $1.50; refundable with purchase

Looking for interesting ways to display your herbal items or plants? Take a look at The Crate Shoppe's catalog! They carry miniature crates in solid oak or pine, miniature bushel baskets, micro mini solid pine crates, reproduction orange crates, bushel basket lids, solid oak apple crates, "old oaken buckets" and other interesting items.

Custom-made crates can be built to your specifications.

Crop King, Inc.
Dan Brentlinger
PO Box 310
Medina, OH 44258

(216) 725-5656
Established 1982
Mail order; wholesale; retail
Catalog $3.00; refundable with order

Crop King carries a full line of supplies for commercial (or smaller) greenhouses along with their hydroponic growing systems, supplies and equipment.

Eon Industries
John H. Noe
315 Dodge St.
Swanton, OH 43558

Established 1982
Mail order; wholesale
Price list free

Eon Industries supplies permanent nursery and garden markers in various styles and sizes. They are made of rust-resistant, galvanized metals with zinc nameplates.

Weatherproof labeling pencils are also available.

Custom sizes may be ordered from Eon Industries. Write or call for details.

Evergreen Garden Plant Labels

Gary Patterson
PO Box 922
Cloverdale, CA 95425

(707) 894-3225
Established 1982
Mail order
Price list for first-class stamp

Evergreen Garden Plant labels are sturdy, all-weather markers made of galvanized steel with a rectangular face that can be marked on with grease pencil, paint or letter-punched adhesive tape (such as Dymo tape). An optional clip-on plate is made of aluminum and is slightly larger than the basic marker. The markers are available in three lengths: 26", 20" and 13". The company also carries rose pegging hooks, bloom stalk supports and tag stakes.

The Gardener's Eye

Harvey Childs
PO Box 100963, Dept. Q
Denver, CO 80210-0963

(800) 624-4192
Established 1988
Mail order; retail
Catalog free

The Gardener's Eye carries many useful tools and items for the gardener, all of which have been selected for their "enhancement of a gardener's enjoyment and knowledge of gardening". The Gardener's Eye will not carry a product if its manufacturer builds or distributes products which have proven to be deleterious to any living matter. The current catalog lists compost bins, tools, sprinkler systems, planters, rain gauges, garden shears, hand-carved granite items, gloves, a kids' gardening kit, garden posters, organic pesticides and books.

Mr. Childs can special-order almost any garden product, from tools to large quantities of organic fertilizers.

Gardener's Kitchen

Betty J. Rafferty
PO Box 412
Farmington, CT 06034

(203) 677-9181
Established 1976
Mail order
Brochure free

Gardener's Kitchen offers canning supplies that are often hard to find when you want them: canning lids and rings (in many sizes), labels, jar lifters, tongs, jelly strainers, food mills, cherry pitters, bean slicers and more.

Gardens Alive!

Natural Gardening Research Center
PO Box 149
Sunman, IN 47041

(812) 623-3800
Established 1984
Mail order
Catalog free

Gardens Alive! sells supplies for organic gardening including natural insect and disease controls, drip irrigation systems, beneficial insects and fertilizers. The informative catalog contains photos of insects for purposes of identification.

Hollowbrook Pottery & Tile

Roger L. Baumann
Box 413, Hollowbrook Rd.
Lake Peekskill, NY 10537

(914) 526-3786
Established 1976
Mail order; wholesale; retail
Brochure free

Roger.Baumann makes handcrafted stoneware tiles and home and garden planters in various sizes and with assorted glazes. The planters are frostproof and will endure "the harshest of winters". Roger will also take custom orders for other sizes of planters and custom decorated tiles.

Hydrofarm

3135 Kerner Blvd.
San Rafael, CA 94901
or 208 Rt. 13
Bristol, PA 19007

(415) 459-7898
Established 1977
Mail order; wholesale; retail
Catalog free

Hydrofarm manufactures indoor gardening equipment for hydroponics. Items available include grow lights, light stands, meters, timers, organic fertilizers, replacement bulbs, various lighting systems, water dispensers, nutrients, rockwool growing medium, trays and climate controllers. Cutting and seedling starter kits are also listed.

Hydro-Gardens, Inc.

PO Box 9707
Colorado Springs, CO 80932

(719) 495-2266 or (800) 634-6362
Established 1972
Mail order; wholesale; retail
Catalog free

Hydro-Gardens, Inc. carries a full line of supplies for commercial greenhouses as well as hydroponic supplies and nutrients.

Land Steward

Megan Hendricks
434 Lower Rd.
Souderton, PA 18964

(800) 848-3043
Established 1990
Mail order; retail
Catalog free

Land Steward supplies a number of "bio rational insect traps" that will also be of use to the herb gardener. Some of the traps include a codling moth trap, a Japanese beetle trap, a garden pest trap and others. Other interesting pest control devices are "Slug Pubs" and aphid/whitefly traps. The Land Steward's "Bug Charm" lures the beneficial insects to your garden.

Mantis Manufacturing Co.

1458 County Line Rd., Dept. K
Huntingdon Valley, PA 19006-9864

(800) 366-6268
Established 1980
Mail order
Catalog free

Mantis offers several gardening tools and accessories. These include the 20-pound Mantis-20 Tiller/Cultivator and attachments, the ChipMate limb chipper, the Mantis GardenGrid self-watering raised bed garden and accessories, a folding garden cart and the Soil Saver Composter.

The Natural Gardening Company

David Baldwin
217 San Anselmo Ave.
San Anselmo, CA 94960

(415) 456-5060
Established 1986
Mail order; retail
Catalog free

The Natural Gardening Company carries a large number of general, "environmentally sound gardening supplies" such as hand tools, snail and slug barriers, rose and cactus gloves, natural pest controls, drip irrigation systems, organic fertilizers, composting supplies, garden carts, a push lawn mower, herb and tomato drying trays and a spider catching device. The Natural Gardening Company is proud to be the first organic nursery in the U.S. They supply a line of totally organically grown perennials, culinary herbs and gourmet vegetables. Several kinds of bulk wildflower seeds are also available.

Necessary Trading Company

One Nature's Way
New Castle, VA 24127-0305

(703) 864-5103
Mail order; wholesale; retail
Catalog $2.00; refundable with purchase

The Necessary Trading Company offers "Natural Solutions for farm, home and garden". These include soil care products (composting supplies, cover crop seeds, soil testing kits, etc.), plant foods, equipment (sprayers, dusters, safety gear, pruners), pest management supplies (beneficial insects, insect traps, biological and botanical controls, oils and soaps) and animal and pet care products.

The Walt Nicke Company

Katrina Nicke
PO Box 433
Topsfield, MA 01983

(508) 887-3388
Established 1960
Mail order
Catalog free

Walt Nicke started his "Garden Talk" tool catalog more than 31 years ago by offering products that he used in his own gardens to other growers and local customers. The list of tools he used grew and so did the business. Katrina Nicke, Walt's daughter, now offers 63 pages of garden tools and supplies including digging tools, dibbles, German hand tools, weeders, pruning shears and saws, propagators, garden frames and greenhouse supplies, a solar-powered fan for greenhouses or garden frames, inexpensive flowerpots, plantpaks, labels and watering devices. Also listed are English garden tools for children, composting supplies, garden stakes and trellises, gardener's work boots, many books on gardening, engraved writing papers, bookplates and labels by Michael Scott of England, bird feeders, a sweet grass bee skep, authentic Sussex trugs and birdhouses. There are wonderful gift ideas for your gardening friends here!

The folks at the Timmouth Channel Farm suggest rubbing the seeds of parsley between two sheets of sandpaper before planting to hasten germination.

Patio Patch Planters

Michael J. Kaminski
PO Box 70281
Seattle, WA 98107-0281

(206) 789-4937
Established 1984
Mail order; wholesale; retail
Catalog free

Patio Patch Planters are an ingenious interlocking stackable planter system for balconies, patios, apartments and any other place you may want to put a container garden. The Patio Patch Planter is a modular system—a series of boxes can be stacked together or placed in any number of arrangements or used individually. The system consists of six sizes of boxes (made of western red cedar fastened with screws) with optional casters or trellis.

Raindrip, Inc.

Patricia Murray
21305 Itasca St.
Chatsworth, CA 91311

(818) 718-8004
Established 1975
Mail order

Raindrip offers drip watering systems and replacement parts, sprinklers, sprayers, filters and soaker hoses. Contact the company for the name of a local retailer. Ms. Murray also offers seminars on drip watering systems for garden clubs and other groups.

Twinholly's

Sandra Nigro
3633 NE 19th Ave.
Portland, OR 97212

(503) 233-2546; FAX (503) 231-6349
Established 1991
Mail order; wholesale
Write for current prices and ordering information.

Twinholly's sells inexpensive glassine seed envelopes for collecting and storing seeds. The envelopes come in three assorted sizes and are packaged in groups of 50 along with a fact sheet about seeds.

3

Publications

THIS CHAPTER INCLUDES MAGAZINES and newsletters on all aspects of herbs—medicinal, herbal crafts and herb gardening. Some are chatty and informal; others are technical and formal. No matter what your interest in herbs, there's a publication here that you can't live without!

American Ginseng Trends

Future Concepts, Inc.
PO Box 1982
Wausau, WI 54402-1982

(715) 675-4898
Established 1989

American Ginseng Trends is a 10-page bimonthly newsletter published for members of the ginseng industry, and is the only international publication of its type. Topics covered include interviews and information on prices, harvests, consumption, research, marketing, new products, etc. A one-year subscription is $28.00 for U.S., Canada and Mexico. Foreign country subscriptions are $38.00. A sample issue is available for $3.00 (U.S. funds).

The American Herb Association Quarterly Newsletter

Kathi Keville, Editor/Director
PO Box 1673
Nevada City, CA 95959

The AHA Quarterly Newsletter is included with membership in the American Herb Association. The 116-page publication covers topics such as the environment, herbs in the news, book reviews, the legalities of herbs and more. (See listing for AHA in Chapter 9.)

The Business of Herbs

Northwind Farm Publications
Paula or David Oliver
Rt. 2, Box 246
Shevlin, MN 56676

(218) 657-2478
Established 1983
Mail order
Brochures SASE

The Business of Herbs is an international bimonthly magazine for the herb businessperson and the serious herb enthusiast. It features articles on growing herbs successfully, marketing herbs and herbal products, interviews, book reviews, business management tips, where to buy hard-to-find herb supplies, the latest information about medicinal herbs and what's happening in the herb world. The subscription price for one year (6 issues) is $20.00.

Comfrey Chatter

Gay Ingram, Editor
PO Box 1096
Big Sandy, TX 75755-1096

Information SASE

Comfrey Chatter is a bimonthly herbal newsletter with a regional flavor. Regular features are recipes, growing tips, herbal news, informative articles about specific herbs, etc. A one-year subscription is currently $10.00; sample issue is $2.00.

Common Scents

American Aromatherapy Association (AATA)
Annette Davis, Secretary
PO Box 3679
South Pasadena, CA 91031

(818) 457-1742
Established 1988
Information SASE

(See entry in Chapter 9.)

Country Thyme Gazette

Theresa Loe
PO Box 3090
El Segundo, CA 90245

(213) 322-6026
Newsletter information SASE
Mail-order book catalog $1.00

The Country Thyme Gazette, edited and published by Theresa Loe, features articles on herbal cooking, gardening and home entertaining with herbs. In addition, each issue covers herbal trends and handy hints for the home gardener and cook. The 14-page quarterly is $17.00/year; a sample issue is $3.00. Foreign rates are available.

Dittany
Herb Federation of New Zealand
PO Box 20022
Glen Eden, Auckland
New Zealand

Dittany is the Journal of the Herb Federation of New Zealand. Published monthly, the subscription rate is currently $30.00 (overseas rate). I did not see a review copy of this journal; write for further information.

Focus on Herbs
The Herb Garden
Kim Fletcher
5 Coorange Place
Legana, Tasmania
Australia 7277

Phone (003) 301493
Established 1984

Kim and Michael Fletcher of the Herb Garden publish *Focus on Herbs*, a quarterly magazine which "covers all aspects of herbal knowledge". The emphasis is on using herbs in the modern world. Included are articles on native Australian herbs, Asian herbs, American herbs, restaurant reviews, a calendar of events, ethnobotany, herbal medicine, cooking, cultivation, and

crafts. Subscription rates are $16.00/year in Australia; $20.00/year Australian funds in New Zealand; $21.00/year Australian funds in Japan; $22.00/year Australian funds in U.S. and Canada; and $23.00/year Australian funds in U.K. or Europe. Kim is the author of *Herbs in Australian Gardens, A Modern Australasian Herbal, 101 Things to Know About Herbs* and *Herbal Craft: A Practical Guide for Pleasure and Profit.*

Foster's Botanical and Herb Reviews
Steven Foster
PO Box 106
Eureka Springs, AR 72632

(501) 253-7309

Steven Foster's quarterly newsletter covers herbal information sources, book reviews, news of the herb world, etc. The current price is $8.00/year.

Garlic News
Fresh Garlic Association
Caryl Saunders
PO Box 2410
Sausalito, CA 94966-2410

(415) 383-5057
Write for information.

Garlic News is the quarterly newsletter of the Fresh Garlic Association. It includes recipes from some of America's finest chefs and the latest news about garlic's use in medicines and cooking. This is a fascinating newsletter, full of interesting information. A one-year membership in the Association is only $5.00 and includes a subscription to *Garlic News*.

The Herb Companion

Interweave Press
Linda Ligon
201 E. Fourth St.
Loveland, CO 80537

(800) 272-2193

Published by the same people who bring you this book, the full-color, beautiful *Herb Companion* magazine is published "in celebration of the useful plants". Recent issues have included articles on Chinese herbs, herbs of the American Southwest, herbal weddings, saffron, spices, herbal papermaking, scented geraniums, soapmaking, preserving herbs, everlastings and other diverse topics.

The bimonthly magazine is $21.00/year in the U.S. and $26.00/year in Canada and overseas foreign countries (U.S. funds).

The Herb Quarterly

Linda Sparrowe
PO Box 548
Boiling Springs, PA 17007-0548

(717) 245-2764
Established 1978
Write for more information.

The Herb Quarterly is an informative, 52-page journal filled with herbal information of all kinds. Regular columns include Herbal Updates (calendar of events), Letters to the Editor and Book Reviews. Articles cover historical herbs, herb garden design, medicinal herbs, single herb profiles, herbal menu planning, many recipes and more. Subscriptions are $24.00/year; 2 years $45.00. (Add $5.00 for foreign addresses.) Sample copies are available for $6.00.

Good huswives in summer will save their own seeds against the next year, as occasion needs: One seed for another, to make an exchange, with fellowly neighbourhood, seemeth not strange.

—from Tusser's Calendar, 1573

The Herb, Spice and Medicinal Plant Digest

Lyle E. Craker
Dept. of Plant & Soil Sciences
University of Massachusetts
Amherst, MA 01003

(413) 545-2347
Established 1980
Write for more information.

The Herb, Spice and Medicinal Plant Digest covers news about herbs in medicinal research, profiles of important people in the herb world, technical articles about the chemistry of herbs, reviews of recent herbal literature and more. The quarterly, published by the Cooperative Extension Department of the University of Massachusetts and prepared by Dr. Lyle E. Craker in the Department of Plant and Soil Sciences is only $8.00/year; back issues are available.

The Herbal Connection

Maureen Buehrle, Editor
3343 Nolt Rd.
Lancaster, PA 17601-1507

(717) 898-3017

The Herbal Connection is the official publication of the Herb Growing and Marketing Network. The bimonthly newsletter includes articles on marketing and production of herbs, herb business tips, book reviews, a calendar of events and more. A one-year subscription is $24.00; a sample issue is $4.00.

The Herbal Review

89 Thornton Crescent
Wendover, Bucks
U.K. HP22 6DQ

Sample copy not reviewed; write for information.

The Herbal Rose Report

Jeanne Rose
219 Carl St.
San Francisco, CA 94117

(415) 564-6337

Jeanne Rose's new newsletter, *The Herbal Rose Report*, covers the medicinal usage of herbs as well as aromatherapy, herbal sports medicine, the environment, animal care and more. It is published eight times a year, and is $20.00 in the U.S. (Canada $28.00; foreign $35.00 in U.S. funds).

HerbalGram

Herb Research Foundation
Rob McCaleb, President
1007 Pearl Street, Suite 200
Boulder, CO 80302
(303) 449-2265

or American Botanical Council
Margaret Wright, Circulation Manager
PO Box 201660
Austin, TX 78720-1660
(512) 331-8868

Call or write for further information.

HerbalGram is the full-color quarterly journal of the American Botanical Council and the Herb Research Foundation. HerbalGram presents research reviews from scientific literature, follows legal issues, market trends and media coverage of herbs. *HerbalGram* is currently $25.00 for four issues. A sample issue is $5.00.

Herban Lifestyles

Christine Utterback
84 Carpenter Road
New Hartford, CT 06057

(203) 489-0567
Mail order; retail; public garden by appointment
Brochure free

Herban Lifestyles is an eclectic bimonthly newsletter that emphasizes "how we live, work and play with herbs". Current sub-scription rates are $18.00/year for six issues; $22.00 annually in Canada (U.S. funds); and $33.00/year foreign (U.S. funds). Sample issues are available for $3.00 (U.S.), $4.00 (Canada) and $5.00 (foreign).

Christine also offers freelance writing services, garden lectures/slide programs and seasonal workshops.

The Herban News

Sherril Steele-Carlin
PO Box 70125
Reno, NV 89570-0125

(702) 972-8111
Mail order
Established 1990

The Herban News is an eight-page newsletter that focuses on one herb per issue. General and historical information are given as well as many original recipes and tips for using the herb. The current subscription price is $13.50 for 12 issues; sample issues are $1.75.

The Herbarist

The Herb Society of America
9019 Kirtland-Chardon Rd.
Mentor, OH 44060

The Herbarist is the annual journal published by The Herb Society of America; it includes articles on all aspects of herbs written by HSA members. Write for more information.

HortIdeas

Greg and Pat Williams
Rt. 1, Box 302
Gravel Switch, KY 40328

(606) 332-7606
Mail order

Greg and Pat Williams' *HortIdeas* monthly newsletter saves readers hours of time by going through hundreds of popular and technical sources to report on the latest research, methods, tools, plants, and books for vegetable, fruit, herb and flower gardeners. The current annual subscription rate is $15.00 for second-class mail or $17.50 for first-class; Canada and Mexico $17.50 for first-class mail; overseas $20.00 for surface mail or $30.00 for air mail. Sample issues are $1.50 in North America or $2.50 overseas by air mail (U.S. funds).

The International Journal of Aromatherapy

Herbal Endeavours, Ltd.
Colleen K. Dodt
3618 S. Emmons
Rochester Hills, MI 48307

(313) 852-0796
Mail order; retail
Call or write for current subscription price.

Colleen K. Dodt of Herbal Endeavours, Ltd., is the U.S. distributor for *The International Journal of Aromatherapy*, published quarterly in Brighton, England, by Maggie and Robert Tisserand. Robert Tisserand is the "father of aromatherapy".

The International Journal of Aromatherapy covers the use of natural, aromatic plant oils in the pursuit of well-being, whether mental, emotional, physical or aesthetic.

Medical Herbalism

Paul Bergner, Editor
PO Box 33080
Portland, OR 97233

(503) 235-5883
Established 1989

Medical Herbalism is a bimonthly clinical newsletter for the herbal practitioner. It covers case reviews by experienced clinicians, analyses of current issues, book reviews, educational resources and more. The subscription price is $24.00/year (Canada $29.00).

MediHerb Newsletter

MediHerb Pty. Ltd.
Michael Hoy
124 McEvoy St.
Warwick, Queensland
Australia 4370

Phone: 0011 61 76 61 4900

The MediHerb Newsletter is published for herbal practitioners only, and includes information on herbal scientific research, therapeutic applications of herbs, herbal profiles and more. MediHerb Pty. is a supplier of dried herbs and extracts. Practitioners should write for more information on their letterhead.

Potpourri from Herbal Acres

Phyllis V. Shaudys
PO Box 428-W
Washington Crossing, PA 18977

Established 1978
Brochure free

Phyllis Shaudys edits a homey, information-packed newsletter that includes hints on growing, harvesting and using herbs. It features contributions from herbal experts and correspondents around the country; herbal crafts for every season; recipes for using herbs in cooking and much more. *Potpourri from Herbal Acres* is currently

$20.00 per year. Ms. Shaudys is the author of *The Pleasure of Herbs* and *Herbal Treasures* (Garden Way Publishing), both of which are compilations of information gleaned from the newsletters for the first 12 years. Each book is available from Ms. Shaudys for $15.95 postpaid or from bookstores. (See Chapter 4 for descriptions of both books.)

Potpourri Party-Line

Berry Hill Press
Dody Lyness
7336 Berry Hill–D4
Palos Verdes, CA 90274-4404

(310) 377-7040

Potpourri Party-Line is a quarterly newsletter that focuses on growing, drying and arranging dried florals and crafting with fragrance. This friendly newsletter is targeted towards those who design with dried flowers and herbs, those who grow or dry the herbs or flowers for the designers and fragrance crafters. Ms. Lyness states that the newsletter does not contain "culinary recipes . . . doggerel verse . . . or herbal puns". Its main purpose is rather to be a "continuing source of marketing and design ideas with flair and focus". Regular features include book and periodical reviews, news and views of herb growers and marketers and carefully screened advertising.

Subscriptions are $15.00/year in the U.S.; $18.00/year in Canada and Mexico; and $27.00/year in all other countries. A sample copy is $3.95. Back issues are available to subscribers at a discount. (Also see listing for Dody Lyness Co. in Chapter 2 and review of Ms. Lyness's booklet *Potpourri . . . Easy as One, Two, Three* in Chapter 4.)

Sage Advice

Dorry Norris
PO Box 626
Trumansburg, NY 14886

(607) 387-6449
Established 1984
Brochure for large SASE

Sage Advice, Dorry Norris's quarterly herbal journal, is personal and includes recipes, growing tips and history. The current subscription price is $10.50/year (4 issues).

Ms. Norris, proprietor of Sage Cottage Bed and Breakfast, is also the author of the new *Sage Cottage Herb Garden Cookbook*, which is available from her at the address above (see Chapter 4 for description).

Seedhead News

Native Seeds/SEARCH
Kevin Dahl
2509 N. Campbell #325
Tucson, AZ 85719

(602) 327-9123 (office phone; no orders)
Established 1983
Mail order; display garden at the Tucson Botanical Gardens
Catalog $1.00

The Seedhead News is the quarterly publication for members of Native Seeds/SEARCH (see listing in Chapter 1). It includes recipes, previews of workshops and other special events, gardening tips, book reviews and feature articles on Native American farmers and crops.

Spice and Herb Arts

Kaye Cude
5091 Muddy Lane
Buckingham, FL 33905

(813) 694-8863

Spice and Herb Arts is an interesting bi-monthly journal about spices, herbs, fruits and vegetables that grow in warm or hot areas. Ms. Kaye Cude, editor and publisher, emphasizes growing, crafting, cooking, preserving and most of all, enjoying, these plants. The current subscription price is $12.50 (plus $.75 for Florida residents) per volume, which includes 6 issues per volume year. All subscriptions begin with the September issue; back issues of the volume ordered will be mailed when the paid subscription is received. (No free sample issues are available.)

The Whole Chile Pepper Magazine

Out West Publishing Co.
PO Box 4278
Albuquerque, NM 87196

This magazine specializes in hot foods, spices and herbs used with these foods, and growing and cooking with peppers. Features fiery cuisine from domestic and international sources. Write for current subscription price.

Wildflower

The Canadian Wildflower Society
1848 Liverpool Rd.
Box 110, Pickering, ON
Canada L1V 6M3

Write for more information.

Wildflower is the quarterly magazine of the Canadian Wildflower Society (see listing in Chapter 9) and a subscription is included in the Society's membership fee. *Wildflower* is devoted exclusively to our continent's native wildflowers and other wild flora such as trees, shrubs, herbs, mosses, lichens and fungi. The profusely illustrated magazine includes articles on wildflower gardening techniques and features native plants suitable for the home garden. Book reviews, a calendar of events and lists of reference books are included. A prominent wildflower artist is profiled in each issue. The magazine also lists sources across North America for seeds and nursery-grown native plants. An extensive seed exchange program is available to members. Regular memberships are $25.00/year (payable in U.S. funds for U.S. subscribers) or $45.00 for two years. Family or library memberships are $30.00/year.

World of Cookbooks

Grace Kirschenbaum
1645 S. Vineyard Ave.
Los Angeles, CA 90019

(213) 933-1645
Established 1986
Write for more information.

World of Cookbooks, The International Cookbook Newsletter, is a unique quarterly that reviews between 60 to 70 cookbooks per issue from large and small publishers all over the world. Many cookbooks are published overseas that we might never hear about in the U.S.—unless we read this newsletter. All kinds of cookbooks are reviewed, and many of these are on herbs.

Individual subscriptions are $40.00/year; overseas subscriptions are $52.00 and corporate subscriptions are $80.00.

Bibliography of Books on Herbs

IN THIS CHAPTER YOU'LL FIND HUNDREDS of books on herb gardening, cooking, medicinal uses, folklore, etc. Most books are categorized by their main subject, although there is usually some overlap in subject matter in books of this sort. For example, many of the herb cultivation books also include recipes.

If you can't find the title you're looking for at your local bookstore, check the list of mail-order booksellers in Chapter 5 or order directly from the publisher. We have included some publishers' addresses at the end of this chapter for your convenience. Books which are out of print can sometimes be ordered from the booksellers listed in Chapter 5. Some of the books can also be ordered directly from the authors in which case their address has also been included in the Directory which follows at the end of this chapter.

Herb Gardening

Adams, James. *Landscaping with Herbs*. Portland, OR: Timber Press, 1987. Probably the most complete book in print on herbal landscaping. Includes cultural requirements and landscaping plans for more than 600 herbs; many useful photos, charts and illustrations. Discusses fragrant gardens, formal gardens, kitchen gardens, a "wild" garden and more.

Andrews, Jean. *Peppers, the Domesticated Capsicums*. Austin, TX: University of Texas Press, 1984. Describes the history of the genus *Capsicum*, its biology, how it is grown, what makes it red and hot, its economic and other uses, and hundreds of fascinating facts about 32 different pepper cultivars. The book is illustrated with beautiful watercolors by the author. Preparation tips and recipes are included.

Bacon, Richard M. *Growing, Gardening and Cooking with Herbs* (The Forgotten Arts Series). Dublin, NH: Yankee Books, 1972. Covers cultivation of more than 30 herbs; garden design; harvesting and drying; making teas, concoctions and drinks; cooking with herbs (with many recipes); making herbal by-products (perfumes, cosmetics, potpourris, dyes, soaps, wreaths, etc.) and herbs as pesticides.

Beston, Henry. *Herbs and the Earth*. Garden City, NY: Doubleday, Doran and Co., (reprint of 1935 edition). A literary excursion through the world of herbs. Recounts the folklore and history of Beston's favorites and offers practical advice on landscaping and cultivation.

Bremness, Lesley. *The Complete Book of Herbs: A Practical Guide to Growing & Using Herbs*. New York: Viking-Penguin, 1988. Includes theme garden plans, information on more than 100 herbs, fresh and dried herbal arrangements, recipes for potpourris, beauty products and more.

Bremness, Lesley, ed. *Herbs—Reader's Digest Home Handbook*. New York: Reader's Digest Press, 1991. Gives details on 90 herbs with growing, harvesting and preserving information; home remedies, cosmetic uses and recipes.

Clarkson, Rosetta E. *Herbs, Their Culture and Uses—The Complete Guide to Planning, Growing, and Harvesting Your Own Herb Garden*. New York: Macmillan, 1942 (republished in 1990). Discusses propagation and cultivation of herbs; unusual herb gardens and plantings; theme gardens (culinary, fragrant, indoor, dye); harvesting and drying. Contains information and recipes on cooking herbs and preparing potpourris, sachets, vinegars and teas. Brief descriptions of 101 herbs are included as are useful reference lists of fragrant herbs, biblical herbs, herbs attractive to bees, herbs with colorful flowers, etc.

Cook, Alan D. *Oriental Herbs and Vegetables*. New York: Brooklyn Botanic Gardens, 1989. How to grow and use many of the "strange sounding" herbs and vegetables that are so popular now at the market.

Crockett, James Underwood and Ogden Tanner. *Herbs*. Alexandria, VA: Time-Life Books, 1977. Includes a general introduction to herbs, herbal landscaping and container gardening, and an illustrated encyclopedia of 126 herbs.

Eldridge, Judith. *Cabbage or Cauliflower? A Garden Guide for the Identification of Vegetable and Herb Seedlings*. Boston: David R. Godine, 1984. This useful book covers 72 plants and includes information on their history and a description of each plant as it grows to maturity. Also includes life-size drawings of the seeds, seedlings, developing and then fully grown plants.

Felton, Elise. *Artistically Cultivated Herbs—How to Train Herbs as Decorative Art*. Santa Barbara, CA: Woodbridge Press, 1990. Step-by-step instruction for creating an herbal standard, developing an herbal "strawberry jar," espalier or bonsai; designing hanging baskets of herbs or herbal window boxes. Illustrated with many useful lists, charts and tables.

Forsell, Mary. *Heirloom Herbs: Using Old-Fashioned Herbs in Gardens, Recipes and Decorations*. New York: Random House, 1991. A full-color, comprehensive guide to growing and using antique herbs. Includes information on the history of herb gardens, herb gardening basics, and cultivation techniques and recipes for more than 45 old-fashioned herbs—culinary, household and medicinal.

Foster, Gertrude B. *Herbs for Every Garden*. New York: Dutton, 1973. A thorough guide to herb growing. Discusses the habitat, history and uses of each herb. Herbal craft projects and recipes are included.

Foster, Gertrude B., and Rosemary F. Louden. *Park's Success with Herbs*. Greenwood, SC: George W. Park Seed Co., 1980. Covers the cultivation, growing and harvesting of herbs as well as herb garden design. A unique feature is the close-up photos of seedlings and mature plants. An A-to-Z listing describes the habits, culture and use of more than 100 herbs. Some herbal crafts and recipes are included.

Fox, Helen Morgenthau. *Gardening with Herbs for Flavor and Fragrance*. New York: Dover, 1972. Covers both gardening and cooking with herbs. Much herbal lore and legend and many recipes. A chapter is devoted to herbal teas.

Garden Way Publishing, eds. *Herbs—1001 Gardening Questions Answered*. Pownal, VT: Storey Communications, 1990. An encyclopedic listing of more than 50 herbs written in question-and-answer format. Includes historical background, uses of herbs and cultivation and harvesting information. Many color photos.

An old Christian tradition says that parsley should be sown on Good Friday between the hours of twelve noon and three o'clock, the time of the Crucifixion. Parsley germinates slowly and this is believed to be because the seed has to return seven times to the devil and back before it can come up in the garden.

—from *The Frugal Housewife*, by Mrs. Child, 1833

Garland, Sarah. *The Herb Garden: A Complete Guide to Growing Scented, Culinary and Medicinal Herbs*. New York: Penguin Books, 1984. Starts with a fascinating account of historical herb gardens: from monastery gardens, medieval gardens, Renaissance gardens and physic gardens to contemporary herb gardens. Includes information on planning a hardy herb border, a wild herb garden, a low-maintenance garden, a cottage garden, a kitchen herb garden, a medicinal garden, a scented herb garden, a garden for bees and butterflies and a dyer's herb garden. Herb garden construction, growing herbs in containers, choosing herbs, and growing and using herbs are discussed in detail.

Gilbertie, Sal. *Herb Gardening at Its Best: Everything You Need to Know about Growing 200 Herbs*. New York: Macmillan, 1980. Basic herb cultivation with instructions for designing 30 specialty gardens, including a tea garden, a potpourri garden, a medicinal herb garden, and a shady garden.

Hepper, F. Nigel. *Planting a Bible Garden*. Kew: Royal Botanic Gardens, n.d. (Available from Unipub.) Discusses gardens and plants mentioned in the Bible as well as designing a Bible garden. Describes 75 of these plants (many of which are herbs) illustrating them with line drawings and color photos.

The Herb Society of America. *The Beginner's Herb Garden*. Concord, MA: The Herb Society of America, 1983. This small booklet covers designing and planting an herb garden and describes herbs in common use.

Hill, Madalene and Gwen Barclay. *Southern Herb Growing*. Fredericksburg, TX: Shearer Publications, 1987. (Available from the authors.) A beautiful, full-color guide to growing more than 130 different herbs in the South. Includes information on garden design, cultivation and harvesting as well as 100 recipes from the Hilltop Herb Farm restaurant in Romayor, Texas.

Hopkinson, Simon and Judith. *Herbs—Classic Garden Plants*. Chester, CT: Globe Pequot, 1989. A presentation of herbs as garden and landscape plants.

Jacobs, Betty E.M. *Growing and Using Herbs Successfully*. Pownal, VT: Storey Communications, 1981. A handy guide to growing, propagating and harvesting herbs for profit. Covers the basics of starting a herb business and markets for herbs and herb products.

Jacobs, Betty E.M. *Growing Herbs and Plants for Dyeing*. Tarzana, CA: Select Books, 1977. (Distributed by The Unicorn Books for Craftsmen.) Includes information on growing 23 herbs that can be used as natural dyes.

Keville, Kathi. *American Country Living: Herbs*. New York: Crescent Books, 1991. This beautiful, full-color book features chapters on designing a country herb garden, cultivating your garden, using herbs in the country kitchen as well as making herbal crafts such as pressed herbs and flowers, herbal and floral wreaths and herbal gifts for a country Christmas. Many recipes and tips for using the herbs.

Kirkpatrick, Debra. *Using Herbs in the Landscape—How to design and grow gardens of herbal annuals, perennials, shrubs and trees*. Harrisburg, PA: Stackpole Books, 1992. Presents design ideas and detailed planting plans for herb gardens from small container gardens and curbside plantings to larger, formal gardens. The book focuses on integrating the herb garden into a total landscaping plan. Detailed growing information is given about each plant along with its culinary and medicinal uses. Lists arranged by plant requirements make it easy to find herbs that grow best in a given situation. Several theme gardens are discussed, including a colonial American garden, a culinary garden, a medicinal garden and a fragrance garden.

Larkcom, Joy. *The Salad Garden*. New York: Viking Press, 1984. Good information on growing, harvesting, and using salad plants, many of which are herbs. Includes recipes.

Lathrop, Norma. *Herbs: How to Select, Grow and Enjoy*. Tucson, AZ: HP Books, 1981. A good introduction to growing and using herbs. Includes landscape planning, container gardening, propagation, an encyclopedia listing several hundred herbs with color photos, information on cooking with herbs, making potpourri, etc.

Meltzer, Sol. *Herb Gardening in Texas*. Houston: Gulf Publishing, 1983. General information on herbal propagation, container gardening of herbs, how to make herbal insect repellents, oils, etc. Lists more than 80 herbs that can be grown in Texas and their cultural requirements.

Miloradovich, Milo. *Growing and Using Herbs and Spices*. New York: Dover, 1986. A complete, compact reference guide to North American culinary herbs and spices. Includes how to plant, transplant, cultivate, harvest, use and preserve "virtually every herb and spice available in North America today".

Phillips, Roger, and Nicky Foy. *The Random House Book of Herbs*. New York: Random House, 1990. Covers more than 400 herbs with notes on cultivation and uses. Hundreds of full-color photographs.

Potts, Leanna K. *From Seed to Serve: A Beginner's Book on Planting and Using Herbs*. Joplin, MO: Leanna K. Potts, 1986. A handy little booklet that covers garden planning, cultivation and harvesting of 10 different herbs and includes seeds of each. Also includes more than 100 recipes.

Potts, Leanna K., and Evangela Potts. *Thyme for Kids*. Joplin, MO: Leanna K. Potts, 1990. Similar in content to the above book, except targeted toward children. Includes seeds and easy-to-make recipes.

Prenis, John. *The Windowsill Herb Garden*. Philadelphia: Running Press, 1990. A beginning guide for herb gardeners. Covers planting, cultivation, harvesting and uses of more than 20 low-maintenance herbs (primarily culinary).

Prenis, John. *Herb Grower's Guide: Cooking, Spicing and Lore*. Philadelphia: Running Press, 1974. An introduction to the history, cultivation and uses of 25 of the most popular herbs.

Riotte, Louise. *Carrots Love Tomatoes: Secrets of Companion Planting for Successful Gardening*. Pownal, VT: Storey Communications, 1981. An "A-to-Z" listing of companion plants which include many herbs (emphasizes vegetables and fruits). Also contains a helpful section on poisonous plants.

Riotte, Louise. *Roses Love Garlic*. Pownal, VT: Storey Communications, 1983. A sequel to the above book; emphasizes companion planting with flowers.

Rohde, Eleanour Sinclair. *A Garden of Herbs*. New York: Dover, 1969 (republication of 1936 edition). A brief history of herb gardens is followed by hints on growing the common herbs. Intended for those who wish to grow an "old-fashioned" herb garden, the book includes many recipes for syrups, conserves, wines, perfumes and herbs as scents (pomanders, ointments, colognes, etc.) A chapter is devoted to the picking and drying of herbs.

Schuler, Stanley, ed. *Simon & Schuster's Guide to Herbs and Spices*. New York: Simon & Schuster, 1990. Covers the origin and history of herbs and spices, the cultivation of herbs as well as their uses in cooking, perfumes and infusions. Descriptions of more than 280 species are given along with their specific uses and 140 full-color photos.

Shaudys, Phyllis V. *The Pleasure of Herbs: A Month-by-Month Guide to Growing, Using and Enjoying Herbs*. Pownal, VT: Storey Communications, 1986. Inspiring information on growing, harvesting and preserving herbs; a brief encyclopedia of herbs; many useful charts on the uses of herbs; a culinary "herb of the month"; many craft ideas and good information on how to package, display, price and promote herbs for resale.

Shaudys, Phyllis V. *Herbal Treasures*. Pownal, VT: Storey Communications, 1990. A sequel to the above-mentioned book and a literal "treasure chest" of information that includes hundreds of month-by-month projects for herbal gardening, cooking and crafts.

Simmons, Adelma Grenier. *Herb Gardening in Five Seasons*. New York: Dutton, 1977. Describes lore and uses of herbs seasonally arranged throughout the year.

Simmons, Adelma Grenier. *Herb Gardens of Delight*. New York: Dutton, 1979. Describes eight different herbal garden plans: for fragrance, culinary and decorative gray and silver gardens, a Shakespeare garden, two saints' gardens, medicinal herb and dye gardens. Fascinating lore and information on the plants are included.

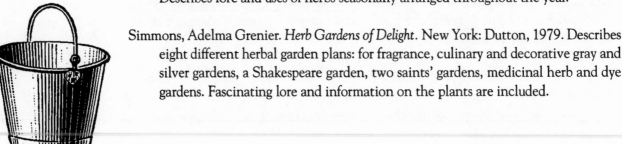

Simmons, Adelma Grenier. *Herbs Through the Seasons at Caprilands*. Emmaus, PA: Rodale Press, 1987. Describes planting an herb garden, summer garden care, harvesting and preserving herbs and planning next year's garden. Many recipes, growing tips and herbal craft suggestions are included.

Sitton, Diane Morey. *Texas Gardener's Guide to Growing and Using Herbs*. Waco, TX: Texas Gardener Press, 1987. Covers the basics of garden layout, design, preparation, container gardening, herbs in companion plantings, cooking with herbs, etc. Introduces 49 herbs that can be grown successfully in Texas, with a short history, description and cultivation requirements. Includes recipes and herbal crafts.

Swanson, Faith H., and Virginia B. Rady. *Herb Garden Design*. Hanover, NH: University Press of New England, 1984. More than 50 herb garden designs created by members of The Herb Society of America and landscape design architects. Includes plans for sunken gardens, knot gardens, dooryard gardens, fragrance gardens, Biblical gardens and others with detailed dimensions, plant lists and structural elements.

Titterington, Rosemary. *Growing Herbs—A Guide to Management*. Swindon, Wiltshire, England: Crowood Press, 1990. (Available from the author at Iden Croft Herbs.) Covers choosing a site and setting up an herb business, growing herbs in pots or as crops, propagating, harvesting, drying and selling the herbs.

Tolley, Emelie, and Chris Mead. *Herbs: Gardens, Decorations and Recipes*. New York: Clarkson N. Potter, 1986. A beautiful, full-color guide to all aspects of herb cultivation and use. Includes recipes, herbal decorations (wreaths, potpourris, etc.), garden design, etc.

Van Atta, Marian. *Growing and Using Exotic Foods*. Sarasota, FL: Pineapple Press, Inc., 1991. Covers the cultivation, harvesting and use of exotic fruits and vegetables. Includes information on the horseradish tree, elderberry, carob, prickly pear, roses, ginger, passion fruit, aloe, gotu kola and others.

Webster, Helen Noyes. *Herbs—How to Grow Them and How to Use Them*. Newton, MA: Charles T. Branford, 1974 (first published in 1939). Fascinating information on colonial herb gardens, growing wild herbs, the doctrine of signatures, medicinal herbs, drying and curing herbs, general directions for growing a herb garden and a chapter on biblical herbs.

Welch, William C. *Antique Roses for the South*. Dallas, TX: Taylor, 1990. Covers the search for old roses, landscaping with antique roses, arranging with old roses, the culture and propagation of old roses and antique roses suitable for Southern gardens. Includes information on rose crafts such as potpourri, waxed roses, etc. Illustrated with hundreds of full-color photos.

Zabar, Abbie. *The Potted Herb*. New York: Stewart, Tabori and Chang, 1988. Covers the basics of herb cultivation and features 18 herbs that are suitable for container growing. Gives detailed information on growing herbal topiaries; some recipes.

SOME NOTES ABOUT HEIRLOOM SEEDS

There has been a lot of attention in the press in recent years to "heirloom" or "traditional" varieties, yet many people are unclear as to just what these terms mean. Since I find no universally accepted definitions among seedsmen and preservation workers, here are the meanings of the terms as I use them:
* Traditional varieties: any variety developed more than 50 years ago. Includes many commercially developed and distributed varieties.
* Heirloom varieties: any variety that owes its existence to its preservation by home gardeners or private individuals, rather than the seed trade. This includes old varieties whose origin is unknown which have been passed down from generation to generation, as well as old varieties developed by seedsmen which at some point were dropped by the seed trade and would have been lost had they not been maintained by home gardeners.

—J. L. Hudson's The 1991 Ethnobotanical Catalog of Seeds

Herbs—General References

Bonar, Ann. *The Macmillan Treasury of Herbs—A Complete Guide to the Cultivation and Use of Wild and Domesticated Herbs*. New York: Macmillan, 1985. Covers herb gardening, container growing, harvesting, recipes and the design of herb gardens. Describes 59 herbs, their history, cultivation and use.

For the love of gardening is a seed that once sown never dies, but always grows and grows to an enduring and ever increasing source of happiness.

—Gertrude Jekyll

Burr, Fearing. *Field and Garden Vegetables of America*. Chillicothe, IL: The American Botanist, Booksellers, 1990 (first published in 1863; this edition was republished from the second edition of 1865). Full descriptions of nearly 1100 species and varieties of vegetables that were grown more than 125 years ago with directions for propagation, culture and use. Many of these varieties have already become extinct and are no longer in cultivation; some are still being grown today under different names. This important volume is invaluable for helping to identify these historic varieties of vegetables. It also describes herbs such as chives, garlic, leeks, onions, rocambole, shallots, amaranthus, black nightshade, nettle, orach, sorrel, salad plants (dandelion, horseradish, mustard, nasturtium, chervil, etc.), medicinal plants and "oleraceous plants" (angelica, anise, balm, basil, clary, coriander, dill, fennel, etc.).

Conrow, Robert, and Arlene Hecksel. *Herbal Pathfinders: A Sourcebook for the Herbal Renaissance*. Santa Barbara, CA: Woodbridge Press, 1983. Biographical information on 27 leading herbalists—their lives, origins, health principles and favorite recipes. Includes Paul Lee, Jeanne Rose, Rosemary Gladstar, James Duke and 23 others.

Cooper, Guy, and Gordon Taylor. *English Herb Gardens*. New York: Rizzoli, 1986. Features 58 herb gardens in England with color photos of each one. Herbal glossary describes 42 plants.

Gips, Kathleen. *The Language of Flowers—A Book of Victorian Floral Sentiments*. Chagrin Falls, OH: Pine Creek Herbs, 1990. A charming dictionary of the meanings of herbs and flowers, trees and shrubs. The information and illustrations were compiled from French, English and American floral dictionaries dating back to 1830; the book cross-references sentiment with plants. A good guide for the tussie-mussie designer or the general flower lover.

Grieve, Mrs. M. *A Modern Herbal*. 2 vols. New York: Dover, 1971 (first published in 1931). An encyclopedia of herbs including everything from "abcess root to zedoary". Information on the medicinal, culinary, cosmetic and economic uses of herbs is presented, along with folklore, cultivation instructions and the chemical constituents of the herbs. Includes directions for making extracts, tinctures, lotions, wines, brandies, etc.

Kowalchik, Claire, and William H. Hylton. *Rodale's Illustrated Encyclopedia of Herbs.* Emmaus, PA: Rodale Press, 1987. An alphabetical presentation of more than 140 herbs and how to grow and use them. Includes additional entries on garden design, herbal symbolism, historical aspects, sources, etc.

Lima, Patrick. *Harrowsmith Illustrated Book of Herbs.* Buffalo, NY: Firefly, 1988. Discusses herbs for the kitchen, for shade and color, for teas and fragrance—all of which are suitable for northern climates.

Lust, John, ed. *The Herb Book.* New York: Bantam Books, 1983. Information on more than 200 herbs and their history, lore and uses (cosmetic, aromatic, and medicinal).

Mabey, Richard. *The New Age Herbalist: How to Use Herbs for Healing, Nutrition, Body Care and Relaxation.* New York: Macmillan, 1988. Covers herb growing and use with an emphasis on natural gardening. Includes herbal alternatives for fragrance, food, cosmetics, medicines, decorations, teas, etc., and a reference glossary listing more than 200 herbs and their cultivation.

Mulherin, Jennifer. *The Macmillan Treasury of Spices & Natural Flavorings.* New York: Macmillan, 1988. Covers traditional uses of spices, spices in history, unusual spices and flavorings, curries and spice mixes around the world, an encyclopedic list of 50 spices and herbs. Also discusses natural flavorings and extracts.

Rinzler, Carol. *Complete Book of Herbs, Spices & Condiments.* New York: Facts on File, 1990. Covers more than 100 herbs, spices and condiments with fascinating information on the uses and medicinal properties of each; how they are used in cooking and the nutritional values; and how the herb or spice affects the human body.

Rose, Jeanne. *Ask Jeanne Rose about Herbs.* New Canaan, CT: Keats, 1984. A small herbal primer of common questions and their answers.

Rose, Jeanne.. *Herbs and Things: Jeanne Rose's Herbal.* New York: Grosset & Dunlap, 1972. A collection of practical and exotic herbal lore.

Stuart, Malcolm., ed. *The Encyclopedia of Herbs and Herbalism.* New York: Crown, 1989. Covers the history of herbalism, the biology and chemistry of plants, the medicinal uses of plants, herbs in the kitchen, the domestic and cosmetic uses of herbs, cultivation, collection and preservation of herbs. A reference section lists 420 of the "most important herbs", each illustrated with a photo or drawing.

Sturdivant, Lee. *Profits from your Backyard Herb Garden.* Friday Harbor, WA: San Juan Naturals, 1988. An introductory guide to the small-scale production and marketing of herbs. Emphasizes 12 basic culinary herbs, edible flowers, greens and flowers. Practical information on packaging, harvesting and business details for the spare-time gardener with a small garden space.

Herbal Health & Beauty Products;
Medicinal Uses of Herbs

Benedetti, Maria Dolores Hajosy. *Earth and Spirit—Healing Lore and More from Puerto Rico*. Maplewood, NJ: Waterfront Press, 1989. This book is an overview of the folk medicine of Puerto Rico. Features interviews with curanderos, midwives, spiritual healers, a farmer who plants by the moon and others. Remedies and lore are presented in an extensive recipe section organized by health condition ranging from "alcohol and drug addiction" to "warts". All plants are cross-referenced in English, Spanish and Latin.

Buchman, Dian D. *The Complete Herbal Guide to Natural Health and Beauty*. New York: Doubleday, 1973. Full of information on cosmetic treatments from head to foot. Includes recipes for facial masks, honey and lemon cleansers, natural deodorants, herbal baths and scrubs. A chart lists the herbs described in the book, the ailments for which they are prescribed and what parts of the body are treated with what herbs.

Cameron, Myra. *Mother Nature's Guide to Vibrant Beauty and Health*. Englewood Cliffs, NJ: Prentice-Hall, 1990. A basic guide to achieving healthy skin, hair, eyes, hands and feet with inexpensive, natural beauty treatments and remedies. Includes recipes for facials, hair colorants, lotions, poultices, etc., and good information on diet, exercise and stress management through the use of natural substances.

Carpenter, Deb. *Nature's Beauty Kit—Cosmetic Recipes for Faces over 21*. Rushville, NB: P.L.A.N Publishers, 1989. This little spiral-bound booklet contains many recipes for natural cosmetics, health and beauty products that can be made at home: facial steams, eye care products, hair care items (shampoos, rinses, conditioners), bath herbs, oils and salts and much more.

Castleman, Michael. *The Healing Herbs: The Ultimate Guide to the Curative Powers of Nature's Medicines*. Emmaus, PA: Rodale Press, 1991. This 436-page, easy-to-use book packs in lots of information on medicinal herbs and their uses. Herbal lore, history, and research on 100 well-known and widely available herbs and more than 200 different medical conditions and diseases are discussed. Other topics include growing the herbs, medicinal applications and the "safety factor".

Coon, Nelson. *Using Plants for Healing*. Emmaus, PA: Rodale Press, 1979. A historical overview of medicinal uses of plants, and the preparation of plants for medicinal use (drying, collecting and preserving). Includes descriptions of plants commonly used as medicines. A handy "Plant Collector's Calendar" lists approximate dates for collecting a selection of wild medicinal plants.

Densmore, Frances. *How Indians Use Wild Plants for Food, Medicine and Crafts*. New York: Dover, 1974. Discusses the methods used by Indians to gather plants and the way they used them in medicine and surgical procedures. Also lists a large number of specific herbs used by Indians, their preparation and administration.

Evelyn, Nancy. *The Herbal Medicine Chest*. Freedom, CA: Crossing Press, 1986. Includes instructions for making your own ointments, oils, teas, infusions, tinctures and extracts and how they have been used traditionally in herbal medicine.

Foster, Steven, and James A. Duke. *A Field Guide to Medicinal Plants: Eastern and Central North America*. New York: Houghton Mifflin, 1990. This guide to the identification of medicinal plants in the wild includes descriptions of 500 plants with detailed line drawings and photos. Lists historical and modern uses of each plant, with a discussion of research and clinical data that supports or discredits traditional medicinal use. Warnings are included about toxic plants.

Gibbons, Euell. *Stalking the Healthful Herbs*. Brattleboro, VT: A. C. Hood, 1989 (first published in 1966). Covers over 40 wild herbs and the manifold uses for each one including food as well as medicine. Wild horseradish, witch hazel, comfrey, nettle, ginseng, wild mints, and horehound are among the herbs discussed.

Grainger, Janette, and Connie Moore. *Natural Insect Repellents for Pets, People and Plants*. Austin, TX: The Herb Bar, 1991. This useful book discusses herbal insect repellents of many kinds to use on all kinds of personal and household pests including fleas, mosquitoes, other insects, head lice, ants, moths and silverfish. A chapter also treats grooming and worming pets.

Graves, George. *Medicinal Plants—An Illustrated Guide to More than 180 Herbal Plants that Cure Disease and Relieve Pain*. New York: Crown, 1990. An abridged version of the original, first published in 1834 as *Hortus Medicus*. Old reproductions of plant illustrations are highly detailed and useful for identification purposes. Short descriptions of each plant are also given.

Green, James. *The Male Herbal: Health Care for Men and Boys*. Freedom, CA: Crossing Press, 1991. This concise book includes guidelines for selection and preparation of herbal formulas for various male health problems along with general historical background on herbalism.

Hoffman, David. *The Holistic Herbal*. Dorset, England: Element Books, 1988. (Available from California School of Herbal Studies). Thorough book on description, actions and chemistry of medicinal plants. Chapters explain the various systems of the body (circulatory, respiratory, digestive, etc.) and the herbs' effects on each of them.

Hutchens, Alma R. *Indian Herbalogy of North America*. Windsor, ON, Canada: Merco, 1973. Subtitled *A Study of Anglo-American, Russian and Oriental Literature on Indian Medical Botanics of North America*, this book covers more than 200 plants used by North American Indians for medicinal, culinary and other purposes. Describes the plants, their medicinal parts, their influence on the body, and their uses in folk medicine and industry.

Kloss, Jethro. *Back to Eden*. Loma Linda, CA: Back to Eden Books, 1939 (revised 1989 by Promise Books). This encyclopedia of herbal preventive medicine and healing by natural means includes information on diet, cooking, nursing and specific instructions for using herbs to treat disease.

Moore, Michael. *Medicinal Herbs of the Desert and Canyon West*. Santa Fe, NM: Museum of New Mexico Press, 1989. Covers 60 species of plants and gives information on their appearance, habitat, collection and preparation, medicinal uses and dosage. Includes many plants which have been neglected in other medicinal herbals.

The word "lavender" is derived from the Latin *lavare* meaning "to wash"; the herb has been used in soaps and bath waters since ancient times.

Nabhan, Gary Paul. *Gathering the Desert*. Tucson, AZ: University of Arizona Press, 1985. A fascinating book that discusses the four seasons in the desert and useful plants specific to each of the seasons. These include creosote bush, mesquite, amaranth, chiltepin, devil's-claw, wild desert gourds and more.

Reader's Digest, eds. *Magic and Medicine of Plants*. Pleasantville, NY: Reader's Digest Association, 1986. Fascinating herbal folklore and history coupled with descriptions of more than 300 plants and their medicinal uses with full-color illustrations.

Rose, Jeanne. *The Herbal Body Book*. New York: Grosset & Dunlap, 1976. An exploration of the external use of herbs and other natural ingredients (honey, vinegar and oil) to promote health and beauty of the entire body from head to toe.

Rose, Jeanne. *Jeanne Rose's Herbal Guide to Food and Health*. North Atlantic Publications, 1989. (Available from the author.) A unique herbal cookbook that explores the use of herbs as foods to promote health, beauty and well-being through their nourishing and medicinal qualities.

Rose, Jeanne. *Kitchen Cosmetics: Using Herbs, Fruit & Flowers for Natural Bodycare*. San Francisco, CA: Herbal Studies/Jeanne Rose, 1990. A comprehensive guide to using plants as cosmetics. Contains recipes and herbal lore, basic cosmetic plants and other ingredients and hints on using plants in cosmetics.

Scheffer, Mechthild. *Bach Flower Therapy—Theory and Practice*. Rochester, VT: Inner Traditions, 1987. The "bible" of flower therapy and the methods of Dr. Edward Bach, a physician who gave up his practice more than 50 years ago to develop his theories on natural healing. These were based on the use of 38 different flower remedies that he felt would restore mental and emotional balance and cure disease.

Spoerke, David G. *Herbal Medications*. Santa Barbara, CA: Woodbridge Press, 1990. Scientific information about more than 200 herbs used in both folklore and modern herbal practice. Includes their active principles, modes of action, potential for toxicity and other comments.

Theiss, Peter and Barbara. *The Family Herbal*. Rochester, VT: Healing Arts Press, 1989. Written by the founders of the largest pharmaceutical herb company in Germany, this book takes a "homey" approach to the authors' personal experience with herbs. It covers more than 40 herbs that are native to Germany and their medicinal uses based on the various body systems.

Thomson, William A.R., M.D. *Herbs that Heal*. New York: Scribners, 1976. Emphasizes the healing possibilities in various herbs and a little history of how the plants have been used as medicines.

Tierra, Michael. *The Way of Herbs—Simple Remedies for Health and Healing*. Santa Cruz, CA: Unity Press, 1980. A guide to the healing properties and uses of herbs, the theories of herbal treatment and therapy. Describes the uses of 98 important medicinal herbs and how to make herbal formulas, with cautionary notes.

Tierra, Michael and Lesley. *Chinese-Planetary Herbal Diagnosis*. Santa Cruz, CA: Michael and Lesley Tierra, 1988. This book is a concise introduction to the principles of traditional Chinese holistic herbal diagnosis used in conjunction with the practice of Chinese herbology. It includes information on traditional Chinese, East Indian and traditional Western herbs which may be used separately or together in the same formula.

Tisserand, Maggie. *Aromatherapy for Women—A Practical Guide to Essential Oils for Health and Beauty*. Rochester, VT: Inner Traditions, 1985. Covers aromatherapy for health and beauty. Emphasizes conditions of pregnancy, childbirth, postnatal care and the treatment of childhood illnesses.

Tisserand, Robert. *The Art of Aromatherapy—The Healing and Beautifying Properties of the Essential Oils of Flowers and Herbs*. Woodstock, NY: Beekman, 1977. The classic work on this subject. Recipes for 29 essential oils for massage, medicinal, cosmetic and bath uses; history of oils from ancient Egyptian times to the present day.

Vogel, Virgil J. *American Indian Medicine*. Norman, OK: University of Oklahoma Press, 1970. A fascinating study of the medical aspects of Indian history, folklore, pharmacology and botany, this book emphasizes "rational therapy", or the non-shamanistic or ritual aspects of Indian medicine. It discusses the influence of Indian medicine on folk medicine, American Indian therapeutic methods, Indian health and disease and American Indian contributions to pharmacology.

Weil, Andrew, M.D. *Natural Health, Natural Medicine: A Comprehensive Manual for Wellness and Self-Care*. Boston: Houghton Mifflin, 1990. Covers preventive health maintenance, specific prevention of heart attacks, strokes or cancer; protecting the immune system and basic natural treatments for specific illnesses. Includes good resource information on alternative types of medical practitioners.

Weiner, Michael A., with Janet Weiner. *Weiner's Herbal: The Guide to Herb Medicine*. Briarcliff Manor, NY: Stein and Day, 1980. An illustrated A-to-Z listing of more than 170 medicinal plants of the world: a layman's guide to traditional herbal treatments.

Weiss, Gaea, and Shandor Weiss. *Growing and Using the Healing Herbs*. Emmaus, PA: Rodale Press, 1985. Gives a short history of herbal medicine and herbal healing traditions in Europe, the East and America. Includes an illustrated section featuring healing plants from alfalfa to yarrow. Contains good information on gathering and using the herbs in lotions, oils, liniments, tinctures, etc.

Yun, Hye Koo (Henry). *Herbal Holistic Approach to Arthritis*. Burnaly, BC, Canada: Dominion Herbal College, 1988. Dr. Hye Koo Yun is the son of Korea's first clinical nutritionist and homeopath. His book covers the traditional and contemporary Oriental and Occidental herbal remedies for arthritis, diagnosis and treatment and selected case studies.

Historical References

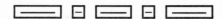

Anderson, Frank J. *An Illustrated History of the Herbals*. New York: Columbia University Press, 1985. A chronological survey of herbals from the 1st through the 16th centuries. Illustrated with drawings from some of the early books.

Bayard, Tania. *Sweet Herbs and Sundry Flowers: Medieval Gardens and the Gardens of the Cloisters*. New York: Metropolitan Museum of Art, 1985. A gift booklet that gives an overview of medieval gardening, with a chapter devoted to the uses of herbs in these gardens. Includes information on the three medieval gardens at the Cloisters in New York.

Clarkson, Rosetta E. *Green Enchantment—The Magic and History of Herbs and Garden Making*. New York: Macmillan, 1991. First published in 1940, this book is a classic and definitive history of herbs and gardening. Includes chapters on the early history of garden design, the herbalists and monastery gardens and early gardening tools. Explores garden lore with chapters on early medicinal and magical herbs, herbs for the witches' garden and "fairy tale" herbs that never existed. The book is illustrated with more than 100 facsimile woodcuts from ancient herbals and garden books.

Rohde, Eleanour Sinclair. *The Old English Herbals*. New York: Dover, 1971 (republication of 1922 edition). A study of the history of herbals from early Anglo-Saxon manuscripts to the "still-room books" of the 17th century with many references to folklore, custom, and the history of medicine, botany and magic. Includes an extensive bibliography on herbals from the 9th Century through 1678.

Woodward, Marcus, ed. *Leaves from Gerard's Herball*. New York: Dover, 1969 (republication of 1931 edition). Selections from John Gerard's *Herball or General Historie of Plantes*, which first appeared in 1597. Herbs are grouped according to time of flowering. Illustrated with many quaint woodcuts after the originals.

In the sixteenth century, nettles were cut just before flowering and placed in a wooden trough. The plants were then covered with rainwater and left to ferment. After about a month the liquid was diluted with more rainwater and sprayed on the ground. Farmers thought that the nettle plant had magic powers—the fact is that the nettle plant takes up nitrogen, iron, protein, phosphate, etc. into its roots and releases it into the soil in the rainwater.

—from *The Frugal Housewife*, by Mrs. Child, 1833

Cooking with Herbs

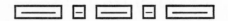

Belsinger, Susan. *Flowers in the Kitchen*. Loveland, CO: Interweave Press, 1991. Describes 25 edible flowers and illustrates (with recipes) how they can be used in butters, vinegars, salads, appetizers, entrees and desserts. Includes a comprehensive chart of 50 edible flowers and a garden plan.

Brooklyn Botanic Garden. *Herbs and Cooking*. New York: Brooklyn Botanic Garden, 1982. Covers culinary herbs and their uses in cooking and garden ornamentation.

Carroll, Ricki and Robert. *Cheesemaking Made Easy*. Pownal, VT: Storey Communications, 1982. Easy-to-understand information on making your own soft cheeses, hard cheeses, whey cheeses, goat's milk cheeses, bacterial and mold-ripened cheeses and cheese spreads. Includes some information on making herbal cheeses.

Claiborne, Craig. *Cooking with Herbs and Spices*. New York: Harper & Row, 1970. Discusses 55 herbs or spices and includes recipes for each of them.

Clark, Marge. *It's About Thyme! An Herb Manual and Cookbook of Herb and Non-Herb Recipes*. West Lebanon, IN: Marge Clark, 1991 (third printing). This delightful book covers a wealth of information on herb garden design, cultivation, harvesting and preservation of herbs, recipes for herb blends, potpourris, oils, etc. The second half of the book includes hundreds of recipes for appetizers and drinks, soups, salads, dressings, fish and seafood, chicken and meat, fruits and vegetables and desserts. The final chapter discusses canning and preserving foods.

Dille, Carolyn, and Susan Belsinger. *Herbs in the Kitchen*. Loveland, Colorado: Interweave Press, 1992. This beautiful book gives historical information and sound advice for growing and using 20 popular culinary herbs. The more than 200 enticing recipes are supplemented with a number of full-page color photographs.

Duke, James A. *Culinary Herbs: A Potpourri*. New York: Trado-Medic Books, 1984. Semitechnical in nature, this book lists some of the most popular culinary herbs and explains their culture, modern uses and traditional uses in folk medicine.

Duke, James A. *Living Liqueurs*. Lincoln, MA: Quarterman, 1987. Gives guidelines for making your own herbal liqueurs; covers herbal combinations, brewing and steeping techniques and alcohol bases; includes the culture, uses and folklore of 50 herbs that can be used in liqueurs.

GARLIC IN EIGHT LANGUAGES

French: ail
Italian: aglio
German: knoblauch
Greek: skortho
Arabic: thum
Spanish: ajo
Turkish: sarmisak
Hebrew: shum

—from *Garlic News*

Ferrary, Jeannette, and Louise Fiszer. *Season to Taste—Herbs and Spices in American Cooking.* New York: Simon & Schuster, 1988. Includes 200 recipes based on 150 herbs and 11 spices used traditionally in American cooking; emphasizes light and healthy eating.

Fischborn, Cynthia, and Cheryl Long. *Easy Microwave Preserving.* Lake Oswego, OR: Culinary Arts, 1989. An introduction to preserving jellies, fruits, sauces, and relishes with the microwave. Includes instructions for drying herbs in the microwave with recipes for their use.

Fresh Garlic Association. *The Garlic Lover's Cookbook.* Berkeley, CA: Celestial Arts, 1982. Covers garlic "history and mystery", good things to know about garlic and many recipes for using garlic in vegetables, salads and dressings, soups, breads and pasta, meats, poultry and seafood. Includes winning recipes from the Gilroy (California) Garlic Festival.

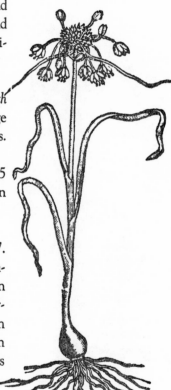

Gilbertie, Sal. *Kitchen Herbs—The Art and Enjoyment of Growing Herbs and Cooking with Them.* New York: Bantam, 1988. How to grow culinary herbs; includes a large collection of recipes (more than 160 pages of them) using both fresh and dried herbs.

Hersey, Jean. *Cooking with Herbs.* New York: Scribners, 1972. A brief introduction to 15 herbs that can be grown in pots and recipes for each of them. Includes a chapter on herb teas and miniature potpourris.

Hutson, Lucinda. *The Herb Garden Cookbook.* Austin, TX: Texas Monthly Press, 1987. (Available from the author.) This concise book covers herbal landscaping, propagation and gardening tips and is a good introduction to herbs of the American Southwest and Mexico. Includes descriptive botanical information, easy-to-understand planting and harvesting instructions, personal observations, and more than 150 recipes using the herbs. Some special features of the book are chapters on Mexican and Oriental herbs, suggested menus and many recipes for herbal vinegars and butters.

Johnson, Marsha Peters. *Gourmet Vinegars: How to Make & Cook with Them.* Lake Oswego, OR: Culinary Arts, 1990. This thorough book covers the basics of gourmet vinegar making. Includes recipes for basic berry, fruit, herb, spice, vegetable, flower and mixed vinegars as well as recipes for using the vinegars.

Kavasch, Barrie. *Native Harvests—Recipes and Botanicals of the American Indian.* New York: Random House, 1979. (Available from the American Indian Archaeological Institute.) Includes hundreds of authentic recipes for soups, salads, vegetables, main dishes, beverages, and breads from American Indians—everything from clover soup to elder blossom fritters. Easy-to-use charts specify the many uses of the plants by the Indians, which parts to use, and when and where to harvest them.

Klein, Erica Levy. *Skinny Spices: 50 nifty homemade spice blends that can make any diet delicious*. Chicago: Surrey Books, 1990. Recipes for 50 herbal blends that can add interest to low-sodium, low-fat or low-calorie diets. They include Salad, Chinese, Hot, and Greek and Mid-Eastern Spice Blends. Each blend is followed by two sample recipes; suggestions are given for their use in salads, dips, main dishes, etc.

Krochmal, Connie and Arnold. *A Naturalist's Guide to Cooking with Wild Plants*. New York: New York Times, 1974. Identifies more than 90 wild plants (many of which are herbs) with photos or drawings and information on when and how to harvest the edible portions. Recipes for cooking them are also included.

Long, Cheryl, and Heather Kibbey. *Classic Liqueurs: The Art of Making and Cooking with Liqueurs*. Lake Oswego, OR: Culinary Arts, 1990. Covers the basics of liqueur making, from equipment and materials to techniques. Contains recipes for making fruit liqueurs as well as nonfruit liqueurs with nuts or herbs. Then, when you've made them, read the recipes for serving and cooking with them.

Mazza, Irma Goodrich. *Herbs for the Kitchen*. Boston: Little, Brown, 1947. A cookbook with many recipes which use herbs; includes chapters on garlic, rice, one-dish meals and herbal salads.

Norris, Dorry Baird. *Sage Cottage Herb Garden Cookbook: Celebrations, Recipes and Herb Gardening Tips for Every Month of the Year*. Chester, CT: Globe Pequot, 1991. (Available from the author.) A nice collection of original herbal recipes developed at the New York Sage Cottage Bed & Breakfast. Organized by month, it includes much fascinating herbal holiday lore.

Owen, Millie. *A Cook's Guide to Growing Herbs, Greens & Aromatics*. New York: Knopf, 1978. Covers not only information on growing herbs, greens and aromatics outdoors and indoors but also foraging for wild greens and herbs, preserving herbs, using fresh mixed herbs. Contains cultivation information for 46 herbs and greens (including milkweed, sorrel, purslane and fiddleheads) with nearly 100 recipes.

Rankin, Dorothy. *Pestos! Cooking with Herb Pastes*. New York: Crossing Press, 1985. Includes 29 pesto recipes using a wide variety of herbs, oils and nuts; winter pestos made from dried herbs and 60 recipes for using the pestos.

Ripperger, Helmut. *Spice Cookery*. New York: George W. Stewart, 1942. Eighty recipes using various spices. (No index or table of contents.)

Rohde, Eleanour Sinclair. *Culinary and Salad Herbs*. New York: Dover, 1972. How to grow, use and store the Asian and Mediterranean herbs that we now use in cooking. Covers their history and lore.

Sawyer, Helene. *Gourmet Mustards: How to Make and Cook with Them*. Lake Oswego, OR: Culinary Arts, 1990. Covers the basics of gourmet mustard making. Includes 20 recipes for wine, herb, spice, fruit and vegetable mustards and more than 50 recipes for using them (even desserts!)

Schmidt, R. Marilyn. *Flavored Vinegars—Herb and Fruit*. Barnegat Light, NJ: 1988. Includes recipes for making 32 vinegars, from simple herb flavors to spice and fruity flavors along with recipes for using them and instructions for vinegar hair rinses and facials.

Shepherd, Renee. *Recipes from a Kitchen Garden*—Vols. 1 and 2. Felton, CA: Shepherd's Garden, 1987. Two collections of recipes from Renee Shepherd, owner of Shepherd's Garden Seeds. Many delicious recipes for vegetables, chili peppers, edible flowers, herbs and more.

Smith, Leona Woodring. *The Forgotten Art of Flower Cookery*. Gretna, LA: Pelican, 1973 (third printing, 1990). One of the first books published on edible flowers, this book includes more than 200 recipes using 26 common garden flowers such as borage, carnation, chives, chrysanthemum, clover, dandelion, daylily, elder, gardenia, lavender, lilac, marigold, rosemary, violet and yucca.

Stobart, Tom. *Herbs, Spices and Flavorings*. Woodstock, NY: Overlook Press, 1970. The history and the scientific basis of flavorings with an alphabetical reference to hundreds of herbs, spices and flavorings—everything from ajowan to zedoary.

Stoval, Edith. *Salt-Free Herb Cookery*. Pownal, VT: Storey Communications, n.d. This little booklet features handy tips for eliminating salt in your diet and using herbs instead. Covers 10 basic culinary herbs with recipes.

Tolley, Emelie, and Chris Mead. *Cooking with Herbs*. New York: Clarkson N. Potter, 1989. A beautifully illustrated book of herbal cuisine from around the world and across the U.S.A.

Townsend, Doris. *How to Cook with Herbs, Spices and Flavorings*. Tucson, AZ: HP Books, 1982. General information and recipes for spices, herbs, seeds, extracts, sauces and stocks, herb and spice compounds, flavored vinegars and oils and condiments.

HOMEMADE GERMAN MUSTARD

1/4 cup dry mustard
2 tablespoons water
1/3 cup cider vinegar
2/3 cup water
 (can substitute flat beer)
2 tablespoons fresh horseradish (optional)
1/4 cup sugar
1/2 teaspoon salt
3 tablespoons white flour

Mix mustard and 2 tablespoons water and set aside. In a 1 quart saucepan, mix well 2/3 cup water, vinegar, sugar, salt and flour. Cook over low heat 3 min. or until smooth. Stir constantly. Remove from heat and stir in mustard until smooth. Cover and refrigerate 24 to 30 hours before using. Leave opened pony bottle in refrigerator overnight. Notes: Put 2/3 cup water and 3 tablespoons flour in shaker and shake well. Electric hand mixer can be used on low speed.

—from Pendery's catalog, Ft. Worth, Texas

Herbal Crafts

Becker, Dotti. *A Concise Guide to Growing Everlastings*. Williams, OR: Goodwin Creek Gardens, 1991. Covers all aspects of sowing, growing and harvesting everlastings including soil preparation and fertilization, transplanting, watering, insect and animal pests, and drying and storing dried flowers. Twenty-seven everlastings are featured, with comprehensive information about each plant.

Black, Penny. *The Book of Potpourri—fragrant flower mixes for scenting and decorating the home*. New York: Simon and Schuster, 1989. A beautiful overview of the craft of making potpourris in full color. Includes information on materials and equipment; fixatives and essential oils; drying flowers and herbs; and potpourri recipes for roses, herbs, garden flowers, spices, seeds, woods, roots, berries and small fruits. Also includes valuable information on conservation of wildflowers and cautions regarding poisonous berries.

Black, Penny. *The Book of Pressed Flowers*. New York: Simon and Schuster, 1988. Covers pressing, drying and arranging herbs and flowers. Step-by-step instructions for pressing a wide variety of plant materials and using them to make greeting cards, floral pictures, sachets, etc.

Bramson, Ann. *Soap—Making It and Enjoying It*. New York: Workman, 1975. Covers the history of soapmaking as well as all aspects of making your own soaps—ingredients, equipment, recipes, troubleshooting, scenting and instructions for making specialty soaps.

Buchanan, Rita. *A Weaver's Garden*. Loveland, CO: Interweave Press, 1987. The only book to cover in detail natural plant resources for the textile artist. Includes information on plant fibers for spinning and stuffing, dyes from plants and soap plants for cleaning textiles as well as fragrant plants to scent and protect textiles and plant materials used to make textile tools. Tells how to create a garden using a variety of these plants.

Crawford, Hester M. *Herbs and Their Ornamental Uses* (#68). Brooklyn, New York: Brooklyn Botanic Garden, 1972. A guide to using herbs as border plants to provide color, texture and interest in the garden.

Cusick, Dawn. *A Scented Christmas*. Asheville, NC: Lark, 1990. Step-by-step directions for making traditional scented garlands, ornaments, wreaths, swags, centerpieces, tussie-mussies—more than 100 projects in all.

Cusick, Dawn, and Rob Pulleyn. *Wreaths 'Round the Year: More Than 90 Inspiring Wreaths to Make and Enjoy*. Asheville, NC: Lark, 1991. Features more than 90 wreaths to make, from simple holiday pieces to more extravagant designer creations. Includes detailed instructions, designer tips, and a list of evergreens, herbs and flowers to use on the wreaths.

Docker, Amanda. *An English Country Lady's Book of Dried Flowers*. New York: Doubleday, 1990. Unusual dried flower arrangements for weddings, kitchen designs, outdoor party decorations and holidays with a British "accent".

Duff, Gail. *Natural Fragrances: Outdoor Scents for Indoor Uses*. Pownal, VT: Storey Communications, 1989. Ideas for using fragrance in every room of your house. Includes instructions for making sachets, potpourris, holiday crafts and projects, scented candles and aromatic blends for closets.

Fettner, Ann Tucker. *Potpourri, Incense and Other Fragrant Concoctions*. New York: Workman, 1977. In-depth information on creating your own potpourris, incenses, toilet waters, scented candles, pomanders, and sachets.

Hillier, Malcolm, and Colin Hilton. *The Book of Dried Flowers*. New York: Simon and Schuster, 1986. A comprehensive guide to drying and arranging herbs and flowers with instructions for making wreaths, topiaries and swags.

Jacobs, Betty E.M. *Flowers That Last Forever: Growing, Harvesting, and Preserving*. Pownal, VT: Storey Communications, 1988. A general book on growing, harvesting and drying 31 everlasting flowers.

James, Theodore, Jr. *The Potpourri Gardener—How to Grow, Harvest & Dry Flowers For Fragrance & Color in Your Home All Year Round*. New York: Macmillan, 1990. Beautiful, full-color book describes how to create a potpourri garden and tells how to grow more than 100 herbs, annuals, bulbs, perennials, roses and shrubs that can be used as potpourri material. Also included are directions for making your own potpourris, with 20 original recipes.

Joosten, Titia. *Flower-Drying with a Microwave*. New York: Sterling, 1989. Helpful hints on drying more than 200 types of flowers in a microwave oven, with many ideas for projects and designs.

Leyel, Mrs. C. F. *Herbal Delights—Tisanes, Syrups, Confections, Electuaries, Robs, Juleps, Vinegars and Conserves*. London: Faber and Faber, 1937. Includes information on aromatic tisanes (teas), cordial herbs, cooling herbs, refreshing herbs, pot herbs and salads, spices and condiments, natural perfumes and cosmetic herbs, together with quotes and recipes for using the herbs.

CHRISTMAS PINE POTPOURRI

1 cup rosemary leaves, dried

1 cup fir balsam or pine needles, dried

1 cup rosebuds and petals, red or pink

1 cup cedar chips

1/2 cup oakmoss

10 drops Christmas pine oil

Place all of the ingredients in a large jar and mix well. Cover and store in a dark place for 2 weeks. Remove and place in plastic bags and tie with red ribbon for Christmas Gifts.

—Hartman's Herb Farm catalog, Barre, Massachusetts

Lyness, Dody. *Potpourri . . . Easy as One, Two, Three!* Palos Verdes Peninsula, CA: Berry Hill Press, 1991. This booklet gives good, easy-to-understand information on the basics of potpourris (both dry and moist) from picking and drying the flowers to mixing the ingredients and displaying your creations. Also tells how to make a flower press and pressed flowers, sachets and tinctures, and how to extract essential oils. There are 20 pages of recipes for dry, simmering, no-fixative and moist potpourri blends.

McRae, Bobbi A. *Nature's Dyepot: A Resource Guide for Spinners, Weavers and Dyers.* Austin, TX: Fiberworks Publications, 1991. Tells where to find seeds and plants for natural dyes, many of which are herbs. An A-to-Z chart of potential natural dye plants is included, along with a large annotated bibliography.

Ohrbach, Barbara M. *The Scented Room: Cherchez's Book of Dried Flowers, Fragrance and Potpourri.* New York: Clarkson N. Potter, 1986. This beautiful book begins with six easy recipes for potpourris and instructions for making sachets, pomanders, floral waters, scent pillows, lavender bottles and more. The second part of the book tells how to make flower and herbal wreaths, door bouquets, tussie-mussies and flower arrangements. Gathering, drying and storage techniques are also discussed.

Petalin, Carol. *The Creative Guide to Dried Flowers.* London: Webb & Bower, 1988. Includes some information on drying and preservation techniques. Focuses on different types of arrangements of dried flowers and everlastings such as wedding displays, trees, garlands and swags, holiday arrangements, etc. Colored photo section is helpful for identifying dried flowers.

Pulleyn, Rob. *The Wreath Book.* Asheville, NC: Lark, 1988. Describes more than 100 types of unusual wreaths from traditional to contemporary—kitchen wreaths, scented herbal wreaths, moth-repellent wreaths, an edible wreath and more. Illustrated in color.

Pulleyn, Rob, and Claudette Mautor. *Everlasting Floral Gifts.* Asheville, NC: Lark, 1991. More than 100 projects with how-to instructions for wreaths, bouquets, evergreen garlands, scented stationery, pressed flower gift tags and more together with information on the language of flowers.

Scobey, Joan, and Norma Myers. *Gifts from Your Garden.* New York: Bobbs Merrill, 1975. Information on harvesting and drying or pressing herbs and flowers; making potpourri (with recipes), culinary gifts (horehound candy, mint drops, herbal vinegars and jellies, dried herbs) and more.

Silber, Mark and Terry. *The Complete Book of Everlastings—Growing, Drying and Designing with Dried Flowers.* New York: Knopf, 1988. A beautiful, full-color guide to all aspects of growing and using 145 varieties of flowers and plants for drying. Includes information on raising annual and perennial everlastings from seed and designing with everlastings.

Simmons, Adelma Grenier. *Country Wreaths from Caprilands: The Legend, Lore & Design of Traditional Herbal Wreaths*. New York: Wieser & Wieser, 1989. Many ideas and designs for holiday and all-occasion wreaths including Victorian and wedding wreaths, kitchen wreaths and more.

Thorpe, Patricia. *Everlastings: The Complete Book of Dried Flowers*. Boston: Houghton Mifflin, 1986. Information on growing, collecting, drying and using more than 90 different everlastings.

Verhelst, Jeannette. *Everlasting Flowers for Pleasure & Profit*. Radville, SK, Canada: Jeannette Verhelst, 1991. Focuses on growing everlastings from buying seed to harvesting the flowers to preservation techniques. Also discusses flowers suitable for drying and the business aspects of marketing everlasting flowers.

Webb, David W. *Making Potpourri, Colognes and Soaps: 102 Natural Recipes*. Blue Ridge Summit, PA: TAB, 1988. A guide to making floral and other scents, drying flowers and making bouquets, potpourris, sachets, soap, candles, bubble baths, shampoos, perfumes, colognes, toilet waters, aftershaves, deodorants and room fresheners.

Wood, Rob and Lucy. *The Art of Dried Flowers: Inspired Floral and Herbal Wreaths, Bouquets, Garlands and Arrangements for Grand Occasions and Simple Celebrations*. Philadelphia: Running Press, 1991. A complete course in selecting, drying and arranging flowers into arrangements such as garlands, wreaths, and bouquets. Step-by-step instructions are accompanied by full-color photographs of the finished designs.

Publishers & Book Distributors

The American Botanist, Booksellers
Keith Crotz
1103 W. Truitt
PO Box 532
Chillicothe, IL 61523
(309) 274-5254

American Indian Archaeological Institute
Susannah Croasdaile
PO Box 1260
Washington Green, CT 06793-0260
(203) 868-0518

Berry Hill Press
Dody Lyness
7336 Berry Hill–D4
Palos Verdes, CA 90274-4404
(310) 377-7040

Brooklyn Botanic Gardens
1000 Washington Avenue
Brooklyn, NY 11225-1099

California School of Herbal Studies
PO Box 39
Forestville, CA 95436

Marge Clark
Rt. 1, Box 69
West Lebanon, IN 47991

Columbia U. Press
562 W. 113th St.
New York, NY 10025

Crescent Books
(Distributed by Crown Publishers, Inc.)
225 Park Avenue South
New York, NY 10003

The Crossing Press
97 Hangar Way
Watsonville, CA 95076

Crowood Press
Gipsy Lane, Swindon, Wiltshire
England SN2 6DQ

Culinary Arts Ltd.
PO Box 2157
Lake Oswego, OR 97035

Dominion Herbal College
7527 Kingsway
Burnaby, BC
Canada V3N 3C1
(604) 521-5822

Doubleday Books
666 5th Avenue
New York, NY 10103

Dover Publications
31 East 2nd Street
Mineola, NY 11501

Facts on File, Inc.
460 Park Avenue South
New York, NY 10016
(212) 683-2244

Fiberworks Publications
Bobbi A. McRae
PO Box 49770WB
Austin, TX 78765-9770
(512) 343-6112

The Fresh Garlic Association
PO Box 2410
Sausalito, CA 94966-2410

Garden Way Publishing
(See Storey Communications)

Globe Pequot Press, Inc.
138 W. Main
Chester, CT 06412
(203) 526-9571

Goodwin Creek Gardens
Jim or Dotti Becker
PO Box 83
Williams, OR 97544
(503) 488-3308

Gulf Publishing Co.
PO Box 2608
Houston, TX 77252-2608

Healing Arts Press
One Park Street
Rochester, VT 05767

The Herb Bar
Connie Moore
200 West Mary
Austin, TX 78704
(512) 444-6251

The Herb Society of America
Leslie Rascan
9019 Kirtland-Chardon Rd.
Mentor, OH 44060

Houghton Mifflin Co.
One Beacon St.
Boston, MA 02108

Madalene Hill and Gwen Barclay
PO Box 1734
Cleveland, TX 77327-1734
(713) 592-9178

Lucinda Hutson
4612 Rosedale
Austin, TX 78756
(512) 454-8905

Iden Croft Herbs
Rosemary Titterington
Frittenden Rd.
Staplehurst, Kent
England TN12 0DH
Phone: 0580 891 432 or Fax 0580 892416

Inner Traditions International Ltd.
One Park St.
Rochester, VT 05767

Interweave Press
Linda Ligon
201 E. Fourth St.
Loveland, CO 80537
(800) 272-2193 (book orders)

Alfred A. Knopf, Inc.
201 East 50th St.
New York, NY 10022

Lark Books
Nine Press
50 College Street
Asheville, NC 28801

Dry roses put to the nose
to smell do comfort the
Brayne and herte and
quickeneth the
spryte.
—Askham's
Herbal, 1550

Little, Brown & Co.
34 Beason St.
Boston, MA 02108

Macmillan Publishing Co.
Front and Brown Streets
Riverside, NJ 08075

Merco
620 Wyandotte East
Windsor, ON
Canada

Museum of New Mexico Press
PO Box 2087
Santa Fe, NM 87504

Dorry Norris
PO Box 626
Trumansburg, NY 14886
(607) 387-6449

North Atlantic Books
2800 Woolsey St.
Berkeley, CA 94705

George W. Park Seed Co.
Cokesbury Rd.
Greenwood, SC 29647-0001
(800) 845-3369

Pelican Publishing Company
1101 Monroe Street
PO Box 189
Gretna, LA 70053
(504) 368-1175

Penguin USA
PO Box 120
Bergenfield, NJ 07621-0120

Pine Creek Herbs
Kathleen Gips
152 S. Main Street
Chagrin Falls, OH 44022

Pineapple Press
PO Drawer 16008
Sarasota, FL 34239
(813) 952-1085

P.L.A.N. Publishers
Deb Carpenter
HC 81, Box 88
Rushville, NE 69360
(308) 327-2064

Clarkson N. Potter
201 E. 50th St.
New York, NY 10022

Leanna Potts
717 Glenview
Joplin, MO 64801

Prentice-Hall, Inc.
Englewood Cliffs
New Jersey 07632

Random House
225 Park Avenue South
New York, NY 10003

Ransom Hill
KJ's Books
Kathy Emmerson
1109 Gem Lane
Ramona, CA 92065
(619) 789-2715

Reader's Digest Association, Inc.
Pleasantville, NY 10570

Rodale Press
33 E. Minor
Emmaus, PA 18098
(215) 967-5171

Jeanne Rose Herbal Studies Course
219 Carl Street
San Francisco, CA 94117

Running Press Publishers
125 S. 22nd St.
Philadelphia, PA 19103

San Juan Naturals
Lee Sturdivant
PO Box 642
Friday Harbor, WA 98250
(206) 378-2648

Shepherd's Garden Publishing
Renee Shepherd
7389 West Zayante Rd.
Felton, CA 95018
(408) 335-5400

Stackpole Books
Donna E. Pope
PO Box 1831
Harrisburg, PA 17112
(717) 234-5041

Sterling Publishing Co.
387 Park Ave. S.
New York, NY 10016

Storey Communications
(Garden Way Publishing)
Liz Z. LaForte
Schoolhouse Rd.
Pownal, VT 05261
(802) 823-5811

Surrey Books
230 East Ohio St., Suite 120
Chicago, IL 60611
(800) 326-4430

TAB Books, Inc.
Blue Ridge Summit, PA 17214-9988

Taylor Publishing Co.
1550 W. Mockingbird Ln.
Dallas, TX 75235

Texas Gardener Press
Suntex Communications, Inc.
Box 9005
Waco, TX 76714
(817) 772-1270

Michael and Lesley Tierra
PO Box 712, Box HC
Santa Cruz, CA 95060
(408) 429-8066

Timber Press, Inc.
9999 SW Wilshire
Portland, OR 97225
(503) 292-0745

The Unicorn Books for Craftsmen
1338 Ross Street
Petaluma, CA 94954-6502
(707) 762-3362
(distributor for Select Books)

Unipub
4611-F Assembly Drive
Lanham, MD 20706-4391

University of Arizona Press
1230 N. Park Avenue, No. 102
Tucson, AZ 85719
(602) 621-1441

University of Oklahoma Press
PO Box 787
Norman, OK 73070-0787
(405) 325-2000

University of Texas Press
PO Box 7819
Austin, TX 78713-7819

University Press of New England
17½ Lebanon St.
Hanover, NH 03755
(603) 646-3349

Jeannette Verhelst
Country Green
PO Box 178
Radville, SK
Canada S0C 2G0
(306) 869-2907

Viking Penguin, Inc.
40 W. 23rd St.
New York, NY 10010

Waterfront Press
52 Maple Ave.
Maplewood, NJ 07040

Woodbridge Press
PO Box 6189
Santa Barbara, California
(800) 237-6053

Workman Publishing Co.
708 Broadway
New York, NY 10003

Yankee Books
PO Box 1248
Camden, ME 04843
(207) 236-0933

Growing mint in your garden will supposedly attract money to your purse.

5

Mail-Order Booksellers

THESE SUPPLIERS CARRY ALL SORTS of books on herbs—cookbooks, gardening books, reference books, craft books, medicinal guides—you name it! Some specialize in out-of-print or rare books, while others sell new or used books. Many of the suppliers in Chapters 1 and 2 also sell books, but may not have as large a selection as these companies.

Abundant Life Seed Foundation

Forest Shomer
PO Box 772
Port Townsend, WA 98368

(206) 385-5660
Established 1975
Mail order; wholesale; retail; public garden
Catalog $1.00

As aromatic plants bestow
No spicy fragrance
    while they grow,
But crush'd or trodden
    to the ground,
Diffuse their balmy
    sweets around.

—Oliver Goldsmith

In addition to its many seeds (see listing in Chapter 1), the Abundant Life Seed Foundation carries many books on herbs, seed growing and collecting, plant and flower craft, food preparation and processing, health and healing, plant identification and use, garden design, biodynamics, trees. Children's books and reference and resource guides are also available here.

agAccess

Jeffrey Harpain
PO Box 2008
Davis, CA 95617

(916) 756-7177
Established 1984
Mail order; retail
Catalog free

agAccess offers the widest selection of agricultural and horticultural books, computer programs and videotapes available from a single source. The agAccess book catalog contains technical references as well as popular titles on agriculture, horticulture, gardening, pest management, water, soil and landscaping. The company sells every agricultural and horticultural book in print and is happy to search for out-of-print books for customers. Computerized book searches for any crop, region, professional interest or title are also available.

The agAcess retail bookstore, located at 603 Fourth St. in Davis, California, stocks thousands of new, used and rare horticultural and agricultural titles. (Also see listing in Chapter 10.)

Alloway Gardens & Herb Farm

Barbara Steele
456 Mud College Rd.
Littlestown, PA 17340

(717) 359-4548 or 359-4363
Established 1984
Mail order; retail
Newsletter $1.00

Barbara Steele of Alloway Gardens & Herb Farm has written, published and edited several books and booklets on herbs. Four booklets are *Potpourri Pleasantries*, *Holiday Herbal Hints*, *Summer Kitchen Herbal Luncheons*, and *Thymely Tips—Cooking with Herbs*. These are $1.75 each. Also available is a booklet titled *Lovely Lavender* ($5.00 + $1.50 postage) and a larger cookbook, *When the Dinner Bell Rings* by Ellie Bennett and Marlene Lufriu ($9.75 + $2.00 postage).

The American Botanist, Booksellers

Keith Crotz
1103 W. Truitt
PO Box 532
Chillicothe, IL 61523

(309) 274-5254
Established 1983
Catalog $5.00; refundable with purchase

The American Botanist, Booksellers, specialize in garden history, herbals, horticulture and landscape architecture. They carry hundreds of old, rare and out-of-print books and publish several garden book classics such as Fearing Burr's *Field and Garden Vegetables of America* (see Chapter 4) and *Gardening for Profit* by Peter Henderson. This company also offers a book appraisal service; call for details.

American Indian Archaeological Institute

Susannah Croasdaile
PO Box 1260
Washington Green, CT 06793-0260

(203) 868-0518
Established 1975
Mail order; wholesale; retail
Brochure SASE

The goal of the AIAI is to research, preserve and share American Indian history and culture through education. *Native Harvests—Recipes and Botanicals of the American Indian* by Barrie Kavasch is available from this source. The retail store has a selection of about 600 books.

American Spice Trade Association, Inc.

Peter Furth
580 Sylvan Ave.
Englewood Cliffs, NJ 07632-3173

(201) 568-2163
Established 1907
Price list SASE

The American Spice Trade Association is a nonprofit organization that provides information on various spices in the form of audiovisual presentations, technical manuals, article reprints, general interest literature, recipe leaflets, charts and brochures—all at very reasonable prices.

Ayer Company Publishers, Inc.

Jeanne Frazier
PO Box 958
Salem, NH 03079-0958

(603) 898-1200
Established 1982
Mail order; retail
Catalog free

Ayer Company Publishers offer books on a variety of subjects by mail order including five by Gertrude Jekyll: *Wood and Garden, Wall and Water Gardens, Colour Schemes for the Flower Garden, Roses* and *Lilies.*

Brooklyn Botanic Garden

Order Department
1000 Washington Ave.
Brooklyn, NY 11225-1099

(718) 622-4433
Established 1910
Write for book list.

The Brooklyn Botanic Garden's handbooks in the Plants & Gardens series are each devoted to a single subject (including bonsai, herbs, roses and bulbs). New books are issued quarterly. Titles of interest to herb lovers include *Culinary Herbs* (#98), *Herbs & Cooking* (#122), *Herbs & Their Ornamental Uses* (#68), and *Oriental Herbs and Vegetables* (#101). Several short gardening videos are also offered.

Brooks Books

Philip & Martha Nesty
1343 New Hampshire Dr.
Concord, CA 94521-3804

(510) 672-4566
Established 1986
Mail order; retail by appointment
Catalog $1.00; refundable with order

Brooks Books specializes in new and used books on botany and ornamental horticulture. A recent catalog lists 501 books but these represent only a fraction of the 3000+ books that the Nestys have in stock.

They try to maintain a good selection of books on herbs and feature them occasionally in a special section of the catalog. The catalogs are issued about three times per year.

Buckeye Naturopathic Press
Karen Echard
623 Neely Manor Blvd.
East Palestine, OH 44413-1650

(216) 426-2600
Established 1988
Brochure free

Buckeye Naturopathic Press publishes books on the history and practice of naturopathic medicine with special emphasis on homeopathy, botanical medicine and hydrotherapy. Two of Buckeye's recent titles are *Herb Doctors* and *Official Herbs, Botanical Substances in the USP: 1820–1990,* both by Wade Boyle, ND.

Calendula
PO Box 930
Picton, ON
Canada K0K 2T0

(613) 476-3521
Established 1987
Catalog free

Calendula specializes strictly in out-of-print and old books on gardening, floriculture, and botany.

Capability's Books, Inc.
Paulette Rickard
2379 Highway 46
Deer Park, WI 54007-7506

(800) 247-8154
Established 1978
Mail order; retail
Catalog free

Capability's Books carries every book on gardening in print. The annual catalog includes books on annuals, arranging and decorating with flowers, bamboos, bats, begonias, birds, botanical illustration, bulbs, container gardening, daylilies, everlastings, ferns, foliage, fragrance, garden plans, geraniums, greenhouses, herbs, hydroponics, landscaping . . . get the idea? As new books are published, they are listed in periodic catalog updates. If, by chance, a book that you want is not listed in the catalog, be assured that special orders are welcomed.

The Cookbook Cottage
Stephen Lee
1279 Bardstown Rd.
Louisville, KY 40204

(502) 458-5227
Established 1986
Mail order; retail
Catalog $3.00

The Cookbook Cottage offers out-of-print herb and gardening books and new and old herb cookery books. Mr. Lee also offers a number of cooking classes through the Cookbook Cottage.

Country Herbs & Flowers
Mary Ann Ireland
RD #7, Box 164, County Rt. 8
Fulton, NY 13069

(315) 593-6683
Established 1989
Call or write for further information.

Mary Ann Ireland of Country Herbs & Flowers has written and published a set of informative booklets titled *Herbs To Know & Grow, A Guide to Hardy Perennials and a Perennial Plant List.* The booklets are currently $2.00 each. Although Ms. Ireland doesn't sell other products by mail order, she sells dried packaged herbs and spices and dried floral material in her retail shop.

Country Thyme Gazette

Theresa Loe
PO Box 3090
El Segundo, CA 90245

(213) 322-6026
Book catalog $1.00; newsletter information for SASE

In addition to publishing the *Country Thyme Gazette* newsletter, Theresa Loe also offers a number of books by mail order on such subjects as herbal lore and cookery, gardening and crafts from the garden.

Fiberworks Publications

Bobbi A. McRae
PO Box 49770WB
Austin, TX 78765-9770

(512) 343-6112
Established 1981
Mail order; wholesale
Catalog $2.00

Fiberworks Publications is owned by Bobbi A. McRae, the author of *The Herb Companion Wishbook & Resource Guide*. Other books available from Ms. McRae include *Nature's Dyepot: A Resource Guide for Spinners, Weavers & Dyers* (sources for hard-to-find natural dyes, seeds and plants) and other books on natural dyeing, herbs and the fiber arts.

Garden Way Publishing

(See listing for "Storey's Books for Country Living")

Gardeners Bookshelf

Don Simons, Manager
PO Box 16416
Hooksett, NH 03106-6416

(603) 268-0461
Mail order
Catalog free

Gardeners Bookshelf offers more than 1200 titles on gardening and horticulture, nature and bird feeding/watching. Among the gardening books are a large number on herbs, dried flowers, wreaths, and potpourri. Gardeners Bookshelf pays shipping and handling charges on all orders of $40.00 and above, and also offers free books or discounts on larger orders.

Great Lakes Herb Company

Ron Holch
PO Box 6713
Minneapolis, MN 55406

(612) 722-1201
Established 1988
Mail order; wholesale; retail
Catalog $1.00

In addition to thousands of herbal products (see listings in Chapters 1 and 2), Great Lakes Herb Company carries a number of books specializing in natural health and healing with herbs.

Greenfield Herb Garden

Arlene Shannon
1135 Woodbine
Oak Park, IL 60302

(219) 768-7110
Established 1980
Mail order; wholesale; retail; public garden
Catalog $1.50

In addition to a large number of herbal products (see listing in Chapter 2), Arlene Shannon also carries more than 300 books on herbs and herb gardening in her catalog.

If a Footman take mugwort and put it into his shoes in the morning, he may goe forty miles before Noon and not be weary.

—William Coles in *The Art of Simpling*, 1656

Harvest Harmony

Denise Rosalia
PO Box 326
Ridge, NY 11961

(516) 924-1772
Established 1990
Mail order
Catalog $3.00

Harvest Harmony is "your complete source of herbal reference" materials—books, videos, posters and calendars.

Kendall/Hunt Publishing Company

Mariel Damaskin
6869 Woodlawn Avenue NE, #114
Seattle, WA 98115

(206) 523-5820
Flyer free

The Kendall/Hunt Publishing Company offers *The Herbal Desk Reference* by F. Joseph Montagna, editor.

KJ's Books

Kathy Emmerson
1109 Gem Lane
Ramona, CA 92065

(619) 789-2715 or (800) 332-8727
Established 1991
Catalog free

KJ's Books (formerly Ransom Hill Press) carries a number of hard-to-find herb books on cooking and diet, stress and cultivation. Also listed in the current catalog are herb books in Spanish, Oriental books, gift books and general gardening books.

Ladybug Press

Lane Furneaux
7348 Lane Park Court
Dallas, TX 75225-2468

(214) 368-4235
Established 1985

Lane Furneaux (also see listing in Chapter 10) has written and published a booklet titled *Heavenly Herbs—Enjoy Them!* Available for $6.95 + $1.05 shipping (Texans add tax), the booklet is filled with herbal tips, delicious recipes and cute illustrations. The booklet can be ordered with covers in various colors.

Laurelbrook Book Services

Doug Paton
5468 Dundas St. West, #600
Toronto, ON
Canada M9B 6E3

(416) 234-6811
Established 1988
Catalog $2.00; refundable with purchase

Laurelbrook Book Services sells new and hard-to-find books on all aspects of gardening including annuals, bulbs, dictionaries and encyclopedias, ground covers, herbs, landscaping, perennials, propagation, roses, seeds, weeds, wildflowers and more.

Meyerbooks, Publisher

Anita L. Meyer
PO Box 427
Glenwood, IL 60425-0427

(708) 757-4950
Established 1976
Mail order; wholesale; retail
Catalog $.50

Meyerbooks offers a number of hard-to-find books on herbs, including many published by Meyerbooks. Among these are *The Herbalist* by Joseph E. Meyer, *The Herbalist Almanac* and *American Folk Medicine* by Clarence Meyer and *The Old Herb Doctor* by Joseph E. Meyer.

Northwind Farm Publications

Paula and David Oliver
Rt. 2, Box 246
Shevlin, MN 56676

(218) 657-2478
Established 1983
Mail order
Brochures for SASE

Northwind Farm Publications offers an extensive list of new herb books for sale by mail order. Also see *The Business of Herbs* in Chapter 3.

Pomona Book Exchange

Mrs. Walda Janson
Rockton PO
Rockton, ON
Canada L0R 1X0

(519) 621-8897
Established 1951
Mail order
Catalog $1.00; includes 1-year subscription

The Pomona Book Exchange offers out-of-print, new and rare books on horticulture, agriculture, natural history, botany and related subjects. Mrs. Janson will purchase libraries, collections or single books on these subjects, and can appraise books for individuals for insurance or estate purposes. Write or call her for further details.

ProNatura, Inc.

Andranik Mehrabian
7616 Lindley Ave., #9
Reseda, CA 91335

(818) 706-0147
Established 1985
Mail order; importer
Catalog free

ProNatura distributes a number of books on herbal health and medicine including Maria Treben's *Health through God's Pharmacy* (available in Spanish, French and German), *The Family Herbal* by Barbara and Peter Theiss, and *Cures* by Maria Treben.

Jeanne Rose

219 Carl Street
San Francisco, CA 94117

(415) 564-6785 (leave message);
FAX (415) 564-6799
Established 1978
Mail order; wholesale; retail
Catalog $2.50; includes gift

Jeanne Rose is a nationally known medical herbalist with a private health consulting practice, an international author, an aromatherapy expert and a lecturer on "all things herbal". She has been called the "grande dame" of the herbal movement and has studied medical herbology and botanical pharmacy for more than 25 years. Ms. Rose is the author of *Herbs & Things* (1969), *The Herbal Body Book* (1976), *Kitchen Cosmetics* (1978), *The Herbal Guide to Inner Health* (1989), *The Modern Herbal* (1987), *The Herbal Studies Course* (1981 and 1988) and *The History of Herbs and Herbalism* (1981). All are available from her at the address above.

Second Life Books, Inc.

Russell Freedman
PO Box 242
Lanesborough, MA 01237

(413) 447-8010
Established 1972
Mail order; retail by appointment
Catalog $1.00

Second Life Books is a good source for used and rare books (from the 16th to the 20th centuries) on Americana, agriculture and horticulture.

Secret Garden Book Source

Vickie Haushild
6306 Mt. Tacoma Dr. SW (at Lakewood Garden & Pet Center)
Tacoma, WA 98499

(206) 584-7898 or 759-8891
Established 1989
Mail order; retail
Write or call for further information.

Vickie Haushild will bring a selection of garden books to your group or club meeting, display them, give a short program, offer the books for sale and donate 10% of the total sale to your group's treasury. Books may also be ordered by mail postage paid, but the 10% donation does not apply.

Sequoyah Gardens

Betty Wold
Rt. 1, Box 80
Gore, OK 74435

(918) 487-5849
Established 1981
Write for more information.

Betty Wold of Sequoyah Gardens has written and published *Speaking of Herbs: Ten Introductory Programs for Speakers*. The spiral-bound book is dedicated to "the thousands of budget minded club officers who must arrange for six to twelve programs annually. Plus, useful tips to calm the fears of the inexperienced, nervous speaker."

Each program is followed by Notes, Bibliography and an herbal craft or recipe to try. The book is $12.95 + $1.50 postage and handling.

The Spencer Book Shop

David Carter
RR #2, Box 143
Spencer, IN 47460

Mail order
Book list for SASE

David Carter offers a huge selection of herb and gardening books by mail order, postage paid.

Stackpole Books

Donna E. Pope
PO Box 1831
Harrisburg, PA 17112

(717) 234-5041
Established 1930
Mail order; wholesale; retail
Catalog $3.00

Stackpole Books publishes a number of books on nature, plants, gardening, fishing, hobbies and crafts.

Storey Communications

(Garden Way Publishing)
Liz Z. LaForte
Schoolhouse Rd.
Pownal, VT 05261

(802) 823-5811
Established 1973
Mail order; wholesale; retail
Catalog free

Storey's Books for Country Living catalog features books on gardening, country skills, crafts, nature and cooking. Many herb books published by Storey Communications are listed, including Phyllis Shaudys's *Pleasure of Herbs* and *Herbal Treasures*, Gail Duff's *Natural Fragrances* and Betty Jacobs's *Growing & Using Herbs Successfully*. *Country Wisdom Bulletins* published by Storey include titles on *Making Liqueurs for Gifts*, *Jams, Jellies & Preserves*, and *Salt-Free Herb Cookery*. Storey also operates a bookstore for damaged books at 1476 Massachusetts Ave., North Adams, MA 01247.

TMI Books

Garth Hartland
PO Box 316
Johnson City, NY 13790-0316

(607) 729-2034
Established 1991
Mail order
Catalog free

TMI Books offers new books at prices at least 15% below the publisher's list price, with additional discounts for volume orders. TMI carries an extensive list of gardening books, including some on herbs.

T. M. Taylor Company

Ted Taylor
PO Box 500544
Malabar, FL 32905

(800) 927-3084
Established 1991
Mail order; wholesale
Brochure for SASE

Ted Taylor offers the 135-page manual *Secrets to a Successful Greenhouse Business and Other Profitable Horticultural Projects* for $19.95 + $2.00 shipping.

Vileniki—An Herb Farm

Gerry Janus
RD #1, Box 345
Olyphant, PA 18447

(717) 254-9895
Established 1979
Mail order; retail
Book catalog $2.00; plant catalog $1.50; both refundable with order

In addition to herb plants, Vileniki also offers a huge listing of books on Chinese and Oriental herbs, culinary herbs and food, herb gardening and cultivation, medicinal herbs, herbal reference, herb teas, Native American herbs and edible and useful wild herbs. Five videos on herbs.

Western Reserve Herb Society

Jenifer P. Richter, Chairman
11030 East Blvd.
Cleveland, OH 44106

(216) 871-0294
Established 1942
Mail order
Write for more information.

The Western Reserve Herb Society has published a series of five cookbooks including *Herbs, A Cookbook and More* ($7.50 + $2.00 postage) and *Cooking with Herb Scents* ($16.95 + $2.50 postage). Write for further information.

Henry VIII's favorite perfume was a mixture of rosewater and oil of roses mixed with musk and ambergris—he didn't buy it for his women, he wore it himself!

The Wine and Food Library

Jan Longone
1207 W. Madison St.
Ann Arbor, MI 48103

(313) 663-4894
Established 1973
Mail order; retail by appointment
Catalog $3.00

The Wine and Food Library is a bookshop devoted to the old, rare, interesting, unusual and out-of-print books on "all matters culinary, gastronomic and oenological"—I had to look it up, too; it means "pertaining to wine or winemaking". Ms. Longone stocks about 15,000 books and will conduct book searches for her customers. She also will do book and library collection development and appraisal.

Wood Violet Books

Debbie Cravens
3814 Sunhill Drive
Madison, WI 53704-6283

(608) 837-7207
Established 1984
Mail order; retail by appointment
Catalog $1.00; refundable with purchase

Debbie Cravens carries a large assortment of books on gardening, horticulture and herbs in her catalog.

Elisabeth Woodburn, Books

Ms. Bradford G. Lyon
Booknoll Farm
PO Box 398
Hopewell, NJ 08525-0398

(609) 466-0522
Established 1946
Mail order; retail by appointment only
Catalogs ($2.50 each) are issued on various subject areas. Send an SASE for listing of available catalogs before ordering.

Elisabeth Woodburn, Books is a good source for both old and new books on horticulture, landscape gardening, herbs and early farming techniques. Ms. Lyon also offers a free horticultural book search service for her customers.

6

Educational Opportunities

THIS CHAPTER LISTS HERB SUPPLIERS who sponsor classes and workshops. You'll find classes in medicinal herbs, herbal crafts, herb gardening—almost any subject you'd care to learn about. It also includes sources for educational herb videos, correspondence schools and several specialty libraries with herb book collections.

Classes/ Workshops

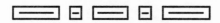

Akin' Back Farm & Gifts of Thyme

Joe and Sybil Kunkel
2501 Hwy. 53 S.
La Grange, KY 40031-9535

(502) 222-5791
Established 1986
Retail; public garden

Joe and Sybil Kunkel offer a number of classes and workshops at their Akin' Back Farm. Some of these are Planning an Herb Garden, Topiary Design with Dried Flowers, Preserving Flowers, and Making a Dried Wreath.

The Kunkels have a number of herb gardens open to the public at their farm. Their retail shop, Gifts of Thyme, specializes in herbal products, original everlasting and herbal designs, gifts and a large number of books.

Alloway Gardens & Herb Farm

Barbara Steele
456 Mud College Rd.
Littlestown, PA 17340

(717) 359-4548 or 359-4363
Established 1984
Retail
Newsletter $1.00

Alloway Gardens offers a number of spring and summer classes at the farm. These include Beginning Your Herb Garden, Everlastings for Fun and Profit, Topiary Workshop, Culinary Herbs, Lovely Lavender, Making an Herb Wreath for the Kitchen and more. Several publications are also available from Alloway Gardens;

see Chapter 5 for listing. Plants and other herb products are available for sale at the retail location.

Alpine Herb Farm

Linda Quintana
6375 Rutsatz Rd.
Deming, WA 98244

(206) 592-5943
Established 1980
Retail
Class schedule for SASE

Linda Quintana offers a number of classes at the Alpine Herb Farm: Herbs for Women, Herbal Spring Tonics, Household Herbs, Planning and Growing an Herb Garden and more.

Antique Rose Emporium

Mike Shoup
Rt. 5, Box 143
Brenham, TX 77833

(409) 836-4293
Established 1983
Mail order; wholesale; retail
Catalog $5.00; includes newsletter subscription which lists activities at the Emporium Retail Center

The Retail Center at the Antique Rose Emporium includes a gift shop (Trellises and Treasures) and is a focus for seminars and lectures throughout the year on the history and cultivation of old roses. A Fall Festival of Roses is held on the first weekend of November each year. (Also see listing in Chapter 1.)

Apothecary Rose Shed

Shawn Schultz
PO Box 194
Pattersonville, NY 12137

(518) 887-2035
Established 1987
Catalog $1.00

Shawn Schultz offers classes on Cooking with Herbs, Dried Flowers and Everlastings, Wreathmaking, Healing with Herbs, Fragrance Crafting and others at the Apothecary Rose Shed.

Back of the Beyond

Bill and Shash Georgi
7233 Lower E. Hill Rd.
Colden, NY 14033

(716) 652-0427
Established 1983
Brochures $.75

Shash Georgi offers a number of herbal lectures, classes, mini-courses and garden tours throughout the year stressing the organic method of growing and using herbs. Back of the Beyond is also a Bed & Breakfast (see listing in Chapter 10).

Bellwether Herbs & Flowers

Gail Ingraham
Rt. 2, Box 210 Shady Lane Rd.
Suttons Bay, MI 49682

(616) 271-3004
Established 1986
Retail; public garden
Class schedule for SASE

Gail Ingraham offers a variety of workshops including Growing and Using Herbs, The Victorian Nosegay, and Garden Inspiration and Ideas. Gail also has a large selection of herbs and perennials for sale at the farm. Gardeners who live in the Grand Traverse Bay area will be interested in the handy "Bellwether Bloom Chart" (currently $6.50), a graphical listing of the bloom dates for 184 perennials grown at Bellwether in 1990.

Berkshire Botanical Garden

Joseph G. Strauch
PO Box 826
(Rts. 102 and 183)
Stockbridge, MA 01262

(413) 298-3926
Established 1934
Write or call for information and calendar.

The Berkshire Botanical Garden offers monthly herb workshops from June through August. Each workshop focuses on one or several herbs, their care and uses and includes a luncheon featuring them. The volunteer Herb Associates meet weekly to grow, harvest and prepare herbs; they welcome new members interested in learning more about herbs. Winter workshops at the Garden have included bonsai, wreathmaking and topiary. (Also see listing in Chapter 8.)

Bittersweet

Stephanie Berk
4033 Skippack Pike
PO Box 432
Skippack, PA 19474

(215) 584-5888
Established 1976
Retail; public garden
Schedule for SASE

Stephanie Berk sponsors a Spring Herb Seminar at Bittersweet each year on Saturday mornings from March through May. Preregistration required.

Bluejay Gardens Herb Farm

Viola Jay
Rt. 2, Box 196
Haskell, OK 74436

(918) 482-3465
Established 1981
Mail order; wholesale; retail; public garden
Catalog $1.00; refundable with purchase

Viola Jay of Bluejay Gardens offers a good listing of herbal crafting classes: Wreathmaking, Making Herbal Garlands, Herbal Thanksgiving or Christmas Arrangements, Making Victorian Sprays and others.

Ms. Jay specializes in planning herbal weddings. Bluejay Gardens also offers herb plants for sale (see Chapter 1).

You can use a clear soda straw to reinforce long stems of cut flowers or herbs for arrangements. When the arrangement is finished, the straws will hardly be noticeable.

Boerner Botanical Gardens

5879 S. 92nd St.
Hales Corners, WI 53130

(414) 425-1130
Established 1930
Public garden
Write or call for further information.

A number of workshops and classes are held at the Boerner Gardens each year. Classes on herbs have included Windowsill Herb Gardening, Herbal Gifts from your Garden, Braided Herbal Swags and Herbal Wreaths. (Also see listing in Chapter 8.)

Brooklyn Botanic Garden

Education Department
1000 Washington Ave.
Brooklyn, NY 11225-1099

(718) 622-4433
Established 1910
Call for schedule of classes.

The Brooklyn Botanic Garden offers courses in botany and related horticultural arts for children and adults as well as public and family programs. The workshops include Natural Pest Control, Perennials in the Landscape, Making a Living Herbal Wreath, A Saturday Afternoon (Herbal) Tea Party and Preserving Flowers and Foliage. (Also see listing in Chapter 8.)

Brookville Gardens

Cindy Brautigan
7885 Brookville Rd.
Plymouth, MI 48170

(313) 455-8602
Established 1982
Catalog $2.00; refundable with purchase

Cindy Brautigan of Brookville Gardens offers a number of interesting classes and workshops from April through December. They include Planting a Strawberry Jar with Herbs, Harvesting & Preserving Culinary & Fragrant Herbs, Cooking with Basil, Make a Culinary Wreath and Make a Grapevine Cornucopia.

Buffalo Springs Herb Farm

Don Haynie
Rt. 1, Box 476
Raphine, VA 24472

(703) 348-1083
Established 1991
SASE for current class schedule

The Buffalo Springs Herb Farm sponsors a number of "herbal happenings" throughout the season (August 1 through December 15). Some of these include Sunday teas, a holiday house tour, herbal luncheons and workshops on Arranging with Fresh Herbs, Making Dried Wreaths, Making a Tussie Mussie Nosegay and others. The retail shop on the premises offers a wide selection of herbal products and garden accessories.

Bulloch Hall Historical Site

Nancy Rittenburg
180 Bulloch Ave.
Roswell, GA 30075

(404) 992-1731 or 993-8137
Established 1984 (recreated garden)
Write for more information.

The Bulloch Hall Historical Site offers classes in gardening, making tussie-mussies, and heritage crafts (soap, candles, etc.), landscape design, soil preparation, and growing and cooking with herbs.

Busha's Brae Herb Farm

Dixie Stephen
Rt. 1, Box 232M
Setterbo Rd.
Suttons Bay, MI 49682

(616) 271-6284
Established 1985
Mail order; wholesale; retail; public garden
Brochure free

In addition to fresh cut herbs, seasonings and herbal products (see listings in Chapters 2 and 8), Busha's Brae offers a variety of programs to individuals and groups. Lectures and seminars given at the farm include Herb Butters and Spreads, Cooking with Herbs, Designing a Culinary Wreath and Designing an Advent Wreath. Ms. Stephen will also travel to other locations and lecture on The Herbs and Flowers of Shakespeare, The Herbs of Christmas, Cultivation of Herbs, Building and Using a Drying Facility (for commercial growers) and Developing Food Products for Retail and Wholesale Production (also for commercial producers).

Butterfly Hill Herbary

Virginia Esposito
PO Box 635
Pine Bush, NY 12566-9611

(914) 744-3040
Established 1987
Write for class schedule and more information.

Butterfly Hill Herbary offers classes and workshops on beginning a herb garden, natural pet care, spring tonics, herbal baths/lotions/shampoos, and cooking with herbs. Children's workshops are also offered, and a quarterly newsletter, *Thymely Advice*, is available.

Caprilands Herb Farm

Darlene Lee
534 Silver St.
Coventry, CT 06238

(203) 742-7244
Established 1953
Mail order; public garden; retail
Catalog free

A number of workshops, special programs and classes are available at Caprilands Herb Farm. Check the catalog for a current schedule. (Also see listings in Chapters 2 and 8.)

Cats in the Cradle

Christine Wittmann
Rt. 140
Alton, NH 03809

(603) 875-7284
Established 1988
Schedule for SASE

Christine Wittmann offers several workshops at Cats in the Cradle each season. Some of these are Herbal Salve Making, Planning an Herbal Tea Garden and Herbal Soap Making. A gift shop (open May through December) carries potted herbs, dried botanicals, herbal salves, tinctures and soaps, books, wreaths, potpourri and more.

Cedarbrook Herb Farm

Terry and Toni Anderson
986 Sequim Ave. S.
Sequim, WA 98382

(206) 683-7733
Established 1968
Mail order; retail; public garden
Catalog $1.00

Interesting herb classes offered at Cedarbrook Herb Farm from March through November include Herb Lore and the Tussie-Mussie, Everlastings, Making a Lavender Wand, Making a Garlic Braid and Bundle and many wreathmaking classes.

Cherry Valley Herb Farm

Susan Carpenter
969 Snake Hill Rd.
N. Scituate, RI 02857

(401) 568-8585
Established 1987
Public garden; retail
Write for more information.

Susan Carpenter offers workshops throughout the season including Growing Everlastings, Vinegar Making, Coil Basketry, Introduction to Herb Gardening, and Making Pressed Flowers and Herbs. Susan also offers custom-made pressed flower wedding invitations.

Clark's Greenhouse & Herbal Country

Wilma Clark
RR 1, Box 15B
San Jose, IL 62682

(309) 247-3679
Established 1985
Mail order; wholesale; retail; public garden
Catalog $1.00; refundable with order

Wilma Clark offers classes and workshops at her greenhouse such as Making Spring Baskets; Making Spring Hats; Planning an Herb, Everlasting and Perennial Garden; and Planting a Container Herb Garden. (Also see listings in Chapters 1 and 8.)

Cornell Plantations

Robison York State Herb Garden
1 Plantations Rd.
Ithaca, NY 14850-2799

(607) 255-3020
Public garden; gift shop
Write or call for current schedule.

Cornell Plantations offers a number of workshops and classes throughout the year. A recent schedule listed classes on gardening, wildflowers, ikebana, plants and their native American uses and more. (Also see listing in Chapter 8.)

Country Green

Jeannette Verhelst
PO Box 178
Radville, SK
Canada S0C 2G0

(306) 869-2907
Established 1984
Brochure for SASE

Jeannette Verhelst of Country Green offers a number of workshops throughout the year. These include Creating a Topiary, Making a Living Wreath, Making a Christmas Swag, Decorating a Summer Hat and others.

Ms. Verhelst is the author of *Everlasting Flowers for Pleasure and Profit* (see Chapter 4), which is currently available from the address above for $6.95 + $2.00 postage and handling (U.S. funds).

Country Road Herb Farm & Gift Barn

Joeann Hudspath
1497 Pymatuning Lake Rd.
Andover, OH 44003

(216) 577-1932
Established 1986
Mail order; wholesale; retail; public garden
Catalog $2.00

Joeann Hudspath's classes at the Country Road Herb Farm have included free medicinal and culinary lectures on Growing and Harvesting Your Herb Garden, Medicinal History of Herbs, Homeopathy Explained and Culinary Magic.

Ms. Hudspath also offers medicinal and culinary herbal consultations. Write or call for further information.

The Country Shepherd

Dell Ratcliffe
Rt. 1, Box 107
Comer, GA 30629

(404) 783-5923
Established 1986
Mail order; retail; public garden
Catalog $1.00

Dell Ratcliffe of The Country Shepherd offers classes throughout the year. A few are Cooking with Herbs, Growing Herbs for Crafting and Introduction to Herb Gardening.

Desert Botanical Garden

Mary Ann Fox and Mary Irish
1201 N. Galvin Pkwy.
Phoenix, AZ 85008

(602) 948-2069
Established 1937
Write or call for current schedule.

The Desert Botanical Garden offers classes throughout the year. They include Flower Pressing and Crafts, Pine Needle Basketry, Desert Spring Edibles, Wall Basket Workshop and Wildflower and Landscape Photography Workshop.

Dreams End Farm

Pat Jenney
8655 Feddick Rd.
Hamburg, NY 14075

(716) 941-3330
Established 1980
Retail; public garden
Class schedule for SASE

Dreams End Farm offers herbal workshops throughout the year. The retail shop is open year-round; call first during the winter months. Ms. Jenney also sponsors annual Spring and Autumn Open Houses at the farm.

ECHO (Eclectic Complementary Health Options)/Healing Heart Herbals

Cindy Parker
2137 Newark-Granville Rd.
Newark, OH 43055

(614) 587-3361
Established 1987
SASE for brochure

Cindy Parker teaches an herbal apprenticeship program and day classes, and leads herb walks both in her garden and in the wild. She sponsors herbal retreats and workshops throughout the year and offers herbal products and booklets through her business, Healing Heart Herbals.

Enchanted Crest

W. Loyd and Carollyn Blackwell
RR #1, Box 216
Belle Rive, IL 62810

(618) 736-2647
Established 1985
Information for SASE

The Enchanted Crest Bed and Breakfast is located in a Victorian mansion that is on the National List of Historic Places. Carollyn Blackwell offers a number of educational workshops including basketmaking, herbal soaps, perfumes and crafts of all kinds. (Also see listing in Chapters 8 and 10.)

England's Herb Farm

Yvonne England
RD #1, Box 706
Honey Brook, PA 19344

(215) 273-2863
Established 1978
Mail order; retail; public garden
Catalog $2.00

Yvonne England offers herbal workshops, lectures and four-week courses at her Herb Farm and at your location. Topics include Herbs: Lore and Legend, Herbal Dyeing, Native American Herbs, Herbs in the Perennial Border, Wreathmaking and others.

The Essential Oil Company

Robert Seidel
PO Box 206
Lake Oswego, OR 97034

(503) 697-5992 or (800) 729-5912
Established 1977

Robert Seidel of The Essential Oil Company (see listing in Chapter 2) offers a six-lesson Aromatherapy Certificate Course. Write or call for details.

The Fragrance Shop

Gail Hayden
RFD 3, Box 476, College Hill Rd.
Hopkinton, NH 03229

(603) 746-4431
Established 1977
Mail order; wholesale; retail; public garden
Catalog free; specify wholesale or retail

Gail Hayden of The Fragrance Shop (also see listing in Chapter 2) offers a large number of workshops at her herb farm including Dried Floral Wedding Creations, Landscaping with Herbs, Designing a Colonial Flower Garden and Making a Colonial Williamsburg Wreath.

Friendship Herb Gardens

Dolly Hanes
3930 McClain Rd.
Lima, OH 45806

(419) 221-3415
Established 1986
Brochure for SASE

Dolly Hanes offers a number of classes and lectures at her Friendship Herb Gardens including Making a Decorated Grapevine Tree, Herbal Landscaping, Making a Williamsburg Table Centerpiece and Herbal Harvest and Potpourris.

Gilbertie's Herb Gardens

Celeste M. and Sal Gilbertie
7 Sylvan Lane
Westport, CT 06880

(203) 227-4175
Established 1969
Retail only
Current schedule for SASE

Gilbertie's Herb Gardens offers a number of workshops, seminars and lectures at their retail store and garden center. Topics include Summer Patio Planting; Decorating with Herbs and Flowers, Fresh and Dried; Fresh Herbal Wreaths and Preparing the Herbal Pantry.

Sal Gilbertie is the author of *Home Gardening at Its Best*, *Herb Gardening at Its Best*, and *Kitchen Herbs*. More than 400 varieties of herb plants are sold at the garden center and are available year round.

Good Scents

Donna Metcalfe
23 South Sixth St.
Redlands, CA 92373

(714) 335-6160
Established 1985
Mail order; wholesale; retail (call for hours)
Catalog $1.00

Donna Metcalfe teaches a number of herb classes and workshops at her retail shop. These include Making Your Own Potpourri, Make a Basket, Tussie-Mussies and the Language of Flowers, Wreathmaking and others.

Green Terrestrial

Pam Montgomery, Herbalist
1651 Rt. 9W
Milton, NY 12547

(914) 795-5238
Established 1986
Mail order
Write for schedule or call for more information.

Pam Montgomery offers herbal apprenticeship programs, workshops and "Women's Weekends" through Green Terrestrial.

Heard's Country Gardens

Mary Lou Heard
14391 Edwards St.
Westminster, CA 92683

(714) 894-2444
Established 1985
Retail; public garden
Write or call for a class schedule.

Mary Lou Heard offers classes throughout the season at Heard's Country Gardens. These include Herbal Oils and Vinegars, Potpourri Workshop, The Art of Pressed Flowers, Making Crystallized Flowers, Herbal Topiaries, Everlastings, Putting Herbs By and Seed Starting.

Heavenly Scent Herb Farm

Kathy Mathews
13730 White Lake Rd.
Fenton, MI 48430

(313) 629-9208
Established 1984
Retail; public garden
Write or call for a current class schedule.

Representative classes offered at Heavenly Scent Herb Farm include Designing an Herb Garden, Making a Willow Wall Basket, Spring Tabletop Arrangements, Designing an Everlasting Garden, Herbal Wall Weaving and Christmas in July. Kathy also has herb plants, topiaries, baskets, scented geraniums and strawberry (herb) jars for sale at the Farm.

The Herb Barn

Nancy Johns
1955 Greenley Ave.
Benton Harbor, MI 49022

(616) 927-2044
Established 1989
Mail order; wholesale; retail; public garden
Catalog $1.00; refundable with purchase

Nancy Johns of The Herb Barn offers a number of interesting classes throughout the year: Pressed Flowers, Discovering the Secret of Youth, Victorian Wreaths, Tussie-Mussies, Making Holiday Swags, Dried Herbal Gardens and Let's Do Topiary are just a few of them.

Nancy offers a unique service—Adopt-a-Garden. You "adopt" an 8' × 8' plot of land at The Herb Barn and all of its herbs, fresh or dried, are yours to enjoy all year. You can participate as much or as little as you want, and can visit your garden any time! Sounds like a great opportunity for those without much space to grow their own herbs! Call or write for more information. (Also see listing in Chapter 2.)

The Herb Cottage

Norma Magneson
3202 Runkie St.
Niles, MI 49120

(616) 663-8952
Established 1980
Retail; classes
Write or call for a current class schedule.

The Herb Cottage offers herb classes and children's nature and gardening classes throughout the year.

Herb Country Gifts & Collectibles

Paula Johnson
63 Leonard St.
Belmont Center, MA 02178

(508) 263-2405
Established 1979
Write or call for more information.

Paula Johnson offers lectures and workshops during the spring and summer at her gardens. These include a Spring Wreath Workshop, a Potted Herb Gardening lecture and a Fresh Mint Wreath and Corsage workshop.

Ms. Johnson is the author of a delightful 40-page booklet, *The Language of Herbs and Their Companions*. It is available for $4.00 + $1.00 postage from the address above.

The Herb Cupboard

Sherri Byrne
PO Box 375
Fort Plain, NY 13339

(518) 993-2363
Established 1974
Write or call for class schedule.

Sherri Byrne of The Herb Cupboard holds classes throughout the growing season on Cooking with Herbs, The Romantic Garden, Planning and Planting the Herb Garden, Harvesting and Storing Herbs and Making Potpourris and Herb Wreaths.

The Herb Haus

Marion Bates
31 Beecham Rd.
Reading, PA 19606

(215) 779-1075
Established 1977
Write or call for schedule.

The Herb Haus offers classes in both spring and fall. Write for further information.

The Herb Market (Rutland of Kentucky)

Mary Peddie
Jail and Green St.
Washington, KY 41096-0182

(606) 759-7815
Established 1971
Wholesale; public garden; retail
Write or call for class schedule.

Mary Peddie of The Herb Market offers a number of herbal "short courses" at her shop: How to Take Successful Cuttings, Herb Identification/Uses, Herbs and the Culinary Arts, How to Make Potpourri and others.

Mrs. Peddie will travel to other locations to give workshops on The Basic Herb Garden, The Culinary Garden, The Pioneer Woman's Herb Garden, Ornamental Herbs and The Scented Geranium.

Herb N' Ewe

Barbara Wade and Susan Mills
11755 National Rd. SE
Thornville, OH 43076

(614) 323-2264
Established 1988
Mail order; retail; public garden
Price list and class schedule for LSASE

A number of garden lectures and luncheon teas are held at Herb N' Ewe throughout the season. Topics include Planning the Herb Garden, Flowers for Drying, Tussie-Mussie workshop, Edible Flowers, Rosebud Topiaries and Planning an Herbal Christmas.

Herbal Endeavours, Ltd.

Colleen K. Dodt
3618 S. Emmons
Rochester Hills, MI 48307

(313) 852-0796
Mail order; retail
Established 1986
Catalog $2.00

Colleen Dodt offers lectures, classes and workshops on herbs and aromatherapy. She is the U.S. contributor to the *International Journal of Aromatherapy*, published in Brighton, England.

Herbal Gardens

George Walsh
PO Box 38
Montara, CA 94037

(415) 728-7683
Established 1981
Catalog free

Herbal Gardens sponsors a number of classes and special activities such as Herbal Body Care, Herbal Medicine, Herbal Child Care and Aromatherapy by Jeanne Rose as well as classes on floral crafts, herbal gardening, herbal cosmetics and more.

To make cologne water: one pint of alcohol, sixty drops of lavender, sixty drops of bergamot, sixty drops of essence of lemon, sixty drops of orange water. to be corked up, and well shaken. it is better for considerable age.

—from *The Frugal Housewife* by Mrs. Child, 1833

The Herbalist, Inc.
Tierney P. Salter
6500 20th NE
Seattle, WA 98115

(206) 523-2600
Established 1984
Mail order; wholesale; retail
Catalog free

Tierney Salter offers a number of special events, classes and workshops at The Herbalist including classes on herbs and iridology. Recent events have included a workshop on Botanical Medicine and Wildcrafting with Michael Moore and an Herbal Retreat with Ryan Drum.

The Herbary & Stuff
Mary Lou Hamilton
Rt. 3, Box 83
Jacksonville, TX 75766

(903) 586-2114
Established 1989
Catalog $2.00

Mary Lou Hamilton of The Herbary & Stuff offers herb seminars from May through July each year. Write or call for a current schedule.

The Herbfarm
Carrie Van Dyck
32804 Issaquah–Fall City Rd.
Fall City, WA 98024

(206) 784-2222
Established 1978
Mail order; retail; public garden
Catalog $3.50 includes plant list; $2.00 refundable with purchase

Besides hundreds of herb varieties, a country store and a restaurant, the Herbfarm hosts more than 250 classes and special events each year. Topics include Make a Living Wreath, Starting from Seed, Create a Salad Garden in a Basket, Gardening for Floral and Herbal Crafts, Designing Your Herb Garden, Bugs: The Good, the Bad and the Ugly, Make a Living Sculpture, Spring Wild Edibles, Make Herbed and Fruit Vinegars and hundreds more. Well-known chefs of the Northwest give cooking classes at the farm. (Also see listings in Chapters 1, 2 and 8.)

The Herbs of Happy Hill
Kathy Chain
14705 Happy Hill Rd.
Chester, VA 23831

(804) 796-2762
Established 1984
Call for class schedule.

Kathy Chain offers a number of herb classes each fall in her shop. These include herbal wreath, harvesting, potpourri and cooking classes.

Hickory Hill Herbs
Paula Jones Hill
307 W. Ave. E.
Lampasas, TX 76550

(512) 556-8801
Call or write for more information.

Paula Jones Hill at Hickory Hill Herbs offers a number of interesting classes, demonstrations and workshops throughout the year. Topics include Herbal Wreathmaking; Pestos, Herbal Vinegars and Potted Herbs for the Windowsill; Herbal Soapmaking; Essential and Fragrance Oils and Potpourris; Herbal Christmas Crafts and Last-Minute Gift Ideas. (Also see listings in Chapters 2 and 10.)

High Hampton Inn & Country Club

Ms. Inas Crisp
198 Hampton Rd.
Cashiers, NC 28717

(704) 743-2411
Established 1924
Call or write for information.

The High Hampton Inn & Country Club offers a number of workshops throughout the season, such as Spring Wildflowers, Summer Wildflowers and Fall Colors and Woodland Harvest. An herb garden adjacent to the inn provides seasonings which are used in the kitchen.

Jane's Herb Farm

Jane Kuitems
1042 State Rd.
Webster, NY 14580

(716) 872-3720
Established 1981
Call or write for current schedule.

Jane's Herb Farm sponsors a number of workshops throughout the year such as Planning Your Garden, The Kitchen Garden, Growing and Drying Everlastings, Cooking with Herbs, Cosmetics from your Kitchen and Reaping the Harvest and Putting the Garden to Sleep.

Kingwood Center

Bill Collins
900 Park Ave. W.
Mansfield, OH 44906

(419) 522-0211
Established 1953
Call or write for schedule.

Kingwood Center sponsors a number of lectures and workshops throughout the year for both adults and children. Topics include Old Garden Roses, Pressed Flower Design, Harvesting and Drying Flowers and Herbal Delights.

la dama maya herb and flower farm

Maureen Messick
Rt. 5, Box 82
Luray, VA 22835

(703) 743-4665
Established 1977
Mail order; wholesale; retail; public garden
Newsletter/brochure free

Workshops and classes are held periodically at the farm. Topics include Planning Your Herb Garden, Simple Herb Cookery, Flowers for Drying and others. Ms. Messick has come up with a wonderful "barter" idea—for four hours of work at the farm, you'll get 15 plants! Call for further information.

Long Creek Herb Farm

Jim Long
Rt. 4, Box 730
Oak Grove, AR 72660

(417) 779-5450
Call or write for schedule.

Jim Long offers a number of workshops and programs for herb and garden clubs as well as Civil War reenactment and historic groups. These include Landscaping with Herbs, Pre-Civil War Folk Remedies and Herbal Medicines, Herbal Folklore of the Ozarks, Safe and Edible Wild Mushrooms, Garden Medicinals and Basics of Herbal and Folk Medicines. Mr. Long researched and designed the Heritage Herb Garden located on the grounds of the Ozark Folk

Center State Park near Mountain View, Arkansas, as well as his own private gardens. For more information on these two gardens, see Chapter 8. Mr. Long has written a series of how-to booklets (*How to Grow and Use Herbs Successfully, How to Use Folk Remedies, How to Use Native Herbs, Dream Pillows/Aphrodisiacs and Love Potions; How to Grow a Southwest Cooking Garden* and others). Each booklet averages 8 to 16 pages and sells for $3.50 + $1.00 postage.

Mari-Mann Herb Farm

Michael L. King
RR #4, Box 7
N. end of St. Louis Bridge Rd.
Decatur, IL 62521-9404

(217) 429-1555
Established 1977
Mail order; wholesale; retail; public garden
Catalog $1.00

The Mari-Mann Herb Farm offers a number of herbal craft and gardening classes throughout the year. Call or write for a current schedule. (Also see listing in Chapter 2.)

Mary's Herb Garden & Gift Shop

Betty Ann Viviano
23825 Priest Rd.
Philomath, OR 97370

(503) 929-6275
Established 1989
Catalog free

Betty Ann Viviano of Mary's Herb Garden & Gift Shop also offers a "Get Herb Help Now!" correspondence course to help you learn the how-tos of planting, growing and harvesting your own herbs. In 12 individual lessons, you will learn the history and uses of 18 different herbs and herbal blends and how to grow and prepare them.

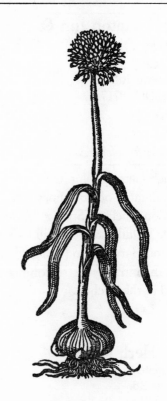

Matthaei Botanical Gardens

TheUniversity of Michigan
Carolyn Patterson and Sandell Bennett
1800 N. Dixboro Rd.
Ann Arbor, MI 48105

(313) 998-7061
Established 1907
Public gardens; gift shop

The Matthaei Botanical Gardens offers a number of adult education classes and workshops. Topics have included classes on wild spring edibles, making stone troughs for your garden, wild mushrooms and medicinal plants. (Also see listing in Chapter 8.)

Meadowbrook Herb Garden

Judy Gagel
PO Box 578
Fairfield, CT 06430-0578

(203) 254-7323 (mail order)
(401) 539-7603 (wholesale or retail location)
Established 1967
Mail order; wholesale; retail; public garden
Catalog $1.00

Meadowbrook Herb Garden sponsors classes and workshops throughout the year on herbs. Topics include Cooking with Herbs, Basketmaking, Medicinal Herbs, Wreathmaking and Organic Gardening. The classes are held at the retail location, Rt. 138 (93 Kingstown Rd.), Wyoming, Rhode Island. (Also see listings in Chapters 1 and 2.)

New Hampshire Farm Museum

Susie McKinley and Melissa Walker
Rt. 16, Plummer's Ridge
PO Box 644
Milton, NH 03851

(603) 652-7840
Established 1969
Public garden; country store
Write or call for a schedule; the Museum is open June through October.

The New Hampshire Farm Museum, formed to promote and preserve New Hampshire's agricultural heritage, sponsors classes, events and workshops, as well as an annual Herb Day.

New Hope Herb Farm

Carolee Bean
Rt. 1, Box 660
Spencer, IN 47460

(812) 829-6086
Established 1985
Catalog $1.00

Carolee Bean of the New Hope Herb Farm offers herbal workshops including an Everlastings Workshop and an Herbal Christ-

mas Workshop. The Farm also sponsors several herb festivals throughout the year. Call or write for further information. Ms. Bean also offers herb plants by mail order; see listing in Chapter 1.

Oak Valley Herb Farm

Kathi Keville
14648 Pear Tree Lane
Nevada City, CA 95959

Established 1971
Catalog $1.00

Kathi Keville, the Director of the American Herb Association and editor of its *AHA Quarterly Newsletter*, offers a number of herb and aromatherapy classes throughout the year. A six-month advanced herbal apprenticeship program in the areas of botany, ecology, aromatherapy, flower essences, ethnobotany, herbal medicine and healing is also available.

Olive's Hearth & Haven

Olive Curtis
5481 Doren Rdd
Acme, WA 98220

(206) 595-2485
Established 1991
Write or call for more information.

Olive Curtis sponsors garden tours by appointment in conjunction with an herbal luncheon or cooking class. The cooking class includes samples substantial enough to constitute a meal in itself. Ms. Curtis, a retired home economist, emphasizes low-calorie, low cholesterol cooking using only fresh products. Herbal sorbets and scented geranium cakes are just a few of her specialties. Every class has herbal crackers and vegetable dishes cooked with herbs.

Olive's herb garden sounds wonderful—it starts from a rose arbor and leads along a curving brick path lined with 95 scented geraniums on one side and climbing heritage roses on the other. An orchard in-

Dandelions are grown in Japan as decorative plants and over 200 varieties in orange, black, white and copper colors are cultivated by florists.

—from *The Frugal Housewife* by Mrs. Child, 1833

cludes pears, apples, grapes, currants, blueberries, kiwis and other berries. The current price for the daylong tour and cooking class is $35.00 per person.

The Ozark Folk Center State Park

Heritage Herb Garden
Tina Marie Wilcox
PO Box 500
Mountain View, AR 72560

Established 1985
Call or write for class schedule and further information.

The Ozark Folk Center State Park Heritage Herb Garden (also see listing in Chapter 7) sponsors a number of special herbal events throughout the year. These include a medicinal plant seminar, an herbal feast, a heritage herb spring extravaganza with workshops, a harvest herbal dinner and an herbal elves holiday workshop.

Peconic River Herb Farm

Cristina Spindler
310C River Rd.
Calverton, NY 11933

(516) 369-0058
Retail; public garden

The Peconic River Herb Farm offers workshops from March through December. Topics include Essential Oils, An Introduction to Herbal Medicine, A Beginner's Herb Garden, Herb Butters and Cheeses, Cooking with Garden Flowers and Herbal Cosmetics.

The Spindlers also offer more than 300 varieties of herbs, native plants and seeds for sale at their retail shop.

Penny Royal Herbs

Penny Anderson
300 Skyline Rd.
Georgetown, TX 78628

(512) 863-8354
Established 1987
Write for more information.

Penny Anderson's herb talks and presentations include Herb Gardening for Scented Gifts and Flavorful Cooking, Backyard Potpourri, The Herb Lore of Love Potions and Pest Control Using Herbs.

Penny's Garden

Penny and Don Melton
PO Box 305 Blacks Creek Rd.
Mountain City, GA 30562

(404) 746-6918
Mail order; wholesale; retail; public garden
Established 1987
Catalog free

Penny and Don Melton offer a number of workshops and special activities at Penny's Garden throughout the season such as Making Your Own Container Garden, Harvesting and Preserving Fresh Herbs, Gardening the Organic Way and others. In addition to the gourmet herbal food products that the Meltons sell by mail order (see listing in Chapter 2), the retail shop has herb plants, scented geraniums, books, dried arrangements, wreaths and garden accessories.

Pettengill Farm

Jan Richenburg
121 Ferry Rd.
Salisbury, MA 01952

(508) 462-3675
Established 1982
Write for class schedule.

Jan Richenburg offers a number of interesting workshops and classes at Pettengill Farm including children's classes, a perennial garden workshop, a window box class and an antique flower garden workshop. Other topics are basic herb gardening, making your own potpourri, dried flower growing and harvesting, making a strawberry jar, harvesting, and drying and storage of herbs. A number of herbal products are available at Pettengill Farm's retail shop.

Rachel Dee Herb Farm

Eugene or Yvonne Brown
40622 196 Ave. SE
Enumclaw, WA 98022

(206) 825-2797
Established 1989
Public garden; retail
Class schedule free

The Rachel Dee Herb Farm offers classes on herb culture, culinary herbs and herbal lore. The gift shop on the premises carries herb vinegars, wreaths, bath oils and other products.

Radcliffe Farms

Cyndy Radcliffe and Maggi Roth
250 Airport Rd.
Bedminster, NJ 07921

(908) 526-0505
Established 1984
Mail order; wholesale (dried flowers and herbs); retail
Price list/workshop schedule for SASE

Cyndy Radcliffe of Radcliffe Farms offers workshops on making herbal wreaths, wall arches and sprays, herbal arrangements, topiaries and baskets.

Rhettland Herbary

Eddie Rhett-Thurston
7867 Burson Rd.
Valley Springs, CA 95252

(209) 786-2667
Established 1986
Gift shop; public garden
Catalog $2.00 (annual subscription fee)

Eddie Rhett-Thurston offers herbal workshops from March through October on such topics as Herb and Garlic Braiding, Lovely Lavender, Introduction to Herbal Cuisine and The Gourmet Wreath Workshop. The Herbary periodically sponsors brunches, open houses and garden tours.

The Rosemary House

Bertha and Susanna Reppert
120 South Market St.
Mechanicsburg, PA 17055

(717) 697-5111
Established 1968
Mail order; wholesale; retail; public garden
Catalog $2.00

The Repperts at The Rosemary House offer many classes, special events and tours throughout the season. Classes include Planning and Planting Your Herb Garden, Potpourri and Potpourri Crafts, Cooking with Herbs, Herb Vinegars, Kitchen Cosmetics and Living Herb Wreaths. "Lectures and Luncheons" are held next door to the Rosemary House at Sweet Remembrances, Nancy Reppert's restaurant. Call for a current schedule and reservations.

Rosemary's Garden

Shondeya Betari
132 North Main St.
Sebastopol, CA 95472

(707) 829-2539
Write for a current schedule.

Rosemary's Garden offers a number of classes including Herbs for the Immune System, Herbs for Children, Women's Self-Help with Natural Remedies, Children's Herbal Crafts and Aromatherapy for Women and Children.

Sage Cottage

Dorry Norris
PO Box 626
112 East Main St.
Trumansburg, NY 14886

(607) 387-6449
Established 1984
Brochure for large SASE

Dorry Norris gives herb programs at her Sage Cottage on every Thursday from May through October. Original herb dishes are prepared for each session, which includes such topics as Eating Your Lawn, Good Spells & Magic Potions, Bride's Food and more. Sage Cottage is also an herbal bed and breakfast; see Chapter 10 for more information.

Sage Mountain Herbs

Rosemary Gladstar and Karl Slick
PO Box 420
E. Barre, VT 05649

(802) 479-9825
Established 1987
Brochure/class schedule free

Sage Mountain Herbs offers in-depth herbal workshops and classes from May through November as well as other special events. The classes include natural cosmetics and skin care, medicinal herbology and herbal preparation, and the edible and medicinal uses of wild plants. Ms. Gladstar has also written a home study course, "Science and Art of Herbology", and is the author of the Sage Healing Ways series of nine herb pamphlets. She is the founder of The California School of Herbal Studies and cofounder of the Traditional Medicinal Herb Tea Company.

San Antonio Botanical Center

Paul Cox
555 Funston Place
San Antonio, TX 78209

(512) 821-5143
Established 1980
Call for more information.

The San Antonio Botanical Center offers classes and workshops throughout the year such as Botanical Drawing, Indian Uses of Native Texas Plants and cooking classes with Cecil Flentge (see listing for Spiceman Enterprises in Chapter 10).

Sea Holly Herbs & Flowers

Doris Davis
Rt. 1, Box 556
Wilmington, NC 28405

(919) 686-7805
Established 1989
Write for current schedule.

Doris Davis sponsors morning or evening herb classes and workshops at her shop throughout the year. These include Making Tussie-Mussies, Making a Scented Swag and Making an Herbal Wreath.

If of thy mortal goods
thou are bereft,
And from thy slender
store two loaves
alone to thee are left,
Sell one, and with the
dole
Buy hyacinths to feed
thy soul.

—attributed to the
Gulistan of Moslih
Eddin Saadi, a
Mohammedan sheik and
Persian poet (1184–
1291). Quoted in *The
Sandy Mush Herb
Nursery Handbook.*

Shady Acres Herb Farm

Theresa Mieseler
7815 Hwy. 212
Chaska, MN 55318

(612) 466-3391
Established 1977
Catalog $2.00; class schedule for SASE

Shady Acres Herb Farm offers a good selection of herb classes and workshops. Topics include Designing a Space for Herbs, Renewing an Established Herb Garden, Everlastings and Herbs, Edible Flowers, Lavender and Its Many Uses, Scented Geraniums and Scented Standards.

The Shaker Messenger

Diana Van Kolken
210 South River Ave.
Holland, MI 49423

(616) 396-4588
Established 1978
Retail
Call or write for current schedule.

The Shaker Messenger offers classes and workshops throughout the year on herbal topics such as wreathmaking and basketmaking. The shop also sponsors an Herb Day and a Wildflower Day every year.

Ms. Van Kolken's gift shop specializes in handmade reproductions of Shaker objects. She carries many herb books, Shaker herbs and teas, wreaths, dried flowers, herb drying racks, etc.

Shelton Herb Farm

Meg Shelton
Rt. 5, Box 499, Goodman Rd.
Leland, NC 28451

(919) 253-5964

Meg Shelton offers a variety of classes and workshops at the Shelton Herb Farm from March through October. Some topics covered are An Herbal Strawberry Jar; Culinary Herbs for the Patio; Making a Thyme, Rosemary and Sweet Myrtle Topiary and Preserving Herbs.

The Silo, Inc.

Ruth and Skitch Henderson
44 Upland Rd.
New Milford, CT 06776-2199

(203) 355-0300
Established 1972
Write or call for information.

The founders of the New York Pops, Ruth and Skitch Henderson are a multitalented couple. They offer classes in herb and other cookery throughout the year at the Silo, their cooking school, gallery and store. Their new book, *Ruth & Skitch Henderson's Seasons in the Country—Good Food for Family & Friends*, is available autographed from The Silo.

Silver Bay Herb Farm

Mary Preus
9151 Tracyton Blvd.
Bremerton, WA 98310

(206) 692-1340
Established 1981
Retail; public garden
Class schedule for SASE

Mary Preus of Silver Bay Herb Farm offers a number of interesting workshops and special events throughout the year. Topics include herbal cooking, medicine, potpourri and wreath making, herbal vinegars and holiday gifts.

The Silver Bay Gift Shop sells a variety of herb plants, herbal products and gifts.

Ms. Preus also offers organically grown, fresh cut herbs and edible flowers for individual and restaurant customers. The Little Book of Herbs series by Mary Preus may be obtained here (write for current price).

Apprenticeships with "hands on" learning experience for those who are seriously interested in herbs are available at Silver Bay Herb Farm. Write or call for more information.

Sinking Springs Herb Farm
Ann Stubbs
234 Blair Shore Rd.
Elkton, MA 21921-8025

(301) 398-5566
Established 1968
Current class schedule for SASE

Ann Stubbs offers a number of special events and workshops at her Farm throughout the season such as an annual spring herb market, a fresh herb wreath workshop, a country Christmas open house and tour and a "Cooking for the Health of It" class.

SouthRidge Treasures & Herbs
Mary Ellen Wilcox, Owner
368A Ridge Rd.
Scotia, NY 12302

(518) 372-2222
Established 1988
Call or write for more information.

The interesting classes and workshops are offered throughout the season at South-Ridge Treasures & Herbs include Crafting with Herbs, Making a Fresh Herbal Wreath, a Potpourri Workshop and Making a Victorian Potpourri Ornament. Ms. Wilcox's 26-page booklet, *Growing Herbs for Enjoyment*, is available from the address above for $2.50.

Spoutwood Farm
Rob and Lucy Wood
RD 3, Box 66
Glen Rock, PA 17327

(717) 235-6610
Established 1987
Write or call for class schedule.

Rob and Lucy Wood offer a large number of classes and workshops at Spoutwood Farm including Introduction to Organic Gardening, Basic Wreathmaking for Beginners, Making Dried Flower Jewelry, Edible Flower Candying, Fresh Herbal Wreathmaking and many others.

The Woods are the authors of the beautiful book *The Art of Dried Flowers: Inspired Floral and Herbal Wreaths, Bouquets, Garlands and Arrangements for Grand Occasions and Simple Celebrations* (see Chapter 4 for a description). An autographed copy may be ordered from the address above for $23.50 postpaid

Spring Brook Farm
Virginia Batchelder
8015 Turin Road
Rome, NY 13440

(315) 337-4707
Established 1983
Write or call for class schedule.

Virginia Batchelder of Spring Brook Farm offers a number of classes and workshops at her shop.

Spring Herb Farm

Nancy Spring
2919 39th St. E.
Bradenton, FL 34208

(813) 748-1524
Established 1988
Retail; public garden
Call for schedule.

Nancy Spring of the Spring Herb Farm offers some interesting classes at her retail shop: Making Candied Violets, Making Old-Fashioned Horehound Candy, Baking Breads with Lemon Herbs and others. Ms. Spring also sponsors special events with visiting chefs and speakers at the Farm.

State Arboretum of Virginia

Anne White
PO Box 175
Boyce, VA 22620

(703) 837-1758
Established 1926
Public garden
Call for current schedule.

The Arboretum sponsors a number of workshops throughout the year, many of which are herb oriented.

Stillridge Herb Farm

Mary Lou Riddle
10370 Rt. 99
Woodstock, MD 21163

(301) 465-8348
Established 1971
Mail order; public garden; retail
Brochure $.75

Mary Lou Riddle offers workshops at her Stillridge Herb Farm on such topics as Growing and Using Culinary Herbs, Growing Your Own Dried Flowers, Making a Victorian Flower Wreath, Planting an Herb Garden for Use and Delight and Planting Herbs in Containers.

Ms. Riddle's 48-page booklet, *Through My Kitchen Window*, a collection of herbal recipes, is available for $3.95 + $1.00 postage and handling.

Summit Lake Herbs

Reitha A. Andersen
12310 Summit Lake Rd., NW
Olympia, WA 98502

(206) 866-2402
Established 1985
Call or write for class schedule.

Classes and special events are held at Summit Lake Herbs throughout the year. Some class titles are: Starting an Herb Garden, Weaving a Berry Basket, Create a Spring Wreath for your Door, Make Herb Vinegars, Harvesting and Drying Herbs, Making Herbal Jellies and Making Kitchen Cosmetics.

Sweethaven Farm

Noreen Driscoll
Weatogue Rd.
Salisbury, CT 06068

(203) 824-5765
Established 1985
Class schedule for SASE

Throughout the year, a wide variety of herbal crafting, gardening and cooking workshops are offered for adults and children at Sweethaven Farm. Special arrangements can be made for garden clubs or group "Tours and Teas" or herbal picnics in Sweethaven Farm's meadow. Special classes are also given for children in the Farm's "Peter Rabbit Garden".

A seventeenth century legend tells that Jehan Gir, the Emperor of India, filled a pool in his garden with rosewater for his wedding day. On top of the water he floated thousands of rose petals for his true love. On the day of the wedding, he and his bride rowed over the water in a little boat. A scum had formed on the top of the water. The Emperor scooped some of the scum into his hands and found that it was a wonderful, oily perfume. The bride named the perfume "Atar Jehangiri", meaning the "perfume of Jehan Gir". This was how attar of roses was first discovered.

—from *The Frugal Housewife* by Mrs. Child, 1833

Thomas Jefferson Center for Historic Plants

John T. Fitzpatrick
Monticello
PO Box 316
Charlottesville, VA 22902

(804) 979-5283
Established 1987
Mail order; retail; public garden
Catalog free

A series of lectures, workshops and walks are presented on Saturdays by the gardens and grounds staff at Monticello. Topics have included Growing and Cooking with Herbs, Winemaking, Dried Flower Workshop, Virginia Cider Making and Old Roses Workshop.

Triple Oaks Nursery

Larraine Kiefer
Box 385
Franklinville, NJ 08322

(609) 694-4272
Established 1974
Current schedule for SASE

Larraine Kiefer offers herbal and craft workshops throughout the year at Triple Oaks Nursery. Some classes available are Basic Centerpieces, Door Wreaths, Herbal Crafts and Making Decorative Brooms. Herbal lectures and luncheons are given for groups of 15–30; topics can include Fragrances—Plants and Potpourri, Culinary Herbs and Flower Arranging.

Tucson Botanical Gardens

Cecily Gill
2150 N. Alvernon Way
Tucson, AZ 85712

(602) 326-9255
Established 1968
Write or call for more information.

The Tucson Botanical Gardens sponsor classes each fall and spring on "Herb Gardening in the Desert".

United Society of Shakers—Workshops

The Shaker Museum
Sabbathday Lake
Poland Spring, ME 04274

(207) 926-4597
Class schedule for SASE

The Shaker Museum at Sabbathday Lake offers interesting herb classes throughout the season. These include Making Herbal Preparations, Herbs for Female Health, Making Herbal Wreaths and Holiday Gifts from Herbs.

The Herb Department at the Museum offers a number of herb products for sale by mail order; see listing in Chapter 2.

University of California Botanical Garden

Bobbie Ohs
Centennial Dr.
Berkeley, CA 94720

(510) 642-3012 or 642-3343
Established 1890
Write or call for current schedule.

The University of California Botanical Garden offers a number of ongoing herbal lectures and classes on such topics as Herbs: How to Begin, Harvesting Your Herbs and Chinese Medicinal Herbs. Periodically, a "Green Stuff Day Camp" is offered for children. (Also see listing in Chapter 8.)

Vileniki—An Herb Farm

Gerry Janus
RD #1, Box 345
Olyphant, PA 18447

(717) 254-9895
Established 1979
Mail order; retail
Plant catalog $1.50; book catalog $2.00; both refundable with order

Vileniki—An Herb Farm gives summer classes on herbal identification, herb vinegars and oils, cooking with flowers, herbal pet care and preparing an herbal medicine chest. (Also see listings in Chapters 1 and 5.)

Village Arbors

Jeannette Frandsen
1804 Saugahatchee Rd.
Auburn, AL 36830

(205) 826-3490
Established 1985
Call for current schedule.

Jeannette Frandsen offers quarterly classes at Village Arbors on perennials, growing and using herbs and wreathmaking.

Whiskey Run Herb Farm

Mary Schenck
188 Locktown-Flemington Rd.
Flemington, NJ 08822-9555

(908) 782-1278
Established 1983
Class schedule for SASE

Herb classes and workshops are given at Whiskey Run from May through December. Topics have included tussie-mussie workshops, flower and herb basket design and how to make everlasting and herbal wreaths.

Betsy Williams—The Proper Season

Betsy Williams
68 Park St.
Andover, MA 01810

(508) 470-0911
Established 1970
Mail order; wholesale; retail
Catalog $1.00

Betsy Williams offers classes and workshops at The Proper Season shop on such topics as Moss Topiary Trees, Making a Dried Flower Topiary, Making a Spring Dried Flower Basket, Beginning Your Herb Garden and Making a Herbal Strawberry Jar. (Also see listing in Chapter 2.)

Windy River Farm/Cottage Garden Herbs

Judy Weiner
PO Box 312
Merlin, OR 97532

(503) 476-8979
Established 1980
Mail order; wholesale; retail; public garden
Catalog $1.00

Windy River Farm offers workshops and classes in herbs and organic gardening. These include Introduction to Medicinal Herbs, Wild Herb Walks and Culinary Herb Growing. The Farm has a gift shop and offers herb products by mail order; see listing in Chapter 2.

Wonderland Tea and Spice Herb Shop

Alpine Herb Farm
Linda Quintana
1305 Railroad Ave.
Bellingham, WA 98225

(206) 733-0517
Established 1976
Mail order; wholesale; retail
Catalog $1.00

Linda Quintana offers a number of classes including Planning and Growing an Herb Garden, Spring Harvest and Identification, Herbs for Women, Herbal Spring Tonics and Household Herbs.

Words About Herbs

Portia Meares
PO Box 559
Madison, VA 22727

(703) 948-6517
Established 1989
Information for SASE

Portia Meares's unique packet of teaching materials titled "The Art and Skill of Teaching about Herbs" was developed over eight years that Portia taught about herbs and wild edible plants. It includes basic instruction on the art and skills that you need to teach others about herbs, a sample syllabus or an outline of a five-week course, a sample class plan, a list of 50 herbs to be identified and used during the course, a glossary of medical terms, a selected bibliography, sample handouts, a sample evaluation form, a sample press release, and a sample flyer that you can use to announce your classes. The packet is currently $20.00 + $1.50 postage and handling.

Schools, Colleges & Correspondence Courses

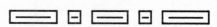

Augusta Heritage Center

Doug Hill
Davis & Elkins College
Elkins, WV 26241-3996

(304) 636-1900
Established 1973
Catalog free

Every July and August, Augusta Heritage Center sponsors a number of wonderful classes on the traditional arts—craft, folklore, dance and music. These include Herbs, Herb Gardening and Herbs and Woodslore. Others that may be of interest to herb enthusiasts are basketry, woodslore and treenware.

Blazing Star Herbal School

Gail Ulrich, Director
PO Box 6
Shelburne Falls, MA 01370

(413) 625-6875
Established 1982
Information forSASE

Gail Ulrich sponsors ongoing herbal workshops throughout the year as well as three- and seven-month herbal apprenticeships at her Blazing Star Herbal School. Weekend intensive classes and private apprenticeships are also offered. Apprenticeships and workshops can focus on the language of plants, methods of herbal preparation, herbal first aid, the culinary uses of herbs, women's herbal health care, wild plant identification, herbal skin and hair care, flower essences and other subjects.

Ms. Ulrich has worked for more than 18 years as an herbalist and 11 years as a certified Flower Essence Practitioner and instructor. She offers consultation in herbal medicine and flower essence therapy; telephone consultations are available by appointment. Gail also sponsors the Women's Herbal Conference in August each year.

California School of Herbal Studies

PO Box 39
Forestville, CA 95436-9706

(707) 887-7457
Established 1977
Catalog $1.00

The California School of Herbal Studies offers a wide variety of residential herbal classes for all levels of interest and expertise, from one-day or weekend tutorials and special events to comprehensive five-month courses for beginning, intermediate or advanced students. Subjects include Therapeutic Herbalism, The Healthy Home and Natural First Aid, Aromatherapy Training, Foundations of Herbalism Essence of Herbalism, and Healing Ways for Women.

Dominion Herbal College

Judy Nelson, President & Registrar
7527 Kingsway
Burnaby, BC
Canada V3N 3C1

(604) 521-5822
Established 1926
Call or write for flyer.

The Dominion Herbal College offers a Chartered Herbalist Degree Program Professional Course through home study that covers human anatomy; symptoms of disease; herbs, roots, and barks used in treat-ment. On-site summer seminars and a 200-hour, in-class Herbal Therapeutics course are also offered to the College's correspondence students and graduates.

East West School of Herbalism

Lesley Tierra, Director
PO Box 712, Box HC
Santa Cruz, CA 95060

(408) 429-8066
Established 1980
Brochure free

The East West School of Herbalism sponsors two home study courses in the art and science of herbology: A Home Study Course in Herbal Medicine and The Professional Herbalist Course. The courses were written and created by Michael Tierra, author of *The Way of Herbs, Chinese-Planetary Herbal Diagnosis* and other books.

Herbal Healer Academy

Marijah McCain
HC 32, Box 97-B
Mountain View, AR 72560

(501) 269-4177
Established 1989
Mail order
Write or call for additional information.

The Herbal Healer Academy offers a 22-lesson correspondence course in herbal healing that is designed to teach students common sense practice in home medicinals. It features "hands-on" experience in making oils, tinctures, herbal baths, teas, salves and cough medicines. The course is not strictly herbal but incorporates other mediums such as bee pollen, spirulina, sprouts and wheatgrass. Another course is a 10-lesson advanced course on Psychic Healing.

The Academy publishes a quarterly newsletter (currently $5.00/year) containing helpful herbal tips and information. A

A poultice made of ginger or of common chickweed, that grows about one's door in the country, has given great relief to the tooth-ache, when applied frequently to the cheek.

—from *The Frugal Housewife* by Mrs. Child, 1833

mail-order catalog of herbs, oils, seeds, massage tables, etc., is available to the Academy's students.

Herbal Studies Course

Jeanne Rose
219 Carl St.
San Francisco, CA 94117

(415) 564-6337
Established 1967
Catalog $2.50; includes $4.00 gift

Jeanne Rose offers an Herbal Studies Course by correspondence that covers "all things herbal" in three volumes and 34 lessons. The course has been approved for 150 units of Continuing Education credit for RN, LVN and PTE, and is Provider Approved by the California Board of Registered Nursing for 150 contact hours. The lessons cover such subjects as herbal body care, basic gardening, herbal sports medicine, history and folklore, astrology and herbs, herbal remedies, herbal foods, etc. Graduates receive a Certificate of Completion and will be able to prepare and use herbal remedies and treatments.

Ms. Rose also offers an intensive advanced course in herbal treatments. Graduates receive a Certificate of Herbal Practitioner. Call for more information.

National Health Care Institute

School of Massage, Nutrition and Herbology
Ryan Drum
350 Mission St. SE
Salem, OR 97302

(503) 585-8912
Write or call for more information.

This school offers, in conjunction with the Dominion Herbal College, a Comprehensive Herbal Studies program with weekend seminars on Waldron Island and in Vancouver, British Columbia.

Pacific Institute of Aromatherapy

PO Box 903
San Rafael, CA 94915

(415) 479-9120
Write for details.

The Pacific Institute of Aromatherapy sponsors several certification courses in San Francisco, California, each year in addition to an international certification course in aromatherapy by correspondence.

Quintessence Aromatherapy, Inc.

Ann Berwick
PO Box 4996
Boulder, CO 80306-4996

(303) 258-3791
Established 1990
Mail order; wholesale; retail
Catalog free

Ann Berwick offers the Quintessence Aromatherapy Correspondence Course as well as a certification course leading to Certification in the Theory and Practice of Holistic Aromatherapy.

Rocky Mountain Herbal Institute

Roger Wm. Wicke
PO Box 579
Hot Springs, MT 59845-0579

(406) 741-3811
Established 1977
Brochure free

The Rocky Mountain Herbal Institute annually offers a one year training program in Clinical Herbal Medicine that is designed for students unable to relocate for full-time study or working health-care professionals. It consists of three five-day residential intensives in Hot Springs, Montana, over a 10-month period preceded by scheduled reading and homework assignments which are completed by correspondence.

The instructor, Roger Wm. Wicke, has taught herbal medicine both to health professionals and to the general public since 1986.

School of Herbal Medicine

Carolyn Eden
PO Box 168-C
Suquamish, WA 98392

(206) 598-3556
Established 1979

The School of Herbal Medicine offers a year-long Correspondence Course in Herbal Studies, covering the philosophy and practice of herbal medicine, human pathology, diagnosis of conditions and a detailed study of native remedies, including their cultivation and preparation.

School of Natural Medicine

Farida Sharan, MDMA, ND, MH
PO Box 7369
Boulder, CO 80306-7369

(303) 443-4882
Established 1978 (in U.K.)
Mail order
Catalog $2.00

Dr. Farida Sharan of the School of Natural Medicine offers several options for correspondence study: a Master Herbalist Diploma Correspondence Course, an Advanced Herbal Medicine Correspondence Course, a Master Iridologist Diploma Correspondence Course and a Naturopathic Correspondence Course. A six-week apprentice training course is also available.

Sierra School of Herbs & Health

Barbara Klokkevold
PO Box 744
Alta, CA 95701

(916) 389-2554
Established 1988
Brochure free

The Sierra School of Herbs & Health offers a certification program in Professional Herbology with a weekend study option, as well as many special events and field trips. A six-month Advanced Apprenticeship program with Kathi Keville is also offered.

Therapeutic Herbalism

David Hoffmann
9304 Spring Hill School Rd.
Sebastopol, CA 95472

(707) 829-3451
Established 1990
Brochure free

Therapeutic Herbalism is an herbal correspondence course designed to be a clinically oriented approach to the use of herbal medicine in North America. The course explores the European practice of Phytotherapy, or plant therapy, and is based on Mr. Hoffmann's training and clinical experience in the United Kingdom. The course material is also available on a "text only" basis.

Wise Woman Center
Susun Weed
PO Box 64
Woodstock, NY 12498-0064

(914) 246-8081
Established 1986
Mail order
Catalog $1.00

Susun Weed of the Wise Woman Center offers a number of workshops, retreats and herbal apprenticeships emphasizing the "wise woman healing tradition". Susun's books, *The Wise Woman Herbal for the Childbearing Year* ($8.95 + $3.00 postage) and *Healing Wise* ($11.95 + $3.00 postage) are available from her at the address above.

Why should a man die who has sage in his garden?

—from *Regimen Sanitatis Salerni*, author unknown, c. 1100

Videos

Earth Herbs
Tom and Betty Tropper
PO Box 23306
Ventura, CA 93002

(805) 659-5158
Established 1975
Mail order
Catalog $2.00

Earth Herbs carries a number of videos on herbs. These include Michael Tierra's "Way of Herbs", Dr. and Mrs. Peter Theiss's "Healing Power of Herbs", Maria Treben's "Health through God's Pharmacy", Jeff Ball's "How to Grow & Cook Fresh Herbs" and many more. This company also offers a large assortment of herbal products (see listing in Chapter 2).

Indiana Botanic Gardens
Tim Cleland
PO Box 5
Hammond, IN 46325

(219) 947-4040
Established 1910
Mail order; wholesale; retail
Catalog free

Indiana Botanic Gardens carries several herb videos in addition to their large line of herbal health and beauty products (see Chapter 2). Titles include "Cooking with Edible Flowers and Culinary Herbs" and "Edible Wild Plants".

Morningstar Publications

Debra Nuzzi
997 Dixon Rd.
Boulder, CO 80302

(303) 440-7422
Established 1985
Mail order; wholesale
Brochure for SASE

Morningstar Publications offers "Herbal Preparations and Natural Therapies: Creating and Using a Home Herbal Medicine Chest", the "video that teaches herbal medicine making from A to Z". The four-hour instructional video covers making your own infusions, salves, ointments, cough syrups and more. It includes a 140-page reference manual. The current price is $95.00.

Natural Organic Farmers Association

Julie Rawson
RFD #2
Barre, MA 01005-9645

(508) 355-2853
Established 1971
Video listing for SASE

The Natural Organic Farmers Association offers videos on such topics as Basic Organic Gardening, Growing Herbs, Greenhouse Management, Principles of Biological Pest Controls, Beekeeping, Growing Garlic, Working with Perennials, Seed Saving, Growing a Cutting Garden for Flowers, Non-Insecticide Pest Control, Dried Flowers and Herbs and Growing for Restaurants. Each video is only $15.00, and most are 90 minutes long. (Also see listing in Chapter 9.)

Video Herbalist

Pearl E. Loyd
PO Box 3694
Terre Haute, IN 47803

(812) 235-3593
Established 1984
Mail order; wholesale
Brochure free

Pearl E. Loyd, herb specialist and restaurateur, is featured in two videos that are available from her at the address above. Volume One, "From Garden to Kitchen", features the basics of growing and using herbs in a step-by-step presentation. Volume Two, "Cooking with Herbs", includes instructions for many herb recipes. Each comes with a supplementary booklet, and costs $24.95 + $3.50 shipping and handling.

Wild Edible Plant Tours

"Cattail" Bob Seebeck
PO Box 236
Drake, CO 80515-0236

(303) 669-9162
Established 1980
Mail order
Write for more information.

"Cattail" Bob Seebeck offers a two-hour videotape on "Thirty-three Wild Edible, Medicinal, Poisonous and Useful Plants of the Rocky Mountains" for $15.00. Mr. Seebeck is also available for educational outdoor hikes, slide presentations, auto tours and overnight backpack tours/wild edible plant walks of the area.

Wise Woman Herbals

Sharol Tilgner
PO Box 328
Gladstone, OR 97027

(503) 239-6573
Established 1988
Information for SASE

A 60-minute video in Dr. Tilgner's Botanical Series, Volume 1, Edible and Medicinal Herbs, is available from Wise Woman Herbals. Current price is $39.95 + $2.50 shipping.

Specialty Libraries with Herbal Collections

Brooklyn Botanic Garden

Plant Information Dept.
1000 Washington Ave.
Brooklyn, NY 11225-1099

(718) 622-4433
Established 1910
Call for further information

The Brooklyn Botanic Garden library houses an extensive, up-to-date horticultural reference collection with 30,000 volumes and more than 600 current periodicals in horticulture, botany, landscape architecture, garden history and ecology. Special collections include more than 3000 current nursery and seed catalogs. The library is open to nonmembers by appointment. Also available is a Plant Information Service which provides telephone and written answers on plant-related questions.

Denver Botanic Gardens Library

Solange G. Gignac, Librarian
1005 York St.
Denver, CO 80206

(303) 370-8014

The Library at the Denver Botanic Gardens has more than 12,000 volumes on botany and horticultural subjects, including some 700 rare books, some dating as far back as the 16th century.

Lloyd Library and Museum

Rebecca A. Perry, Librarian
917 Plum St.
Cincinnati, OH 45202

(513) 721-3707
Established 1864
Call for further information

The Lloyd Library is a scientific library which was originally the company library of the Lloyd Brothers, a pharmaceutical firm. It has an extensive collection of literature on botany, pharmacy, plant chemistry, pharmacognosy, medicinal plants and eclectic medicine, natural history, chemistry, and zoology. The Lloyd's collection of herbals is outstanding.

The Library boasts one of the world's largest and most complete collection of pharmacopoeias, formularies and dispensatories, and its collection of pharmacy books and serials dates from 1493.

The Lloyd Library provides reference and bibliographical services and maintains contact with other libraries by computer and interlibrary loan. Anyone may use the Library free of charge. Information is also provided by mail or phone.

Santa Barbara Botanic Garden Library

1212 Mission Canyon Rd.
Santa Barbara, CA 93105

(805) 682-4726

The library at the Santa Barbara Botanic Garden features more than 7000 books and houses a herbarium containing more than 86,000 specimens.

Smithsonian Institution

Office of Horticulture Branch Library
Arts & Industries Bldg., #2401
Washington, DC 20560

(202) 357-1544

The Smithsonian Office of Horticulture Branch Library focuses on the history of gardening and design. The collection comprises more than 15,000 nursery and seed catalogs, more than 3500 books and 250 periodicals. Researchers may use the library by appointment.

Herbs and Etymology

Is a herbarian the offspring of a barbarian and an herbalist? What is the difference between an herbarian and herbarium? Do you have an herbary or herbour? What is an herblet? Are you herbiferous or herbless? Is this book herbose? Is an herbal accolade an herbelade?

The word herb itself is derived from the Latin *herba*, meaning green crops, or more literally, herbage. It is this meaning of herb that is used in Genesis 1:11, "the herb yielding seed." However, talk to a botanist, and you will hear the word herb used to describe any plant that is not woody, something called herbaceous. In turn, a horticulturist will use the definition that is most familiar to us: a plant which may be used for scent, flavor, medicine, or dye.

The following are some herb-enlightenments or a little herberized dictionary gleaned from the *Oxford English Dictionary*:

herbaceously: with a flavoring of herbs.

herbage: (1) herbaceous growth, (2) herbs for garnishing a dish, or (3) the green, succulent part of herbaceous plants.

herbal: (1) a book containing the names and descriptions of plants with their properties and virtues, (2) a collection of botanical specimens (= herbarium), (3) belonging to or consisting of herbs, or (4) the nature of an herb.

herbalism: the science of herbs or plants.

herbalist: (1) one versed in the knowledge of herbs, (2) a collector or writer on plants, or (3) a dealer in medicinal herbs.

herbalize: to collect medicinal herbs.

herbarian: one skilled in the knowledge of herbs (= herbalist).

herbarism: the knowledge of herbs (= herbalism).

herbarist: one skilled in herbs (= herbalist).

herbarium: (1) a collection of dried plants systematically arranged, (2) a book or case contrived for keeping such a collection, or (3) the room or building in which it is kept.

herbarize = herbalize = herborize.

herbary: (1) one skilled in herbs (= herbalist), (2) a collection of dried plants (= herbarium), (3) a place where herbs are grown, (4) a treatise on herbs (= herbal), or (5) the science of herbs.

herbelade = kind of pork-sausage mixed with herbs and baked in a crust.

herbar, herber (-e, -eior, -our): middle English forms of arbor, especially in its earlier senses, a green plot (herb- or flower-garden, orchard).

herberie, erberie: collection of herbs, a herb-market, provision, or store of herbs.

herbescent: growing like an herb (herbaceous).

herbid: grassy.

herbiferous: bearing or producing herbs.

herbish: resembling an herb; greenish.

herbist, herbister: herbalist.

herbless: destitute of herbs.

herblet, herbling: a little herb.

herb-man: one who deals in herbs.

herborist = herbarist = herbalist.

herborization: one who herborizes; a botanical excursion.

herborize: (1) to tend herbs or plants or (2) to gather herbs (botanize).

herbose: abounding in herbs or herbage.

herbous: belong to or of the nature of an herb.

pot-herb: an herb grown for boiling in the pot; any of the herbs cultivated in a kitchen-garden.

And how could we forget the most hotly debated linguistic conundrum in herbdom (the world of herbs)—how do you pronounce herb? In Old French and Middle English, it was only occasionally spelled with an "h" after the Latin, and is found written that way regularly after 1475. However, the "h" was mute until the nineteenth century in England and has remained so among most Americans.

From *The Herb Grower's Companion* by Arthur O. Tucker and Thomas DeBaggio. To be published by Interweave Press in 1993.

7

An Herbal Calendar

BEFORE PLANNING A TRIP to these events, check with the contact person for current dates and schedules, as dates of annual festivals may vary from year to year. Many of the herb societies and clubs listed in Chapter 9 also sponsor annual activities; write or call them for more information. We realize that we have only scratched the surface in compiling this information. If your club, society, shop, etc. sponsors an ongoing annual event, please let us know so that we may include it in future editions of this book.

January

The saving grace of January for herb gardeners is that it heralds the arrival of seed catalogs. Brighten January's dark, cold days by browsing through Chapter 1 of this book and ordering seed and plant catalogs and making wish lists for spring.

National Environmental Policy Act.

Anniversary of its enactment in 1970.
January 1

St. Basil's Day

An Eastern Orthodox church observance which includes serving St. Basil cakes. (These do not contain basil, and the day relates to the herb in name only.)
January 1

George Washington Carver's birthday (1864–1953)

Noted agricultural chemist whose work with potatoes paved the way for such culinary delights as Rosemary Potatoes and Dill Potato Salad.
January 5

National Pizza Week

A week ripe for celebration by herb enthusiasts. Can you imagine pizza without oregano?
Third week in January

February

Often considered the cruelest month, T.S. Eliot notwithstanding. February is the time when over-eager gardeners in northern climes start seedlings too early indoors, while those in warmer parts of the country plant spring greens and even harvest the first chives.

Groundhog Day and Candelmas Day

"If Candelmas is fair and clear, There'll be two winters to the year." If the groundhog sees his shadow, six more weeks of winter are in store.
February 2

Frances Moore Lappe's birthday (1944–)

Author of Diet For a Small Planet *and crusader for eating off the bottom of the food chain. A fine day for tofu with herbs.*
February 10

Annual Midwest Herb Show

Herbs for Health & Fun Club
c/o Treasa Brookman
R.R. #1, Box 396
Opdyke, IL 62872
(618) 756-2271

Herbal crafts, books, herb talks and workshops, demonstrations.
Second weekend of February

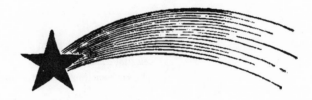

March

Whether it comes in like a lion or not, March is a hopeful month because the days *do* get longer and spring *does* arrive, at least officially. It's definitely time for those in cooler climates to finally start flats of herb seeds, and for everyone to go foraging for sorrel.

Luther Burbank's birthday (1849–1926)
American horticulturist who developed a host of new plant varieties.
March 7

St. Patrick's Day
Traditional time for gardeners in many parts of the country to plant potatoes.
March 17

Vernal Equinox
That point in time when the sun crosses the celestial equator.
Occurs sometime between March 20–22

Fragrance Day
A special day to be aware of the perfumes and bouquets of the world around us.
March 21

National Nutrition Month
Celebrate healthful herbs in your diet; create your own herbal salt substitute.

April

Named for Aphrodite, goddess of love, April can be the month that truly heralds spring, or breaks your heart with late storms. Daylight Savings Time takes effect on the fourth Sunday, and we all "spring forward" to later sunsets.

350 Acres of Spring at Longwood Gardens

Contact: Longwood Gardens
Kennett Square PA 19348

Sunday afternoon organ and chamber music concerts all month amid blooming spring bulbs and flowering shrubs and trees.

National Garden Week

National Garden Bureau
1311 Butterfield Road, Suite 310
Downer's Grove IL 60615

Second full week in April

Arbor Day

Many different dates are designated for tree plantings and celebrations around the country; the first Arbor Day was celebrated on April 22, 1872, in Nebraska.

Earth Day

Contact: Environmental Protection Agency
Office of Public Awareness
401 M Street SW
Washington, D.C. 20460

First observed on April 22, 1970, with the slogan, "Give Earth a Chance".

Easter Egg Week

The implications are obvious; be sure to add chives, basil and chervil. First full week after Easter, of course.

Annual Herb Fare

Peace Tree Farm
Contact: Lloyd R. Traven
Box 65, RD 2
Kintnersville, PA 18930
(215) 847-8152

Mattoon, Illinois, Herb Festival

Contact: Mattoon Chamber of Commerce
1701 Wabash
Mattoon, IL 61938

Annual festival held the last Saturday in April

Annual Herbal Affair & Festival

Contact: City of Sand Springs Festival Committee
908 North Main St.
Sand Springs, OK

Annual Herb Day

Contact: South Texas Unit, The Herb Society of America
PO Box 6515
Houston, TX 77265
(713) 859-9599

May

"Rough winds do shake the darling buds of May", but even so, this is a prime gardening month. Seedlings are still bigger than weeds, and spring salads of young greens, chives, tender basil tips and sprinklings of violets and johnny-jump-ups are a special treat.

Colonial Medicine Workshop
Contact: Special Events Coordinator
Yorktown Victory Center
PO Box 1976
Yorktown, PA 23690

National Wildflower Week
First full week in May. On May 1, be sure and hang a basket of flowers on the door of a special friend.

Herbs at the Hendricks
Contact: Indiana State Museum
202 E. Walnut Street
Corydon, IN 47112

Sale of exotic and indigenous herbs, usually on the second Saturday.

Kentucky Derby
Whether you follow the horses or not, have a mint julep, with or without the whiskey, on the first Saturday in May.

Spring Herb Festival
Alwerdt's Pheasant Farm & Gardens
Contact: Nik Alwerdt
Rt. 1, Box 152-A
Altamont, IL 62411
(618) 483-5798

Annual Herb Festival
Contact: New England Unit, The Herb Society of America
88 Marshall Street
Leicester, MA 01425

Annual Herb Festival
Contact: Green Briar Nature Center
6 Discovery Hill
East Sandwich, MA 02537
(508) 888-6870

Baltimore Herb Festival
Contact: Mary Louise Wolf, Chairman, Planning Committee
2301 Pickwick Road
Baltimore, MD 21207
(301) 448-0406

Annual festival held on the Saturday of Memorial Day weekend

Hedgehog Hill Farm Annual Three-Day Festival
Contact: Mark or Terry Silber
RFD 2, Box 2010
Buckfield, ME 04220-9549
(207) 388-2341

la dama maya herb and flower farm Herbalfest
Contact: Maureen Messick
Rt. 5, Box 82
Luray, VA 22835
(703) 743-4665

Annual festival on the second Saturday in May

Annual Herb Festival
Contact: Herb Society of Greater Fort Worth
5216 Rector Ave.
Ft. Worth, TX 76133

Annual Herb Fair and Sale
Contact: Goose Creek Herb Guild
Betty Fleming
PO Box 2224
Leesburg, VA 22075

June

Time to start harvesting the earliest herbs—mints, chives, dill and such—and plant second crops of others such as cilantro. Early roses will be yielding petals for next fall's potpourris. Summer officially arrives this month, with the longest day of the year falling on the 20, 21 or 22.

National Ragweed Control Month

"Get Ragweed Before It Gets You" is the motto of this observance. That goes for all the other weeds, too.

Annual Herb Day

New Hampshire Farm Museum
Contact: Susie McKinley or Melissa Walker
Rt. 16, Plummer's Ridge, PO Box 644
Milton, NH 03851
(603) 652-7840

Annual Herb Festival

Contact: Larraine Kiefer
Triple Oaks Nursery, Box 385
Franklinville, NJ 08322
(609) 694-4272

Festival held first weekend in June.

Annual Open House and Gardens

The Rosemary House
Contact: Susanna Reppert, Manager
120 South Market St.
Mechanicsburg, PA 17055
(717) 697-5111

Annual Festival of Shaker Crafts and Herbs

Contact: The Museum at Lower Shaker Village
Enfield, NH
(603) 632-5533 or 632-4838

Annual Herb Festival

New Hope Herb Farm
Contact: Carolee Bean
Rt. 1, Box 660
Spencer, IN 47460
(812) 829-6086

Annual Herb Fest

Rasland Farm
Contact: Sylvia Tippett
NC 82 at US 13
Godwin, NC 28344-9712
(919) 567-2705

Wheat Weaving Week

Contact: Marie Olinger
Illinois Association of Wheat Weavers
RR 6, PO Box 59
Galesburg, IL 61401

Celebrated the third week in June, when wheat is at its prime for this traditional craft.

Annual Herb Festival

Vileniki—An Herb Farm
Contact: Gerry Janus
RD #1, Box 345
Olyphant, PA 18447
(717) 254-9895

Annual Herbal Delights Symposium at Albright College

Contact: Pennsylvania Heartland Unit, The Herb Society of America
Yvonne Snyder
3830 Admire Rd.
Dover, PA 17315

July

═ □ ═ □ ═

July is the month of vacations, travel, picnics and high summer laziness. Celebrate National Picnic Month and National Ice Cream Month with the creative and festive addition of appropriate herbs. It's also the month when your garden will get away from you if you don't watch out. Try to strike a balance between leisurely glasses of herbal iced tea on the verandah and attentive weeding, watering and harvesting.

St. Swithin's Day
"St. Swithin's Day, if thou dost rain, for 40 days it will remain; St. Swithin's Day, if thou be fair, for 40 days, 'twill rain nae mair." July 15.

Gilroy Garlic Festival
Contact: Gilroy Garlic Festival Association
Box 2311
Gilroy, CA 95021

A harvest celebration in "The Garlic Capital of the World", complete with cook-off, food booths, and Garlic Queen. Celebrated the last weekend in July.

Take Your Houseplants for a Walk Day
Some think your houseplants will be more thrifty if they get in touch with their environment. Walk them around the neighborhood. Show them the sights. Introduce them to folks. (This is a recognized national holiday; we are not making this up.) Last Friday in July.

Annual Midsummer Herb Festival
Well-Sweep Herb Farm
Contact: Louise Hyde
317 Mt. Bethel Rd.
Port Murray, NJ 07865
(908) 852-5390

Annual Herb Fair
Tucson Botanical Gardens
Contact: Cecily Gill, Herb Garden
2150 N. Alvernon Way
Tucson, AZ 85712
(602) 326-9255

Annual National Herb Growing and Marketing Conference
International Herb Growers & Marketers Association
1201 Allanson Rd.
Mundelein, IL 60060
(708) 566-4566

August

Take cuttings of tender herbs in August—scented geraniums, fringed lavenders, rose-mary—and you should have well-rooted plants by first frost. August is the peak season for basil in many parts of the country, so take advantage of the bounty to freeze batches of pesto.

Sneak Some Zucchini Onto Your Neighbor's Porch Night
August 8 or thereabouts.

Izaak Walton Day (1593–1683)
What is stuffed trout without either tarragon or fennel?
August 9.

St. John's Mint Festival
Contact: Chamber of Commerce
Box 61
St. Johns, MI 48879

A time to honor mint farmers in the area.
Second weekend in August.

Annual Women's Herbal Conference
Contact: Gail Ulrich, Director
Blazing Star Herbal School
PO Box 6
Shelburne Falls, MA 01370

September

This is the month of back to school, Labor Day and the autumnal equinox. You'll notice that the light comes in your south and east windows in a new, fallish way, and you'll feel urges to pot up plants for your winter windowsill garden. Watch for the "Harvest Moon" late this month or in October. It's the first full moon after the autumnal equinox.

la dama maya herb and flower farm
Annual Flowerfest
    Contact: Maureen Messick
    Rt. 5, Box 82
    Luray, VA 22835
    (703) 743-4665

Annual Herb Festival
    Quailcrest Farm
    Contact Libby or Deborah Bruch
    2810 Armstrong Rd.
    Wooster, OH 44691
    (216) 345-6722

    Annual festival held the Saturday after Labor Day

Herb & Garden Fair
    Sunnybrook Farms Nursery
    Contact: Timothy Ruh
    9448 Mayfield Rd.
    Chesterland, OH 44026
    (216) 729-7232

Fall Herb Festival
    Midwest Michigan Herb Association
    Box 662
    Rockford, MI 49341
    (616) 942-1251

October

If you live in New England, you can revel in the vivid colors of fall foliage. Bring those potted herbs in before first frost, and spend a crisp fall afternoon stripping down the bundles of herbs you dried in late summer; start mixing potpourris and other herbal blends for the holidays, so they'll have plenty of time to mellow. Hope for Indian summer.

Ginkgo Day

This ancient Chinese medicinal tree has the odd habit of dropping all its leaves simultaneously, usually in the month of October. See if you can guess when Ginkgo Day will be in your area.

World Vegetarian Day

North American Vegetarian Society
PO Box 72
Dolgeville, NY 13329

Where would vegetarians be without herbs? Picking at bland beans and tofu. Celebrated on October 1

Herb Harvest Fall Festival

The Ozark Folk Center State Park
Heritage Herb Garden
Tina Marie Wilcox
PO Box 500
Mt. View, AR 72560

Annual Herb Festival

Lewis Mountain Herbs & Everlastings
Judy Lewis
2345 St. Rt. 247
Manchester, OH 45144
(513) 549-2484

Held second week in October

Annual Chile Festival

Tucson Botanical Gardens
2150 N. Alvernon Way
Tucson, AZ 85712
(602) 326-9255

Annual Herb Fair

Huntsville Herb Society
Botanical Garden Administration Bldg.
4747 Bob Wallace Ave.
Huntsville, AL

November

If you live in the South, November is the month to plant cold-weather herbs for an early spring harvest. In colder climates, it's time to stay indoors, drink herb tea and watch for early holiday herb sales.

National Pea Soup Week

What's pea soup without a bay leaf?
Celebrate this classic combination the first
full week in November.

Fall Festival of Roses

Contact: Mike Shoup
Antique Rose Emporium
Rt. 5, Box 143
Brenham, TX 77833
(409) 836-4293

Held the first weekend in November each year

Annual Christmas Herb Sale

Contact: Carol Pflumm
The Herb Farm
Barnard Rd.
Granville, MA 01034
(413) 357-8882

Held the last weekend in November

Fall Herb Market

Contact: Connie Moore
The Herb Bar
200 West Mary St.
Austin, TX 78704
(512) 444-6251

Annual Herb Market held in early
November.

December

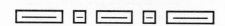

Rosemary is the Christmas herb: this month, make a rosemary wreath, decorate a large specimen in place of a Christmas tree, slip sprigs of this fragrant favorite in your holiday cards, and brew a bit in a cup of tea. Enjoy the fragrance of spices as you bake for the holidays. On December 21, take heart that the days will start getting longer.

Santa Lucia Day

Bake traditional saffron buns in celebration of this Swedish national holiday.
December 13

Boston Tea Party

Colonists demonstrated against tea taxes by dumping a British shipment of tea in Boston Harbor. Using native American herbs in place of Thea chinensis *became a patriotic act. Brew a cup of your favorite on December 16.*

A Grower's Guide to Favorite Culinary Herbs

COMMON NAME (Botanical Name)	Cold Hardy To Approx.	Life Cycle	Height in Feet	Light Needs	Inches Apart	House Plant
BASIL (Ocimum basilicum)	35° F	A	2	FS	18	❧
BAY (Laurus nobilis)	15° F	P	40	FS	—	❧
CHERVIL (Anthriscus cerefolium)	25° F	A	2	PS	9	❧
CHIVES (Allium schoenoprasum)	–40° F	P	1½	FS	12	❧
CORIANDER (Coriandrum sativum)	33° F	A	3	FS,PS	18	
CRESS (Nasturtium officinale)	–20° F	P	1	PS	6	
DILL (Anethum graveolens)	29° F	A	3	FS	12	
GARLIC (Allium sativum)	–40° F	P	2	FS	6	
LEMON BALM (Melissa officinalis)	–20° F	P	2	FS,PS,S	18	❧
MARJORAM (Origanum majorana)	30° F	P	1	FS	10	
MINT (Mentha species)	–20° F	P	2	FS,PS	15	❧
OREGANO (Origanum vulgare)	–20° F	P	2	FS	12	❧
PARSLEY (Petroselinum crispum)	20° F	B	1½	FS,PS	12	❧
ROSEMARY (Rosmarinus officinalis)	15° F	P	6	FS,PS,S	36	❧
SAGE (Salvia officinalis)	–10° F	P	2½	FS	24	
SAVORY, SUMMER (Satureja hortensis)	33° F	A	1½	FS	12	
SAVORY, WINTER (Satureja montana)	–10° F	P	1½	FS	12	❧
SORREL (Rumex acetosa)	–20° F	P	2	FS,PS	12	
TARRAGON (Artemisia Dracunculus sativa)	–20° F	P	2	FS,PS	24	
THYME (Thymus vulgaris)	–20° F	P	1	FS,PS	18	❧

KEY: P = perennial, B = biennial, A = annual, FS = full sun, PS = part sun, S = shade

From *Herbs In the Kitchen* by Carolyn Dille and Susan Belsinger (Interweave Press, 1992).
Information courtesy of Thomas DeBaggio, T. DeBaggio Herbs, Arlington, Virginia

8

Public Gardens
with Herb Collections

IN THIS CHAPTER, we have listed more than 100 public gardens with herb collections. Some of the gardens are small; some are large. We have included as much information about these gardens as possible. Some of them do not have catalogs or brochures, and many are only open seasonally, or have reduced hours or staffs during certain months of the year. Please call for their current schedules and for traveling directions before visiting. For a list of additional herb gardens (including private gardens), see the *Traveler's Guide to Herb Gardens* published by The Herb Society of America. Directors and curators of gardens not mentioned here are welcome to send in information on their gardens for future editions of this book.

Gardens are listed by state at the end of this chapter.

Abigail Adams Smith Museum
421 East 61st St.
New York, NY 10021
(212) 838-6878

This Colonial Dames of America head-quarters museum features a historic house with a small, authentic 18th-century walled herb garden.

Agecroft Hall
Sandi Barnette
4305 Sulgrave Rd.
Richmond, VA 23221-3256
(804) 353-4241

Agecroft Hall is an authentic Tudor and Early Stuart (1485–1650) English country house that was rescued from destruction by a prominent Richmond businessman, T.C. Williams, Jr. Mr. Williams brought Agecroft Hall across the Atlantic Ocean to its present site, recreated it as his home, and filled it with authentic furnishings. Today Agecroft Hall is a museum with a formal garden and a sunken garden that is a copy of the "pond garden" at Hampton Court in England. An herb garden contains only herbs grown during the reign of Elizabeth I; there is also a knot garden, a cutting garden and numerous boxwood walks.

The 85+ culinary and medicinal varieties of herbs grown at Agecroft Hall include hops, lamb's-ears, black fennel, pot marigold, larkspur and hollyhocks. Bee skeps lead the way to a stone walk and to the Still House, where herbs and fragrances would have been dried and processed for home use.

Bouquets garnis are little bundles of herbs and spices used to flavor soups, stews, and sauces. The idea is to keep the herbs contained so that flavor, and not flecks, will permeate the food. Traditionally, bouquets garnis contain parsley, thyme, and bay with occasional additions of whole peppercorns, whole allspice, whole cloves, celery leaves, tarragon, or marjoram. Bouquets garnis can be made ahead in cheesecloth bundles and frozen. Add them to simmering food directly from the freezer.

—a tip from Heard's Country Gardens

American Clock and Watch Museum
Joyce Stoffers, Managing Director
100 Maple St.
Bristol, CT 06010
(203) 583-6070

The American Clock and Watch Museum has a small garden with a sundial and some herbs. The garden, kept "in the spirit" of the 1801 house beside it, contains a number of old-fashioned flowers.

American Indian Archaeological Institute
Rt. 199, Box 260 (38 Curtis Rd.)
Washington, CT 06793
(203) 868-0518

A native plant trail through 15 acres features plants used by American Indians for food, dyes and medicine.

Antique Rose Emporium
Mike Shoup
Rt. 5, Box 143
Brenham, TX 77833
(409) 836-4293

The Antique Rose Emporium is located at the site of an early settler's homestead that has been restored and planted with a variety of gardens featuring old roses and perennials (including many herbs). A Fall Festival of Roses is held here on the first weekend of November each year, and a gift shop, Trellises and Treasures, is located on the premises. (Also see listing in Chapter 1.)

Arkansas School for the Blind

Garden of Exploration
2400 West Markham
Little Rock, AR 72201

The Garden of Exploration at the Arkansas School for the Blind features a sunken oval garden that includes raised planting beds with aromatic herbs and brightly colored flowers.

Arkansas Territorial Restoration Medicinal Garden

3rd and Scott Sts.
Little Rock, AR 72201

The medicinal garden features plants used by early settlers in Arkansas during the Territorial Period (1819–1836).

Atlanta Botanical Garden

Piedmont Park at the Prado
Atlanta, GA 30357

The Atlanta Botanical Garden contains several floral fragrance and herb gardens.

Bayberry Hill Herb Emporium

Barbara McHugh
3364E US 22-3
Morrow, OH 45152
(513) 899-4779
Established 1988

The gardens at Bayberry Hill Herb Emporium have been designed to represent gardens of the 19th century. They include a formal herb garden, an English cottage garden, a bird and butterfly garden, a collection of old roses, perennials and shrubs and a wildflower collection.

W. J. Beal Botanical Garden

Curator, Division of Campus Park and Planning
Michigan State University
412 Olds Hall
East Lansing, MI

The W. J. Beal Botanical Garden is an outdoor laboratory for the study and appreciation of plants. More than 5000 different kinds of plants can be found on the five-acre site. The garden, established in 1873 by Professor William James Beal, is the oldest continuously operated botanical garden of its kind in the United States. There are four main collections—systematic (plant family groupings), economic, ecological (native Michigan plants) and landscape plants. You'll find perfume plants, fiber plants, dye plants, oil plants, honey plants, flavoring plants, injurious plants, Indian food plants, vegetables and wild relatives and medicinal plants. There is even a weed garden!

Berkshire Botanical Garden

Joseph G. Strauch, Jr.
PO Box 826
(Rts. 102 and 183)
Stockbridge, MA 01262
(413) 298-3926

The 15-acre Berkshire Botanical Garden features perennial gardens, a terraced herb garden, an 18th-century farmhouse, adjoining rock garden, as well as vegetables growing in raised beds. Also featured are primroses, daylilies and a pond surrounded by wildflowers. A Garden Gift Shop offers herb products produced on-site.

Birmingham Botanical Gardens
2612 Lane Park Rd.
Birmingham, AL 35223
(205) 879-1227

The 67½-acre Birmingham Botanical Garden is a municipally owned public garden with a large vegetable and herb garden. The latter, maintained by volunteers, includes scented geraniums, creeping thymes, upright and prostrate rosemaries, culinary herbs, and a "sweet and sour" theme garden with lavenders, monardas and lemon herbs. The gardens are open daily from sunrise to sunset.

Black Creek Pioneer Village
1000 Murray Ross Parkway
Downsview, ON
Canada M3J 2P3
(416) 661-6610 (recording)

This restored village features several herb gardens: the Doctor's Medicinal Garden, an authentic 19th-century kitchen garden and a dye garden for weavers.

Boerner Botanical Gardens
5879 S. 92nd St.
Hales Corners, WI 53130
(414) 425-1130

The Boerner Botanical Gardens is a display garden that has been in operation since the 1930s. An herbal display garden contains more than 300 species of annuals, biennials, perennials and woody plants. The Garden also features more than 350 varieties of roses (3500 plants). The Boerner Botanical Gardens have published a handy *Herb Information Handbook*, compiled by Ruth D. Wrensch. The book currently retails for $4.95 + $1.25 postage. (Also see listing in Chapter 6.)

Boscobel Restoration
Margaret Eibsen
Rt. 9D
Garrison, NY 10524
(914) 265-3638
Established 1963

The Boscobel Restoration is one of the nation's leading museums of the decorative arts of the Federal period. The gardens at the Restoration include an apple orchard, formal rose gardens, an orangerie and an herb garden that includes a variety of culinary, medicinal and aromatic herbs. A gift shop on the premises carries garden ornaments, books and topiaries.

Brooklyn Botanic Garden
Dept. of Public Relations
1000 Washington Ave.
Brooklyn, NY 11225-1099
(718) 622-4433

The Herb Garden at the Brooklyn Botanic Gardens includes more than 300 kinds of medicinal, culinary, fragrant and ornamental herbs and features a 16th-century Elizabethan knot garden. Other specialty gardens include a Fragrance Garden (the first of its kind in the country), which features raised beds holding plants with fragrant flowers, aromatic and textured foliage and culinary herbs; all of these are accessible to the handicapped. A Shakespeare Garden, styled after an English cottage garden, exhibits plants mentioned in the playwright's works. (Also see listing in Chapter 6.)

Busha's Brae Herb Farm

Dixie Stephen
Rt. 1, Box 232M
Setterbo Rd.
Suttons Bay, MI 49682
(616) 271-6284

Busha's Brae (means "Grandma's Hillside" in Polish and Scottish) Herb Farm is a working farm and all the gardens have been named after the Stephens's children: St. Anne's Garden of Biblical herbs, Bill's Shakespearean garden, the Kent of Canterbury cottage garden with perennial flowers and herbs and Busha's Garden (a production garden). Gardens in progress include the Chad, Bishop of Lichfield Garden, a monastic cloister garden, and the King David I Garden with plants native to the Scottish highlands. The gardens are open to visitors from June through September. A Holiday Open House is held from Thanksgiving through the first weekend in December each year.

Group teas and luncheons may be scheduled from May 15 through December 15. Inquire for more details. (Also see other listings in Chapters 2 and 6.)

The Butchart Gardens

Box 4010, Station A
Victoria, BC
Canada V8X 3X4

Among the 50-acre Butchart Gardens are a Sunken Garden and an English Rose Garden.

Canterbury Shaker Village

288 Shaker Rd.
Canterbury, NH 03224
(603) 783-9511

The Canterbury Shaker museum features two large herb gardens containing more than 95 varieties of medicinal, culinary, fragrance and dye herbs.

Caprilands Herb Farm

Darlene Lee
534 Silver St.
Coventry, CT 06238
(203) 742-7244

Caprilands Herb Farm comprises 31 different gardens, including an identification garden, a dye garden and more. The gardens contain more than 300 varieties of herbs and scented geraniums. On the premises are also an 18th-century farmhouse, a bookshop, a restored 18th-century barn, a greenhouse gallery and a bouquet and basket shop. Garden tours and programs are presented daily by Adelma Simmons or her assistants. (Also see listing in Chapters 2 and 6.)

Chicago Botanic Garden

Lake Cook Rd., east of Edens Expressway
PO Box 400
Glencoe, IL 60022
(708) 835-5440

The 300-acre Chicago Botanic Garden includes the Farwell Herb Garden with more than 225 varieties of herbs, a knot garden, culinary, dye, medicinal and informal herb gardens.

Clark's Greenhouse & Herbal Country

Wilma Clark
RR 1, Box 15B
San Jose, IL 62682
(309) 247-3679

Clark's Greenhouse & Herbal Country has an extensive number of tour gardens that are open to the public from spring through fall. The gardens consist of 36 plots where many culinary herbs are grown for fresh cut sales and a display garden of medicinal, bee, kitchen, tea, Biblical, fragrant, witches' and dye herbs, thymes, sages, mints and scented geraniums. A craft store on the premises offers a wide selection of herb products and other crafts. (See listings in Chapters 1 and 6.)

The Cloisters

Metropolitan Museum of Art Medieval Herb Garden at Bonnfont Cloisters
Fort Tryon Park
New York, NY 10040
(212) 233-3700

The Cloisters features more than 250 varieties of plants and herbs which were known and used in medieval times within monasteries. These include medicinal, dye, aromatic and culinary herbs.

Cobblestone Farm

2781 Packard Rd.
Ann Arbor, MI 48104
(313) 994-2928

Cobblestone Farm is a living history farm museum with an 1844 farmhouse and an heirloom herb, flower and vegetable garden of plant species grown before 1865.

Colonial Williamsburg

Williamsburg, VA 23185
(804) 220-7645

Colonial Williamsburg is a living history museum with a number of authentic herb gardens on the premises.

Cornell Plantations

Robison York State Herb Garden
Diane Miske
1 Plantations Rd.
Ithaca, NY 14850-2799
(607) 255-3020

Cornell Plantations comprises 2800 acres and includes an arboretum, botanical garden and the natural area surrounding Cornell University. One of the specialty gardens is the one-acre Robison York State Herb Garden, which contains about 400 exotic and common herbs divided into 16 theme areas: herbs of the ancients, herbs in literature, bee herbs, herbs of the settlers, herbs of Native Americans, medicinal herbs, simples and worts, culinary herbs, economic herbs, dye herbs, tea herbs, fragrant herbs, sacred herbs, savory seed herbs, tussie-mussie and nosegay herbs and scented geraniums (more than 30 species and cultivars).

Cornell Plantations' informative guide to the herb gardens, *An Herb Garden Companion*, is available from the gift shop or by mail; write for the current price.

Country Roots Shop & Gardens

Gloria Harris
203 Keller Dr.
Stroudsburg, PA 18360
(717) 992-5557

Country Roots Shop & Gardens offers a wide variety of herbal products and botanical collectibles in their circa 1775 log cabin shop. Gloria Harris offers classes and lectures and a number of special events throughout the year. The public garden is open from April through December. (Also see listing in Chapter 10.)

Cox Arboretum

6733 Springboro Pike
Dayton, OH 45449
(513) 434-9005

The Cox Arboretum has an herb garden featuring more than 185 species of plants, as well as a separate everlasting garden.

Cranbrook House & Gardens

380 Lone Pine Rd.
Bloomfield Hills, MI 48013
(313) 645-3149

Cranbrook, a National Historic Landmark, is located 25 miles northwest of Detroit. The English manor house is surrounded by formal herb gardens enhanced by fountains and sculptures; a more informal kitchen herb garden is also on the property.

Crocker Hill Studios

Gail and Steve Smith
RR #3, Ledge Rd.
St. Stephen, NB
Canada E3L 2Y1
(506) 466-4251

Crocker Hill Studios consists of three acres of paradise along the St. Croix River, across the U.S. border from Calais, Maine. The Smiths grow more than 100 varieties of herbs and perennials in specialty tea, scent, culinary and medicinal gardens. A gift shop on the premises offers herbal items, potpourris and a variety of dried botanicals grown in the gardens. The gardens are open to visitors from June through September, or by appointment.

Cushing House Museum

Historical Society of Old Newbury
Eleanor Bailey
98 High St.
Newburyport, MA 01950
(508) 462-2681

The 19th-century Cushing House Museum period garden features herbs and old roses.

Dallas Civic Garden Center

PO Box 26194, Fair Park
(Martin Luther King Jr. Blvd.)
Dallas, TX 75226
(214) 428-7476

The Dallas Civic Garden Center is located in Fair Park, the site of the 1936 Texas Centennial World's Fair and of the annual Texas State Fair. Specialty herb gardens in the Center include a Shakespearean Garden, a Rose Garden, and an herb and fragrance garden labeled in Braille.

Speak not
Whisper not,
Here bloweth
Thyme and Bergamot;
Softly on thee every hour
Secret herbs
their spices shower.

—Walter de la Mare

Damside Garden Herbs

Sheena Cruickshank
Damside Johnshaven
Montrose, Angus
Scotland DD10 0HY
0561-61496

If you happen to be in the neighborhood, drop in on Damside Garden Herbs' public herb garden. Although the gardens are fairly new, there is still plenty to see: a Celtic and knot garden, an Elizabethan garden, a Roman and Monastic garden, juniper and heather collections, a bog garden, a chamomile lawn and more.

Denver Botanic Gardens

909 York St.
Denver, CO 80206-3799
(303) 370-8014

The Herb Garden at the Denver Botanic Gardens includes a wide variety of culinary, dye, medicinal and fragrance plants. A rock garden of creeping thymes is another highlight. The library at the Gardens has more than 100 volumes on herbs and is open to the public.

Des Moines Botanical Center

909 E. River Rd.
Des Moines, IA 50316
(515) 283-4148

The collections at the Des Moines Botanical Center include a large herb garden with fragrance, medicinal and culinary herbs as well as herbal shrubs, ground covers and trees.

Devonian Botanic Garden

Gillian Ford
University of Alberta
Edmonton, AB
Canada T6G 2E1
(403) 987-3054

The three-quarter-acre herb garden at the University of Alberta's Devonian Botanic Garden features seven large island beds enclosed in pathways of brick. Medicinal, domestic and economic herbs, wild edible, culinary and poisonous herbs are represented. A companion booklet, *Herbs of the Garden*, describes all the herbs in the herb garden and is available for $4.25 (Canadian funds) from the address above (Canadian residents add GST).

Early American Museum and Gardens

Cheryl Kennedy, Director
PO Drawer 669
(1/2 mile north of Mahomet on Rt. 47)
Mahomet, IL 61853
(217) 586-2612

The Gardens at the Early American Museum include several small herb gardens as well as a waterfall and woodland gardens.

Eden Vineyards Winery & Park

19850 State Rd. 80
Alva, FL 33920
(813) 728-9463

The Eden Vineyards Winery & Park has a spice and herb garden that is open to the public on weekends. Ms. Kaye Cude, editor and publisher of *Spice & Herb Arts* (see listing in Chapter 3), maintains the garden for the Winery and sells herb and spice plants, rhizomes and planting materials there.

Enchanted Crest

W. Loyd and Carollyn Blackwell
RR #1, Box 216
Belle Rive, IL 62810
(618) 736-2647

The Enchanted Crest is a Victorian mansion that is surrounded by a four-acre lawn with 20 herb gardens consisting of more than 300 varieties of herbs and perennials, an original pear and pecan orchard, park area, nature walks and pines surrounding a two-acre lake. Carollyn Blackwell welcomes visitors to the Crest and the gardens by appointment. Groups of any size can be accommodated, from five to a busload. Included is a lavish Victorian tea, a tour of the garden and grounds, a tour of the mansion with 50 quilts on display, a barn and gift shop.

According to the season of the year, you will be entertained with herb talks and herbal craft demonstrations. (Also see listings in Chapters 6 and 10.)

Fairie Herb Gardens

Steve Taylor or Dave Baird
6236 Elm St. SE
Tumwater, WA 98501
(206) 754-9249

Fairie Herb Gardens is situated on one-half acre and comprises several specialty gardens. The Fragrance Garden, the unusual Blue/Yellow Garden, a Medieval Paradise Garden and the Culinary Garden contain more than 340 varieties of herbs. The Gardens are open from April through October. A drying shed and shop on the premises offer a variety of herbal products; workshops and special events are also given at the Garden.

The Fairie Herb Garden Growing Guide, a 36-page handbook on the growing and using of more than 300 herbs in the maritime Northwest area, is available for $4.00 from the address above.

Farmington Historic Home and Garden

3033 Bardstown Rd.
Louisville, KY 40205
(502) 452-9920

This historic home, designed by Thomas Jefferson in 1840, features experimental herb gardens and a restored 19th-century kitchen garden, among others.

Fernbank Science Center Garden

156 Heaton Park Dr., NE
Atlanta, GA 30307

The garden at the Fernbank Science Center includes more than 50 varieties of herbs and many scented geraniums.

Filoli

Canada Rd.
Woodside, CA 94062
(415) 364-2880

Filoli is a 654-acre estate set against the California Coastal Range. A Property of the National Trust for Historic Preservation, Filoli is well known for its 16 acres of formal gardens (including an herbal knot garden and antique roses) and historic 43-room mansion. A gift shop is on the premises.

Henry Ford Museum at Greenfield Village

Oakwood Blvd.
Dearborn, MI 48120-1970
(313) 271-1620

The Henry Ford Museum at Greenfield Village features a heart-shaped lavender garden designed by Mrs. Henry Ford as well as several other smaller gardens which contain a number of common and uncommon herbs.

Fort Worth Botanic Garden

3220 Botanic Garden Dr. North
Fort Worth, TX 76107
(817) 870-7689

The Fort Worth Botanic Garden features several specialty gardens on its 114 acres, including European-designed rose gardens, a Fragrance Garden for the Blind, a Japanese Garden and a Perennial Garden.

Foster Botanic Gardens

180 N. Vineyard Blvd.
Honolulu, HI 96817
(808) 533-3406

The Foster Botanic Gardens, on the island of Oahu, includes a large collection of exotic trees and palms, a Wild Orchid Garden of more than 10,000 plants, a Bromeliad Garden and an Economic Herb Garden.

Fullerton Arboretum

California State University at Fullerton
Fullerton, CA 92634
(714) 773-3579

The 26-acre Fullerton Arboretum features many specialty gardens including a large Rose Garden with gazebo, a Historical Orchard and an 1890s-style garden with annuals, scented geraniums, vegetables and herbs.

Gatehouse Herbs

Carol Gates
98 Van Buren St.
Dolgeville, NY 13329
(315) 429-8366

Gatehouse Herbs is located on a 12-acre estate with a 19th-century house and gift shop. Carol Gates has designed several gardens around the shop, using traditional plants that were available when the house was built: a culinary garden, perennial borders inspired by English gardens and containing old roses, a Bible Garden, a Wildflower Garden and a Silver Garden. Ms. Gates gives garden tours and teas featuring fresh-baked scones for $3.00 per person. Classes and workshops are offered throughout the year.

If you want to know if your lover is thinking of you, blow on a dandelion seedhead—also known as a "blowball". If all of the seeds disperse, you're out of luck—but if any of the seeds are left, the answer is yes!

Many books, herbal vinegars, teas, antique botanical prints, Crabtree & Evelyn and Scarborough & Co. products, plants and garden accessories are available at the gift shop that are not listed in the Gatehouse Herbs mail-order catalog. (Also see listing in Chapter 2.)

J. Paul Getty Museum

17985 Pacific Coast Hwy.
Malibu, CA 90265-5799
(213) 458-2003

The J. Paul Getty Museum is modeled on an ancient Roman villa; the plantings around the Museum represent plants and herbs that were used by the Romans for culinary, medicinal and religious purposes. Terraces, an atrium garden and a walled garden are on the premises.

Gourmet Gardens Herb Farm

Diane and Dick Weaver
14 Banks Town Rd.
Weaverville, NC 28787-9200
(704) 658-0766
Established 1990

More than 150 varieties of herbs fill the traditional knot herb garden at the Gourmet Gardens Herb Farm. A culinary garden includes 42 edible herbs and flowers, and an everlasting garden surrounds the shop. Herb plants and seeds are sold at the shop, as well as wreaths, soaps, books, beauty items, herb butters, vinegars and mixes.

Hancock Shaker Village

Rt. 20
Hancock, MA 01237
(413) 441-0188

Hancock Shaker Village features an authentic herb garden with culinary and medicinal plants, as well as the plants that the Shakers grew for their seed company.

General William Hart House

Old Saybrook Historical Society
Mrs. William O'Connor
350 Main St.
Box 4
Old Saybrook, CT 06475

The authentic period herb garden at the General William Hart House has received awards from the Federated Garden Clubs of Connecticut. Tours of the gardens along with a lecture are available for interested groups for a fee. Write for more information.

Hedgehog Hill Farm

Mark or Terry Silber
RFD 2, Box 2010
Buckfield, ME 04220-9549
(207) 388-2341

Hedgehog Hill Farm is a small, diversified organic farm located in the western mountains of Oxford County, Maine. Its 160 acres are mostly wooded, with eight acres of cleared fields where the Silbers harvest a variety of herbs and flowers, perennials, everlastings and vegetables. Garden tours are offered.

The Herb and Everlasting Shop at Hedgehog Hill sells a variety of products and gifts made from the Silbers's harvests. (Also see listing in Chapter 2.)

The Herbfarm

32804 Issaquah–Fall City Rd.
Fall City, WA 98024
(206) 784-2222

The Herbfarm comprises 17 theme gardens containing more than 400 varieties of herbs.

Hilltop Garden

Indiana University
Bloomington, IN 47401

The Hilltop Garden on the Indiana University campus is the first children's garden in the United States. It features gardens with roses, vegetables and herbs in a research lab setting.

Hilltop Herb Farm

Beverly Smith
Daniels Ranch Rd. (farm road 787)
Romayor, TX 77368
(713) 592-5859

Established in 1957 by Jim and Madalene Hill, Hilltop Herb Farm features approximately one-half acre planted with more than 200 different varieties of herbs. A specialty of the farm is an all-white herb garden and a lovely gift shop.

Historic Bartram's Garden

Helen DiCaprio
54th St. and Lindbergh Blvd.
Philadelphia, PA 19143
(215) 729-5281

John Bartram was a colonial Quaker botanist, farmer and plant explorer. Self-educated, he learned Latin to study botany books. He traveled north to New York, south to Florida and as far west as the Ohio River, bringing back seeds and roots, planting them in his garden, observing, propagating them and then shipping them abroad. Bartram's fame spread, and in 1765, George III appointed him Royal Botanist. Even Linnaeus spoke of Mr. Bartram as "the greatest natural botanist in the world". Historic Bartram's Garden (together with his house), preserved by his descendants, friends and the Garden Club Federation of Pennsylvania, today is America's oldest surviving botanical garden. The "upper kitchen garden" contains seven beds of herbs organized by plant family. Other beds consist of plants used in cooking and medicines, which Bartram would have obtained by foraging, and herbs used for refreshment and medicines in the form of tisanes.

Historical Society of Glastonbury's Welles Shipman Ward House

Nancy Berlet, Exec. Director
972 Main St.
PO Box 46
Glastonbury, CT 06033
(203) 633-6890

The Welles Shipman Ward House, built in 1755, has an 18th-century-style back-door kitchen herb garden.

Honor Heights Park

Regency Hill
Muskogee, OK 74401

Honor Heights Park is the setting of the tribal museum of the Creek Confederacy. Herbs are included in the landscaping around the Park and Museum.

Houston Garden Center

1500 Hermann Dr.
Houston, TX 77004
(713) 529-5371

The Houston Garden Center features a Chinese pavilion, an All-America Rose Garden with more than 2000 bushes and fragrance, herb, perennial and wildflower gardens.

Huntington Botanical Gardens

1151 Oxford Rd.
San Marino, CA 91108
(818) 405-2100

The traditionally designed Herb Garden at the Huntington Botanical Gardens has specialty gardens of medicinal, culinary, salad and dye herbs.

Stan Hywet Hall & Gardens

714 North Portage Path
Akron, OH 44303
(216) 836-5533

The 70-acre gardens at Stan Hywet Hall & Gardens were created between 1912 and 1928 as the center of a 3000-acre estate. They include an English walled garden, a sunken garden, rose gardens and a Japanese garden. The 65-room manor is furnished with original family collections.

Iden Croft Herbs

Rosemary Titterington
Frittenden Rd.
Staplehurst, Kent
England TN12 0DH
Phone: 0580 891 432; FAX 0580 892416

Iden Croft Herbs is a fresh culinary herb farm located in the heart of the "Garden of England". The farm features acres of herbs bordered by grass paths, a large walled garden and a variety of demonstration gardens containing more than 450 varieties of herbs. One has a thyme path that attracts so many butterflies on a warm day that it is said to resemble a Persian carpet. An "Access to All" aromatic garden has been designed for the enjoyment of blind and disabled visitors. A National Origanum Collection garden was designated in 1983. A small shop houses potpourris, herbal salves, bath herbs, books, terra-cotta pots, lavender and seeds. (Also see listing in Chapter 1.)

Inniswood Metro Gardens
Herb Garden
Leslie Dybiec or Kim Wood
940 Hempstead Rd.
Westerville, OH 43081
(614) 891-0700

The specialty of the Inniswood Herb Garden is its significant botanical collection of thyme plants. The plants were once part of a dissertation project by Harriet Flannery Phillips of Cornell University. When Ms. Flannery's project was completed, the Central Ohio Unit of The Herb Society of America "rescued" the plants and moved them to Inniswood Metro Gardens. Fifty-three thymes are represented in the gardens, and include a thyme lawn, a thyme seat, thyme ground covers and plantings between paving stones. The gardens were featured in the April/May 1991 issue of the *Herb Companion* magazine.

Seven other specialty gardens include a Blue-Gray garden, a Culinary Garden, a Medicinal Garden, a Fragrance Garden, a Bee Garden, a Bible Garden and a Shade Garden.

Iowa State University Horticultural Garden
Iowa State University
Ames, IA 50001
(515) 294-2751

The one-acre ISU Horticultural Garden is an All-America Rose selections test garden which also includes many antique roses. There are also a formal herb garden with medicinal, culinary, fragrant, beverage and dye plant collections and a knot garden of annual and perennial herbs.

Jenkins Estate
Tualatin Hills Park & Recreation District
Beaulah Payne or Sharon Burns
PO Box 5868
Aloha, OR 97006
(503) 642-3855 or 649-9624

The Jenkins Estate features an old-fashioned herb garden, antique roses and a large scented geranium garden near a 19th-century farmhouse.

Kingwood Center
Bill Collins
900 Park Ave. West
Mansfield, OH 44906
(419) 522-0211
Established 1953

Kingwood Center was formerly the private estate of the late Charles Kelley King, an Ohio industrialist. Today, the private, non-profit educational institution sponsors workshops, flower shows, a horticultural reference library and public lectures. The herb gardens at Kingwood Center are grouped according to usage: culinary, medicinal, tea and fragrance, ornamental and dyeing.

Leeds Castle

Miss Sara J. White, Merchandise Manager
Leeds Castle, Maidstone
Kent, England ME17 1PL
Phone: 0622 765400; FAX: 0622 35616

Leeds Castle is one of the most romantic and most ancient castles in the United Kingdom. Rising from its two small islands in the middle of a lake, it is surrounded by 500 acres of rolling parkland containing lakes, streams, waterfalls, a wild Woodland Walk and the Culpeper Garden—a traditional English Garden of old-fashioned flowers, collection of catmint, bergamot and fragrant plants. The herbalist Nicholas Culpeper was a distant kinsman of the family who lived at Leeds in the 17th century, and the Culpeper Garden has been planted to honor him. There's more—13 greenhouses, an aviary, a topiary maze, an underground grotto and an ancient vineyard from which the Castle's own wine is produced. A Flower Festival is held most years at the castle in September.

Living History Farms

Miriam Dunlap
2600 NW 111th
Des Moines, IA 50322
(515) 278-5286
Established 1967

Living History Farms is a 600-acre, open-air museum that tells the story of midwestern agriculture with authentic buildings, planting methods and livestock and gardens. The farms include many historic gardens, all authentic to the time periods presented.

Long Creek Herb Farm

Jim Long
Rt. 4, Box 730
Oak Grove, AR 72660
(417) 779-5450

Long Creek Herb Farm is the working farmstead of Jim Long, the former publisher of *The Ozarks Herbalist* regional newsletter. The gardens include native Ozark plants as well as cultivated and imported culinary and medicinal herbs (more than 180 varieties in all). Jim uses many of the herbs in the seasonings, teas and crafts that he sells through The Herb Shop at Long Creek, and through a yearly Christmas catalog. The gardens are also open by reservation for "picnic and painting parties" for artists, garden clubs or other groups. Call for details. (Also see listing in Chapter 6.)

Longwood Gardens

PO Box 501
Kennett Square, PA 19348-0501
(215) 388-6741

Longwood Gardens is part of a 1050-acre estate that features 20 conservatories, fountains, a Children's Garden and an Idea Garden. The herb garden contains more than 130 varieties divided into four main collections: medicinal, fragrant, culinary and industrial.

Los Angeles State and County Arboretum
301 N. Baldwin Ave.
Arcadia, CA 91006
(818) 821-3222

The Los Angeles State and County Arboretum's Garden of Herbs contains native, Oriental and Mexican herbs as well as culinary, medicinal, fragrant and decorative herbs. Also included are a knot garden, a Shakespearean garden, a Shaker garden and a Native garden.

George L. Luthy Memorial Botanical Garden
Pam Grant
2218 N. Prospect
Peoria, IL 61603-2193
(309) 686-3362

The George L. Luthy Memorial Botanical Garden includes a rose garden containing hundreds of plants and varieties, a flowering shrub garden, annual beds and an herb garden featuring fragrant and flavorful herbs.

Harold L. Lyon Arboretum
University of Hawaii at Manoa
Karen E. Shigematsu
3860 Manoa Rd.
Honolulu, HI 96822
(808) 988-3177

The Harold L. Lyon Arboretum is a 124-acre research and education unit of the University of Hawaii. Two of its special collections are the Beatrice H. Krauss Ethnobotanical Garden and the Herb and Spice Garden, which is being developed by the Hawaii Herb Association. The Arboretum also offers a number of classes throughout the year; write for details.

Mary's Herb Garden & Gift Shop
Betty Ann Viviano
23825 Priest Rd.
Philomath, OR 97370
(503) 929-6275

Betty Ann Viviano has designed a unique display garden of ten herb gardens: Mary's Garden, with herbs dedicated to St. Mary; the Culinary Herb Garden made up of cooking herbs; a Thyme Garden; a Tea Garden (with 12 different mints); a Silver and Gray Garden; Sage and Basil Gardens; an Aromatic Garden; a Mexican Garden; and the Garden of the Saints.

Matthaei Botanical Gardens
The University of Michigan
Carolyn Patterson and/or Sandell Bennett
1800 N. Dixboro Rd.
Ann Arbor, MI 48105
(313) 998-7061

The Matthaei Botanical Gardens is a teaching and research facility of The University of Michigan. Its many outstanding features include a conservatory that houses about 2000 plant species gathered from around the world and a formal medicinal garden, rock garden and an herb knot garden. (Also see listing in Chapter 6.)

Of all the garden herbs, none is of greater virtue than sage.

—Thomas Cogan in *Haven of Health*, 1596

McDowell House and Apothecary Shop

Carol Johnson
125 S. 2nd St.
Danville, KY 40422
(606) 236-2804

The McDowell House, a National Historic Landmark owned by the Kentucky Medical Association, has been opened to the public as a museum since 1939. It is the accurately restored and furnished house and apothecary shop of pioneer surgeon Ephraim McDowell. A guided tour of the house, shop, flower and physic gardens shows the everyday life and culture of early Kentuckians.

Mercer Arboretum and Botanic Gardens

Lee Ann Toles, Director, or
Linda Gay, Garden Manager
22306 Aldine Westfield
Humble, TX 77338

The Mercer Arboretum Herb Garden contains many varieties of culinary, medicinal and fragrant herbs as well as an everlasting flower garden, Texas native plants and a color and perennial garden.

Michigan 4-H Children's Garden

Jane L. Taylor, Curator
Michigan 4-H Foundation
4700 South Hagadorn Rd.
East Lansing, MI 48823
(517) 353-6692
Established 1991

The one-half-acre Michigan 4-H Children's Garden is part of the new 7½-acre Horticultural Demonstration Gardens on the Michigan State University campus. The garden is being designed with the wants and needs of children in mind. Children even helped design it, and asked that plants from Peter Rabbit stories be included as well as flowers in a rainbow of colors and a place to watch butterflies. They suggested that no "NO" signs be included. Instead, the signs will say "please gently touch". Especially exciting are the herb gardens, which include a cloth (fiber) and color (dye) garden, a pizza garden, an oriental stir-fry garden, a taco garden and kitchen and cottage gardens where vegetables are harvested and cooked. The gardens will be accessible to children with special needs. A special demonstration raised bed will be wheelchair accessible, and a treehouse will be accessible by a ramp, for a bird's-eye view of the gardens from the air.

Construction was begun on the Children's Garden in the summer of 1991, but already there is a lot to see. Funds are still being sought from organizations and individuals; dedication of the garden is set for 1993.

The Horticultural Demonstration Gardens are open from dawn to dusk daily; there is no admission charge.

Mission Mill Village and Museum
1313 Mill St., SE
Salem, OR 97301
(503) 585-7012

The herb gardens of the Mission feature mid-19th-century pioneer medicinal, culinary and dye herbs. The museum is a woolen mill and has quilters and weavers demonstrating their skills.

Missouri Botanical Garden
2101 Tower Grove Ave.
PO Box 229
St. Louis, MO 63166

The Missouri Botanical Gardens feature a Victorian-design herb garden with medicinal, dye, culinary and fragrant herbs. Other features of the garden are a Scented Garden for the blind and a Renaissance Knot Garden.

Monticello
Thomas Jefferson Center for Historic Plants
John T. Fitzpatrick
PO Box 316
Charlottesville, VA 22902
(804) 979-5283

Thomas Jefferson's restored residence has large herb and vegetable gardens. Large flower gardens contain everlastings, old-fashioned flowers and heirloom plants.

Montreal Botanical Garden
4101 Sherbrooke St. East
Montreal, Quebec
Canada H1X 2B2

The Montreal Botanical Garden features medicinal and poisonous herb gardens as well as many special theme gardens.

Mount Vernon
The Mount Vernon Ladies' Association of the Union
Mt. Vernon, VA 22121
(703) 780-2000

Mount Vernon's large formal kitchen garden contains herbs and antique roses.

Museum of Alaska Transportation and Industry
PO Box 909
Palmer, AK 99645
(907) 745-4493

The Museum of Alaska Transportation and Industry has many planting beds scattered around the grounds filled with many varieties of herbs as well as annual flowers such as poppies, cosmos, salvias, snapdragons and others. (Most of the plants bloom in August here.)

Nani Mau Gardens
421 Makalika St.
Hilo, HI 96720
(808) 959-3541

The 17-acre Nani Mau Gardens, set in the Panaewa rain forest, include large collections of orchids, ginger groves, allspice trees, a Japanese garden, thousands of tropical flowering plants and a rare Hawaiian herb garden.

The National Herb Garden

U.S. National Arboretum
3501 New York Ave., NE
Washington, DC 20002
(202) 472-9259

The two-acre National Herb Garden, a joint project of The Herb Society of America and the National Arboretum, features three large sections with more than 1000 varieties of herbs: a formal sunken knot garden, a historic rose garden and a group of ten herbal theme gardens. The theme gardens include a dye garden, an early American garden, a medicine garden, an oriental garden, a culinary garden, an American Indian garden and others.

New York Botanical Garden

Luce Herb Garden
Marilyn Ratner, P. R. Coordinator
200th St. and Souther Blvd.
Bronx, NY 10458-5126
(212) 220-8700

The Luce Herb Garden at the New York Botanical Garden was designed by prominent English garden designer and author Penelope Hobhouse. It features twin knots of clipped boxwood with planting beds of ornamental herbs.

Ogden House

1520 Bronson Rd.
Fairfield, CT 06430
(203) 259-6356

Ogden House, a mid-18th-century farmhouse, features more than 50 species of herbs in an authentic herb and kitchen garden.

Old Slater Mill Museum

PO Box 727
Roosevelt Ave.
Pawtucket, RI 02862
(401) 725-8638

The Old Slater Mill Museum features a small garden of fiber, textile and dye plants.

Old Sturbridge Village

Susan Rogers
1 Old Sturbridge Village Rd.
Sturbridge, MA 01566
(508) 347-3362

Old Sturbridge Village, a living history museum, features several kitchen, flower and herb gardens. These contain more than 400 varieties of herbs and plants grouped according to their use. The Center Village flower gardens have been planted to show styles of garden layout likely to be found in New England in the 1830s. Lots of heirloom flowers and vegetables can be seen in specialty garden beds throughout the property. A Museum Gift Shop and New England Bookstore are on the premises.

Old Westbury Gardens

71 Old Westbury Rd.
Old Westbury, NY 11568
(516) 333-0048

Listed on the National Register of Historic Places, Old Westbury Gardens features eight formal gardens, demonstration gardens, boxwood, cottage and walled gardens; includes many herbs. A mansion on the property is furnished with 18th-century antiques and English paintings.

HOMEMADE YOGURT HERB DRESSING
Makes four 1/4-cup servings (approximately 30 calories per serving)

3/4 cup homemade yogurt
1/4 cup peeled minced cucumber
1/2 teaspoon parsley flakes
1/4 teaspoon garlic salt
1/4 teaspoon onion powder
1/8 teaspoon dry mustard
1/4 teaspoon granulated sugar

In mixing bowl, add all ingredients to yogurt. Mix gently until well blended. Serve as a dressing for salad or as a raw vegetable dip. For extra zip, substitute some horseradish for the dry mustard.

—contributed by the New England Cheesemaking Supply Co., Inc., Ashfield, MA

The Ozark Folk Center State Park

Heritage Herb Garden
Tina Marie Wilcox
PO Box 500
Mt. View, AR 72560
(501) 269-3851

The Heritage Herb Garden at the Ozark Folk Center State Park was formed to preserve and interpret the herbal lore of the Ozark folk community. Designed by Jim Long of Long Creek Herb Farm, the Garden comprises a Yarb Garden, Dye Plant and Textile Garden, Terraced Garden, Garden for the Physically Challenged, Young Pioneer Garden and Native Plant Wildlife Garden. An Herb Cabin on the property is a demonstration and herb drying area. Special herbal events are scheduled throughout the year at the Folk Center and a gift shop is also located in the Park.

William Paca Garden

Romey Curtis
1 Martin St.
Annapolis, MD 21401
(410) 267-6656

William Paca was a signer of the Declaration of Independence and a Revolutionary War governor in Maryland. The restored William Paca Garden includes a Garden House or pavilion, boxwood topiary trees, an authentic 1761 kitchen garden with herb edgings and a physic garden of medicinal plants.

Park & Tilford Gardens

BCE Development Corporation
440-333 Brooksbank Ave.
North Vancouver, BC
Canada V7J 3S8
(604) 984-8200

The Park and Tilford Gardens include many theme gardens, including a formal rose garden, a flower garden and an herb garden with medicinal and culinary herbs.

Parkview School for the Blind

3300 Gibson St.
Muskogee, OK 74401

The Parkview School for the Blind has a small garden of herbs to smell and to feel that are marked with Braille labels.

Plimoth Plantation

Plymouth, MA 02360
(617) 746-1662

This 17th-century style Pilgrim's village reconstruction contains authentic herb kitchen and vegetable gardens.

Putnam Cottage

Betsy Cullen, Curator/Caretaker
243 East Putnam Ave.
Greenwich, CT 06830
(203) 869-9697

A small 18th-century kitchen herb garden has been planted on the grounds of this historic house (formerly the Knapp Tavern) and museum.

Quail Botanical Gardens

230 Quail Gardens Dr.
Encinitas, CA 92024
(619) 436-3036

The Quail Botanical Garden features more than six acres of herbs, including a medieval herb garden, Latin American and Southeast Asian herb gardens.

The Red Barn

Jeanita or Jerome Ives
HCR30, Box 96C
Pelsor, AR 72856-9801
(501) 294-5284

The Red Barn is located in the northwest Arkansas Ozark Mountains. The Iveses have two herb gardens. One is designed around picnic grounds, and the other is part of a Heritage Cabin on the property. The Red Barn comprises 12 acres of meadows and woods, a restaurant, general store, country gift shop and camping facilities. The facilities are available for groups who wish to have a group workshop in a camp-type setting. Write or call for details.

Rhettland Herbary

Eddie Rhett-Thurston
7867 Burson Rd.
Valley Springs, CA 95252
(209) 786-2667

The Rhettland Herbary consists of two acres of herbal display gardens; call or write for further information.

Rodef Shalom Biblical Botanical Garden

Irene Jacob, Director
4905 Fifth Ave.
Pittsburgh, PA 15213
(412) 621-6566
Garden guide $5.00

The Rodef Shalom Biblical Botanical Garden is located adjacent to the Rodef Shalom Temple and includes plants of ancient Israel and plants with Biblical names. These include bay laurel, henna, madder, flax, wheat, barley, millet, saffron, safflower, chamomile, chicory, cinnamon, coriander, dandelion, lemongrass, thyme, olives, dates, pomegranates, figs, cedars and many others.

Rue Ja's Herb Collection Farm

Ruth or James Stryker
1849 Woodard Rd.
Webster, NY 14580-9725
(716) 265-0169

Ruth and James Stryker's Rue Ja's Herb Garden focuses on culinary herbs mixed with perennial flowers. The doorway is flanked by two large myrtle topiaries. A Gazebo Colonial Garden contains fragrant herbs and flowers that are attractive to bees, butterflies and hummingbirds. Other gardens on the premises include roses, lavenders, everlastings, fruits and vegetables. In all, the gardens include more than 200 varieties of herbs. The Herb Shoppe sells dried flowers, arrangements, wreaths, baskets and potpourri supplies.

St. Thomas Episcopal Church
1486 SW Levens
Dallas, OR 97338
(503) 623-8522

The Vicar's Garden at the St. Thomas Episcopal Church includes a Biblical herb garden.

San Antonio Botanical Center
Paul Cox
555 Funston Place
San Antonio, TX 78209
(512) 821-5143

The San Antonio Botanical Center features many specialty gardens that include herbs. Some of these are the Rose Gardens with its hybrid teas, climbers, floribundas and antiques; an Old-Fashioned Garden of annuals and perennials; a Garden for the Blind, featuring plants chosen for their texture and scent; and an Herb Garden, which includes herbs used by settlers for medicinal and culinary purposes.

Here's your sweet lavender,
Sixteen sprigs a penny,
Which you will find,
    my ladies,
Will smell as sweet as any.

— Old London street cry

San Diego Wild Animal Park
Off Hwy. 78
Escondido, CA (619) 234-6541 or 480-0100

The San Diego Wild Animal Park features more than 200 varieties of medicinal, culinary, ornamental and fragrant herbs interspersed with herds of camels, zebras, elephants, lions and other wild animals.

Santa Barbara Botanic Garden
1212 Mission Canyon Rd.
Santa Barbara, CA 93105
(805) 682-4726

The Santa Barbara Botanic Garden is part of a 65-acre preserve in the foothills of the Santa Ynez Mountains. The Garden features large collections of irises and native California herbs and plants, many of which are rare or endangered.

Santa Fe Trail Center
Ruth Olson, Director
Rt. 3
Larned, KS 67550
(316) 285-2054

The Santa Fe Trail Center has a small annual and perennial herb garden surrounded by a walled courtyard that was planted and is maintained by the local herb guild.

Selsley Herb Farm
Peter or Gillian Wimperis
Water Lane, Selsley Common
Stroud, Gloucestershire, England GLS SLW
0453 766682

The Selsley Herb (and Goat) Farm attracts many visitors each year. It includes a nursery offering a wide variety of herbs and aromatic plants, a garden open to the public for a small charge, a barn shop with herbal products for sale along with a variety of farm animals to amuse the children. A traditional cart wheel and ladder are planted with herbs. A long herbaceous border is also planted entirely with herbs.

Shaker Museum
Old Chatham, NY 12316
(518) 794-9100

The Shaker Museum features Shaker folk art and artifacts as well as an herb garden.

Shakertown at Pleasant Hill
3500 Lexington Rd.
Harrodsburg, KY 40330
(606) 734-5411

A medicinal Shaker herb garden is featured at this restored site of a Shaker community.

Shelburne Museum
Rt. 7
Shelburne, VT 05482
(802) 985-3344

The Shelburne Museum has several gardens including medicinal, culinary, dye and fragrance herbs. An interesting Apothecary's Shop is also part of the Museum.

Shepherd's Garden Seeds
Renee Shepherd
6116 Highway 9
Felton, CA 95018
(408) 335-6910

Renee Shepherd opens her trial gardens for educational tours twice weekly during the spring and summer. (Also see listing in Chapter 1.)

Stanley-Whitman House Museum
Jean Martin, Director/Curator
37 High St.
Farmington, CT 06032
(203) 677-9222

The Stanley-Whitman House, a National Historic Landmark, is one of the best-known examples of early New England framed architecture. The Museum gardens are currently being restored to reflect a typical "dooryard garden" of the 18th century, with herbs and flowers appropriate to the time.

State Arboretum of Virginia
Anne White
PO Box 175
Boyce, VA 22620
(703) 837-1758

The State Arboretum of Virginia (the Orland E. White Arboretum) covers nearly 135 acres and contains more than 6000 trees and woody shrubs. Specialty gardens include: an herb garden, a perennial garden, an azalea garden and a large boxwood garden.

Free guided tours starting about March 15 are offered by appointment to adult and children's groups, including school classes. Call to reserve tour times. The Arboretum also sponsors a number of workshops throughout the year.

State Botanical Garden of Georgia
Jeannette Coplin, Herb Garden Curator
2450 S. Milledge Ave.
Athens, GA 30605
(404) 542-1244

The State Botanical Garden of Georgia, located about two miles south of the University of Georgia campus, encompasses more than 300 acres. The Garden's specialty gardens and plant collections include several herb gardens.

The State of New Hampshire

Urban Forestry Center
45 Elwyn Rd.
Portsmouth, NH 03801
(603) 431-6774

The Urban Forestry Center is a demonstration urban forest that is being used and developed by the Division of Forests and Lands, New Hampshire Department of Resources and Economic Development. The forested and wetland tract is made up of many preserved areas, one of which is an herb garden. The garden is a traditional 19th-century design, and the herbs have been placed in informal groupings. Borders of lavender, artemisia, alpine strawberries and thymes outline the beds. Herbs include anise, bee balm, borage, caraway, comfrey, costmary, lungwort, lovage, parsley, wild ginger, woad, lamb's-ears and hundreds more.

Strawbery Banke Museum

Anne M. Masury
454 Court St.
PO Box 300
Portsmouth, NH 03801
(603) 433-1100

The Strawbery Banke Museum includes several period display gardens, including an early herb and vegetable garden of the early 1720s.

Strybing Arboretum & Botanical Gardens

Walden R. Valen, Director
9th Ave. and Lincoln Way (Golden Gate Park)
San Francisco, CA 94122
(415) 753-7089

The Garden of Fragrance at the Strybing Arboretum is filled with plants (many of which are herbs) that have been chosen for their fragrance, color, texture and usefulness.

The Sundial Herb Garden

Ragna Tischler Goddard
59 Hidden Lake R.d
Higganum, CT 06441
(203) 345-4290

Visitors to the Sundial Herb Garden will find three gardens—a knot garden, an 18th-century-style garden and a topiary garden. The gardens, modeled after 17th- and 18th-century designs, show a variety of herbs planted in formal settings. At "Tea Talks" on Sunday afternoons from June through September, herb teas and desserts are served and a brief talk on herbs is given. In addition, three "High Teas" and other special events are scheduled each year. Advance reservations are required for these events; call or write for details.

Herb programs or teas for groups can also be arranged by appointment, and the Sundial Herb Garden can also accommodate small weddings.

Boyce Thompson Southwestern Arboretum

Kim Stone
PO Box AB
Superior, AZ 85273
(602) 689-2723

The Boyce Thompson Southwestern Arboretum (located on U.S. 60, 60 miles east of Phoenix) specializes in plants for drought tolerance and hardiness in hot, dry climates. The 1076-acre Arboretum includes desert and woodland plantings of yuccas, saguaros and a eucalyptus grove with more than 50 different species.

Thyme Garden Seed Company

Rolfe or Janet Hagen
20546 Alsea Hwy.
Alsea, OR 97324
(503) 487-8671

The Thyme Garden Seed Company (see listing in Chapter 1) has more than one-half acre planted with medicinal herbs, dye plants, moon garden plants and a large number of culinary herbs. Janet and Rolfe Hagen, owners, eventually plan to develop different "thyme" gardens, focusing on different eras—Roman, medieval, etc.

Tucson Botanical Gardens

Cecily Gill Herb Garden
2150 N. Alvernon Way
Tucson, AZ 85712
(602) 326-9255

The Tucson Botanical Gardens contains a small Kitchen Herb Garden with culinary and medicinal herbs, a Heritage Rose Garden, a Spring Wildflower Garden, a Native Seeds/SEARCH Garden, a Sensory Garden and other specialty collections. A Gift Shop and Chile Room sells lots of botanically inspired gifts, with one room dedicated entirely to items with a "chili" theme.

John J. Tyler Arboretum Garden for the Blind

515 Painter Rd.
Lima, PA 19060

The John J. Tyler Arboretum Garden for the Blind features a large variety of herbs planted along two display borders.

University of California at Berkeley Botanical Garden

Bobbie Ohs
Centennial Drive
Berkeley, CA 94720
(510) 642-3012 or 642-3343
Established 1890

The University of California Botanical Garden includes a Chinese Herb Garden, a collection of culinary, aromatic, medicinal and ornamental herbs, a Hummingbird garden and more. (Also see listing in Chapter 6.)

University of California at Davis Arboretum

University of California, Davis Campus
Davis, CA 95616
(916) 752-2498

The University of California at Davis Arboretum features a large medicinal herb garden, specialty gardens and a number of culinary herbs in informal gardens throughout the UC Campus.

University of California at Riverside Botanical Gardens

University of California
Campus Drive
Riverside, CA 92521
(714) 787-4650

The 37-acre University of California at Riverside Botanical Gardens displays more than 3500 species of plants from all over the world, including antique roses and culinary herbs.

University of Minnesota Landscape Arboretum

3675 Arboretum Drive
Chanhassen, MN 55317
(612) 443-2460

The University of Minnesota Landscape Arboretum grows a large variety of herbs that can live through the cold Minnesota winters. Gardens include a 16th-century English knot garden, a Cloister garden and others containing a large number of medicinal, culinary, ornamental and fragrant herbs.

University of Rhode Island Medicinal Plant Garden

J. Peter Morgan, Supervisor;
Dr. Yuzuru Shimizu, Director
College of Pharmacy
Department of Pharmacognosy
Kingston, RI 02881-0809
(401) 792-2751, ext. 2849

The Medicinal Plant Garden at the University of Rhode Island contains many popular plants that are used as herbs and spices, over-the-counter drugs and cosmetics. An International Seed Exchange program is sponsored by the Garden.

University of Washington Medicinal Herb Garden

Volunteer Coordinator
Friends of the Medicinal Herb Garden
Dept. of Botany, KB-15
University of Washington
Seattle, WA 98195
(206) 543-1126

The Medicinal Herb Garden at the University of Washington is located in the heart of the campus and is the largest collection of its kind in the western hemisphere. Established in 1911 by the UW School of Pharmacy, the first one-acre garden was expanded during World War I to help offset a critical national shortage of belladonna, digitalis and other natural drugs. Over the years, the gardens have been expanded, moved and neglected until 1984, when a newly formed volunteer group, Friends of the Medicinal Herb Garden, adopted the site. They are working to preserve, maintain and improve the garden, which is now being used to train students of pharmacy, botany, landscape architecture, urban horticulture, art and anthropology.

Washington National Cathedral Gardens

Wisconsin and Massachusetts Ave.
Washington, DC 20016-5098
(202) 537-6263

The gardens of the Washington National Cathedral include an Herb Cottage and garden, an Herb Bed filled with native bee balm, aromatic herbs and a Peace Rose planted in 1954 and The Hortulus, or "little garden", which has been planted with monastic kitchen and infirmary herbs used during the 9th century. Herbs and scented geraniums may be purchased at the Greenhouse at Washington Cathedral, and herb plants are available by mail order (see listing in Chapter 1). The gardens are open every day from dawn to dusk.

Western Reserve Herb Garden

Garden Center of Greater Cleveland
11030 East Blvd. (University Circle)
Cleveland, OH 44106

The Western Reserve Herb Society maintains the second largest herb garden in the United States adjacent to the Garden Center of Greater Cleveland. The garden, now more than 22 years old, features several hundred herb varieties in the knot garden and herbal theme gardens accented with stone walls, ironwork, mill wheels, etc.

Henry Whitfield State Historical Museum

Michael A. McBride, Director/Curator
Old Whitefield St.
PO Box 210
Guilford, CT 06437
(203) 453-2457

The gardens of the Henry Whitfield State Hictorical Museum feature herbs which were in use during the 17th and 18th centuries.

Zilker Botanical Garden

Zilker Park
2200 Barton Springs Rd.
Austin, TX 78746
(512) 477-8672

The Herb Gardens at Zilker Park feature more than 100 varieties of culinary, medicinal and fragrant herbs.

HERBS, USEFUL IN COOKERY

Thyme, is good in soups and stuffings.
Sweet Marjoram, is used in Turkeys.
Summer Savory, ditto, and in Sausages and salted Beef, and legs of Pork.
Sage, is used in Cheese and Pork, not generally approved.
Parsley, good in soups, and to garnish roast Beef, excellent with bread and butter in the spring.
Penny Royal, might be more generally cultivated in gardens, and used in cookery and medicines.
Sweet Thyme, is most useful and best approved in cookery.

—from *American Cookery* by Amelia Simmons, 1796

Geographic Index to Gardens

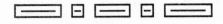

Alabama

Birmingham Botanical Gardens

Alaska

Museum of Alaska Transportation and Industry

Arizona

Boyce Thompson Southwestern Arboretum
Tucson Botanical Gardens

Arkansas

Arkansas School for the Blind
Arkansas Territorial Restoration Medicinal Garden
Long Creek Herb Farm
Ozark Folk Center State Park Heritage Herb Garden
The Red Barn

California

Filoli
Fullerton Arboretum
J. Paul Getty Museum
Huntington Botanical Gardens
Los Angeles State and County Arboretum
Quail Botanical Gardens
Rhettland Herbary
San Diego Wild Animal Park
Santa Barbara Botanic Garden

Shepherd's Garden Seeds
Strybing Arboretum & Botanical Gardens
University of California at Berkeley Botanical Garden
University of California at Davis Arboretum
University of California at Riverside Botanical Gardens

Colorado

Denver Botanic Gardens

Connecticut

American Clock and Watch Museum
American Indian Archaeological Institute
Caprilands Herb Farm
General William Hart House
Ogden House
Putnam Cottage
Stanley-Whitman House Museum
The Sundial Herb Garden
Welles Shipman Ward House
Henry Whitfield State Historical Museum

District of Columbia

The National Herb Garden
Washington National Cathedral Gardens

Florida

Eden Vineyards Winery & Park

Georgia

Atlanta Botanical Garden
Fernbank Science Center Garden
State Botanical Garden of Georgia

Hawaii

Foster Botanic Gardens
Harold L. Lyon Arboretum
Nani Mau Gardens

Illinois

Chicago Botanic Garden
Clark's Greenhouse & Herbal Country
Early American Museum and Gardens
Enchanted Crest
George L. Luthy Memorial Botanical
  Garden

Indiana

Hilltop Garden

Iowa

Des Moines Botanical Center
Iowa State University Horticultural
  Garden
Living History Farms

Kansas

Santa Fe Trail Center

Kentucky

Farmington Historic Home and Garden
McDowell House and Apothecary Shop
Shakertown at Pleasant Hill

Maine

Hedgehog Hill Farm

Maryland

William Paca Garden

Massachusetts

Berkshire Botanical Garden
Cushing House Museum
Hancock Shaker Village
Old Sturbridge Village
Plimoth Plantation

Michigan

W. J. Beal Botanical Garden
Busha's Brae Herb Farm
Cobblestone Farm
Cranbrook House & Gardens
Henry Ford Museum at Greenfield
  Village
Matthaei Botanical Gardens
Michigan 4-H Children's Garden

Minnesota

University of Minnesota Landscape
  Arboretum

Missouri

Missouri Botanical Garden

New Hampshire

Canterbury Shaker Village
The State of New Hampshire Urban
   Forestry Center
Strawbery Banke Museum

New York

Abigail Adams Smith Museum
Boscobel Restoration
Brooklyn Botanic Garden
The Cloisters—Metropolitan Museum of
   Art Medieval Herb Garden at
   Bonnfont Cloisters
Cornell Plantations—Robison York
   State Herb Garden
Gatehouse Herbs
New York Botanical Garden—Luce
   Herb Garden
Old Westbury Gardens
Rue Ja's Herb Collection Farm
Shaker Museum

North Carolina

Gourmet Gardens Herb Farm

Ohio

Bayberry Hill Herb Emporium
Cox Arboretum
Stan Hywet Hall & Gardens
Inniswood Metro Gardens Herb Garden
Kingwood Center
Western Reserve Herb Garden

Oklahoma

Honor Heights Park
Parkview School for the Blind

Oregon

Jenkins Estate
Mary's Herb Garden & Gift Shop
Mission Mill Village and Museum
St. Thomas Episcopal Church
Thyme Garden Seed Company

Pennsylvania

Country Roots Shop & Gardens
Historic Bartram's Garden
Longwood Gardens
Rodef Shalom Biblical Botanical Garden
John J. Tyler Arboretum Garden for the
   Blind

Rhode Island

Old Slater Mill Museum
University of Rhode Island Medicinal
   Plant Garden

Texas

Antique Rose Emporium
Dallas Civic Garden Center
Fort Worth Botanic Garden
Hilltop Herb Farm
Houston Garden Center
Mercer Arboretum and Botanic Gardens
San Antonio Botanical Center
Zilker Botanic Gardens

Vermont

Shelburne Museum

Virginia

Agecroft Hall
Colonial Williamsburg
Monticello
Mount Vernon
State Arboretum of Virginia

Washington

Fairie Herb Gardens
The Herbfarm
University of Washington Medicinal
    Herb Garden

Wisconsin

Boerner Botanical Gardens

CANADA
Alberta

Devonian Botanic Garden

British Columbia

The Butchart Gardens
Park & Tilford Gardens

Montreal

Montreal Botanical Garden

New Brunswick

Crocker Hill Studios

Ontario

Black Creek Pioneer Village

UNITED KINGDOM
Gloucestershire

Selsley Herb Farm

Kent

Iden Croft Herbs
Leeds Castle

Scotland

Damside Garden Herbs

Cooking with Favorite Culinary Herbs

HERB	COMBINES BEST WITH THESE HERBS	USE FRESH WITH	USE IN COOKED DISHES
BASIL	bay, chives, cress, dill, garlic, marjoram, mint, parsley, oregano	salads, cheeses, tomatoes, pastas, vegetables, vinegars, oils	marinades, sauces, meat; cooked briefly—soups, vegetables, eggs, seafood, pastas
BAY	compatible with all	bouquets garnis, marinades	meat, fish, fowl, stuffings, breads, puddings, soups, stews
CHERVIL	chives, cress, dill, lemon balm, parsley, sorrel, tarragon	salads, eggs, avocados, vegetables, melons, cheeses	cook only briefly—fish, oysters, poultry, eggs, sauces, vegetables
CHIVES	bay, chervil, coriander, cress, dill, lemon balm, marjoram, oregano, parsley, sorrel, tarragon, thyme	salads, cheeses, eggs, vegetables, butters, mayonnaise, vinegars, sour cream	needs little cooking—sauces, soups, stews, eggs, vegetables, potatoes, seafood
CORIANDER	chives, garlic, marjoram, oregano, parsley; often used alone	salads, sauces, salsas, cheeses, escabeches	fish, shellfish, curries, fowl, pork, lamb, sauces, soups, beans, stir fries, Mexican dishes
CRESS	chervil, chives, dill, garlic, parsley, sorrel, tarragon	best raw in salads; with vegetables, grains, pastas	cook briefly—soups, sauces, fish, chicken, pasta, grains, potatoes
DILL	basil, bay, chervil, chives, cress, garlic, mint, parsley, sorrel, tarragon	best raw in salads; with vegetables, pastas, grains, seafood, eggs, slaws, sour cream, cheeses	cook briefly—soups, sauces, vegetables, fish, potatoes, baked goods, pickles
GARLIC	compatible with all; but use sparingly with chervil, chives, lemon balm, mint	rubbed on bread, in salads, sauces, marinades; with pastas, grains, seafoods, cheeses	goes well with every type of food except desserts and sweets
LEMON BALM	chervil, chives, mint, parsley; use sparingly with garlic	salads, fruits, macerated fruits, beverages, butters, sorbets	vegetables, grains, fish, chicken, desserts, tea
MARJORAM	basil, bay, chives, coriander, garlic, oregano, mint, parsley, rosemary, sage, summer savory, tarragon, thyme, winter savory	salads, eggs, rice, pastas, cheeses, vegetables	sauces, soups, stews, pasta, meat, fish, poultry, vegetables, cheeses
MINTS	basil, cress, dill, lemon balm, parsley, tarragon	beverages, salads, vegetables, desserts, ices, ice creams, fruits	tea, sauces, jellies, preserves, baked goods, meat, soups, vegetables, fish
OREGANO	basil, bay, chives, coriander, garlic, marjoram, mint, parsley, sage, summer savory, tarragon, thyme, winter savory	salsas, pastas, cheeses, tomatoes, vegetables	sauces, soups, stews, pasta, meat, beans, vegetables, cheeses
PARSLEY	compatible with all	salads, dressings, bouquets garnis, sauces, cheeses, pastas, vegetables	soups, stews, vegetables, poultry, fish, meat, pasta, grains; everything but desserts
ROSEMARY	bay, garlic, marjoram, oregano, parsley, sage, summer savory, thyme, winter savory	cheeses, breads, marinades, beverages, vegetables, oils	roast meats, game, poultry, fish, soups, stews, potatoes, legumes, bread
SAGE	bay, garlic, marjoram, oregano, parsley, rosemary, summer savory, thyme, winter savory	cheeses, marinades	tea, soups, stews, meat, poultry, breads, vegetables, beans, apples
SORREL	basil, chives, dill, garlic, parsley, tarragon	best raw in salads; mayonnaise, grains, legumes	lightly cooked soups, sauces, eggs, vegetables, shellfish, fish, poultry
SUMMER SAVORY	basil, bay, garlic, marjoram, oregano, parsley, rosemary, sage, tarragon, thyme	beans, tomatoes, bouquet garnis, salads, vegetables, cheeses	vegetables, soups, beans, corn, eggs, potatoes
WINTER SAVORY	basil, bay, garlic, marjoram, oregano, parsley, rosemary, sage, tarragon, thyme	beans, bouquet garnis, marinades	soups, stews, meats, poultry, beans, vegetables
TARRAGON	bay, chervil, chives, cress, dill, garlic, mint, sorrel, summer savory, thyme, winter savory	salads, dressings, eggs, vegetables, seafood	sauces, fish, eggs, chicken, meats, soups, vegetables, vinegars, pickles
THYME	basil, bay, chives, garlic, marjoram, oregano, parsley, rosemary, sage, summer savory, tarragon, winter savory	grains, vegetables, bouquet garnis, salads, cheeses	soups, sauces, stews, meat, poultry, fish, shellfish, vegetables, mushrooms, breads, marinades

From *Herbs In the Kitchen* by Carolyn Dille and Susan Belsinger (Interweave Press, 1992).

9

Herb Membership Groups

WE HAVE LISTED REGIONAL GROUPS, clubs and societies first, including all units of The Herb Society of America. These are followed by state organizations and then national and international membership organizations. Get involved with a group! Herb societies and clubs are fun places to meet new friends, learn about herbs and have a good time.

Regional Herb Societies/Clubs

Contact each group directly for meeting times and places. Herb societies usually do not have big budgets for postage, so be sure to enclose a self-addressed stamped envelope with your request for information. You might also want to contact these groups when moving into or traveling to a different area of the country to check on meeting times or special events, annual festivals, etc., sponsored by the groups.

Adirondack Herb Society
Jane Desotelle, President
RR 2
Chateaugay, NY 12920
(518) 563-4777

Andover Herb Society
Mary Elizabeth Russell
17 Boardman Ln.
Hamilton, MA 01936

Anne Hathaway Herb Society
Tulsa Garden Center
2435 S. Peoria
Tulsa, OK 74114

Ark-La-Tex Herb Society
Gay Ingram
PO Box 1096
Big Sandy, TX 75755-1096

Austin Herb Society
Colleen Belk
908 Arroweye Trail
Austin, TX 78733

or Bobbi A. McRae
PO Box 49770
Austin, TX 78765

Baton Rouge Herb Society
Patsy McGrew
30181 Smith Drive
Walker, LA 70785

Birmingham Herb Society
Mary Jean Morawetz
Birmingham Botanical Gardens
2612 Lane Park Rd.
Birmingham, AL 35223

Central Ohio Unit Herb Society of America
Mrs. Betsy Warner
145 E. South St.
Worthington, OH 43085

Central Texas Herb Society
Paula Jones Hill
307 W. Ave. E
Lampasas, TX 76550
(512) 556-8801

Chattahoochee Unit, The Herb Society of America
Mrs. Preston Miller
PO Box 52754
Atlanta, GA 30305

Columbus Herb Society
Fleta Jonassen, President
510 8th St.
Columbus, IN 47201
(812) 372-3030

Covered Bridge Herb & Garden Club
Joan Balder Cook
Mallory Rd., RR 1, Box 320
Sauquoit, NY 13456

Delaware Valley Unit, The Herb Society of America
Joan Noveske
6278 Groveland Rd.
Pipersville, PA 18947

Des Moines Herb Study Group
Kathy Drew
3321 E. 9th St.
Des Moines, IA 50316

or Kim Sova
1431 41st St.
Des Moines, IA 50311

Evening Herb Society of the Palm Beaches
PO Box 17318
West Palm Beach, FL 33416-7318

Fireland's Herb Study Unit
c/o Lois Gunn
3505 St. Rt. 113
Milan, OH 44846

Fort Worth Herb Society
PO Box 60245
Fort Worth, TX 76115

Frankenmuth Mid-Michigan Unit, The Herb Society of America
Marianne Dafoe
1895 S. Beyer Rd.
Saginaw, MI 48601-9437

or Gloria Rodammer
7749 W. Swaffer Rd.
Vassar, MI 48768

Glastonbury Garden Club
Dorothy Pittman
Fairview Terrace
South Glastonbury, CT 06073

Goose Creek Herb Guild
Betty Fleming
PO Box 2224
Leesburg, VA 22075

Grosse Pointe Unit, The Herb Society of America
Mrs. Molly Valade
21 Westwind
Grosse Pointe Farms, MI 48236

Herb Guild Unit, The Herb Society of America
Ms. Margaret Turk
8402 Vera Dr.
Broadview Heights, OH 44147

Herb Society of Deep East Texas
423 Moody
Lufkin, TX 75901

Herb Society of Greater Fort Worth
5216 Rector Ave.
Fort Worth, TX 76133

Herb Society of Old City Park
1717 Gano St.
Dallas, TX 75215

The Herb Society of South Central Kansas
1214 Coolidge
Wichita, KS 67203

Herb Study Group of The Friends of The Matthaei Botanical Gardens
University of Michigan
1800 N. Dixboro Rd.
Ann Arbor, MI 48105-9741
For information, call (313) 998-7061 or 769-9414

If they would drink
nettles in March
And eat mugwort in May,
So many fine maidens
Wouldn't go to the clay
—old proverb

Herbs for Health & Fun Club
Treasa Brookman
RR #1, Box 396
Opdyke, IL 62872

Hoover Historical Unit, The Herb Society of America
Ms. Bettie Kehl
725 Bellaire
Louisville, OH 44641

Inland Herb Society
Nick Waddell
PO Box 8657
Riverside, CA 92515-8657

Kentuckiana Unit, The Herb Society of America
Barbara Warf
9 Martin Dr.
New Albany, IN 47150

Kingwood Herb Society
Heidi Apger, President
Rt. 8, Bass Rd.
Mansfield, OH 44904

Knoxville Herb Society
Lizz Cook
11126 Sonja Dr.
Knoxville, TN 37922

Kyana Herb Society
Gwen Van Wyk
PO Box 521
Pewee Valley, KY 40056

Long Island Unit, The Herb Society of America
Robin H. Brown
1280 N. Parish Dr.
Southold, NY 11971

Low Country Herb Society
PO Box 174
Pawleys Island, SC 29585

Lower Cape Fear Herb Study Guild
Sea Holly Herbs and Flowers
Doris Davis
Rt. 1, Box 556
Wilmington, NC 28405

Madison Herb Society
Ohlbrich Gardens
Atwood Ave.
Madison, WI 53704

or PO Box 8733
Madison, WI 53708

Maple Hill Gardeners
Beaver Brook Association
117 Ridge Rd.
Hollis, NH 03049
(603) 465-7787

Memphis Herb Society
PO Box 241321
Memphis, TN 38124

Midwest Michigan Herb Association
Gale Newton, President
Box 662
Rockford, MI 49341
(616) 942-1251

Nashville Herb Society
Mrs. A. Welling LaGrone
Shady Borene
2408 Old Natchez Trace
Franklin, TN 37064

Nashville Unit, The Herb Society of America
Marianne Byrd
4419 Harding Place
Nashville, TN 37205

New England Unit, The Herb Society of America
88 Marshall St.
Leicester, MA 01425

North & Central Texas Unit, The Herb Society of America
Kay S. Nelson
8418 Swananoah Rd.
Dallas, TX 75209

Northeast Seacoast Unit, The Herb Society of America
Tanya Jackson, Corresponding Secretary
45 Elwyn Rd.
Portsmouth, NH 03801

or Ms. Shirley MacDougall
108 1st Crown Point
Rochester, NH 03867

Northern California Unit, The Herb Society of America
Jack and Karen Mahshi
3503 Half Moon Ln.
Concord, CA 94518

Northern Illinois Unit, The Herb Society of America
Diane Johnson
1615 Walnut
Wilmette, IL 60091

Northern New Jersey Unit, The Herb Society of America
Mrs. David G. Cassa
602 Fairmount Ave.
Chatham, NJ 07928

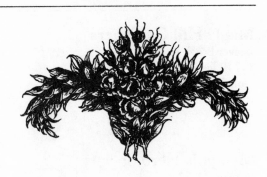

Old City Park Herb Society
1717 Gano St.
Dallas, TX 75215

Pennsylvania Heartland Unit, The Herb Society of America
Yvonne Snyder
3830 Admire Rd.
Dover, PA 17315

Old Dominion Herb Society
3920 W. Franklin St.
Richmond, VA 23221

Peoria Herb Guild
Jane Look
7710 S. Gerdes Rd.
Mapleton, IL 61547

Owensboro Herb Society
Betty Jo Kaelin
1206 Holly Ave.
Owensboro, KY 42301

Philadelphia Unit, The Herb Society of America
Caroline Amidon
Box 201, Nantmeal Rd., RD 1
Glenmoore, PA 19343

Ozark Herb People
Janice Vigh
PO Box 465
Leslie, AR 72645

Ozark Hills Herb Society
Sue or John Thaxter
HCR 2, Box 1040
Hollister, MO 65672
(417) 335-2792

Potomac Unit, The Herb Society of America
Bernice Pivarnik
8611 Regor Lane
Annandale, VA 22003

Ozarks Herb Growers & Marketers Association
Jim Long, Founder
Long Creek Herbs
Rt. 4, Box 730
Oak Grove, AR 72660
(417) 779-5450

Prince George's Herb Society
J. Cmero
3707 37th Place
Cottage City, MD 20722

Rochester Herb Society
Ruth Stryker
1849 Woodard Rd.
Webster, NY 14580-9725
(716) 265-0169

San Joaquin Herb Society
Eddie Rhett-Thurston
7867 Burson Rd.
Valley Springs, CA 95252
(209) 786-2667

Slo Thymes Herb Society
Christine Hill
1072 San Adriano
San Luis Obispo, CA 93406

Smokey Mountain Herb Society
1743 W. Broadway, Suite 173
Maryville, TN 37801

Somerset Herb Club "Herbal Gems"
Laurel Art
PO Box 414
Somerset, PA 15501

South Central Kansas Herb Society
Frank Good
1214 Coolidge
Wichita, KS 67203

South Texas Unit, The Herb Society of America
Lois Jean Howard
7623 Troulan
Houston, TX 77074

Southern California Unit, The Herb Society of America
Kirby Davis
1833 West 247th Place
Lomita, CA 90717

Southern Michigan Unit, The Herb Society of America
Laura Principe
1134 Eton Cross
Bloomfield Hills, MI 48304

Southern Ontario Unit, The Herb Society of America
Mrs. A. (Janet) van Nostrand
Nordlands RR 1
Gormley, ON
Canada L0H 1G0

Susquehanna Herb Guild
Kerry A. Morton
PO Box 534
Mt. Gretna, PA 17064

Susquehanna Unit, The Herb Society of America
Bonita H. Miller
2140 Landis Valley Rd.
Lancaster, PA 17601

Thymely Herb Group
Janet Waite, President
334 Goode St.
Burnt Hills, NY 12027
(518) 885-9738

Tidewater Unit, The Herb Society of America
Ms. Jeanne Pettersen
5520 Del Park Ave.
Virginia Beach, VA 23455

HINTS FOR USING WINE VINEGARS

- Substitute wine vinegars in any recipes where you would use wine or lemon juice
- Try several tablespoons of vinegar in any commercial spaghetti sauce, soup or gravy.
- Use a little vinegar to deglaze your wok when stir-frying.

—from Chicama Vineyards catalog

Tulsa Herb Society
Janetta Williamson
1230 E. Hazel Blvd.
Tulsa, OK 74114

or Tulsa Garden Center
2435 S. Peoria
Tulsa, OK 74114

Chinese call the dandelion plant "earth nail" because of its long taproot.

Virginia Commonwealth Unit, The Herb Society of America
Mrs. Robert (Marianne) Quinnell
PO Box 1120
Kilmarnock, VA 22482

Wabash Valley Herb Society
1225 Maple Ave.
Terre Haute, IN 47804

West Central Illinois Herb Guild
Marilyn Fedder
54 N. Main
Winchester, IL 62694

Western Pennsylvania Unit, The Herb Society of America
Mrs. Leslie (Corrine) Lockard
703 Old Clairton Rd.
Clairton, PA 15025

Western New York Herb Study Group
6195 Bunting Rd.
Orchard Park, NY 14127

Western Reserve Unit, The Herb Society of America
Mrs. Eugene (Jennifer) Richter
3073 Fairfax Rd.
Cleveland Heights, OH 44106

Members-at-Large Regional Vice-Chairmen, The Herb Society of America

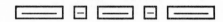

These regions cover areas where distance might prohibit regular attendance at The Herb Society of America's Unit meetings.

Region I
Sherri Byrne
The Herb Cupboard
Box 375
Fort Plain, NY 13339

Region II
Betty Anne Eliason
PO Box 870
Chestertown, MD 21620

Region III
Ann Harris
Rt. 5, Box 230
Versailles, KY 40383

Region IV
Helen Kovach
5381 Cleves-Warsaw Pike
Cincinnati, OH 45238

Region V
Linda Wells
588 Cherry Ct.
Birmingham, MI 48009

Region VI
Ms. Helen Chandler
151 Gayland, #51
Escondido, CA 92027

State Organizations

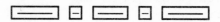

Arkansas Unit, The Herb Society of America
Mrs. W. Gerald Foster
PO Box 2896
Batesville, AR 72501

Colorado Native Plant Society
Gayle Weinstein, President
PO Box 200
Ft. Collins, CO 80522

Connecticut Unit, The Herb Society of America
Betty H. Stevens
46 Keighley Pond Rd.
Cobalt, CT 06414

Delaware Herbalists
Sinking Springs Herb Farm
Ann Stubbs
234 Blair Shore Rd.
Elkton, MD 21921-8025
(301) 398-5566

Illinois Herb Association
Una M. French, President
R. 1, Box 245
Dixon, IL 62830
(618) 266-7351

Kentucky Herb Growers and Marketers Association
Jean Hynes
PO Box 43611
Louisville, KY 40243

Maryland Herb Association
PO Box 388
Millington, MD 21651-0388

or Sinking Springs Herb Farm
Ann Stubbs
234 Blair Shore Rd.
Elkton, MD 21921-8025
(301) 398-5566

Michigan Herb Associates
Judith Bradley
136N Behnke Rd.
Coldwater, MI 49036

Michigan Herb Business Association
Dixie Stephen, President
Rt. 1, Box 232M
Setterbo Rd.
Suttons Bay, MI 49682
(616) 271-6284

or 7885 Brookville Rd.
Plymouth, MI 48170

Minnesota Herb Society
3675 Arboretum Drive
Chanhassen, MN 55317

New Hampshire Herb Society
PO Box 482
Contoocook, NH 03229

New York Unit, The Herb Society of America
Mrs. Richard Dailey
301 East 66th St., 7M
New York, NY 10021

North Carolina Herb Association
Maggie Houston
904 D Norwalk St.
Greensboro, NC 27407

or Rt. 1, Box 65
Godwin, NC 28344

North Carolina Unit, The Herb Society of America
Dorothy Bonitz
146 Great Oak Drive
Hampstead, NC 28443

Oklahoma Herb Growers and Marketers Association
7010 S. Yale, Suite 117
Tulsa, OK 74136

Oklahoma Herb Growers Association
Howard LeLeeux
2087 E. 71st St., #114
Tulsa, OK 74136

Texas Herb Grower's & Marketer's Association
Janis Teas, Treasurer
32920 Decker Prairie Rd.
Magnolia, TX 77355

Virginia Herb Growers & Marketers Association
PO Box 1176
Chesterfield, VA 23832

Wisconsin Chapter, The Herb Society of America
Patricia Buch
5608 W. Washington Blvd.
Milwaukee, WI 53208

or Jane Cole
1002 Twilight Dr.
De Pere, WI 54115

National/International Organizations

American Aromatherapy Association (AATA)
Annette Davis, Secretary
PO Box 3679
South Pasadena, CA 91031

(818) 457-1742
Established 1988
Information for SASE

The American Aromatherapy Association was formed to further the understanding of essential oils in the U.S. and Canada. Memberships are offered to both lay persons and professionals. The association's goals are to establish quality standards, offer a networking service, provide an information exchange and work toward a recognized licensing procedure in the field of aromatherapy. Contact the organization for current membership information. *Common Scents* is the AATA's quarterly publication.

American Botanical Council
Margaret Wright
PO Box 201660
Austin, TX 78720-1660

(512) 331-8868
Founded 1983

The American Botanical Council is a nonprofit educational organization that strives to provide accurate information about herbs and medicinal plant research. The ABC publishes *HerbalGram* (see listing in Chapter 3) in conjunction with the Herb Research Foundation. The Council also publishes a series of Botanical Booklets written by Steven Foster on echinacea, Siberian ginseng, Asian ginseng, ginkgo, milk thistle, peppermint, chamomile, American ginseng, goldenseal, feverfew, garlic and valerian. The booklets are currently $9.95/set or $1.00 each. A one-year membership in the Council is currently $25.00, and includes a subscription to *HerbalGram*.

American Herb Association

Kathi Keville, Director
PO Box 1673
Nevada City, CA 95959

Founded 1981

The American Herb Association is a national membership organization that strives to keep its members informed about the latest developments in the herbal world—legal, educational, scientific, etc. The AHA offers literature searches, manuscripts, herb analysis, legal services and herbal product development for its members, among other services.

Regular memberships are $20.00/year; supporting members $35.00; foreign members $28.00. A subscription to the *AHA Quarterly Newsletter* is included with membership (see Chapter 3).

American Herbalists Guild

Roy Upton
PO Box 1683
Soquel, CA 95073

Established 1989
Write for more information.

The American Herbalists Guild is a professional organization for medical herbalists. Members represent a wide range of backgrounds including Native American, Chinese, Western Folkloric, European and Ayurvedic practices. The main goal of the AHG is to promote high-quality training in Herbal Medicine. The group provides educational and networking opportunities as well as herbal practitioner referrals. A yearly seminar and symposium are also sponsored by the AHG.

The British Herb Trade Association

The Administrator
The National Farmers Union
Agriculture House
London SW1
England

The British Herb Trade Association comprises herb specialists from all areas of herbal production—fresh herbs, dried herbs, retail herb shops, aromatic and scientific researchers, among others. Write for membership details or more information. The BHTA has available a map of herb farms, gardens and shops in Britain.

The Canadian Wildflower Society

1848 Liverpool Rd.
Box 110
Pickering, ON
Canada L1V 6M3

Write for more information.

The Canadian Wildflower Society serves as a communication link among native plant societies, botanical gardens and native plant research centers across North America. The Society publishes a quarterly magazine, *Wildflower* (see description in Chapter 3). An extensive seed exchange program is available to members. Regular memberships are $25.00/year (payable in U.S. funds for U.S. subscribers) or $45.00/two years. Family or library memberships are $30.00/year.

Flower and Herb Exchange

Diane Whealy
RR 3, Box 239
Decorah, IA 52101

(319) 382-5990
Write or call for information.

The Flower and Herb Exchange is dedicated to the preservation of flowers, wildflowers, ornamentals and herbs that are family heirlooms or are unavailable commercially. The FHE is a project of the Seed Savers Exchange (a nonprofit organization working to save heirloom vegetable and fruit varieties from extinction). The main goal of The Flower and Herb Exchange is to provide information for those who want to preserve and exchange seeds of these endangered flowers and herbs. Names of members are listed in an annual directory, which members use to exchange and/or order seeds. The annual membership fee is currently $5.00.

Fresh Garlic Association

Caryl Saunders
PO Box 2410
Sausalito, CA 94966-2410

(415) 383-5057
Newsletter $5.00/year

The Fresh Garlic Association supports the use of fresh garlic in both medicinal and gastronomic uses. New members of the FGA receive an introductory kit of garlic recipes, garlic source list and a subscription to *Garlic News*, a quarterly newsletter.

The Association also publishes several books and pamphlets. The pamphlets *Garlic and Vegetables Go Together* and *Garlic and Pasta Go Together* are available free with a self-addressed stamped envelope. A cookbook, *Great Garlic Recipes from Great American Restaurants* is $1.00. Volumes I and II of *The Garlic Lovers' Cookbook* are $9.95 each (see Chapter 4 for description).

Herb Growing & Marketing Network

Maureen Buehrle
3343 Nolt Rd.
Lancaster, PA 17601-1507

(717) 898-3017

The Herb Growing & Marketing Network was begun to help small herb businesses obtain the wholesale or commercial information that they need. The Network consists of three services—a bimonthly newsletter, *The Herbal Connection* (see listing in Chapter 3); *The Herbal Green Pages*, an annual business and resource guide; and an information service. The price for the package is currently $40.00/year; a subscription to *The Herbal Connection* alone is $24.00; *The Herbal Green Pages* is $15.00.

Herb Research Foundation

Rob McCaleb, President
1007 Pearl St., Suite 200
Boulder, CO 80302

(303) 449-2265
Call or write for further information.

The Herb Research Foundation is an independent, nonprofit educational and research organization dedicated to providing reliable scientific botanical information for its members, the public and the media. The HRF encourages research on common botanicals, folk medicines and other herbal products. The Foundation is also strongly committed to helping save potential medicinal plants from extinction.

Members of the HRF receive *The HerbalGram* quarterly (see listing in Chapter 3). Bibliographies and other publications concerning herbs and pharmacognosy are also available.

In the Middle Ages in France, each family supposedly had their own still for distilling their own lavender water. Eventually professional distillers would travel around the countryside with their stills and work from the public marketplaces making lavender water for the townspeople. This became a form of entertainment for the people, who had come for miles around in order to get their turn at using the still. Unfortunately, the custom finally died out during World War I and today most lavender water is mass produced in commercial distilleries.

—from *The Frugal Housewife* by Mrs. Child, 1833

The Herb Society

77 Great Peter St.
London SW1P 2EZ
England

Write for details.

The Herb Society of America

Leslie Rascan
9019 Kirtland-Chardon Rd.
Mentor, OH 44060

The Herb Society of America was founded in Massachusetts in 1933 for the purpose of furthering the knowledge and use of herbs. THSA is mainly concerned with the cultivation of herbs, their history and their uses (both past and present) as flavoring agents, medicinal, fragrant and dye plants; ornamentals in garden design; household aids and as economic plants. Among the projects of THSA is the establishment of herb gardens, both private and public, including the National Herb Garden at the National Arboretum in Washington, D.C. (see listing in Chapter 8).

The Herb Society of America comprises sponsored members organized into units and currently has 34 units in 23 states as well as six member-at-large regions. As membership in The Herb Society of America is by invitation only, interested persons should contact Ms. Rascan for further information.

THSA also publishes a useful booklet, *The Beginner's Herb Garden* (currently $3.00 + $.75 postage).

Heritage Rose Foundation

Charles A. Walker, Jr.
1512 Gorman St.
Raleigh, NC 27606

The Heritage Rose Foundation is a non-profit organization that works for the permanent preservation of old roses. Current membership fees are $10.00/year. Write to Mr. Walker at the address above for more information. He can also provide information about the Heritage Rose Group, which has regional membership groups.

Heritage Seed Program

Heather Apple, President
RR 3
Uxbridge, ON
Canada L0C 1K0

(416) 852-7965
Write for further information.

The Heritage Seed Program is a project of the Canadian Organic Growers. Its goal is to seek out and preserve heirloom and endangered varieties of food crops, including herbs. Membership in the Program is open to anyone—backyard gardeners, farmers, historical sites, botanical gardens, horticultural historians and interested individuals in Canada, the U.S. and other countries.

Members receive a magazine three times a year, and in December all members receive a list of seeds which are being offered by members. From it you can choose varieties which you are interested in growing and preserving. Members are asked to make the commitment to learn proper seed-saving techniques, grow the plant and then make some of its seed available to other members at no cost. All are welcome to join the Program even if they do not want to become a grower.

The 1990 Seed Listing lists only 15 varieties of herbs along with wildflowers, everlastings, vegetables, fruits and grains. President Heather Apple says that the group is interested in expanding their work with herbs. Various levels of memberships are available: regular members (Canadian) $10.00; U.S. and foreign $15.00; fixed income $7; supporting member $20.00 annually.

International Herb Growers and Marketers Association

1201 Allanson Rd.
Mundelein, IL 60060

(708) 566-4566

The International Herb Growers and Marketers Association is a networking organization for people who want "herbs to be a business as well as fun". Call or write for membership information.

Marigold Society of America

Jennette Lowe, Secretary
PO Box 112
New Britain, PA 18901

Membership information for SASE

The Marigold Society of America, a friendly association of people interested in the culture and uses of marigolds, distributes information about their use and encourages the development of new varieties.

A quarterly newsletter contains marigold-related articles. Members receive marigold seeds with the spring issue each year. The current membership fee is $12.00 for regular members.

Native Seeds/SEARCH

Kevin Dahl
2509 N. Campbell #325
Tucson, AZ 85719

(602) 327-9123 (office phone; no orders)
Established 1983
Mail order; display garden at the Tucson
Botanical Gardens
Catalog $1.00

Membership dues are currently $10.00/year for low-income persons or students; $18.00/year for associates, $30.00/year for families. Other levels of membership are available. Contributions to the "Land Fund" are also welcomed. (See additional information about the group in Chapter 1 under Native Seeds/SEARCH and in Chapter 3 under *Seedhead News*.)

Natural Organic Farmers Association

Julie Rawson
RFD #2
Barre, MA 01005-9645

(508) 355-2853
Established 1971
Information for SASE

The Natural Organic Farmers Association (NOFA) is a group of farmers and supporters of organic farming throughout the northeastern U.S. The group practices, and encourages others to practice, agriculture which reflects natural ecosystems. The group publishes a useful, informative newspaper, *The Natural Farmer*. Various membership levels are available; call or write for further details. (Also see listing in Chapter 6.)

Rocky Mountain Herbalists Coalition

Catherine Hunziker
Box 1304
Boulder, CO 80306-1614

(303) 665-9508

The Rocky Mountain Herbalists Coalition is a group of herbalists, herb growers, wildcrafters, teachers, researchers and manufacturers primarily from the Boulder/Denver area in Colorado. The group meets monthly to exchange information and to work on herbal issues beyond the members' individual concerns. Membership is open to anyone seriously interested in herbs. The Coalition sponsors special events, maintains a city-sponsored educational herb garden and is involved in other activities. The membership fee is currently $25.00/year. For more information, contact Catherine Hunziker at the address above.

Royal Horticultural Society

Vincent Square
London SW1P 2PE
England

Write for details.

Other

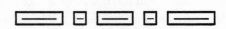

Danimose Foundation for Research and the Promotion of Herbal Medicine

Adolphus Akahedbi Oparah, Herbalist
PO Box 325
Nkwogwu-Mbaise, Owerri
Federal Republic of Nigeria
West Africa

or PO Box 71
TIKO
Republic of Cameroon
West Africa

The Danimose Foundation is a family business that orders herbs, seeds and herbal books from all over the world for its use and for resale in retail shops in West Africa. Mr. Oparah would like to correspond with any interested persons in the U.S.

10

Additional Resources

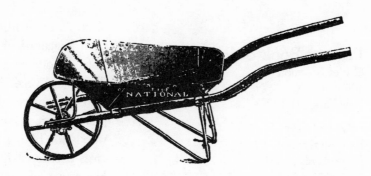

THIS CHAPTER CONTAINS AN ECLECTIC MIXTURE of those companies and services that really didn't fit in any of the other chapters. Here are sources for antiquarian herbal books and prints, herbal bed and breakfasts and lodging, miscellaneous services, garden designers, herbal computer software, garden tours, herbal clip art, an herbal restaurant, writers, special services, lecturers and more.

Books/Prints

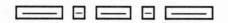

Florilegium
Oriel Eaton Antique Prints
Oriel Eaton
One Union Square West, Studio 802
New York, NY 10003

(212) 255-2218
Established in 1980
Mail order; retail by appointment
Catalog $4.00

Oriel Eaton offers a large choice of antique botanical prints, watercolors and books.

Pageant Book & Print Shop
Shirley Solomon
109 E. 9th St.
New York, NY 10003

(212) 674-5296
Established in 1945
No mail order; retail

Pageant Book & Print Shops buys and sells antiquarian herbal books and prints.

Herbal Bed & Breakfasts/Lodging

Back of the Beyond
Bill and Shash Georgi
7233 Lower E. Hill Rd.
Colden, NY 14033

(716) 652-0427
Established 1983
Brochures $.75

Bill and Shash Georgi's Back of the Beyond Bed & Breakfast is located in the Boston hills and ski area of western New York, 25 miles from Buffalo and 50 miles from Niagara Falls. Various accommodations are offered among the organic herb, flower and vegetable gardens maintained on the country mini-estate. Also on the premises are a large pond for swimming, woods for hiking and a private trail for cross-country skiing. A greenhouse and Herbtique gift shop are part of the complex.

Country Roots Shop & Gardens
Gloria Harris
203 Keller Dr.
Stroudsburg, PA 18360

(717) 992-5557
Established 1984

Write or call for further information. (Also see listing in Chapter 8.)

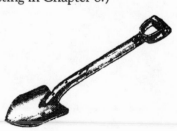

Enchanted Crest

W. Loyd and Carollyn Blackwell
RR #1, Box 216
Belle Rive, IL 62810

(618) 736-2647
Established 1985
Information for SASE

The Enchanted Crest Bed and Breakfast is located in a three-story, 18-room Victorian mansion that is on the National List of Historic Places. The house is surrounded by a four-acre lawn with 20 herb gardens consisting of more than 300 varieties of herbs and perennials, an original pear and pecan orchard, park area, nature walks and pines surrounding a two-acre lake.

Hartman's Herb Farm

Lynn or Pete Hartman
Old Dana Rd.
Barre, MA 01005

(508) 355-2015
Established 1975
Mail order; wholesale; retail; public garden
Catalog $2.00

Write or call for information. (Also see listing in Chapter 2.)

Long Creek Herb Farm

Jim Long
Rt. 4, Box 730
Oak Grove, AR 72660

(417) 779-5450
Call or write for current rates.

Jim Long offers guesthouse lodging on his Herb Farm in addition to his educational workshops and garden tours listed in Chapters 6 and 8. The lodging is available either with or without workshops or programs included for variable rates. (Optional cat included upon request.)

Sage Cottage Bed and Breakfast

Dorry Norris
PO Box 626
112 E. Main St.
Trumansburg, NY 14886

(607) 387-6449
Established 1984
Brochure for large SASE

Dorry Norris' Sage Cottage Bed and Breakfast has four Victorian guest rooms, appointed with period furnishings. All rooms have private baths. (Also see listings in Chapters 3 and 6.)

Sinking Springs Herb Farm

Ann Stubbs
234 Blair Shore Rd.
Elkton, MD 21921-8025

(301) 398-5566
Established 1968
Call or write for more information.

Ann Stubbs offers bed and breakfast "garden cottage accommodations" on her Sinking Springs Herb Farm.

SouthRidge Treasures & Herbs

Mary Ellen Wilcox, Owner
368A Ridge Rd.
Scotia, NY 12302

(518) 372-2222
Established 1988
Call or write for more information.

Sweet Woodruff Farm

Evelyn or Mel Shahan
Rt. 27
Boothbay, ME 04537

(207) 633-6977
Established 1989
Write or call for information.

Miscellaneous Services and Other Resources

agAccess

Jeffrey Harpain
PO Box 2008
Davis, CA 95617

(916) 756-7177
Established 1984
Mail order; retail
Catalog free

In addition to supplying every book in print on agriculture or horticulture, agAccess also operates a custom research service for clients. The service can investigate specific questions on these subjects or locate any document in a fast, cost effective manner. (Also see listing in Chapter 5.)

Dr. John Alloway, DC

9927 Brixton Lane
Bethesda, MD 20817-1525

(301) 469-8150
Established 1981
Write or call for information.

Dr. John Alloway, DC, offers services as a lecturer, practicing herbalist, producer of seminars and herbal consultant. His monograph *Herbs in Hydrotherapy* is available for $5.00 from the address above.

Cody Catering and Crafts

Paula Cody
606 Mercury St.
W. Palm Beach, FL 33406

(407) 686-1982
Established 1982

Paula Cody of Cody Catering and Crafts offers herbal catering services as well as herb garden planning, development and design. All work is done on an individual basis emphasizing personal service. Call for further details.

Falcor

Steve Blake, NDD Sc.
PO Box 873
Ben Lomond, CA 95005

(408) 336-2442
Established 1981
Mail order
Brochure free

Steve Blake of Falcor offers a unique service—he provides herbal software for your computer. Four programs are currently available: Globalherb (an herbal reference library), Planetherb (lists more than 490 herbs and formulas covering more than 1700 health conditions), Proherb (an electronic library listing the 15 most authoritative herbal references) and Homeherb (a simple program to make using herbs in the home easy). Software is available for both IBM and Macintosh computers. Mr. Blake also sells computers with the herbal software included.

The Flavour Connection

Madalene Hill and Gwen Barclay
PO Box 1734
Cleveland, TX 77327-1734

(713) 592-9178
Established 1957 (as Hilltop Herb Farm),
1988 as The Flavour Connection
Call or write for information.

Madalene Hill served as President of The Herb Society of America from 1986 to 1988 and received the prestigious Medal of Honor from the Society in 1978. The Knot Garden at the National Herb Garden in Washington, D.C., was donated and dedicated in Madalene and Jim Hill's honor. Ms. Hill is also the founder of Hilltop Herb Farm in Romayor, Texas. Her daughter, Gwen Barclay, is the current president of the Texas Herb Growers and Marketers Association. The couple wrote the book *Southern Herb Growing*, which is available from the address above. Through their current company, The Flavour Connection, Madalene Hill and Gwen Barclay are available to give lectures and demonstrations, teach classes, seminars and workshops, do freelance writing and herbal consulting. They can provide references for any interested group (as if they needed any!)

Flora & Fauna Tours, Inc.

Thomas H. Driscoll
718 Swedesford Rd.
Ambler, PA 19002-1908

(215) 699-9577
Established 1982
Brochure free

Flora & Fauna Tours sponsors horticultural and natural history tours to international destinations such as the South Pacific (Tahiti, Australia, New Zealand, Fiji), China and Africa.

Frieda's, Inc.

Marketing Department
PO Box 58488
Los Angeles, CA 90058

(213) 627-2981
Established 1962
Catalog free

Frieda's supplies specialty produce to retailers across the nation. The company offers a small, useful brochure titled "Fresh Herb Know-How" free when you send an SASE and request one, mentioning this book. The brochure includes growing tips, recipes and more.

GARDENFIND

Judy Magelssen
PO Box 2703
Lynnwood, WA 98036-3912

Established 1989
Mail order
Brochure free

GARDENFIND is a unique computer program/index (for IBM computers) that finds information in any of more than 3000 entries from 108 gardening magazines for the years 1989 through 1990. GARDENFIND, which is updated every year, indexes *Organic Gardening*, *Flower & Garden*, *National Gardening*, *Horticulture*, *Fine Gardening*, and *American Horticulturist*.

Green Landing Nursery

Maggie Sliker
5810 Green Landing Rd.
Upper Marlboro, MD 20772

(301) 952-0593
Established 1968
Wholesale; retail
Call for information.

Maggie Sliker of Green Landing Nursery designs and plants knot gardens to her customers' specifications. She also sells over 60 varieties of herbs at the nursery.

Within the garden's
peaceful scene
Appear'd two lovely foes,
Aspiring to the rank of
queen
The Lily and the Rose.

—William Cowper

HerbLine

American Botanical Council
PO Box 201660
Austin, TX 78720-1660

(900) 226-4545

The American Botanical Council has a 900+ access number available to those who are interested in news of current events in the field of medicinal plants and information about various commercially popular herbs and medicinals. Messages are updated on a regular basis, usually every five to six weeks. The charge for the messages is $.95 per minute.

Herbscapes by Lane Furneaux

Lane Furneaux
7348 Lane Park Court
Dallas, TX 75225-2468

(214) 368-4235
Established 1985

Lane Furneaux is the "herbal expert" of Dallas, Texas. She has been profiled in *Better Homes and Gardens, Garden Ideas,* and *Outdoor Living and Country Homes.* Her beautiful private herb garden is depicted in *Southern Herb Growing* by Madalene Hill and Gwen Barclay. Ms. Furneaux is available to design symbolic herb gardens and consult by appointment for others. She also writes and lectures, specializing in fresh herb cookery and bouquets (tussie-mussies are her specialty). Call or write for further information; references are available.

Hickory Hill Herbs

Paula Jones Hill
307 W. Ave. E.
Lampasas, TX 76550

(512) 556-8801
Established 1987
Mail order; retail; public garden
Write for more information

Paula Jones Hill of Hickory Hill Herbs offers a number of services through her company. These include custom herb garden design and water garden design. Paula also takes special orders for wreaths, baskets, etc. (Also see listings in Chapters 2 and 6.)

Hilltop Herb Farm

(at Chain-O-Lakes Resort)
Beverly Smith
PO Box 325
Romayor, TX 77368

(713) 592-5859
Established 1957
Free brochure, or call for reservations.

The Hilltop Herb Farm (also see listings in Chapters 1 and 2) Restaurant serves traditional dinners and lunch buffets, by reservation. The meals are cooked from scratch using fresh seasonings and ingredients, many of which are grown on the premises. The Hilltop Herb Farm was founded by Madalene Hill and Gwen Barclay, authors of *Southern Herb Growing.*

Lucinda Hutson

4612 Rosedale
Austin, TX 78756

(512) 454-8905
Write or call for more information.

Lucinda Hutson is the author of *The Herb Garden Cookbook* (see description in Chapter 4). She is a food and garden writer for many national and regional magazines, and is available to give lectures for special events. An autographed copy of Lucinda's book is available from her at the address above for $19.95 + $2.50 shipping/handling.

Libenn Aroma, Inc.

PO Box 201
Granger, IN 46530

(800) 526-8212
Wholesale only
Call for information.

Libenn Aroma specializes in the manufacture of natural and synthetic flavors and fragrances. All formulas are custom-designed for specific uses and customers. Libenn works with many herb and botanical suppliers to produce potpourris, sachets, teas and other products.

National Agricultural Library

United States Department of Agriculture
Lending Branch, ILL, 6th Floor
Public Services Division
Beltsville, MD 20705-2351

(301) 344-3755

The National Agricultural Library can supply copies of agricultural materials and information not found elsewhere. Individuals should submit requests for information first to local or state libraries before asking NAL. The NAL offers Loan Service to other U.S. libraries and Document Delivery Service.

Natural Apothecary

Maggie Houston
7306 Haw Ridge Rd.
Summerfield, NC 27358

Write for more information.

Maggie Houston is an herbal consultant, workshop leader and freelance writer. She writes articles on herbs for newspapers or newsletters.

Nature's Herb Farm

Mary Dunford
5803 Angie
San Antonio, TX 78240

(512) 688-9421
Established 1983
Call for more information.

Nature's Herb Farm sells a large variety of fresh cut herbs to restaurants. Inquire about opening a "fresh cut account" with Ms. Dunford.

Saga International Holidays

120 Boylston St.
Boston, MA 02116

(800) 343-0273
Call for a current schedule.

Together with White Flower Farm, Saga International Holidays sponsors garden tours, both in the U.S. and overseas.

In France, santolina was called *garde de robe* because it was used in wardrobes and chests to protect the contents against insects.

—Family Receipt Book, 1819

Jeri Schwartz Antiques

Jeri Schwartz
555 Old Long Ridge Rd.
Stamford, CT 06903

(203) 322-7854
Mail order; wholesale; retail
Call for details.

Jeri Schwartz Antiques specializes in fine 19th-century silver pieces, smalls and vertu. Her booklet titled *Tussie Mussies: Victorian Posey Holders* is available from her for $7.95 + $1.00 postage.

Shelly's Petals and Herbs, Etc.

Linda Antoine and Joseph Neal
PO Box 496
Port Sulphur, LA 70083

(504) 564-3697
Established 1988
Wholesale
Write or call for further information.

Shelly's Petals and Herbs is operated by the Plaquemines A.R.C. as a vocational rehabilitation program for mentally retarded adults in the parish of Plaquemines, Louisiana. The group wholesales culinary herbs (cut and packaged) to grocery stores in the New Orleans metropolitan area.

Diane Morey Sitton

Rt. 1, Box 384
Colmesneil, TX 75938

(409) 837-5416

Diane Morey Sitton is a freelance garden writer and the author of *Texas Gardener's Guide to Growing and Using Herbs* (Texas Gardener Press, 1987). See Chapter 4 for a description of the book.

Spiceman Enterprises

Cecil Flentge
6834 Neston
San Antonio, TX 78329

(512) 656-8673
List of classes for SASE

Cecil Flentge teaches a wide variety of cooking classes, including cuisine from around the world. In all of his presentations, he emphasizes the use of fresh herbs and spices. Mr. Flentge is available to teach classes or give cooking demonstrations to herb groups, schools or other interested groups. Possible topics include Seasoning Seafood, Cooking with Herbs and Spices and "See" Food and More "Sea" Food. Additionally, he can adapt a class to a theme of the students' (or group's) choice.

Sylvia's Originals

Sylvia Churchbaugh
8010 Conser, Box 4001
Overland Park, KS 66204

(913) 831-3236
Established 1984
Brochure for LSASE

Artist and calligrapher Sylvia Churchbaugh does custom logo rubber stamps, specializing in herb designs, flowers, etc. She also can do custom artwork for signs, tags and advertisements.

Tamblyn-Groves Communications

Karen Groves
28350 Douglas Park
Evergreen, CO 80439

(303) 670-1275
Established 1987

Karen Groves specializes in graphic design, public relations and marketing services, as well as brochure and catalog design. She has worked with herbal businesses in the past to produce line drawings and help design their brochures and catalogs.

Traditional Tours

Svevo Brooks
PO Box 564
Creswell, OR 97436

(503) 895-2957
Established 1979
Brochure free

Svevo Brooks of Traditional Tours sponsors international tours to destinations where you can study traditional medicine, craft and village life.

Wheeler Arts

Paula Wheeler
66 Lake Park
Champaign, IL 61821-7101

(217) 359-6816
Established 1973
Mail order; retail
Catalog $2.95 (includes free sample jumbo sheet of art); refundable with purchase

Paula Wheeler offers a unique service for people who produce herb catalogs, ads, books and brochures. She publishes a collection of herbal "Quick Art" on a computer diskette for Macintosh computers. Disks available include Farm, Holidays, Food, Horticulture, Herbs and Pets. "Jumbo Sheets" of line art are also available. Write for current price and further information.

During the time of the ancient Greeks, some people earned their living by gathering wild roots for doctors. These people were called rhizotomoi, or root gatherers. In order to discourage others from going into the business and becoming competition, the root gatherers made up tall tales about the horrible dangers of their life. For instance, they claimed that if the mandrake root was dug up, it would shriek with pain, causing the digger to go insane. Peony roots, they claimed, had to be dug at night lest woodpeckers come to peck their eyes out!

—from *The Frugal Housewife* by Mrs. Child, 1833

Appendix

THIS STATE-BY-STATE LISTING of herb businesses includes seed and plant suppliers, purveyors of botanicals and other supplies, and businesses and institutions that offer instruction. Look for additional listings in the geographic guide to public gardens (page 218), and in the chapters on publications and publishers.

Remember that many of the businesses listed here are manufacturing and/or mail order only; if you would like to visit them, be sure to call first to see if this is appropriate and to check hours. Businesses that engage only in walk-in retail business are not listed in this guide. There are many hundreds of them nation-wide; check the yellow pages under "Herbs", "Greenhouses", "Nurseries", "Crafts", and other appropriate headings.

ALABAMA

Auburn, Village Arbors

ARKANSAS

Indian Springs, Illuminations
Eureka Springs, Patricia's
Kingston, Ozark Basketry Supply
Mountain View, Herbal Healer Academy
Mountain View, The Ozark Folk Center
State Park
Mountain View, Legacy Herbs
Oak Grove, Long Creek Herb Farm
Rogers, Clement Herb Farm

ARIZONA

Bullhead City, Creative Craft House
Congress, Taylor's Herb Garden of Arizona
Cottonwood, Canyon Country Herbs
Phoenix, Windrose Aromatics
Phoenix, Desert Botanical Garden
Tucson, Native Seeds/SEARCH
Tucson, Tucson Botanical Gardens
Tumacacori, Santa Cruz Chili and Spice Co.

CALIFORNIA

Alameda, Health Concerns
Alta, Sierra School of Herbs & Health
Aptos, Cadillac Mountain Farm
Auburn, Dry Creek Herb Farm
Berkeley, University of California Botanic
Garden
Berkeley, Solargraphics
Berkeley, Food for Thought Posters
Beverly Hills, Marilyan Roberts Collection
Cambria, Heart's Ease Herb Shop & Gardens
Camino, Herbs and Heirlooms
Carmel Valley, Bay Laurel Farm
Chatsworth, Raindrip
Cloverdale, Evergreen Garden Plant Labels

Costa Mesa, The Snuggery Culinary Herb
and Spice Blends
Culver City, Jason Natural Products
Diamond Springs, Rose Acres
Emeryville, Nature's Herb
Fair Oaks, Leydet Oils and Aromatherapy
Products
Fairfax, Magic Garden Herb Co.
Felton, Shepherd's Garden Seeds
Forestville, California School of Herbal
Studies
Forestville, Simplers Botanical Co.
Fort Bragg, Heritage Rose Gardens
Garberville, Greenmantle Nursery
Guerneville, Heirloom Garden Seeds
Hayward, Clyde Robin Seed Co.
La Jolla, Bloomsaver, Ltd.
Laguna Hills, Belle Star
Laguna Beach, Next to Nature
Los Altos, Blue Springs
Los Angeles, Lady of the Lake
Mendocino, Mendocino Arts & Gifts
Mendocino, Wind & Weather
Montara, Herbal Gardens
Monterey, Herbal Effect
Morgan Hill, Aviva Design
Morro Bay, Moon Mountain Wildflowers
Nevada City, Oak Valley Herb Farm
Newberry Springs, High Desert Growers
Wholesale
North Hollywood, Herb Products Co.
Oakland, G.B. Ratto & Co. International
Grocers
Palos Verdes, Dody Lyness Co.
Redlands, Good Scents
Redway, Wild Weeds
Redway, Mountain Rose Herbs
Redwood City, J.L. Hudson, Seedsman
Redwood City, Redwood City Seed Company
Sacramento, Lavender Lane
San Ardo, Barbree Beans
San Diego, American Indian Herb Co.
San Francisco, New Age Creations (Ritual
Works!)
San Rafael, Earthrise Company
San Rafael, Original Swiss Aromatics
San Rafael, Pacific Institute of Aromatherapy

San Anselmo, The Natural Gardening
Company
San Francisco, The Herbal Body Works
Santa Barbara, There's Always the Garden
Santa Barbara, Santa Barbara Botanic
Garden Library
Santa Cruz, East West School of Herbalism
Sebastopol, Rosemary's Garden
Sebastopol, Sandy Smith's Magical Herbs
Sebastopol, Therapeutic Herbalism
Sonora, Havasu Hills Herb Farm
Valley Springs, Rhettland Herbary
Valley Springs, The Country Gardener
Ventura, Earth Herbs
Vista, Taylor's Herb Garden
Watsonville, Roses of Yesterday and Today
Westminster, Heard's Country Gardens
Willits, Bountiful Gardens

COLORADO

Boulder, Quintessence Aromatherapy
Boulder, School of Natural Medicine
Boulder, Herbs of Grace
Boulder, WishGarden Herbs
Boulder, Nature's Apothecary
Carbondale, Mt. Sopris Scents and
Seasonings
Colorado Springs, Hydro-Gardens
Denver, The Gardener's Eye
Denver, Denver Botanic Gardens
Longmont, Blossoms & Bevels
Loveland, Hubble Hill Herbs
Loveland, Rabbit Shadow Farm
Rocky Ford, D.V. Burrell Seed Growers Co.
Saguache, J. Gaunt Woodman Co.

CONNECTICUT

Colebrook, Bird of Paradise Designs
Coventry, Caprilands Herb Farm
Danielson, Logee's Greenhouses
East Hartford, Tide-Mark Press
Fairfield, Meadowbrook Herb Garden
Fairfield, Meadowbrook Herb Garden
Farmington, Gardener's Kitchen
Litchfield, White Flower Farm
Marion, Preserve the Memories
Milford, The Silo
Salisbury, Sweethaven Farm

Union, Select Seeds—Antique Flowers
West Hartford, Sunrise Enterprises
Westport, Gilbertie's Herb Gardens
Wethersfield, Comstock, Ferre & Co.

DISTRICT OF COLUMBIA

Smithsonian Institution
Washington National Cathedral Gardens

DELAWARE

Wilmington, Claudia Simeone

FLORIDA

Bradenton, Spring Herb Farm
Destin, The Flower Press
Eustis, McCrory's Sunny Hill Herbs
Fort Myers, Sanders Unlimited
Kathleen, Val's Naturals
Lake Park, The Pepper Gal
Port Charlotte, PolyBags Plus

GEORGIA

Comer, The Country Shepherd
Dawsonville, Norfold Lavender Ltd.
Duluth, Raven's Nest
Flowery Branch, The Flowery Branch Seed
Company
Mountain City, Penny's Garden
Roswell, Bulloch Hall Historical Site
Whitesburg, International Manufacturing
Co.

HAWAII

Aiea, Honolulu Community Action Program
Hilo, Heartscents
Kalaheo, Kauai Flower Perfumes
Keaau, Island Aromatics

IOWA

Fairfield, LongHerb Health Products
Grimes, The Farmhouse
Lamoni, The Florist Brokerage
Marshalltown, Herbs-Liscious
Norway, Frontier Cooperative Herbs
Shenandoah, Henry Field's Seed & Nursery
   Co.

IDAHO

Boise, John's Gourmet Gardens
Boise, Seeds Blum
Ketchum, High Altitude Gardens
Moscow, NORTHPLAN/Mountain Seed

ILLINOIS

Batavia, Shady Hill Gardens
Belle Rive, Enchanted Crest
Decatur, Mari-Mann Herb Farm
Dix, Windy Pines Natural Herb Farm
Dongola, Fragrant Fields
Laura, Herb'n'Renewal
Malta, Meadow Everlastings
Oak Park, Greenfield Herb Garden
Peoria, Stone Well Herbs
San Jose, Clark's Greenhouse & Herbal
   Country

INDIANA

Crawfordsville, Davidson-Wilson
   Greenhouses
Goshen, The Secret Garden
Hammond, Indiana Botanic Gardens
Seymour, Cactus Patch Herbs
South Whitley, Spices 'N Things
Spencer, New Hope Herb Farm
Sunman, Gardens Alive!

KANSAS

Bunker Hill, Cross Seed Co.
Cheney, The Country Merchants
Lenexa, Midwest Seed Growers
St. George, Ebert's Herbs & Wheat
Udall, Country Bloomers Nursery

KENTUCKY

La Grange, Akin' Back Farm & Gifts of
   Thyme
Louisville, Dabney Herbs
Murray, Story House Herb Farm
Perry Park, Hundley Ridge Farm
Washington, The Herb Market
Wickliffe, Hillhouse Naturals Farm

LOUISIANA

Baton Rouge, Good Scents of Louisiana
Baton Rouge, Magnolia Herbs
Lafayette, The Bayou Blending Co.
Opelousas, Louisiana Nursery
Violet, Down to Earth

MASSACHUSETTS

Andover, Betsy Williams/The Proper Season
Ashfield, New England Cheesemaking
   Supply Company
Barre, Hartman's Herb Farm
Belmont Center, Herb Country Gifts &
   Collectibles
Cambridge, Spice It Up
Elkton, Sinking Springs Herb Farm
Marblehead, Old Hill Herbs
Middleboro, Wyrttun Ward
Salisbury, Pettengill Farm
Shelburne Falls, Blazing Star Herbal School
South Yarmouth, Mr. McGregor's Garden
Southboro, The Sunny Window
Stockbridge, Berkshire Botanical Garden
Topsfield, The Walt Nickle Company
West Tisbury, Chicama Vineyards

MARYLAND

Baltimore, D. Landreth Seed Co.
Bowie, St.-John's Herb Garden
Millington, Maryland's Herb Basket
Prince Frederick, Calvert Homestead
Uniontown, Nathan's Forge
Walkersville, Glade Valley Nursery
Woodstock, Stillridge Herb Farm

MAINE

Albion, Johnny's Selected Seeds
Boothbay, Sweet Woodruff Farm
Buckfield, Hedgehog Hill Farm
Camden, Merry Gardens
Freeport, Good Earth Farm
Litchfield, Daystar
Lubec, Botanical Impressions
New Gloucester, Pinetree Garden Seeds
Poland Springs, United Society of Shakers
Waldoboro, Fox Fern Herb Farm
Wells, Teasel Weed
West Paris, Maine Balsam Fir Products
West Rockport, Avena Botanicals

MICHIGAN

Allegan, Maple Hill Farm
Ann Arbor, Matthaei Botanical Gardens
Benton Harbor, The Herb Barn
Brighton, Vital Energy
Detroit, Rafal Spice Company
East Jordan, Circle Herb Farm
Fenton, Heavenly Scent Herb Farm
Freeland, Warmbier Farms
Grand Rapids, Harvest Health
Hartford, May Apple
Holland, The Shaker Messenger
Niles, The Herb Cottage
Otisville, The Gathered Herb
Parma, Fox Hill Farm
Plymouth, Brookville Gardens
Rochester Hills, Herbal Endeavours, Ltd.
Sutton's Bay, Bellwether Herbs & Flowers
Suttons Bay, Busha's Brae Herb Farm
Tecumseh, Whole World Recycled
   Stationery
Traverse City, Flowers & Spice World
White Pigeon, Out of the Woods

MINNESOTA

Chaska, Shady Acres Herb Farm
Faribault, Farmer Seed & Nursery
Mapleton, Maple River Herb Gardens
Minneapolis, Present Moment Books and
   Herbs
Minneapolis, Great Lakes Herb Company
Isswa, Northstar Freeze Dry
Winona, Prairie Moon Nursery

MISSOURI

Ava, Blessed Herbs
Brixley, Elixir Farm Botanicals
Duenweg, The Ultimate Herb & Spice
   Shoppe
Kansas City, Herb Gathering
Liberty, The Need'l Love Company
Montgomery City, Barney's Ginseng Patch
Raytown, Litl' Mack's Herb Shoppe

MONTANA

Hamilton, Mountain Valley Farms
Hot Springs, Rocky Mountain Herbal
   Institute
Kalispell, Country Garden Dried Flowers and
   Herbs

NORTH CAROLINA

Boone, Boone Drug Co.
Cashiers, High Hampton Inn & Country
   Club
Chapel Hill, Niche Gardens
Fletcher, Holbrook Farm and Nursery
Godwin, Rasland Farm
Hamlet, The Complete Body Shop
Leicester, Sandy Mush Herb Nursery
Leland, Shelton Herb Farm
Moravian Falls, Brushy Mountain Bee Farm
Pilot Mountain, The Herb Garden
Pineola, Gardens of the Blue Ridge
Wilmington, Sea Holly Herbs & Flowers

NEBRASKA

Fort Calhoun, The Fragrant Path
Omaha, DeGiorgi Seed Company
Wayne, Garden Perennials

NEW HAMPSHIRE

Alton, Cats in the Cradle
Center Tuftonboro, Spider Web Gardens
Francestown, Country Thyme
Hopkinton, The Fragrance Shop
Marlow, Baudelaire
Milton, New Hampshire Farm Museum
Pittsfield, Strawberry Meadow Herb Farm
Richmond, Herbitage Farm
Warner, Andalina, Ltd.
Warner, Twin Ridge Farm

NEW JERSEY

Bedminster, Radcliffe Farms
Bloomsbury, Herbalist & Alchemist
Changewater, Herbally Yours
Flemington, Whiskey Run Herb Farm
Franklinville, Triple Oaks Nursery
Haddonfield, Gail Grisi Stenciling
Lawrenceville, Wisteria Press
Port Murray, Well-Sweep Herb Farm
Sewell, Orol Ledden & Sons

NEW MEXICO

Albuquerque, Chili Pepper Emporium
Albuquerque, Old Southwest Trading Company
Placitas, Clear Light Cedar Co.
Santa Fe, Plants of the Southwest
Torreon, Golden Earth Herbs

NEW YORK

Babylon, Van Bourgondien Bros.
Bearsville, Hill Crest House, Ltd.
Brooklyn, Brooklyn Botanical Gardens
Buffalo, Stokes Seeds
Calverton, Peconic River Herb Farm
Colden, Back of the Beyond

Congers, Weleda
Cooperstown, The Farmer's Museum
Dolgeville, Gatehouse Herbs
Fort Plain, The Herb Cupboard
Hamburg, Dreams End Farm
Ithaca, The Hollow, Orchids & Herbs
Ithaca, Cornell Plantations
Lake Peekskill, Hollowbrook Pottery & Tile
Lynbrook, Ellon Bach USA
Lynbrook, United Communications
Mayville, Thistle Hill
Milton, Green Terrestrial
New York, Pageant Book & Print Shop
New York, Cambridge Chemists
New York, Paprikas Weiss Importer
New York, Florilegium
New York, Pecos Valley Spice Co.
Olean, Dragon's Lair
Pattersonville, Apothecary Rose Shed
Pennellville, Tanglewood Gardens
Pine Bush, Butterfly Hill Herbary
Pleasant Valley, Preservations
Potsdam, Sunfeather Handcrafted Herbal Soap Co.
Rome, Spring Brook Farm
Rye, Euroflax, Inc.
Scotia, SouthRidge Treasures & Herbs
Southampton, Select Origins
Southhampton, Emelie Tolley's Herb Basket
Staten Island, Sultan's Delight
Syracuse, Homespun Gatherings
Trumansburg, Sage Cottage
Waterville, Frog Park Herbs
Webster, Jane's Herb Farm
West Babylon, New Forest Gardens
Woodstock, Wise Woman Center

OHIO

Akron, Becker Greenhouse & Herb Farm
Alliance, River's Bend Farm
Andover, Country Road Herb Farm & Gift Barn
Athens, Companion Plants
Bluffton, The Herb House
Chagrin Falls, Pine Creek Herbs
Chesterland, Sunnybrook Farms Nursery
Chillicothe, Bunch's Herbs & Gifts
Cincinnati, Lloyd Library and Museum
Delaware, Gooseberry Patch Company
Kipton, The Crate Shoppe

Laura, Country Flower Bin
Lima, Friendship Herb Gardens
Litchfield, Diana's Design
Madison, Bluestone Perennials
Manchester, Lewis Mountain Herbs & Everlastings
Mansfield, Kingwood Center
Medina, Crop King, Inc.
Mentor, Garden Place
Minerva, Lily of the Valley Herb Farm
New Philadelphia, Liberty Seed Co.
Newark, ECHO/Healing Heart Herbals
Newark, The Studio of Claudia Walker
Painesville, Historical Roses
Seaman, Samuel Wells & Co.
Seville, Bittersweet Farm
St. Paris, Woodspirits Soap
Swanton, Eon Industries
Thornville, Herb N'Ewe
Yellow Springs, No Common Scents
Youngstown, Johanna's

OKLAHOMA

Haskell, Bluejay Gardens Herb Farm

OREGON

Albany, Nichols Garden Nursery
Alsea, Thyme Garden Seed Company
Canby, Western Comfrey, Inc.
Cave Junction, Simply De-Vine
Corvallis, Peace Seeds
Cottage Grove, Territorial Seed Company
Eugene, Hilary's Comfort Beads
Gladstone, Wise Woman Herbals
Grant's Pass, Pacific Botanicals
Hillsboro, Lynn's
Lake Oswego, The Essential Oil Company
Merlin, Windy River Farm/Cottage Garden Herbs
Merlin, Merlin of the Rogue Valley
Philomath, Mary's Herb Garden & Gift Shop
Portland, Twinholly's
Portland, Liberty Natural Products
Portland, Vine Arts
Portland, Allen's Basketworks
Roseburg, Elderflower Farm
Salem, National Health Care Institute
South Beach, A Kiss of the Sun Nursery

Williams, Herb-Pharm
Williams, Goodwin Creek Gardens
Williams, Forestfarm

PENNSYLVANIA

Bath, The Little Farm Press
Bristol, Hydrofarm
Carlisle, The Herb Merchant
Columbia, Cramers' Posie Patch
Easton, The Banana Tree
Emporium, Timber Rock Farms
Gardenville, Gingham 'n Spice, Ltd.
Glen Rock, Spoutwood Farm
Greeley, Dorothy Biddle Service
Honey Brook, England's Herb Farm
Huntingdon Valley, Mantis Manufacturing Co.
Kane, Edgewood Herbs
Lititz, The Herb Shop
Littlestown, Alloway Gardens & Herb Farm
Mansfield, Krystal Wharf Farms
McGrann, Fox Hollow Herbs & Heirlooms
Mechanicsburg, The Rosemary House
Mechanicsburg, Ashcombe Farm and Greenhouses
Olyphant, Vileniki—An Herb Farm
Philadelphia, Haussmann's Pharmacy
Philadelphia, Gaia Botanicals
Philadelphia, Penn Herb Co., Ltd.
Reading, The Herb Haus
Rockton, In Harmony With Nature
Shippensburg, The Berry tree
Skippack, Bittersweet
Souderton, Land Steward
Spraggs, Shields Organic Herb & Flower Farm
Stroudsburg, Country Roots Shop & Gardens
Titusville, Victoria's Herb Shoppe
Trevose, Otis S. Twilley Seed Company
Trout Run, The Herb Barn
Warminster, W. Atlee Burpee & Company
Washington Crossing, Bowman's Hill Wildflower Preserve
Wexford, Kingfisher
Wilkes-Barre, Mary Hughes Designs
Willow Street, Sugar 'n Spice

RHODE ISLAND

Coventry, Camelot Herb Gardens
North Scituate, Cherry Valley Herb Farm

SOUTH CAROLINA

Greenwood, George W. Park Seed Co.
Hodges, Wayside Gardens

SOUTH DAKOTA

Mitchell, Will's Garden of Knowledge
Yankton, Gurney Seed & Nursery Co.

TENNESSEE

Butler, McFadden's Vines & Wreaths
Chattanooga, Graven Images
Cookeville, Hidden Springs Herbs
Flag Pond, American Ginseng Gardens
Franklin, Hyssop Hill
Memphis, Arpe Herb Chopper
Ripley, Owen Farms

TEXAS

Austin, The Herb Bar
Austin, Devonshire Apothecary
Brenham, Antique Rose Emporium
Burleson, Aunt Betty's Herbalicious
    Seasonings
Dallas, Mozzarella Company
Dallas, Horticultural Enterprises
Dallas, Golden Meadows Herb Farm &
    Emporium
Eagle Lake, Wildseed
El Paso, Brooks Enterprises
Eldorado, J.J. Fuessel Custom Tile
Forney, Nature's Acres
Fort Worth, Herbal-Ease
Fort Worth, Petite Fleur Essence
Fort Worth, Pendery's
Fort Worth, Herbal Gardens
Fredericksburg, Fredericksburg Herb Farm
Georgetown, Penny Royal Herbs
Jacksonville, The Herbary & Stuff
Lampasas, Hickory Hill Herbs

Manchaca, It's About Thyme
Mesquite, Texas Gunpowder
Pasadena, Our Family's Herbs & Such
Romayor, Hilltop Herb Farm
San Antonio, Woodland Herbs
San Antonio, San Antonio Botanical Center

UTAH

Ephraim, Pressed for Time
Helper, Progressive Self-Care Systems

VIRGINIA

Amherst, Rose Hill Herbs and Perennials
Boston, Boston Spice and Tea
Boyce, State Arboretum of Virginia
Burke, Nature's Finest
Charlottesville, Thomas Jefferson Center for
    Historic Plants
Chester, The Herbs of Happy Hill
Floyd, Amrita Herbal Products
Luray, la dama maya herb and flower farm
Madison, Words About Herbs
Madison, Swinging Bridge Pottery
Middleburg, Lowelands Farm
New Castle, Necessary Trading Company
North Garden, Southern Exposure Seed
    Exchange
Raphine, Buffalo Springs Herb Farm
Sperryville, Country Manor

VERMONT

Bethel, Rathdowney, Ltd.
East Barre, Sage Mountain Herbs
Londonderry, The Cook's Garden
Middletown Springs, Herb Patch Ltd.
Post Mills, Chef's Pantry
Putney, Putney Nursery
St. Johnsbury Center, Le Jardin du Gourmet
Tinmouth, Tinmouth Channel Farm

WASHINGTON

Acme, Olive's Hearth & Haven
Bellingham, Wonderland Tea and Spice
    Herb Shop

Bremerton, Silver Bay Herb Farm
Deming, Alpine Herb Farm
Enumclaw, Rachel Dee Herb Farm
Fall City, The Herbfarm
Issaquah, The Country Herb
Kennewick, Perseus Gourmet Products
Kent, Ed Hume Seeds
Okanogan, Filaree Farm
Olympia, Summit Lake Herbs
Orient, Pan's Forest
Oroville (Chesaw), Good Seed Company
Port Townsend, Abundant Life Seed
    Foundation
Seattle, Molbak's Seattle Garden Center
Seattle, Patio Patch Planters
Seattle, Barker Enterprises
Seattle, The Herbalist
Seattle, Countryside Fragrances
Sequim, Cedarbrook Herb Farm
Snohomish, Stonegate Gardens
South Bend, Keepsake Hearts & Flowers
Suquamish, School of Herbal Medicine
Trout Lake, Trout Lake Farm
Vashon, Sweet Woodroffe Herb Farm
Waldron Island, Island Herbs

WISCONSIN

Friesland, McClure & Zimmerman
Hales Corner, Boerner Botanical Gardens
Hartland, Nu-Life Cards
Madison, The Soap Opera
Madison, Alyce's Herbs & Gourmet Herb
    Vinegars
Milwaukee, Northwestern Coffee Mills
North Lake, Prairie Seed Source
Randolph, J.W. Jung Seed Company
Seymour, K&S Horseradish
Tony, Dried Floral Creations
Wausau, Hsu's Ginseng Enterprises

WEST VIRGINIA

Berkeley Springs, Wrenwood of Berkeley
    Springs
Elkins, Augusta Heritage Center
Fairmont, Potpourri by Martha
Shenandoah Junction, Rocky Retreat Herb
    Farm
Weston, Smoke Camp Crafts

AUSTRALIA

New South Wales, Bermagui South,
    Herbamed Medicinal Herb Nursery
New South Wales, Erina, The Fragrant
    Garden
Victoria, Warragul, Botanic Ark Nursery
Victoria, Northcote, Potpourri and Sachet
    Supplies
Victoria,Hawthorn, Auroma

CANADA

Alberta, Bowden Alberta Nurseries & Seeds,
    Ltd.
British Columbia, Hornby Island, Peter
    Rabbit Herbal
British Columbia, Burnaby, Dominion
    Herbal College
Manitoba, Winnipeg, T&T Seeds, Ltd.
Nova Scotia, Truro, Rawlinson Garden Seed
Ontario, Waterdown, Hortico, Inc.
Ontario, Goodwood, Richters
Ontario, Puslinch, Country Lane Herbs &
    Dried Flowers
Ontario, Dundas, William Dam Seeds
Ontario, Colgan, The Spice Cabinet
Ontario, Markham, Magnolia's
Ontario, Newmarket, Herbs Unlimited
Ontario, Sydenham, Amaranth Stoneware,
    Ltd.
Saskatchewan, Radville, Country Green

ENGLAND

Kent, Staplehurst, Iden Croft Herbs
Cambridgeshire, Cambridge, Culpeper Ltd.
Lincolnshire, Candlesby, Spilsby, Candlesby
    Herbs

Index

A

Abigail Adams Smith Museum 224
absinthe 46
Abundant Life Seed Foundation 10, 168
acacia gum 113
achillea
    pressed 50
aconite 38–39, 44, 117
acupuncture
    books 116
Adams, James 140
adonis 23, 38
agAccess 168, 274
agastache 34
Agecroft Hall 224
ageratum
    dried 51, 60
agrimony 13, 21, 23–24, 32, 38, 44, 46
Ahrenhoerster, Robert 36
ajuga 12, 20
ajwain 37
Akin' Back Farm & Gifts of Thyme 178
Alberta Nurseries & Seeds, Ltd. 10
alder 114
alfalfa 16, 22–23, 38–39, 117, 122
    pressed 50
alkanet 21–23, 34
Allen, J. Stafford 88
Allen's Basketworks 48
allheal 38
alliums See specific plants
Alloway Gardens & Herb Farm 168, 178
Alloway, John 274
allspice tree 11
allspice berries 51
allspice 84, 85, 121
almond meal 54
aloe vera 21, 24, 28, 32, 34, 37, 39, 42
Alpine Herb Farm 178
alpine plants 37
alumroot 21
Alyce's Herbs & Gourmet Herb Vinegars 118
alyssum 24
    pressed 50

amaranth 10, 21, 23, 28, 33, 35–37, 43
    dried 48, 52–53, 55, 58, 60, 103
Amaranth Stoneware, Ltd 87
ambrosia 10, 28, 32–35, 43, 46
    dried 48, 53, 57, 63
American Aromatherapy Association 132, 265
American Botanical Council 135, 265, 276
American Botanist, Booksellers 162, 168
American Clock and Watch Museum 224
American Ginseng Gardens 10
American Ginseng Trends 132
American Herb Association 132, 266
The American Herb Association Quarterly Newsletter 132
American Herbalists Guild 266
American Indian Archaeological Institute 162, 169, 224
American Indian Herb Co. 110
American Spice Trade Association, Inc.
ammobium 12, 30
    dried 48, 55, 60, 63, 103
Amrita Herbal Products 110
anchusa 24
Andalina, Ltd. 87
Andersen, Reitha A. 197
Anderson, Frank J. 153
Anderson, Tauna 103
Anderson, Toni and Terry 14, 89, 182
Andre, Michele 42
Andrews, Jean 140
Andrews, Tracy 31
angelica 11–15, 17, 19–21, 23–24, 29–30, 32, 34–35, 38–39, 42–44
    root 58
anise 11–14, 16–17, 19–20, 27, 29–31, 34–35, 37, 41, 43–44, 76, 84, 103, 121, 122
anise hyssop 14, 117
    See also hyssop
annatto 121, 122
annuals 15, 17, 20, 22, 24–25, 30–31, 33, 35, 39, 41, 99
Anthemis tinctoria 30
Anthony, Joanne 97

Antoine, Linda 278
antique plants *See* old-fashioned plants
Antique Rose Emporium 11, 178, 220, 224
Apple, Heather 268
Apothecary Rose Shed 179
archangel 44
arches 58, 60
Arkansas School for the Blind 225
Arkansas Territorial Restoration Medicinal Garden 225
arnica 35, 38
aromatherapy
    American Aromatherapy Association 132, 265
    books 151, 173
    classes/workshops 75, 184, 187, 191, 194, 201, 202
    magazines and newsletters 132, 135, 136
    products 64–76, 91, 111, 115, 116
Arpe Herb Chopper 126
arrowroot 78, 121, 122
artemisia 12–13, 15–17, 20–24, 26, 28–32, 38, 44–45
    dried 48, 51, 53, 55, 58, 61, 63
arugula 23, 27–28, 34, 44
asafetida 10, 15, 45, 122
Ashcombe Farm and Greenhouses 48
assegai poles 56
aster 36
astilbe 24
Atlanta Botanical Garden 225
Augusta Heritage Center 200
Aunt Betty's Herbalicious 118–119
Auroma 64
Avena Botanicals 64
Aviva Design 48
Ayer Company Publishers, Inc. 169
Ayurvedic herbs 67, 116

B

baby products 70, 75, 101, 114
baby's-breath 12, 15, 19–20, 22, 24, 26, 30, 32, 34, 37, 39–40,

43–45, 55, 57, 60–61, 63, 103, 104
    pressed 50
Bach, Ellen, USA 111
bachelor-button 34, 43
Back of the Beyond 87, 179, 272
Bacon, Richard M. 140
Badertscher, Kerrie 50
bags
    See containers and bags
Bailes, Michael 66
Bailey, Julie 101
Bair, Liz 29
Baird, Cave 231
Baker, Mary E. 85
Baldwin, David 129
Bales Linda C. 78
balloon flower 21, 23, 44
ballota 29
balm of Gilead 34, 42
balsam 32, 57, 59, 62, 64
Banana Tree 11
Bancroft, Betzy 114
Bannerman, Annita 84
Barbree Beans 76
Barbree, Penny 76
Barclay, Gwen 142, 163, 275
Barker Enterprises 48
Barker, Mabel 48
barley grass 112
Barlow, Marilyn 40
Barnes, Diane 28
Barnes, Judy 123
Barnette, Sandi 224
Barney's Ginseng Patch 11
basil 10, 12–17, 19–20, 22–34, 36–38, 40–46
    dried 51, 60–61, 76, 84, 121
basketmaking supplies 58
baskets 27, 48–49, 51–52, 55–58, 60–61, 63, 68, 88, 90, 95, 97, 98, 100, 102, 106, 109, 243
Batchelder, Virginia 196
Bates, Marion 187
bath products 53–54, 58, 61, 64–76, 77–82, 84, 88, 90, 92, 94, 97, 99–101, 103, 104, 106–109, 111, 113, 121, 233, 235
Batts, Peggy 55
Baudelaire, Inc. 64
Bauer, Chuck 74
Baumann, Roger L. 128
bay 15, 17, 21, 23, 28, 37, 45,

49, 84, 121
Bay Laurel Farm 49
bayberry 29, 39
    branches 53
Beyberry Hill Herb Emporium
    225
Bayard, Tania 153
Bayou Blending Co. 64
bed and breakfasts 272–273
beads 96
Beal, W. J., Botanical Garden
    225
Beall, Steve and Ann 23, 67
Bean, Carolee 34, 191, 215
bearded iris 11
beauty products See body
    products
Becker, Dottie 21, 158, 163
Becker Greenhouse & Herb
    Farm 49
Becker, Jan 49
Becker, Jim 21, 163
bedstraw 14, 23, 38, 46
bee balm 19–22, 25, 28, 31–32,
    34, 36–37, 39
beekeeping supplies 13, 42, 50,
    88, 90–92, 95, 100, 103, 104,
    119, 120, 129
bees 13, 17
beeswax 53–54
begonia 31
Bell, Julia 40
belladonna 15, 38
Belle Star, Inc. 65
bellflower 20
bells-of-Ireland 16, 34
    dried 57, 60
Bellwether Herbs & Flowers 179
Belsinger, Susan 154
Benedetti, Maria Dolores
    Hajosy 148
beneficial insects See insects
Bennett, Ellie, 168
Bennett, Sandell 190, 238
benzoin gum powder 56, 86
bergamot 11, 17, 32, 36–37, 46,
    110
bergamot flowers
    dried 57
bergenia 34
Berggren, Chris 10
Bergner, Paul 136
Berk, Stephanie 179
Berkshire Botanical Garden
    179, 225
Berlet, Nancy 234
Berry Hill Press 137, 162
Berry Tree 49
Berwick, Ann 73, 202

Beston, Henry 140
Betari, Shondeya 194
betony 15, 19, 23–24, 29, 32
biblical herbs 140, 142, 145,
    227, 228, 232, 236, 243, 244
biennials 15
bindweed
    pressed 50
birch bark 122
Bird of Paradise Designs 87
birdhouses 91, 94, 95, 105, 129
biriyani 121
Birmingham Botanical Gardens
    226
Bisso, Wayne 83
bittersweet 12, 20, 31, 36
Bittersweet 179
Bittersweet Farm 88
bladder wrack 114
Black Creek Pioneer Village 226
Black, Penny 158
black pepper vine seeds 11
blackberry root 63
black-eyed Susan 34
Blackwell, W. Loyd and
    Carollyn 184, 231, 273
Blake, Steve 274
Blazing Star Herbal School
    200–201, 217
bleeding heart 24
Blessed Herbs 111
Bliss, Gilbert A. 46
bloodroot 11, 21, 35, 38, 44, 63,
    110
Bloomsaver Ltd. 126
Blossoms & Bevels 50
Blue Springs 11, 76
Bluejay Gardens Herb Farm 12,
    180
Bluestone Perennials 12
Blüm, Jan 40
Bobo, Barbara 76
body care products 54, 59, 61,
    64-77, 79, 70, 82, 85, 86, 89,
    90, 97, 99, 101, 108, 110,
    113, 114, 116, 118, 119, 124,
    233
Boerner Botanical Gardens 180,
    226
bog plants 26
Bonar, Ann 146
boneset 14, 21, 36, 43, 110, 111
book distributors 162–166,
    168–176
book reviews 132–134, 136–138
books 10–13, 15, 17, 19–22, 25,
    27–29, 31, 33, 35–36, 38–43,
    49, 53–56, 58–59, 61, 65–73,
    75, 77–86, 89–92, 94–96,

100, 103, 105, 107–109,
    111–117, 119, 120, 122, 125,
    127, 129, 133, 136–176, 206,
    207, 233, 235, 272, 274
Boone Drug Co. 50
Boonstra, W.N. 12
Booth, Nancy M. 53
borage 10, 12, 14–20, 22, 25,
    27–28, 30–32, 35–37, 41,
    43–44, 46
Borchard, Peter and Susan 15
Boscobel Restoration 226
Boston Spice and Tea Company
    77
Botanic Ark Nursery 12
Botanical Impressions 88
botanicals, dried 23, 39, 55–56,
    60, 64, 65, 67, 68, 76–86
Bountiful Gardens 12
bouquet garni 79, 81, 103, 104,
    119
bouquets 48, 50, 51, 55, 57, 60,
    62, 67, 69, 94, 103
Bowman's Hill Wildflower
    Preserve 13
Boyle, Wade 170
Bradd, Wayne 121
Bradley, Pam 64
Bramson, Ann 158
Brandt-Meyer, Eric and Ann 53
Brautigan, Cindy 180
breadseed 22, 36
Bremness, Lesley 140
Brentlinger, Dan 126
Bridenbaugh, Sandy 51
British Herb Trade Association
    266
Brooklyn Botanic Garden 154,
    162, 169, 180, 206, 226
Brooks Books 169
Brooks Enterprises 111
Brooks, Marilyn R. 111
Brooks, Svevo 279
Brookville Gardens 180
broom 114
Brown, Eugene and Yvonne 193
Brown, Marilyan 104
Bruneau, Betsy and Bill 12
Brushy Mountain Bee Farm,
    Inc. 13, 50
Buchanan, Rita 158
Buchman, Dian D. 148
buchu 117
Buckeye Naturopathic Press 170
Buehrle, Maureen 134, 267
Buffalo Springs Herb Farm 180
bugleweed 23, 26, 31, 35
Bulloch Hall Historical Site 181
Bulloch, Nancy 15

Bunch, Kathie M. 50
Bunch's Herbs & Gifts 50
burdock 10, 17, 35, 37
    root 63, 111
Burk, Murray 119
burnet 11, 14–15, 20, 25, 34,
    39–42, 44, 46
Burnett, Barbara 88
Burns, Sharon 236
Burpee, W. Atlee, & Company
    13
Burr, Fearing 146, 168
Burrell, D. V., Seed Growers Co.
    13
Burrell, Rick 13
Bush, Allen 25
Bush, Katharine 79
Busha's Brae Herb Farm 119,
    180, 227
business and industry
    Annual National Herb
        Growing and Marketing
        Conference 216
    books 142, 147, 175
    British Herb Trade
        Association 266
    Herb Growing and
        Marketing Network 134,
        267
    International Herb Growers
        and Marketers
        Association 269
    magazines and newsletters
        132, 134
    services for 279
    See also marketing
The Business of Herbs 132
Butchart Gardens 227
Butel, Jane 125
Butterfly Hill Herbary 181
butterfly weed 21, 34, 37, 40,
    43, 45
Byrne, Sherri 187

C

cactus 31
Cactus Patch Herbs 14
Cadillac Mountain Farm 51
calamint 21
calamus 66
calendula 12, 15, 19, 25, 28, 32,
    43–44
    dried 60, 110–112, 114, 117
Calendula 170
California School of Herbal
    Studies 162, 201

calla lilies
dried 60
calligraphy 39, 90, 278
Calvert Homestead 88
Cambridge Chemists, Inc. 51
Camelot Herb Gardens 77
Cameron, Myra 148
Cameron, Patricia 56
Campbell, Renee Troyer 73
Campbell, Sam 115
campion 23
Canadian hemlock cones 50
Canadian Organic Growers 24
Canadian Wildflower Society 266
candlemaking supplies 48, 50
candles 48, 54, 66, 67, 74, 75, 77, 80, 83, 100, 107
Candlesby Herbs 88
candytuft 18, 45
canning supplies 127
Canterbury bells 24
Canterbury Shaker Village 227
Canyon Country Herbs 77
Capability's Books, Inc. 170
capers 119
Caprilands Herb Farm 77, 181, 227
caraway 11–12, 14, 17, 19–20, 22, 27, 30, 34, 40, 43, 46, 84, 122
cardamom 29, 38–39, 84, 122
cardoon 11, 15, 19, 21, 29–30, 34, 41, 43
Carlson, Shelley 21, 66
Carmichael, Paul and Melinda 31, 81
carnations
dried 52, 60, 63
carob 19, 35, 78
Carpenter, Deb 148, 164
Carpenter, Susan 182
Carroll, Ricki and Robert 58, 154
Carter, David 174
Casey, Carol 15
caspia 55
dried 48, 53
cassia buds 122
Castleman, Michael 148
castor bean 38
Castro, Armida G. 125
catchfly 34
catering 274
catmint 10, 38, 41
catnip 13, 15–16, 18–20, 22–23, 25, 27, 29–31, 36–37, 39, 41, 43, 45, 53, 54
dried 61

toys 78, 92, 94, 106
Cats in the Cradle 181
cattails 56
cedar chips 51, 58
Cedarbrook Herb Farm 14, 89, 182
cedronella 37
celandine 21
celeriac 32
cellulose 58
celosia 12, 28, 32
dried 48, 52–53, 55, 61, 63
centaury 24
Chain, Kathy 188
Challand, Sharon 57
chamomile 12–13, 17–18, 20–22, 24–25, 30, 37–39, 43–44, 46, 111, 125
Chantal, Katherine 110
Chapman, Cynthia D. 90
chaparral 117
Chavis, Susan C. 89
cheesemaking supplies 58
Chef's Pantry 119
Cherry Valley Herb Farm 182
chervil 11, 14, 19–20, 22, 28–30, 32, 37, 40, 42–44, 84
chia 10, 26, 33, 36
Chicago Botanic Garden 227
Chicama Vineyards 119
chickweed 10, 23, 110, 112
chicory 20, 24, 30–31, 33, 37–38, 45, 122
children's activities 180, 181, 186, 189, 192, 194, 197, 198
children's books 94, 143, 168
children's gardens 234, 237, 239
Childs, Harvey 127
Chili Pepper Emporium 14, 124
chili powder 86
chilis 26–27, 33, 36, 122
Chinese herbs 77, 79, 81, 100, 104, 113, 114, 116, 134
Chinese lantern 12, 21, 32, 63
Chinese pink flower 17
Chinese rhubarb 33
chives 12–17, 19–20, 22, 25, 28, 30–32, 36–38, 40–41, 43–46, 84
dried 52
chlorella 112
Christmas items 49–50, 53, 58–59, 61–62, 77, 81, 87, 89, 93, 106–108, 120, 220
Churchbaugh, Sylvia 278
cilantro 12, 15, 23, 25–26, 28, 32–33, 41, 44, 84, 125
cinnamon 84
apple slices, dried 55

bark 51
chips 103
sticks 53, 57, 106, 121
tree 11
cinquefoil 36, 46
Circle Herb Farm 14
citronella 21, 29
Claiborne, Craig 154
Clark, Marge 162
Clark, Wilma 14, 182, 228
Clark's Greenhouse & Herbal Country 14, 182, 228
Clarkson, Rosetta E. 140, 153
clay 54, 61, 65, 75, 86, 113, 117
cleaning screens 10
Clear Light Cedar Co. 89
Cleland, Tim 97, 204
Clement, Diane 78
Clement Herb Farm 78
Cline, Martha 59
Cloisters, The 228
cloth bags 10
clove pinks 20
clover 16–17, 22, 33, 35, 38, 45, 117
cloves 84, 103, 121
Clyde Robin Seed Co. 15
Cobblestone Farm 228
cockscomb 18
cocoa butter 54
coconut oil 113
Cody Catering and Crafts 274
Cody, Paula 274
coffee 66, 67, 71, 79, 81, 83, 86, 95, 111, 122–124
coffee plant 15
cohosh 20–21, 38, 40, 111, 112, 117
cohosh bugbane 13
Cole, Linda 107
Collins, Bill 189, 236
Colonial Williamsburg 228
coltsfoot 10, 24, 34
Columbia University Press 162
columbine 22, 36, 40, 43
pressed 50
comfrey 10, 12, 17, 23, 29, 32, 36–37, 44, 108, 110, 112, 114, 117
Comfrey Chatter 132
Common Scents 132
companion plants 27, 28, 144, 145, 186
Companion Plants 15
compass plant 17
Complete Body Shop 89
computer software 115, 274, 275
Comstock, Ferre & Co. 15
Condon, Glory H. 49

Condon, Linda 117
coneflower 11–13, 15–17, 19–21, 24, 26, 28, 33–37, 39–40, 43–45
cones 51, 57, 86
alder 58
birch 62
Canadian hemlock 50
Carolina hemlock 57
pinecones 51, 54, 57, 62, 93
Coney, Norma and Dennis 106
Conneen, Jane 99
Conrow, Robert 146
containers and bags 10, 50, 53, 55, 59, 60, 66, 67, 70, 71, 74, 75, 78, 80, 81, 84–86, 92, 101, 103, 105, 106, 122
Cook, Alan D. 141
Cook's Garden 15
Cookbook Cottage 170
cookbooks 41, 78, 107, 108, 118, 119, 123, 125, 137, 138, 140, 141, 143–145, 147, 154–157, 168–172, 174–176
cooking with herbs
classes/workshops 125, 179–181, 183, 187–189, 191–195, 197–200
magazines and newsletters 132, 133, 136, 138
videos 204, 205
Coon, Nelson 148
Cooper, Guy 146
Copley, Diane 80
Coplin, Jeannette 245
coral root 114
coreopsis 12, 17, 20, 26, 31–36, 45
coriander 11, 13, 15, 17, 19, 27, 30, 32, 34, 37, 40, 43–44, 122
corn
dried 60
Indian 60
salad 15
silk 117, 122
cornflower 22, 33
dried 51
Cornell Plantations 182, 228
cosmos 45
costmary 14, 29, 37–39, 41, 44
cota 36, 112
cotton 33, 38
Country Bloomers Nursery 15
Country Flower Bin 51
Country Garden Dried Flowers and Herbs 51
Country Gardener 89
Country Green 166, 182
Country Herb 89

Country Herbs & Flowers 170
Country Lane Herbs & Dried
    Flowers 16
Country Manor 90
Country Merchants 78
Country Road Herb Farm &
    Gift Barn 111, 183
Country Roots Shop & Gardens
    90, 229, 272
Country Shepherd 52, 183
Country Thyme 78
Country Thyme Gazette 132, 171
Countryside Fragrances, Inc. 90
cover crops 12, 36
Cox Arboretum 229
Cox, Paul 194, 244
Craft, Terry 104
crafts
    books 140–146, 158–161,
        168, 171, 174
    classes/workshops 60,
        178–200
    newsletters and magazines
        133, 136–138
    supplies 20, 48–63, 69, 82, 85
Craker, Lyle E. 134
Cramer, Ralph L. 52
Cramers' Posie Patch 52
cramp bark 111
Cranbrook House & Gardens
    229
Crate Shoppe 126
Cravens, Debbie 176
Crawford, Hester M. 158
Creative Craft House 52
Crescent Books 162
cress 13, 20, 31
    See also watercress
Crisp, Inas 189
Croasdaile, Susannah 162, 169
Crocker Hill Studios 229
Crockett, James 141
crocus 24, 29
Crop King, Inc. 126
Cross, Dale K. 16
Cross Seed Co. 16
Crossing Press 162
cross-stitch See stitchery
Crotz, Keith 162, 168
Crowood Press 162
Cruden, Loren 115
Cruickshank, Sheena 230
crystallized flowers 119, 122
crystals 91
Cude, Kaye 138, 230
Culinary Arts Ltd. 162
culinary herbs 10, 12, 16, 24,
    27, 29, 31, 33, 37–40, 42–43,
    49, 53–54, 61–62, 65, 67, 68,

71, 73, 75–89, 92, 93, 99,
    100, 103, 104, 111–113, 117,
    118–124, 129
    books 140–144, 146, 147,
        154–157, 169, 175, 176
    classes/workshops 178, 180,
        183, 187, 193, 195,
        197–200
    videos 204
    See also cooking with herbs
Cullen, Betsy 242
Culpeper Ltd. 65
cultivation See growing herbs
Culver's root 17
cumin 10–12, 16, 19, 28–29, 37,
    40, 43–44, 84, 125
Cummings, Susan Rose 97
curly dock
    dried 48
curry 14, 23, 37, 42, 44, 119, 121
Curtis, Olive 102, 191
Curtis, Romey 242
Cushing House Museum 229
Cusick, Dawn 158, 159
custom growing service 24
Czerwinski, Jeannette 60

D

Dabney, Davy 16, 90
Dabney Herbs 16, 90
Dahl, Kevin 33, 137, 269
daisies 12, 18–19
Dallas Civic Garden Center 229
Dam, Rene W. 16
Dam, William, Seeds 16
Damaskin, Mariel 172
damassia 33
Damian, Kate 75
Damside Garden Herbs 230
dandelion 16, 30, 35, 41, 110,
    114, 117
Danimose Foundation for
    Research and the Promotion
    of Herbal Medicine 270
Davidson-Wilson Greenhouses
    16
Davis, Annette 132, 265
Davis, Doris 194
Davis, Margo 87
daylilies 20
Daystar 17
DeGiorgi Seed Company 17
DeLong, Richard and Rose 52
Demits, Joyce 24
demonstrations and lectures 79,
    90, 96, 135, 174, 229, 231,

274–278
Demorest Harry 83
Densmore, Frances 149
Denver Botanic Gardens 206,
    230
De Paola, A. J. 126
Des Moines Botanical Center
    230
Desert Botanical Garden 183
devil's-claw 38
Devonian Botanic Garden 230
Devonshire Apothecary 65
de Vries, Harry A. 26
Diana's Designs 17
dianthus 12, 20–21, 29, 33, 39
DiCaprio, Helen 234
dill 12–14, 19, 23, 25, 27–28,
    30–32, 34, 37, 41, 43–44, 53,
    60, 76, 84
    pressed 50
Dille, Carolyn 154
dittany 19, 23, 44
Dittany 133
Dobmeier, John and Bonnie 66
Docker, Amanda 159
Dodson, Lynne 49
Dodt, Colleen K. 136, 187
dogwood
    dried 55
dolls 54, 77, 93, 98, 107
Dominion Herbal College 162,
    201
Donohue Michele 73
Dorothy Biddle Service 49
Doubleday Books 162
Dover Publications 162
Down to Earth, Inc. 111
Downey-Butler, Louise 103
Dragon's Lair 91
Dreams End Farm 183
Dremann, Craig and Sue 37
Dried Floral Creations 91
dried flowers 12, 16, 34, 48–57,
    60–62, 68, 69, 88, 93, 98,
    108, 137, 111, 120
dried herbs 15, 23–24, 30, 38,
    42, 48, 50–54, 56, 60–62,
    66–69, 72, 76–86, 89, 92, 93,
    95, 96, 98, 99, 103, 104,
    111–115, 124
Driscoll, Noreen 197
Driscoll, Thomas 275
Drum, Ryan 114, 202
Dry Creek Herb Farm 65
drying racks 96, 101–103
Duff, Gail 159, 175
Duhnoski, Kathy 43
Duke, James A. 149, 154
Dunford, Mary 277

Dunlap, Miriam 237
Dunn, Jan 23
Duran, Barbara 112
Durio, Ken 31
dusty miller
    dried 51
    pressed 50
Dybiec, Leslie 236
dye
    books 142, 158, 160, 171
    classes/workshops 184
    plants 37–39, 42
    public gardens 224–228, 230,
        235, 236, 239–242, 245,
        247
dyer's broom 21, 38

E

Early American Museum and
    Gardens 230
Earth Herbs 66, 204
Earthrise Company 112
earthworms 13
East West School of Herbalism
    201
Eaton, Oriel 272
Ebert, Carol 78
Ebert's Herbs & Wheat 78
Echard, Karen 170
echinacea 12, 17, 22, 29, 41,
    110, 112, 117
ECHO/Healing Heart Herbals
    183
edelweiss 29
Eden, Carolyn 203
Eden Vineyards Winery & Park
    230
Edgewood Herbs 79
edible flowers 14–15, 24, 28, 41
edible seeds 10
Edwards Victoria 70
Eibsen, Margaret 226
Egyptian onion 21
elderberry 19, 112
Elderflower Farm 119
elderflowers 110
Eldridge, Judith 141
elecampane 10, 19, 23, 44
elephant garlic 12, 21–22, 39
Elixir Farm Botanicals 17
Emmerson, Kathy 165, 172
Enchanted Crest 184, 231, 273
Engel, Nancy 106
Engeland, Ron 18
England, Yvonne 79, 184
England's Herb Farm 79, 184

English, Billy E. 10
environment 132, 135, 210
Eon Industries 126–127
epazote 14, 22–23, 27–28, 33, 36–37, 40–41, 43, 121, 125
ephedra 15, 19, 35, 38, 111
epsom salts 54
Erickson, Ann R. 97
Esposito, Virginia 181
Essential Oil Company 91, 184
ethnobotany 133
eucalyptus 11, 19, 21, 28
    dried 34, 48, 52–53, 55, 60–61, 112
    tree 88
Euroflax, Inc. 18
Evelyn, Nancy 149
events 210–221
Everglades ball grass 62
Evergreen Garden Plant Labels 127
everlastings 10, 12–16, 18–22, 27–32, 34, 36, 38–39, 41–44, 46, 81, 99, 134
    dried 48–49, 51, 53–55, 57, 60–61, 63, 67, 73, 79, 82, 86, 93, 94
extracts 59, 64, 66, 67, 69, 72, 75, 81–83, 85, 96, 104, 108, 110–115, 118, 119, 122

F

Facts on File, Inc. 163
Fairie Herb Gardens 231
Fajack, JoAnne 98
Falco, Sue 14
Falcor 274
Fallon, Sandi 89
Farkouh, Charles 123
Farmer Seed & Nursery 18
Farmers' Museum 112
Farmhouse, The 91
Farmington Historic Home and GArden 231
Felton, Elise 141
fennel 10–14, 17, 19–20, 23, 25, 27, 30, 32, 34, 37–38, 41–44, 84
Fennell, Beverly 69
fenugreek 10, 15–17, 20, 37, 41, 121
Fergeus, John 64
Fernbank Science Center Garden 231
ferns 25, 31
Ferrary, Jeannette 155

Fettner, Ann Tucker 159
feverfew 12, 14, 20, 24, 30, 38, 40, 43–44
    dried 48, 53
Fiberworks Publications 171, 163
Field's, Henry, Seed & Nursery Co. 18
Filaree Farm 18
Filoli 232
fines herbes 79, 81, 119
Fischborn, Cynthia 155
Fishman, Marissa 22
Fiszer, Louise 155
Fitzpatrick, John T. 43, 198, 240
fixatives 55, 56, 59, 62, 68, 79, 82, 103, 113, 122
Flavour Connection 275
flax 11–12, 14–15, 18, 22, 35, 37, 39, 43
    dried 52, 63
fleabane 34
Flentge, Cecil 278
Fletcher, Kim 133
Fletcher, Michael 133
Flora & Fauna Tours, Inc. 275
Florilegium 272
Florist Brokerage, Inc. 52
Flower and Herb Exchange 267
flower holders 49
Flower Press, The 91
flower presses 17, 36, 49, 62, 87, 94, 108
flowering shrubs 10
Flowers and Spice World 18
Flowery Branch Seed Company 19
Focus on Herbs 133
Food for Thought Posters 92
Ford, Gillian 230
Ford, Henry, Museum at Greenfield Village 232
Forestfarm 19
forget-me-not 40
Forrest, Steve 13, 50
Forsell, Mary 141
Fort Worth Botanic Garden 232
Foster Botanic Gardens 232
Foster's Botanical and Herb Reviews 133
Foster, Gertrude B. 141
Foster, Steven 133, 149
Fowler, Becky 95
Fox Fern Herb Farm 79
Fox, Helen Morgenthau 141
Fox Hill Farm 19
Fox Hollow Herbs & Heirlooms 19
Fox, Mary Ann 183
foxglove 12–13, 15, 24, 26,

33–34, 40, 43, 45–46
foxtail grass
    dried 61
Foy, Nicky 143
Fragrance Shop 92, 184
Fragrant Garden, The 66
Fragrant Fields 20, 53
fragrant flowers and herbs 16, 20–21, 31, 37, 42
Fragrant Path, The 20
frangipani 35
frankincense 51, 66, 69, 74, 76, 86
Frandsen, Jeannette 199
Frazier, Jeanne 169
Fredericksburg Herb Farm 92
Freedman, Russell 174
freelance writing 135, 275, 277, 278
freeze-dried botanicals 52, 60
freeze-drying machines 52, 58
French, Norman and Una M. 117
Fresh Garlic Association 133, 155, 163, 267
Frieda's, Inc. 275
Friendship Herb Gardens 184
Frog Park Herbs 66
Frontier Cooperative Herbs 79
Frowine, Steven 45
Frye, Barney L. 11
Fu, Lucia 42
Fuessel, J. J., Custom Tile 92
Fuhrer, Carolyn 43
fuller's teasel 12, 15, 30
Fullerton Arboretum 232
Furneaux, Lane 172, 276
Furth, Peter 169
Future Concepts, Inc. 132

G

Gagel, Judy 32, 71, 191
Gaia Botanicals 80
Gaige, A. John 29
Gallagher, Robert 116
Gang, Chris and Greg 126
garam masala 121, 122
Garcia, Janet Scigliane 87
garden art 17, 62, 89, 90, 97, 99, 103–105, 108, 233, 272
garden design
    books 140–147, 153, 154, 168, 207
    classes/workshops 181, 184, 186, 188, 195
    magazines and newsletters

134
    services 28, 118, 275, 276
garden markers 27, 67, 69, 87, 92, 94, 95, 99, 100, 105, 106, 126, 127
Garden Perennials 20
Garden Place 20
Garden Way Publishing 141, 163, 171
Gardener's Eye 127
Gardener's Kitchen 127
Gardeners Bookshelf 171
GARDENFIND 275
gardening
    books 140–146, 168–175, 206–207
    classes/workshops 178–200
    newsletters and magazines 132, 134, 136–138
    supplies 11, 13, 15, 17, 18, 21, 28, 29, 35, 36, 38, 41–43, 126–130
    tools 126–130
    videos 204, 105
    See also organic gardening
Gardens Alive! 127
Gardens of the Blue Ridge 20
gardens for the blind 225, 229, 232, 235, 240, 242, 244
Garland, Sarah 142
garlic 16–18, 20–22, 25, 27–28, 30, 32, 36–38, 42, 55, 62, 84, 112, 117, , 120–123
    books 144, 146, 155, 156
    braid 62, 89, 93, 100, 103
    Fresh Garlic Association 133, 155, 163, 267
    Garlic News 133
    Gilroy Garlic Festival 216
    keepers 78, 79, 99, 106
    press 78
garlic chives 37, 42, 44
Garlic News 133
Gastrell, Shirley 30
Gatehouse Herbs 92, 232
Gates, Carol 232
Gathered Herb 21, 66
Gay, Linda 239
Georgi, Bill and Shash 87, 179, 171
geraniums 32, 40, 134
    See also scented geraniums
Gerber, Meri 61
Gerlach, Nancy 124
germander 12, 23–24, 28, 32, 34, 38, 46
Gervaise, Norma B. 107
Getty, J. Paul, Museum 233
Gibbons, Euell 149

Gibbs, Mary and Charlie 38
Gignac, Solange, G. 206
Gilbertie, Celeste M. 185
Gilbertie, Sal 142, 155, 185
Gilbertie's Herb Gardens 185
Gill, Cecily 198, 216, 247
ginger 20, 22, 24, 84, 121
    crystallized 120
    rhisomes 11
gingerroot 63, 111, 122
Gingham 'n Spice, Ltd. 53
gingko 24, 111, 219
ginseng 10–11, 21, 26, 31, 35,
    38, 61, 63, 67, 69, 72, 79–81,
    86, 132, 111, 113, 115, 117
    American Ginseng Trends
    132
Gips, Kathleen 103, 146, 164
Glade Valley Nursery 21
Gladstar, Rosemary 194
globe artichoke 30
Globe Pequot Press, Inc. 163
glycerin 49, 54, 68, 117
goatsbeard 34
Goddard, Ragna Tischler 246
Golden Earth Herbs 112
Golden Meadows Herb Farm &
    Emporium 80
goldenrod 34, 36, 43
    dried 55
goldenseal 10–11, 110, 117
goldenseal root 63
Gomez, Rae Ann 72
Good Earth Farm 53
Good Scents 53, 185
Good Scents of Louisiana 80
Good Seed Company 21
Good-King-Henry 12, 39, 43–44
Goodwin Creek Gardens 21, 163
Gooseberry Patch Company 93
Gordon, Sharon 15
Gorius, C.H. and Ruth 37
gotu kola 21, 31, 33, 122
gourds 18, 23, 27, 33
    dried 51
gourmet foods 25, 30, 39, 40,
    76–86, 95, 118–124
Gourmet Gardens Herb Farm
    233
Grainger, Janette 149
grains 10, 12, 16, 40, 43, 86
Grant, Pam 238
grapevines 55, 61
grasses 12, 15, 17, 20, 25–27, 29,
    34, 36, 45
Graven Images 93
Graves, George 149
Great Lakes Herb Company 22,
    67, 171

Green, James 116, 149
Green Landing Nursery 275
Green, Mindy 116
Green Terrestrial 112, 185
Greenfield Herb Garden 54, 171
Greenmantle Nursery 22
Grieve, Mrs. M. 146
Griffin, Judy 59
grindelia 114
grinding mills 67, 84, 124
Grisi, Gail, Stenciling, Inc. 93
Gross, Anita 22
ground covers 12, 31
Groves, Karen 279
growing herbs 23, 28, 46
    newsletters and magazines
    132–134, 136–138
guar powder 86
guarijio conivari 33
Guizar, Miquel 21
Gulf Publishing Co. 163
gum arabic 113
gums, resins and waxes 56, 64,
    72, 65, 86, 97, 113, 123
Gurney Seed & Nursery Co. 22
gypsophila
    dried 54

H

Haag, Rosalyn 14
Hackimer, John and Flora M. 46
Hadd, Br. Arnold 86
Hagen, Rolfe and Janet 43, 247
Haggerty, Patrick 121
Hamilton, Mary Lou 24, 188
Hamilton, Rudy 21
Hampstead, Marilyn 19
Hancock Shaker Village 233
Hanes, Dolly 184
Hansen, Kay 122
Hanson, Carol 20, 53
Harpain, Jeffrey 168, 274
Harris, Gloria 90, 229, 272
Hart, General William, House
    233
Hartland, Garth 175
Hartman, Lynn and Pete 22, 93,
    273
Hartman's Herb Farm 22, 93,
    273
Harvest Harmony 172
Harvest Health, Inc. 112
Hatcher, Valerie 62
hats 50, 57, 88, 93, 94, 98, 106
Haushild, Vickie 174
Haussmann's Pharmacy, Inc. 113

Havasu Hills Herb Farm 23
Hawkes, Barbara D. 83
Hawks, Kim and Bruce 34
Hawley, Jane 101
Hayden, Gail 92, 184
Haynie, Don 180
heather 21, 39
    dried 53
Heidgen, Charles F. 40
Healing Arts Press 163
Health Concerns 113
Heard, Mary Lou 185
Heard's Country Gardens 185
Heart's Ease Herb Shop &
    Gardens 94
Heartscents 94
Heavenly Scent Herb Farm 186
Hecksel, Arlene 146
Hedgehog Hill Farm 94, 214,
    233
Heirloom Garden Seeds 23
heirloom plants and seeds
    10–12, 35, 40–41, 228, 240,
    241, 267
    See also old-fashioned plants
heliotrope 20, 24, 28–29, 32,
    40, 42–43
henbane 44
Henderson, Peter 168
Henderson, Ruth and Skitch 195
Hendricks, Megan 128
henna 28, 32
Henry Field's Seed & Nursery
    Co. 18
Hepper, F. Nigel 142
Herb Bar 95, 163, 220
Herb Barn 23, 67, 186
herb chopper 126
Herb Companion 134, 236
Herb Cottage 186
Herb Country Gifts &
    Collectibles 186
Herb Cupboard 187
Herb Federation of New
    Zealand 133
Herb Garden 23, 133, 67
Herb Gathering, Inc. 95
Herb Growing and Marketing
    Network 134, 267
Herb Haus 187
Herb House 95
Herb Market 187
Herb Merchant 95
Herb N' Ewe 96, 187
Herb 'n' Renewal 68
Herb Patch Ltd. 80
Herb-Pharm 113
Herb Products Co. 96
Herb Quarterly 134

Herb Research Foundation 135,
    267
Herb Shop 81
Herb Society 268
Herb Society of America 135,
    142, 163, 223, 236, 241, 268
Herb, Spice and Medicinal Plant
    Digest 134
Herbal Bodyworks 54
Herbal Connection 134
Herbal-Ease (OHR & Assoc.)
    114
Herbal Effect 81
Herbal Endeavors, Ltd. 136, 187
Herbal Gardens 54, 187
Herbal Healer Academy 201
Herbal Review 134
Herbal Rose Report 135
Herbal Studies Course 165, 202
Herbalgram 135
Hebalist & Alchemist, Inc. 114
Herbalist, Inc. 114, 188
Herbally Yours 68
Herbamed Medicinal Herb
    Nursery 23
Herban Lifestyles 135
Herban News 135
Herbarist 135
Herbary & Stuff 24, 188
Herbfarm 24, 68, 188, 234
Herbitage Farm 54
HerbLine 276
Herbs and Heirlooms 69
herbs by region
    alpine 19
    Asia 133
    Australia 133
    Blue Ridge Mountains 21
    China 77, 79, 81, 100, 104,
        113, 114, 116, 134
    desert 33, 138, 150, 246
    eastern Europe 18
    England 28
    France 11
    Hawaii 26
    high-altitude 25
    Mexico 26
    native American 21, 34, 36,
        133, 137
    New England 17
    North America 36
    North Pacific Rim area 10
    northern U.S. 18
    northwestern Mexico 33
    Oriental 17, 42
    Pennsylvania 13
    Siberia 25
    southeastern U.S. 34
    southeastern Wisconsin 36

southern U.S. 142
southwestern U.S. 33, 36, 134
Soviet Republic of Georgia 18
Texas 46, 143, 145, 239
western U.S. 43
Herbs-Liscious 24, 69
Herbs of Grace 114
Herbs of Happy Hill 188
Herbs Unlimited 69
Herbscapes by Lane Furneaux 276
heritage plants 15, 25, 268
See also old-fashioned plants
Heritage Rose Foundation 268
Heritage Rose Gardens 24
Heritage Seed Program 24, 268
Hersey, Jean 155
Hickory Hill Herbs 96, 188, 276
Hidalgo, Mary 11, 76
Hidden Springs Herbs 25
Higgins, Judy 57
High Altitude Gardens 25
High Desert Growers Wholesale 54
High Hampton Inn & Country Club 189
Hilary's Comfort Beads 96
Hill Crest House 97
Hill, Doug 200
Hill, Madalene 142, 163, 275
Hill, Paula Jones 96, 188, 276
Hillhouse Naturals Farm 55
Hilliard, Robert J. 18
Hillier, Malcolm 159
Hilltop Garden 234
Hilltop Herb Farm 25, 120, 276
Hilton, Colin 159
Hilton, Richard 81
Historic Bartram's Garden 234
Historical Roses 25
Historical Society of Glastonbury's Welles Shipman Ward House 234
history of herbs
books 140–142, 144–147, 153, 168, 173, 206, 207
classes/workshops 178, 183, 190
magazines and newsletters 134, 135, 137
Hoffman, David 149, 203
Houghton Mifflin Co. 163
hoja santa 28
Holbrook Farm and Nursery 25
Holch, Ron 22, 67
Holder, Frank 60
Hollopeter, Donna 28

Hollowbrook Pottery & Tile 128
Hollow, Orchids & Herbs, The 26
hollyhock 22, 26, 39–40, 43
Holway, Joyce 101
home brew supplies 34
home entertaining 132
Homespun Gatherings 97
honesty 43
honey 50, 61, 77, 80, 94, 119–121, 124
Honolulu Community Action Program, Inc. 26
Honor Heights Park 235
Hopkinson, Simon and Judith 142
Hopper, Virginia 24
hops 21–22, 41, 112, 117, 122
horehound 10, 12–14, 17, 29, 37–38, 46
dried 57
drops 122
horseradish 18, 22–24, 35, 120, 121
Hortico, Inc. 26
HortIdeas 136
Houston Garden Center 235
Houston, Maggie 277
Hovar, Julie 72
Hoy, Michael 136
Hsu's Ginseng Enterprises 26
Hubble Hill Herbs 27
Hubble, Roselynn 27
Hudson, J. L., Seedsman 27
Hudson, Kevin 50
Hudspeth, Joeann 111, 183
Huffman, Vicki 32
Hughes, Mary, Designs 97
Hume, Ed, Seeds 27
Humenick, Muriel and William 38
Hundley Ridge Farm 27
Hundley, Tom and Loretta 27
Hunt, Peter and Anna 59
Huntington Botanical Gardens 235
Huntington, Carol 85
Hunziker, Catherine 118, 270
Hurt, Pat 54
Hutchins, Alma R. 150
Hutson, Lucinda 155, 163, 277
hyacinth bean 43
Hyde, Cyrus and Louise 45, 108, 216
hydrangea
dried 60
Hydrofarm 128
Hydro-Gardens, Inc. 128

hydroponic supplies 126, 127
Hylton, William H. 147
hyssop 13–15, 17, 21, 27, 30, 35–37, 39–40, 43
dried 52–53, 57, 60, 122
Hyssop Hill 69
Hywet, Stan, Hall & Gardens 235

I

Iden Croft Herbs 28, 163, 235
Illuminations 97
immortelle 23
In Harmony with Nature 28
incense 60, 65–68, 70, 72, 83, 89, 95, 100
Indiana Botanic Gardens 97, 204
indigo 13, 22, 28, 33, 36
Ingraham, Gail 179
Ingram, Gay 132
Inner Traditions International Ltd. 163
Inniswood Metro Gardens 236
insects 12, 36, 38, 127
See also bees
See also organic gardening
interior design 50, 98
International Herb Growers and Marketers Association 269
International Journal of Aromatherapy 136
International Manufacturing Co. 55
Interweave Press 134, 164
Iowa State University Horticultural Garden 236
Ireland, Mary Ann 170
Irish, Mary 183
Irwin, Barbara 94
Island Aromatics 98
Island Herbs 114–115
Israel, Burt 29
It's About Thyme 28
Ives, Jeanita and Jerome 243

J

Jack, Jenny 35
Jacob, Irene 243
Jacob's-ladder 46
Jacobs, Betty E. M. 142, 159, 175
James, Theodore, Jr. 159
jams and jellies 24, 65, 67, 77, 82–84, 98–100, 119–122, 124

Jane's Herb Farm 189
Janson, Mrs. Walda 173
Janus, Gerry 44, 175, 199, 215
Janus, Pamela 58
jasmine 42
Jason Natural Products 70
Jay, Viola 12, 180
Jayne, Fairman and Kate 39
Jekyll, Gertrude 169
Jenkins Estate 236
Jenney, Pat 183
Jerusalem oak 34
jewelry 65, 68, 80, 94, 98, 103, 106, 109
jimsonweed 36, 43
Joe-Pye weed 10, 13, 34, 36, 43
Johanna's 98
John's Gourmet Gardens 29
Johnny's Selected Seeds 28
Johnny-jump-up
pressed 50
Johns, Nancy 67, 186
Johns, Tom 43
Johnson, Carol 239
Johnson, Marsha 155
Johnson, Pamela 29
Johnson, Paula 186
Johnson, Ron 93
Johnston, Rob 28
jojoba 21, 35, 38
Jones, Loring M. 34
Jones, Shatoiya 54
Joosten, Titia 159
journals 133–135, 137
See also magazines and newsletters
Jung, J. C. 29
Jung, J. W., Seed Company 29
juniper berries 51, 121, 125

K

K & S Horseradish 120
Kaminski, Mark A. 41
Kaminski, Michael J. 130
Kapla, William 112
Kapuler, Alan M. 35
Kauai Flower Perfumes 70
Kavasch, Barrie 155, 169
Keeney, Allen 48
Keepsake Hearts & Flowers 98
Kelso, Murry 123
Kendall/Hunt Publishing Company 172
Kennedy, Barbara 28
Kennedy, Cheryl 230
Kestner, Arlene 80

Keune Produce and Veal Farm
Keune, Steven J.
Keville, Kathi 132, 142, 191, 266
Kibbey, Heather 156
Kiefer, Larraine 198, 215
King, Marilyn 87
King, Michael L. 82, 190
Kingfisher, Inc. 29
Kingwood Center 236
Kirkpatrick, Debra 143
Kirsch, Eugene and Margery 82
Kirschenbaum, Grace 138
Kiss of the Sun Nursery 29
KJ's Books 165, 172
Klein, Erica Levy 156
Klokkevold, Barbara 203
Kloss, Jethro 150
Klug, Robert J. 72
van Kluyve, Bob 106
Knopf, Alfred A., Inc. 164
knotweed 24
Konzen, Patly 79
Korn, Gail 20
Koval, Max 117
Kowalchik, Claire 147
Krochmal, Connie and Arnold 156
Kuitems, Jane 189
Kunkel, Joe and Sybil 178
Krystal Wharf Farms 29

L

la dama maya herb and flower farm 98, 189, 214, 218
La Valley, Steve 12
Lacko-Beem, Carol 24, 69
Lady of the Lake 70
lady's-mantle 12, 21, 26, 37, 40–42, 44–46
Ladybug Press 172
LaForte, Liz Z. 165, 174
Lalicker, Cathleen 41
Lambert, Paula 121
lamb's-ears 11, 20, 27, 37, 43, 104
lamb's-quarters 10
lamium 44
Lander, Kathleen 25
Landreth, D., Seed Co. 30
landscaping
    books 140–143, 145, 155, 168, 170, 172, 176, 206
    classes/workshops 180, 181, 184, 189
    services 34, 35, 106

Land Steward 128
Langley, Jean 42
Lapour, Keith 18
Lark Books 164
Larkcom, Joy 143
larkspur 43–44, 48
    dried 48, 51, 61
Lathrop, Norma 143
Lauahi, Lono M. 26
Laurelbrook Book Services 172
lavender 13–16, 19–20, 22–23, 26, 28–32, 34, 37–39, 41, 43–45
    dried 51, 61, 88
Lavender Lane 55
Lawhorn, Janette 108
Lawrence, Korby 54
Le Jardin du Gourmet 30, 120
lecithin 78
Ledden, Donald 30
Ledden, Orol, & Sons 30
Lee, Darlene 77, 181, 227
Lee, Stephen 170
Leeds Castle 237
leeks 16, 22, 30, 32, 36, 42, 122
Legacy Herbs 99
legal issues 132, 135
legumes 34
lemon balm 11–13, 16, 22, 24–25, 28, 37, 43
lemon peel 51
lemon verbena
    See verbena
lemon zest 84
lemongrass 15, 22–23, 37, 42, 44
leopard flower 17
Levengood, Alberta 85
Levine, Patty 102
Levy, Nancy "J.J."65
Lewandowski, Philip A. 44
Lewis, Judy 30, 55, 219
Lewis Mountain Herbs & Everlastings 30, 55, 219
Leydet Oils and Aromatherapy Products 70
Leyel, Mrs. C. F. 159
liatris 44
    dried 53, 60
Libenn Aroma, Inc. 277
Liberty Natural Products, Inc. 71
Liberty Seed Co. 31
libraries 206–207, 230, 236, 274, 277
Ligon, Linda 134, 164
lilac
    dried 52
Lily of the Valley Herb Farm 31, 81
lily-of-the-valley 26, 44

Lima, Patrick 147
Linchester Linda M. 68
Litl' Mack's Herb Shoppe 99
Little, Brown & Co. 164
Little Farm Press 99
Littlefield-Fortin, Darr 106
Living History Farms 237
Lloyd Library and Museum 207
lobelia 19, 63, 110
    pressed 50
Loe, Theresa 132, 171
Logee's Greenhouses 31
Long, Cheryl 155, 156
Long Creek Herb Farm 189, 237, 273
Long, Jim 189, 237, 273
LongHerb Health Products, Inc. 115
Longone, Jan 176
Longwood Gardens 237
loosestrife 20
Los Angeles State and County Arboretum 238
lotus pods 56
Louisiana Nursery 31
lovage 10, 12–14, 19–21, 28–29, 34, 37–38, 46, 122
love-in-a-mist 12
    dried 61
Lovejoy, Sharon 94
Lowe, Jeannette 269
Lowe, Rick and Karen 120
Lowelands Farm 120
Loyd, Pearl E. 205
luffa 16, 18, 35, 38
    sponges 49, 72, 104
Lufriu, Marlene 168
Lukens, Sue 99
lunaria 23, 30, 37
lungwort 44
lupine 36
Lust, John 147
Luthy, George L., Memorial Botanical Garden 238
Lyness, Dody 56, 137, 160, 162
Lyness, Dody, Co. 56
Lynn's 100
Lyon, Bradford G. 176
Lyon, Harold L., Arboretum 238

M

Mabey, Richard 147
mace 29, 121
Macklin, Lisa 99
Macmillan Publishing Co. 164
madder 22, 38–39

magazines 72, 131–138
    See also journals and newsletters
Magelssen, Judy 275
Magic Garden Herb Co. 115
Magneson, Norma 186
magnolia 31
Magnolia Herbs 56
Magnolia's 56
Main, Gerda 50
Maine Balsam Fir Products 57
Maine, Sandy 74
mallow 19–20
mandrake 38, 45
Mantis Manufacturing Co. 128
Maple Hill Farm 71
Maple River Herb Gardens 81
Marcus, Kristi 91
Marigold Society of America 269
marigolds 23, 27, 33, 45
    pressed 50
Mari-Mann Herb Co., Inc. 82, 190
marjoram 11, 16, 27, 30–32, 37, 43–44
    dried 52–53
marketing 132, 134–135, 137, 216, 267, 269, 279
    See also business and industry
Marks, Joe 64
Martin, Jean 245
Martin, Jo Ann 93
Martin, Joy Logee 31
Martin, Robin and Kevin 84
Mary's Herb Garden & Gift Shop 32, 190, 238
Maryland's Herb Garden & Gift Shop 100
massage tools 66
    See also oils
Massey, Maryland 100
mastic gum 123
Masury, Anne M. 246
Matheny, Zin Marie 62
Mathews, Kathy 186
Mathiesen, Catherine 119
Matthaei Botanical Gardens 190, 238
Mautor, Claudette 160
May Apple 82
mayapple 11
maypop 22
Mazza, Irma Goodrich 156
McBride, Michael A. 249
McCain, Marijah 201
McCaleb, Rob 135, 267
McClure & Zimmerman 32
McCrory, Dolores 32

McCrory's Sunny Hill Herbs 32
McCully, Ruth 98
McDorman, Bill 25
McDowell House and
    Apothecary Shop 239
McFadden, Betty, Joe and
    Tammy 57
McFadden's Vines & Wreaths 57
McGee, Rose Marie 34
McIntyre, Lydia 82
McHugh, Barbara 22572
McKinley, Susie 191, 215
McKinney, Lavinia 17
McRae, Bobbi A. 160, 163, 171
Meadow Everlastings 57
Meadowbrook Herb Garden 32,
    71, 191
Meares, Portia 200
meadowsweet 13, 26, 34
media coverage 132, 135
Medical Herbalism 136
medicinal herbs 10, 16–17, 20,
    23, 33, 37, 49, 53, 66, 70, 77,
    80–82, 99, 110–118
    books 114, 116, 118,
        141–152, 168–173, 175
    classes/workshops 178, 179,
        181, 183, 187–189, 191,
        192, 194, 198–204
    magazines and newsletters
        133–136
    organizations 265–267
    videos 204–206
MediHerb Newsletter 136
Mediherb Pty. Ltd. 136
Mehrabian, Andranik 173
Meiners, Dick 36
Melendy, Casel 114
Melton, Penny and Don 122,
    192
Meltzer, Sol 143
Mendocino Arts & Gifts 100
menu planning 134
Mercer Arboretum and Botanci
    Gardens 239
Merco 164
Merlin of the Rogue Valley 121
Merry Gardens 32
Mescher, Jen 58
Messick, Maureen 98, 189, 214,
    218
Metcalfe, Donna 53, 185
Meyer, Anita L. 173
Meyer, Clarence 173
Meyer, Joseph E. 173
Meyerbooks, Publisher 173
Mexican mint marigold 33
Michaud, Karen 16
Michaux, Peter 116

Michigan 4-H Children's
    Garden 239
Midwest Seed Growers 32
Mieseler, Theresa 195
mignonette 23, 29, 40
milkweed 10, 23, 34–36
Miller, Barbara 23
Miller, Karen 86
Miller, Marylou 98
Mills, Susan 96, 187
Miloradovich, Milo 143
mint 12–25, 27–32, 34–35,
    37–42, 44–46
    St. John's Mint Festival 217
Mission Mill Village and
    Museum 240
Missouri Botanical Garden 240
Mr. McGregor's Garden 101
Molbak's Seattle Garden Center
    33
mole-plant 25
Molenock, Joane 26
money plant 12
monkshood 40, 44–45
Montgillion, Dot 84
Montgomery, Pam 112, 185
Monticello 240
Montreal Botanical Garden 240
Moon Mountain Wildflowers 33
Moore, Connie 95, 149, 163,
    220
Moore, Michael 150
Moore, Teesha 68, 89
Morgan, J. Peter 248
Morgan, Penny 122
Morningstar Publications 205
mortar and pestle 67, 69, 79–82,
    88, 95, 99, 103, 104, 106, 124
moss 31, 49, 56, 60
    Spanish 57, 62
moth repellent 53–54, 66,
    77–79, 87, 92, 95, 101, 106,
    107, 114
motherwort 46
Mott, Barbara Starr 72
Mt. Sopris Scents and
    Seasonings 82
Mount Vernon 240
Mountain Rose Herbs 101
Mountain Valley Farms 57
Mozzarella Company 121
mugwort 11, 16–17, 37
Mulherin, Jennifer 147
mullein 12, 15–17, 19, 24, 35,
    43, 110
Murphy, Christine 75
Murray, Patricia 130
Museum of Alaska
    Transportation and Industry

240
mustard 16–17, 37, 42
    flour 121
    seed 76, 121, 122
mustards 69, 71, 77, 79, 85,
    119–122, 124
Myers, Norma 160
Myrick, Val 23
myrrh 66, 69, 74, 76, 110
myrrh beads 54
myrtle 29

N

Nabhan, Gary Paul 150
Nani Mau Gardens 240
Nanneman, Renee 102
nasturtium 17, 20, 23, 36–37,
    41, 43
Nathan's Forge 101
National Agricultural Library
    277
National Health Care Institute
    202
National Herb Garden 241
national/international herb
    organizations 265–270
Native Seeds/SEARCH 33, 269
Natural Apothecary 277
Natural Gardening Company
    129
Natural Gardening Research
    Center 127
Natural Organic Farmers
    Association 205, 269
Nature's Acres 101
Nature's Apothecary 115
Nature's Finest 58
Nature's Herb 82
Nature's Herb Farm 277
Neal, Greaner and JoAnn 77
Neal, Joseph 278
Necessary Trading Company 129
Need'l Love Company, Inc. 102
Nelson, Judy 201
Nelson, Sandy 23
Nesty, Philip and Martha 169
nettles 40, 46, 115, 117
New Age Creations 71
New England Cheesemaking
    Supply Company, Inc. 58
New Forest Gardens 83
New Hampshire Farm Museum
    191, 215
New Hope Herb Farm 34, 191,
    215
New Jersey tea 36

New York Botanical Garden 241
New Zealand 133
Newcomer, Timothy L. 95
Newmeyer, Wendy and Jack 57
newsletters 10, 33, 56, 132–138
    See also magazines and
        journals
Next to Nature 72
Niche Gardens 34
Nichols Garden Nursery 34
Nicke, Katrina 129
Nicke, Walt, Company 129
Nieder, Nancy J. 86
nigella 48, 51, 53, 57
    pods 51
Nigro, Sandra 130
No Common Scents 83
Noe, John H. 126
Norfolk Lavender Ltd. 72
nori 115
Norris, Dorry 137, 156, 164,
    194, 273
North Atlantic Books 164
North Pacific Rim Area 10
NORTHPLAN/Mountain Seed
    34
Northstar Freeze Dry 58
Northwestern Coffee Mills 83
Northwind Farm Publications
    132, 173
Nu-Life Cards 102
nutmeg 51, 121
    grater 78, 79, 86, 106
    whole 76
Nuzzi, Debra 115, 205

O

oak-leaf
    dried 55
oak moss 56
Oak Valley Herb Farm 191
oats
    dried 48, 63
ocotillo 112
Ogden House 241
Ogden, Shepherd and Ellen 15
Ohr, Viola 114
Ohrbach, Barbara 160
Ohs, Bobbie 198, 247
oils 23, 38, 56, 64, 79, 96, 98,
    110, 111, 136
    essential 42, 49, 53–54, 56,
        58, 60, 62, 64–75, 77–83,
        85, 86, 91, 93, 95, 99,
        100, 103, 104, 106, 108,
        112, 114, 116, 117, 122

fragrance 49, 51, 53–56, 58, 77, 80–83, 85, 86, 90, 92, 93, 95, 104, 108
  massage 55, 86, 89, 91, 114
  potpourri refresher 49, 53, 82, 88, 112, 122
  precious 100
old-fashioned plants 10, 11, 18–20, 24–25, 28, 40–41
  books 141, 144, 145, 153
  classes/workshops 178, 192–193, 198
  Flower and Herb Exchange 267
  Heritage Seed Program 268
  public gardens 224, 228, 236, 237, 240, 241, 244
Old Hill Herbs 83
Old Slater Mill Museum 241
Old Southwest Trading Company 124
Old Sturbridge Village 241
Old Westbury Gardens 241
Olive's Hearth & Haven 102, 191
Oliver, Paula and David 132, 173
Olson, Ingrid 36
Olson, Ruth 244
onions 24, 30, 32–33, 41, 44, 46, 120
Oparah, Adolphus Akahedbi 270
open-pollinated seeds 10, 17, 25, 27, 40, 41
orach 23, 35, 43
orchid 31
Oregon Grape root 115
oregano 12–14, 16–17, 19–20, 25, 28, 30, 32–36, 38–41, 43, 45
  dried 51–52, 57, 76, 125
organic controls 33, 36, 127–129
organic gardening
  classes/workshops 179, 191, 192, 196, 199
  supplies 12, 28, 126–130
  videos 205
organically grown plants 14, 16–17, 21–22, 24, 29, 35–36, 41–43, 65, 196
Original Swiss Aromatics 72
ornamental grasses 12, 27, 34
  dried 51
ornamental plants 13, 31
orris 38, 42, 44, 51, 53
orrisroot 31, 53, 56, 58, 66, 113
osage orange 19
osha 10, 36, 110, 112

Our Family's Herbs & Such 102
Out of the Woods, Inc. 58
Out West Publishing Co. 138
Owen Farms 35
Owen, Lillian and Edric 35
Owen, Millie 156
Owens, Jacque 80
Owens, Kerry 68
Ozark Basketry Supply 58
Ozark Folk Center State Park 192, 219, 242

P

Paca, William, Garden 242
Pacific Botanicals 115
Pacific Institute of Aromatherapy 202
Pageant Book & Print Shop 272
Pailler, Dean 19
Palama, Kathy S. 70
Palmer, Lena 110
Pan's Forest 115
pansy 33
  dried 56
  pressed 50
papermaking 134
paprika 123
Park & Tilford Gardens 242
Park, George W., Seed Co. 35, 102, 164
Parker, Cindy 183
Parkview School for the Blind 242
parsley 12–14, 18–19, 21, 23, 25, 37–38, 41–42, 44
passiflora 31
patchouli 16, 21, 29, 31, 37, 66
Patio Patch Planters 130
Paton, Doug 172
Patricia's 102
Patterson, Carolyn 190, 238
Patterson, Gary 127
Paul, Irene 113
Pauser, Alice Petlock 118
Payne, Beaulah 236
Peace Seeds 35
Peconic River Herb Farm 192
Pecos Valley Spice Co. 125
Peddie, Mary 187
Peine, Joshua 89
Pelican Publishing Company 164
Penguin USA 164
Petalin, Carol 160
Pendery's 121
Penn Herb Co., Ltd. 72

penny cress
  dried 63
Penny Royal Herbs 192
Penny's Garden 122, 192
pennyroyal 11–13, 15–16, 22, 28, 30, 44
  dried 52
peony
  dried 62
Pepper Gal 35
pepperberries 49, 62
peppercorns 84, 119, 123
peppergrass 36, 49
peppermint
  See mint
peppers 14, 18–19, 21, 24, 26–27, 30, 33, 35–37, 41, 44, 55, 58, 83, 121, 122, 124, 125
  Annual Chile Festival 219
  books 125, 140, 157
  Whole Chili Pepper Magazine 138
perennials 11–15, 17–22, 25–31, 34–35, 37–39, 41–42, 44–46, 81, 99
perfumes 54, 59, 65, 66, 69, 70, 73–75, 82, 83, 90, 91, 94, 98, 112, 122
perilla 12, 17, 24, 28, 34, 37, 40, 42
Perry, Rebecca A. 207
Perseus Gourmet Products 122
pet products 49, 53–54, 61, 64, 66–68, 71, 75, 77, 80–82, 95, 103, 104, 129, 135
Peter Rabbit Herbal 116
Peters, Philip L. 108
Petite Fleur Essence 59
Pettengill Farm 59, 192–193
Pfeifer, Hilary 96
Pflumm, Mark 32
Phelps, Norma 104
Phenicie, Joyce 102
Phillips, Harriet Flannery 236
Phillips, Roger 143
pickling spices 122
pimpernel 23–24, 42, 44
Pineapple Press 164
Pine Creek Herbs 103, 164
Pinetree Garden Seeds 36
Pinnell, Janice 125
P.L.A.N. Publishers 164
planning a garden 17
planting charts 17
Plants of the Southwest 36
Plimouth Plantation 242
plumosa
  dried 61
poke root 30, 111

Policar, Joseph 51
PolyBags Plus, Inc. 59
pomanders 49, 54, 57, 59–60, 65, 77–80, 91–93, 101, 106, 122
pomegranate
  dwarf 23
Pomona Book Exchange 173
Poole, Susan 107
Poot, Inge 38
Pope, Donna E. 165, 174
poppy 24, 29, 36
  dried 51, 60
poppyseed 20, 22
Porter, Tom and Carol 19posters 87, 88, 92, 108
posters 38, 53, 69, 72, 80, 87, 88, 92, 108, 127
potpourri 11, 34, 38, 49–51, 53–60, 62, 64–108, 111–113, 121, 122, 137, 235
  accessories 49, 56, 62, 66, 85, 88, 93, 103–106, 108, 109, 243
  simmering 49, 58, 65, 66, 68, 71, 75, 82, 84, 85, 88, 90, 92, 100, 101, 104, 106, 107, 122
Potpourri and Sachet Supplies 59
Potpourri by Martha 59
Potpourri from Herbal Acres 136
Potpourri Party-Line 137
Potter, Clarkson, N. 164
Potts, Leanna K. 143, 164
Powers, Jan 105
Prag, Ray and Peg 19
Prairie Moon Nursery 36
prairie sage 115
Prairie Seed Source 36
Prenis, John 143, 144
Prentice-Hall, Inc. 164
Present Moment Books and Herbs 116
Preservations 60
preservatives 49
Preserve the Memories 60
preserving flowers and herbs 23, 49, 52, 58, 61, 134
pressed flowers 50, 53, 90, 91
Pressed for Time 103
Preus, Mary 195
prices 132
prickly pear 22, 34
primrose 110
Prodoehl, Don 18
production 134
Progressive Self-Care Systems 73
ProNatura, Inc. 173

psyllium 38
Puckett, Patty 113
public gardens 10, 14–16, 20–22, 24, 25, 27–34, 37, 39, 43, 45, 46, 49, 52–55, 57, 60, 62, 63, 65–69, 71, 75, 77–80, 82, 88–90, 92–96, 98, 100, 103, 104, 107, 108, 111, 112, 118, 119, 122, 124, 135, 224 -253
publishers 162–166
Pulleyn, Rob 160
pulmonaria 44
Purdin, Mary 83
purslane 12, 35
Purvis, Linda Lee 56
Putnam Cottage 242
Putney Nursery, Inc. 37
Pylant, Leslie 46
pyrethrum 12, 16, 18–19, 22, 37, 95
pyrethrum daisies 12, 18–19

Q

Quail Botanical Gardens 243
Queen-Anne's-lace 34, 37–38
quinine 17
Quinn, Betty Jo 78
Quintana, Linda 86, 178, 200
Quintessence Aromatherapy, Inc. 73, 202

R

Rabbit Shadow Farm 38
Rachel Dee Herb Farm 193
Radcliffe Farms 60, 193
Radcliffe, Cyndy 60, 193, 193
Rady, Virginia B. 145
Rafal, Donald 122
Rafal Spice Company 122
Rafferty, Betty J.
Raiche, Debra A. 81
Raindrip, Inc. 130
rampion 29
ramps 16
Random House 165
Rankin, Dorothy 156
Ransom Hill 165
Rascan, Leslie 163, 269
Rasland Farm 37, 103, 215
Rasmussen, Ed 20
Ratcliffe, Dell 52, 183
Rathdowney, Ltd. 103

Ratner, Marilyn 241
Ratto, G. B., & Co. International Grocers 122
Raven's Nest 104
Rawlinson, Bill 37
Rawlinson Garden Seed 37
Rawson, Julie 205, 269
Raysor, Arie 23
Reader's Digest Association, Inc. 150, 164
Reagin, Joyce 35, 102
Red Barn 243
Redwood City Seed Company 37
Reed, Kay 92
regional/state herb organizations 256–265
Reid, Debra 112
repellents 39, 71, 83, 88, 95
 See also moth repellents
Reppert, Bertha 39, 104, 193
Reppert, Nancy 105, 193
Reppert, Susanna 39, 104, 193, 215
research 132, 136
research services 112, 274
research reviews 135
resinoids 64
restaurant reviews 133
restaurants 105, 193, 276
retail 136
Rhettland Herbary 193, 243
Rhett-Thurston, Eddie 194, 243
Rhudy, Linda 91
Rich, Charlene 21
Richenburg, Jan 59, 192
Richter, Jennifer P. 175
Richters 38
Rickard, Paulette 170
Riddle, Mary Lou 197
Rinzler, Carol 147
Riotte, Louise 144
Ripperger, Helmut 156
Rittenburg 181
River's Bend Farm 60
Robbins, Betty H. 20
Roberts, Marilyan, Collection 104
rocambole 20, 39
rocket 20
Rocky Mountain Herbal Institute 202
Rocky Mountain Herbalists Coalition 270
Rocky Retreat Herb Farm 104
Rodale Press 165
Rodef Shalom Biblical Botanical Garden 243
Rogers, Barabara Radcliffe 54

Rogers, Mary 109
Rogers, Susan 241
Rohde, Eleanour Sinclair 144, 153, 156
roquette 30
Rosalia, Denise 172
Rose Acres 38
Rose Hill Herbs and Perennials 38
rose hips 52–53, 115
Rose, Jeanne 54, 71, 135, 147, 150, 173, 202
Rose, Jeanne, Herbal Studies Course 165, 202
rose petals 51, 59
rosebuds 51, 52, 57, 60
rosemary 11–12, 16, 19–20, 22–26, 28–32, 36–38, 41–42, 44–46
Rosemary House 39, 104–105, 193, 215
Rosemary's Garden 194
roses 11, 15–16, 18, 22, 24–26, 38–39, 45
 books 144, 145, 159, 169, 172
 classes/workshops 178, 189, 198
 dried 48, 51–52, 54, 56, 60, 62, 104
 Fall Festival of Roses 220
 Heritage Rose Foundation 268
 public gardens 224–226, 229, 232, 234, 236, 240, 243, 248
Roses of Yesterday and Today, Inc. 39
Ross, Mary Ellen 32
Roth, Maggi 60, 193
Rothemich, Joan R. 38
Royal Horticultural Society 270
rubber stamps 93, 95
rue 12, 20, 25, 28, 36–37, 43–44, 46
Rue Ja's Herb Collection Farm 243
Ruh, Timothy 42, 218
Ruilova, Mary Jo 105
Running Press Publishers 165
Rutter, Kim 65
Ryan, Marty 62
Ryason, Diane 126

S

sachets 49, 53, 59, 62, 65, 69, 72, 77–79, 81–83, 86, 88–90, 92–94, 99, 100, 104–107, 121, 122
Sacrison, LeAna 51
safflower 11, 13, 15, 20, 37, 40, 43
 dried 48, 125
saffron 78, 84, 119, 120, 122, 123, 134
 bulbs 39
 Spanish 76, 121–123
Saga International Holidays 277
sage 14, 16, 18–21, 23, 25, 27, 30–32, 34, 36–37, 40–41, 43–45, 76, 84
 dried 51–54, 57, 112
Sage Advice 137
Sage Cottage Bed and Breakfast 137, 194, 273
Sage Mountain Herbs 194
St.-John's Herb Garden, Inc. 39, 60
St.-John's wort 16, 21, 24, 44, 110
St. Thomas Episcopal Church 244
salad burnet See burnet
salad greens 15
salsa 79, 123–125
salsify 42
Salter, Tierney P. 114, 188
salt-free herb blends 53, 66, 69, 78–81, 83, 84, 86, 104, 118–121, 123, 125
saltpeter 113
salvia 12, 16, 20–21, 30–31, 33–35, 38
 dried 48, 51–53, 55, 61
Salzler Kate 77
Sammataro, Diana 17
samphire 29
Samuel Wells & Co., 63
San Antonio Botanical Center 194, 244
San Diego Wild Animal Park 244
San Juan Naturals 165
Sanders Unlimited 105
Sandy Mush Herb Nursery 39
Santa Barbara Botanic Garden 207, 244
Santa Cruz Chili and Spice Co, 125
Santa Fe Trail Center 244
santolina 11–12, 38, 44, 48
sarsaparilla 38

root 63
sassafras 19, 63
Saunders, Caryl 133, 267
savory 11, 13–14, 18, 20, 30–31, 40, 42–44
 dried 51, 53
Sawyer, Helene 157
saxifrage 24
scabiosa 20
scent rings 53, 58, 65, 66, 74, 78, 85, 90–92, 104, 106
scented geraniums 12, 14–16, 20–25, 27–32, 34, 37–42, 45–46, 77, 81, 103, 134, 226–228, 231, 232, 236, 249
Scheffer, Mechthild 150
Schenck, Mary 199
Schmelzl, Ernestine 59
Schmidt, R. Marilyn 157
School of Herbal Medicine 203
School of Natural Medicine 203
Schuler, Stanley 144
Schultz, John 20
Schultz, Shawn 179
Schuster, Janet 63
Schwartz, Jeri, Antiques 278
Scobey, Joan 160
sea holly 28, 44
Sea Holly Herbs & Flowers 194
sea lettuce 115
Seaman, Delia 70
Seaver, Kathleen 51
Second Life Books, Inc. 174
Secret Garden 73
Secret Garden Book Source 174
sedges 36
Seebeck, "Cattail" Bob 205
seed exchanges 12, 27, 138, 248, 267
seed starting supplies 13, 29, 128
seed threshers, hand operated 10
Seedhead News
Seeds Blüm 40
Seidel, Robert 91, 184
Select Origins, Inc. 123
Select Seeds—Antique Flowers 40
self-heal 24, 43
Selsley Herb Farm 244
senna 13, 20, 36, 46
Sequoyah Gardens 174
sesame 11, 13, 16, 20, 30, 37, 84
Shady Acres Herb Farm 195
Shady Hill Gardens 40
Shahan, Evelyn and Mel 74, 273
Shaker Messenger 195
Shaker Museum 244
Shakertown at Pleasant Hill 245
Shakespearean herbs 29, 144,

226, 227, 229, 238
shallots 16, 22, 30, 32, 37, 41, 84, 120
Shannon, Arlene 54, 171
Sharan, Dr. Farida 114, 203
Shaudys, Phyllis, V. 136, 144, 175
shave grass 115
Shelburne Museum 245
Shelly's Petals and Herbs, Etc. 278
Shelton Herb Farm 195
Shelton, Meg 195
Shepherd, Renee 40, 157, 165, 245
Shepherd's Garden Seeds 40, 245
Shepherd's Garden Publishing 165
shepherd's-purse 38
Shigamatsu, Karen E. 238
Shields Organic Herb & Flower Farm 61
Shields, Leigh 61
Shimizu, Yuzuru 248
Shomer, Forest 10, 168
Shoup, Mike 11, 178, 220, 224
shrubs 10, 12, 17, 34–36, 45
Sierra School of Herbs & Health 203
Silber, Mark and Terry 94, 160, 214, 233
silica gel 49, 54, 56, 60
Silo, Inc. 195
Silver Bay Herb Farm 195–196
Simeone, Claudia 61
Simmons, Adelma Grenier 77, 144–145, 161, 227
Simons, Don 171
Simplers Botanical Co. 116
simples 116
Simply De-Vine 61
Sims, Lana 102
Sinking Springs Herb Farm 196, 273
Sitton, Diane Morey 145, 278
skin care
 See body care products
skirret 31
skullcap 37, 44
Slick, Karl 194
slide programs 33, 135
 See also demonstrations and lectures
Sliker, Maggie 275
slippery elm bark 63, 111
Smith, Beverly 25, 120, 234, 276
Smith, Gail and Steve 229
Smith, Jerry 71

Smith, Karl L. 112
Smith, Leona Woodring 157
Smith, Margaret M. 79
Smith, Mark 25
Smith's (Sandy) Magical Herbs 73
Smithsonian Institution 207
Smoke Camp Crafts 84
smoking blends 115
smudge sticks 53, 112
sneezewort 35
Snuggery Culinary Herb and Spice Blends 123
Soap Opera 74
soapmaking 74, 134
soaps 53, 54, 64–71, 74–76, 84, 86, 87, 89, 90, 94, 95, 101, 111, 233
 See also bath products
soapwort 15, 21, 32, 40, 42
Solargraphics 62
Solomon, Shirley 272
Solsrud, Denise 91
sorrel 16, 20, 37–38, 41, 43
Soule, Deb 64
soup mixes 76, 81, 85
Southern Exposure Seed Exchange 41
southernwood 11, 14, 41
SouthRidge Treasures & Herbs 196, 273
Southwick, Laurie 77
Sovola, Shelley 70
Sparrowe, Linda 134
spearmint
 See mint
speedwell 10, 28, 32, 46
Spencer Book Shop 174
Spice and Herb Arts 138
Spice Cabinet 84
Spice It Up 84
Spices 'N' Things 85
Spiceman Enterprises 278
Spider Web Gardens 62
spiderwort 17, 31, 36
Spindler, Cristina 192
spirulina 112
Spoerke, David G. 151
sports medicine 135
Spoutwood Farm 196
Spring Brook Farm 196
Spring Herb Farm 197
Spring, Nancy 197
Square, Vincent 270
Stackpole Books 165, 174
Stanley-Whitman House 245
starflower
 dried 61
State Arboretum of Virginia

197, 245
State Botanical Garden of Georgia 245
State of New Hampshire 246
statice 12, 21, 24, 28, 32, 41, 43
 dried 48, 51–55, 57, 60–61, 63, 103
stationery products 40, 62, 77, 78, 87–97, 102, 104, 105, 107–109
stearic acid 113
Steele, Barbara 168, 178
Steele-Carlin, Sherril 135
Stelzer, John and Kelly 119
stencils 93
stephanotis
 dried 60
Stephen, Dixie 119, 181, 227
Sterling Publishing Co. 165
Stevenson, Thomas 13
Stillridge Herb Farm 197
Stinson, Mary and Glenn 100
stitchery 97, 102
Stobart, Tom 157
stock 24
Stockman, William L. 62
Stoffers, Joyce 224
Stokes Seeds, Inc. 41
Stone, Kim 246
Stonegate Gardens 62
Stone Well Herbs 105
Storey Communications 165, 174–175
Storey House Herb Farm 41
Stoval, Edith 157
Stratton, Cynthia 23
Strauch, Joseph G. 179, 225
straw 60
strawberries, alpine 22, 29, 43
Strawberry Banke Museum 246
Strawberry Meadow Herb Farm 85
strawflower 18, 21, 28, 43
 dried 48, 51–53, 57, 60–61, 63, 103
Strybing Arboretum & Botanical Gardens 246
Stryker, Ruth and James 243
Stuart, Malcolm 147
Stubbs, Ann 196, 273
Studio of Claudia Walker 105
Sturdivant, Lee 147, 165
Stutz, Denise 58
succulents 31
Sugar 'n Spice 85
sugar-free herb blends 53, 78, 118, 123, 125
Sultan's Delight, Inc. 123
sumac 123

summer savory
　See savory
Summit Lake Herbs 197
Sundial Herb Garden 246
sundials 94, 109
Sunfeather Handcrafted Herbal
　Soap Co. 74
sunflower 16–19, 33, 36, 38, 41
Sunnybrook Farms Nursery 42,
　218
Sunny Window 106
Sunrise Enterprises 42
sunscreens and tanning oils
　70–72
　See also body care products
Surrey Books 165
swags 50–51, 57–58, 61, 74, 88,
　93, 106
Swanson, Faith H. 145
sweet Annie
　dried 52–53, 58, 60–61
sweet grass braids 115
sweet William 40, 45
Sweet Woodroffe Herb Farm 85
sweet woodruff 15, 30, 35,
　37–38, 43–44
Sweet Woodruff Farm 74, 273
sweet marjoram
　See marjoram
sweet flag 37–38
sweet cicely 14, 29–30, 43–44
Sweethaven Farm 197
Swindler, Phyllis 90
Swinging Bridge Pottery 106
Sylvia's Originals 278

T

TAB Books, Inc. 165
T & T Seeds, Ltd. 42
T-shirts 13, 68, 75, 81, 89, 93,
　96, 100, 107, 109, 125
Tamblyn-Groves
　Communications 279
Tanglewood Gardens 106
Tanner, Ogden 141
tansy 12, 19, 23, 25, 28, 30, 32,
　38, 40–41, 44
　dried 52
tarragon 16, 22, 44–45
tatume squash 26
Taylor, Gordon 146
Taylor, Jane L. 239
Taylor, Kathryn 33
Taylor, Paul 30, 120
Taylor Publishing Co. 165
Taylor, Steve 231

Taylor, Ted 175
Taylor's Herb Garden, Inc. 42
Taylor's Herb Garden of
　Arizona, Inc. 42
tea tree 19, 70, 113
teas 14, 16, 29, 34, 42, 49, 53,
　55, 61, 64–70, 73, 75, 77–88,
　90–92, 94, 95, 97, 99–104,
　108, 110–115, 118, 120–122,
　124, 233
teasel
　dried 51
Teasel Weed 106
Territorial Seed Company 43
Texas Gardener Press 165
Texas Gunpowder, Inc. 125
Theiss, Barbara and Peter 151,
　173
Therapeutic Herbalism 203
There's Always the Garden 107
thistle 43–44
　dried 48, 61, 63, 111, 117
Thistle Hill 107
Thomas, Ian 65
Thomas Jefferson Center for
　Historic Plants 43, 198
Thomas, John R. 45
Thomas, Mari 88
Thompson, Boyce,
　Southwestern Arboretum 246
Thompson, Duane 17
Thomson, William A.R. 151
Thorpe, Patricia 161
thyme 11–17, 20–30, 32, 34–38,
　40–45, 132
　creeping 13, 28, 37
Thyme Garden Seed Company
　43, 247
tickseed 45
Tide-Mark Press 107
Tierra, Lesley 166, 201
Tierra, Michael 151, 166
tiles 92, 128
Tilgner, Sharol 117, 206
Timber Rock Farms 62
Timber Press, Inc. 166
tinctures 17, 64, 65, 67, 69, 82,
　95, 96, 110, 113, 115–118,
　121
Tinmouth Channel Farm 43
Tippett, Dick and Sylvia 37,
　103, 215
Tisserand, Maggie 136, 151
Tisserand, Robert 136, 151
Titterington, Rosemary 28, 145,
　163, 235
TMI Books 175
T. M. Taylor Company 175
toadflax 45

tobacco 22, 35, 40, 115
Toles, Lee Ann 239
Tolley, Emelie 107, 145, 157
Tolley's (Emelie) Herb Basket
　107
tomatillos 26
tonka beans 51, 113
tools 136
topiaries 38, 56–57, 60, 63, 91,
　102, 105, 106, 109, 126
Town's End Herb Farm, Ltd.
　118–119
Townsend, Betty Ann 118
Townsend, Doris 157
Traditional Tours 279
tragacanth powder 86
travel and tours 275, 277, 279
Treben, Maria 173
trees 17, 34–36, 45
trellis 94
Triple Oaks Nursery 198, 215
tropical plants 11
Tropper, Tom and Betty 66, 204
Trout Lake Farm 117
Tucson Botanical Gardens 198,
　216, 219, 247
turmeric 32
tussie-mussies 49, 56–57, 67, 69,
　91–93, 96, 102, 103
　holders 54, 57
Twilley, Otis S., Seed Company,
　Inc. 44
Twinholly's 130
Twin Ridge Farm 86
Twomey, Kevin 42
Tyler, John J., Arboretum
　Garden for the Blind 247

U

Ulrich, Gail 200, 217
Ultimate Herb & Spice Shoppe
　86
Unicorn Books for Craftsmen
　166
Unipub 166
United Communications 108
United Society of Shakers 86,
　198
University of Arizona Press 166
University of California
　Botanical Gardens 198,
　247–248
University of Massachusetts
　Craker, Lyle E. 134
　Dept. of Plant & Soil
　　Sciences 134

University of Minnesota
　Landscape Arboretum 248
University of Oklahoma Press
　166
University of Rhode Island
　Medicinal Plant Garden 248
University of Texas Press 166
University of Washington
　Medicinal Herb Garden 248
University Press of New
　England 166
unpetroleum jelly 54
Upton, Roy 266
Utterback, Christine 135
uva-ursi 112

V

Vaiano, Donna 33
Val's Naturals 62
Valen Walden R. 246
Valentine, Canela 75
valerian 41–44
Vallentyne, Sydney 39, 60
Van Atta, Marian 145
Van Bourgondien Bros. 44
Van Bourgondien, Debbie 44
Van Dyck, Carrie 24, 68, 188
Van Kolken, Diana 195
vanilla bean 53, 59, 83–85, 119,
　121, 123
Varney, Bill and Sylvia 92
Vash, Ernest J. 25
vegetable seeds and plants
　10–13, 15–17, 19, 23, 25–27,
　29–32, 34–37, 39–43, 45, 129
verbena 11, 20–21, 23, 34,
　37–38, 44
Verhelst, Jeannette 161, 166,
　182
vervain 10, 44
vetiver 31
vials 50, 55, 59
　See also containers and bags
Victoria's Herb Shoppe 75
Video Herbalist 205
videocassettes 49, 66, 68, 94,
　168, 204–206
Vietnamese balm 38
Viking Penguin, Inc. 166
Vileniki—An Herb Farm 44,
　175, 199, 215
Village Arbors 199
Vilneff, M. 69
Vincent, Nick 101
Vine Arts 63
vinegars 65, 67–69, 71, 76–80,

82, 83, 85, 86, 92, 94, 98, 100, 114, 118–124, 233
vines 56–58, 60–61
violets 11, 29, 36–37, 40
Vital Energy 117
Viviano, Betty Ann 32, 100, 190, 238
Vogel, Virgil J. 151
Voigts, Karen and Tom 71
Voiron, Elena 122
Volchok, Michael 111

W

Wade, Alan 36
Wade, Barbara 96, 187
Wagener, Jacqueline 69
Walker, Claudia 105
Walker, Donna 93
Walker, Melissa 191, 215
Walsh, George 187
Walsh, Marjorie A. 17
Warmbier Farms 63
Warmbier, Mary Ellen 63
Washington Crossing Historic Park 13
Washington National Cathedral Gardens 44, 249
wassail and mulling spices 77, 85, 88
watercress 13, 16, 42
    See also cress
Waterfront Press 166
Wayside Gardens 45
Weaver, Diane and Dick 233
Weaver, Kathryn 48
weavers' plants 17
Webb, David W. 161
Webster, Helen Noyes 145
wedding supplies 56, 62, 67, 88, 92, 93, 104, 106, 109, 134
Weed, Susun 204
Weil, Andrew 152
Weiner, Janet 152
Weiner, Judy 124, 199
Weiner, Michael A. 152
Weiss, Edward 123
Weiss, Gaea 152
Weiss, Paprikas, Importer 123–124
Weiss, Shandor 152
Welch, William C. 145
weld 15, 42, 44
Weleda, Inc. 75
Well-Sweep Herb Farm 45, 108, 216
Westerink, Claire C. 18

Western Comfrey, Inc. 108
Western Reserve Herb Society 175, 249
Whealy, Diane 267
wheat grass 112
Wheeler Arts 279
Wheeler, Mark 115
Wheeler, Paula 279
Wheeling, Victoria 75
Whiskey Run Herb Farm 199
Whitaker, Garyanna 111
White, Anne 197, 245
White Flower Farm 45
White, Sara J. 237
Whitfield, Henry, State Historical Museum 249
Whole Chile Pepper Magazine 138
Whole World Recycled Stationery 108
Wicke, Roger Wm. 202
Wilcox, Mary Ellen 196, 219, 242, 273
Wilcox, Tina Marie 192
Wildflower 138
wildflowers 10, 13, 15–17, 23, 25–26, 28, 34, 36–38, 45–46, 129, 138
    Canadian Wildflower Society 266
    public gardens 225, 232, 247
    See also specific flowers
Wild Edible Plant Tours 205
wild lettuce 114
Wildseed, Inc. 45
Wild Weeds 75
Wiley, Patricia 39
Williams, Betsy/The Proper Season 109, 199
Williams, Greg 136
Williams, Pat 136
Willoughby, Lori 109
Will's Garden of Knowledge 109
Wilson, Barbara 16
Wimperis, Peter and Gillian 244
Winchester, Paula 95
Wind & Weather 109
Windrose Aromatics, Inc. 75
Windy Pines Natural Herb 117
Windy River Farm/Cottage Garden Herbs 124, 199
Wine and Food Library 176
winemaking supplies 34, 50
winter savory
    See savory
Wiseheart, Susan 17
Wise Woman Center 204
Wise Woman Herbals 117, 206
WishGarden Herbs 118
Wisteria Press 109

witch hazel 21, 111
Wittig, Audrey 62
Wittman, Christine 181
woad 15, 24, 30, 42, 44
Wold, Betty 174
Wonderland Tea and Spice Herb Shop 86, 200
Wood, Kim 236
Wood, Rob and Lucy 161, 196
wood chips 51, 58, 60, 66, 103
Wood Violet Books 176
Woodbridge Press 166
Woodburn, Elisabeth, Books 176
Woodland Herbs 46
Woodman, J. Gaunt, Co. 110
Woodman, Janet 110
Woodroffe, Pam 85
Woodspirits Soap 76
Woodward, Marcus 153
Words About Herbs 200
Workman Publishing Co. 166
workshops and classes 16, 54, 60, 64, 73, 75, 79, 87, 94–96, 98, 105, 125, 135, 178–204, 229, 273
    See also demonstrations and lectures
World of Cookbooks 138
wormwood 11–13, 16, 25, 28, 30, 35, 37, 44
wreath bases 49, 55, 57, 103
wreaths 12, 24, 48–53, 55–62, 68, 69, 73–75, 77–82, 88–98, 100, 102, 103, 106, 109, 233, 243
Wrenwood of Berkeley Springs 46
Wright, Margaret 135, 265
Wright, Paula 63
Wu, Sean 115
Wuthrick, Becky 60
Wyrttun Ward 46

Y

Yankee Books 166
yarrow 11–15, 17, 19–20, 22–23, 26, 28, 30–33, 35–40, 44–46
    dried 51–52, 55, 60, 61, 115
yellow dock 110
yerba buena 15, 22
yerba santa 35, 97, 111
yucca 112
Yun, Hye Koo (Henry) 152

Z

Zabar, Abbie 145
zatar 45, 122
Zilker Botanical Garden 249
Zimmerman, Ron 24, 68
Zink, Barbara 81
zubrovka 39

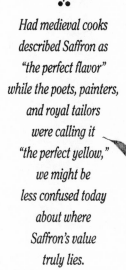

*Had medieval cooks
described Saffron as
"the perfect flavor"
while the poets, painters,
and royal tailors
were calling it
"the perfect yellow,"
we might be
less confused today
about where
Saffron's value
truly lies.*

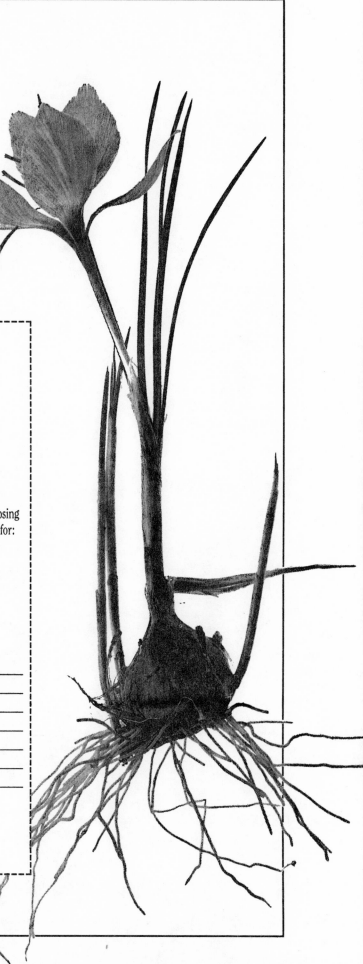